Developing Teams and Organizations

A Practical Handbook for Managers and Consultants

Developing Teams and Organizations

A Practical Handbook for Managers and Consultants

Uri Merry

The Applied Social Research and OD Institute

Melvin E. Allerhand

REM Associates

Addison-Wesley Publishing Company
Reading, Massachusetts
Menlo Park, California • London • Amsterdam • Don Mills, Ontario • Sydney

ISBN 0-201-04531-1
CDEFGHIJKL-MA-89876543210

Preface

People enter consulting or management from different biological, cultural, and educational backgrounds. The authors of this handbook are no different. We represent two educational backgrounds—sociology and psychology; we represent two development currents—one organizational development and the other management and personal consultation; we represent two styles—one more oriented to self and the printed word and the other more oriented to others and the oral word. We share four key common denominators: we have worked together for five years as facilitators and organizational specialists within social and industrial organizations; we have developed an approach for managers and leaders who have a minimum of sophistication in consultation and appropriate training experiences; we have a mutual respect and trust for each other's ideas, styles, and practice; and last but not least, we have a common tendency to combine theory and experience in the service of practical results.

We have built on the ideas of many others and have tried to appropriately recognize their contribution, wherever we used their ideas, within the book.

We are deeply indebted to the team of The Applied Behavioral Sciences Institute of the Ichud and Meuchad Kibbutz Federations, who collaborated with us in developing most of the interventions in this book.

We are especially indebted to U. Osri, E. Chagi, M. Hurwitz, S. Cina, J. Handlon, and J. Shoup, whose ideas and work contributed to creating these processes.

The remarks, corrections, style improvements, typing, and encouragement of Ann Abrahami helped us immeasurably.

Last but not least, we owe much to our wives Ruth and Revel for encouraging us, relieving us of other problems during periods of heavy writing, and assisting in all possible ways to complete the handbook.

We gratefully acknowledge the cooperation of Gulf Publishing Company and University Associates Publishers, Inc., for allowing reprints of illustrations and excerpts.

Maagan Michael, Doar Menashe, Israel   U.M.
South Euclid, Ohio   M.E.A.
November 1976

Contents

Guide in using the handbook

CHAPTER OBJECTIVE

To assist you in using the Handbook as a tool.

GETTING ACQUAINTED WITH THE HANDBOOK

Like the designers of any tool or instrument, we firmly believe that you must get a sense of this instrument—its range of usefulness and its limitations. A key step is to determine how it can be of practical use to you. Ask yourself: "How can I increase my effectiveness through the use of this Handbook?"

We suggest that you consider the following steps in this "getting-acquainted" process:

1. Review the Table of Contents—item by item. What does each intervention mean to you just on the basis of its title?

2. If one intervention strikes your fancy, turn to that section and see what it is like.

3. Then, just page through the Handbook and get a better sense of the way in which the interventions are presented and discussed. Are there any of them that you have already tried? In what way was your experience similar to or different from ours?

4. As you are looking at an intervention that you have not tried or experienced, think about how it might feel if you were in a situation in which it was being tried. Now think about the intervention as though you were the facilitator. How does that feel?

USING THE HANDBOOK IN YOUR WORK

1. *What to think about before going to the Handbook*

    a. *What* is your central concern at this time? Specifically, what is the problem needing a solution; what is the unexpected change that needs attention; what skill do you want to develop? At this point the Handbook will be more useful if you can be as specific and as targeted as possible.

    b. *Who* is the person or group involved with the issue or problem? Must you think of getting a cross-section of the department involved? Is it important to have people of different skills, different backgrounds? What about including representatives from the formal and informal power bases to help ensure implementation?

    c. *Why* must you depart from the usual practice of the group or unit or task force and apply a different type of intervention? Thinking over established procedures and approaches may help you become clearer about the optimal intervention. A *new* (for the group) intervention always requires some preparation to overcome the built-in resistance to change. Thus, when an established procedure can do the job, that procedure is the best starting point.

2. *Entering the Handbook*

    a. With the issue in front of you, select the intervention that seems most appropriate and realistic. Carefully examine the "When to Use" section of the intervention as you are thinking through the options.

    b. *Who* is the ideal, *available* person to function as facilitator in implementing the intervention? Can you do it yourself or does the situation require the assistance of another person in the company or possibly an external consultant? If you decide to use the intervention yourself, should you first try it out on a less critical audience—or possibly role-play the procedure until you are more accustomed to the intervention?*

    c. *When* is the optimal time for attempting the intervention? Would it not be worthwhile to assess the *readiness* of the individual or group to receive and use the intervention? With most interventions, we dis-

---

*   See Appendix II on Basic and Standard Methods for discussion of use of role-play.

cuss the ways of testing the readiness, or circumstances indicating the readiness, of the people involved.

d. *Where* should the intervention take place? As you think about the application, can the unit or group learn best during the regular working day, or will it interfere too much with normal operations? Is something important gained by working with the group away from the work site?

e. *How* do you introduce the intervention to the group or person? Each of the interventions in the Handbook requires a different type of preparation for the people involved—getting the participants warmed up to the experience; clarifying the purpose; thinking about expected results, etc.

f. Finally, *what* might be the anticipated repercussions? The intervention is likely to have some impact, and so people other than just the direct participants might well feel the ripple effect. It is useful to think of the interfacing groups or individuals within the same unit and try to anticipate their reactions. Considering such aftereffects may well help you modify the intervention to better fit the uniqueness of your organization.

SOME USEFUL GUIDELINES

- Who can use these interventions?
- Format in which interventions are presented
- How much structuring should you use?
- Creating your own variations
- Use of journal as a developmental tool
- Problem of jargon

1. *Who can use these interventions?* "Facilitator," "consultant," "leader" —we use these names interchangeably to designate the person who is doing or leading the intervention. The use of these words does not mean that the person leading the intervention must be a trained behavioral scientist or an organizational consultant. These are the names we choose to use to differentiate the person leading the intervention from the people who are participating in the intervention.

At the beginning of each intervention there is a section headed "Who Can Use." In this section we specify who, in our opinion, can use the particular intervention, viz. a trained consultant, a facilitator with some experience, a manager, or anyone. Many of the interventions can be used by sensitive, intelligent people who have had no training or experience in applied behavioral or human sciences. A sizable number of the processes can be experienced and practiced by people doing them on their own just to increase their managerial effectiveness.

2. *Format in which interventions are presented.* Throughout the book we have tried, as much as is reasonably possible, to maintain a similar format in presenting the interventions. The format is:

  a. When to use
  b. Who can use
  c. Purposes
  d. Participants
  e. Materials
  f. Time
  g. Steps in process
  h. Detailed process
  i. Variations

Items a through d are guidelines which might help decide whether or not to use the intervention: Are you the person? Is it the right group? Does it fit your goals?

Items e and f are practical details regarding the materials that need to be prepared and the length of time needed for the entire process.

Items g and h outline the steps and give the detailed process with considerations connected with each step.

Item i gives alternative ways of doing the intervention.

3. *How much structuring should you use?* An intervention may be *more* prestructured or *less* prestructured. In a *more prestructured* intervention:

 ▪ The steps of the process may be all preplanned in detail and within a specified time frame.

 ▪ The participants are led from one stage to another in a predetermined order.

 ▪ The instructions and illustrations may be already written up on newsprint paper and/or printed on handouts.

 ▪ The facilitator has prepared lecturettes which he or she will deliver at designated points with the main points written on newsprint paper or prepared on slides.

 ▪ The *advantages* are that it:
   —has greater chance of achieving the preplanned objectives,
   —gives the participants a more secure feeling that things are in hand,
   —gives the facilitator, who is using the intervention for the first time, a feeling of security in using a tested method, and
   —is easier for inexperienced leaders.

In a *less prestructured* intervention:

 ▪ The steps in the process and much of the content are dependent on the developments that take place during the intervention.

- The participants are given more opportunity to influence the process.
- Illustrations and instructions are presented orally or written in the presence of the participants while their content is being explained.
- Lecturettes are more informal or might be replaced by asking the participants to give their ideas about the subject under consideration and noting them down on newsprint paper.
- the *advantages* are that it:
  —may achieve important objectives that were not preplanned but developed during the process,
  —gives deeper meaning and learning experience to participants who learn through their own efforts and experience, and
  —allows greater flexibility, freedom, and comfort to the experienced and creative facilitator.

In presenting the interventions we have first described each one in its most structured form. In notes in the middle and variations at the end of these descriptions we point out possibilities of less structured approaches.

4. *Creating your own variations.* The detailed steps in the interventions, the choice of lecturettes, instructions, questionnaires, etc., are the results of our experience with various groups and organizations. We have built on the work of others and developed processes that seem to be answering the needs of our clients. We *think* that many of the processes can be useful for most teams or groups in a modern *Western* culture. We *know* that you must treat the intervention steps only as guidelines. You must make the necessary corrections to fit your group.

5. *Use of journal as a developmental tool.* In some of the interventions, we have specifically referred to a journal or a notebook. In our definition of a journal, we include:

- an on-going recording of what has been learned during an intervention,
- a place where you can note ideas or suggestions that are connected with changes you are trying to make in yourself or in your organization, and
- a place where you can keep handouts, articles, etc. that are connected with management or organizational development.

We suggest that the journal be separated by dividers into different sections. The sections may relate to different skills you are trying to develop, such as listening, problem-solving, systems control, etc. Some sections may be devoted to changes in yourself as a manager, such as managerial style, better use of time, etc. As you can well imagine, a journal can ultimately become a series of notebooks.

Some people have found that during an intervention the journal takes on the form of a "diary," that is, they write down thoughts and notes on what is being presented in the order that their ideas or experiences occur. At some later time the ideas are sorted out and written into the different sections of the journal. This process seems to allow for useful reflection, clarification on what has been learned, and—most important—*how what has been learned can be applied in the work situation.*

6. *Problem of jargon.* In any area of study or work, we are confronted with the words of the trade, or *jargon.* Behavioral science (or organizational development) certainly has its share even though we are strongly committed to *communication* and being clear about what is being communicated.

In Appendix I there is a glossary of the jargon frequently used in the Handbook. We have tried to keep these special words to a minimum. We hope we were successful.

Team and organization assessment

2

CHAPTER OBJECTIVE

To offer a series of methods that might help managers and consultants gain a clearer picture of an organization's problems or the problems and issues concerning individuals and teams within the organization. The methods suggested help people pinpoint the problems and thus make it more likely that they will accept the data and be prepared to take action steps to begin dealing with their problems.

GUIDE TO APPLYING INTERVENTIONS

What is team and organization assessment?

- Team and organization assessment includes a number of organized ways of collecting information about a team or an organization.
- The purpose of collecting information may be to: see if there are problems that need dealing with and define what these problems are; focus on key issues of problems and determine whether interventions may be initiated to deal with them.
- The information is collected and problems are defined by the team or organization members who may later have to take part in activities aimed at dealing with these problems.

- Involving people in defining the problems of their organization or team is one of the strong methods available to increase commitment in dealing with these problems.

- The information collected does not serve an external consultant in giving a research report and recommendations. The data are fed back to those involved, serving them both as a stimulant to begin to do something about their problems and as an aid in deciding what to do and where to begin.

- The approach of the interventions described here is based on a "systems" viewpoint. This viewpoint recognizes that each part of the organization is, in some way, dependent on all other parts. In collecting the information and dealing with the problems, the systems viewpoint must be taken into account.

- Each organized assessment, of the kind described here, is an intervention in its own right. It raises people's expectations that changes will come about and possibly matters will improve.

- Consideration should be given to the aspect of raised expectations before deciding on the use of a particular assessment procedure.

- The assessment also serves as the first entry point and link between an external consultant and the team or organization. Relationships and trust established at this stage will later serve as the foundation for collaboration in change efforts.

- In deciding which of these interventions to use, a manager or consultant will have to decide on the scope of the assessment—whether in a team, between teams, in a department, or covering the whole organization.

- A decision will need to be made as to the purpose of the assessment— whether to pinpoint problems, fix priorities among problems, assess organizational functioning, assess functioning in one particular aspect of organizational life, etc.

About the interventions in this chapter

We have often found that many organizations and managers do not know where to start when so many issues and concerns face them. There is some question that "just talking" will be an inefficient use of time; or, at a different level, that it might open up "a can of worms" which would become more than could be handled. Thus, some formal method of assessment is attractive. Still other people are unsure of their readiness to take an important action step until and unless they are very clear about where they are going.

These interventions are about midway between a formal "objective" scientific research report and the other extreme—that of deciding what to do and initiating changes without first collecting information from those involved. The "midway" point makes these forms of diagnosis and assessment useful to a wide range of managers and organizations.

In a workshop setting, managers can have an opportunity to assess and think about their team or organization *without* the pressure of the day-to-day work. Managers and their team members can assess their department and determine its problems. They may begin to look at the impact of the problems and set up some steps to deal with them back on the job.

In the work setting, a more extensive approach to assessment can be organized. Representatives from the total organization can be involved in the procedure. While there is the disadvantage of raising expectations that more will be done than is realistically possible, involving people from different parts of the organization in the assessment has considerable merit.

The interventions

1. *Problem-sensing with groups.* This intervention was developed as an entry to a team or an organization. Oftentimes the top manager would come to discuss the many problems he or she and the organization faced. This process then served as the first diagnostic step in deciding what to begin working on. In smaller organizations, we found we could use this process with groups covering the total organization membership. The method has been developed from experience with many managers and teams.

2. *Individual interviews and group feedback.* A commonly used approach to any team, including managers, a group partnership, or a group of top executives of a large organization, this intervention allows each person to reflect privately and independently on both team and personal issues. It serves as a guide to the team members in deciding which problems to focus on in their work together. Further, it helps the consultant determine the readiness of the group for change.

3. *Questionnaires and feedback.* This intervention demands considerable commitment from the organization. Initiating it requires careful thought by top management and the consultant. We found that going through the process has resulted in a more effective, long-range planning and change process.

4. *Assessment of the organization as a system.* This technique assesses whether or not the organization is carrying out all the functions necessary to keep it going effectively. This is a modification of a method developed by Joseph Handlon and Melvin Allerhand.

Intervention	Use	Who can use	Time demand
Problem-sensing with groups	Pinpointing team or organizational problems; fixing priorities among them	Manager; facilitator; consultant	2–4 hrs
Individual interviews and group feedback	Sensing problems on level of team and between teams for feedback	Mainly outside consultant or facilitator; parts by manager not with own team	8–10 hrs
Questionnaires and feedback	Assessing total organization for *problems* as basis for feedback	Outside consultant	6–12 months
Assessment of the organization as a system	Assessing total organization for how it *functions*	Manager with practice (not with own team); consultants	9–10 hrs

Possible outcomes

1. More awareness of the problems and issues within a team, a department or an organization.
2. More involvement in problem detection.
3. More participation in problem-solving.
4. More awareness of the way a large organization operates.
5. Increased readiness to work on problems and take action steps.
6. Greater acceptance of feedback about problems as opposed to hiding from such problems or concerns.
7. Increased care in defining what and where a problem exists.
8. Increased use of appropriate help from others in the organization.
9. More creative ways of looking at changing the organization.
10. Greater ability to fix priorities among many problems.

Recommended readings

1. Lawrence, P. R., and J. W. Lorsch, *Developing Organizations: Diagnosis and Action* (Reading, Mass.: Addison-Wesley, 1969).

2. Mahler, W. R., *Diagnostic Studies* (Reading, Mass.: Addison-Wesley, 1974).

3. Pfeiffer, J. W., and R. Heslin, *Instrumentation in Human Relations Training* (LaJolla, Calif.: University Associates, 1972).

PROBLEM-SENSING WITH GROUPS

Used with a group so that its members may identify problems, more clearly understand them, and build readiness to solve them.

When to use

This is a most useful process that is often utilized by us as an entry intervention into an organization. The usual circumstances are that a manager or people from top management of an organization come to us to find out whether we can help them. A visit of this kind is generally precipitated by management's feeling that things are not going satisfactorily. There are many problems that management wishes to deal with and is not sure where to begin. Sometimes managers can state what they think the major problems are. At other times they are not sure.

In these circumstances, we would suggest a problem-sensing meeting with:

1. top management, or
2. top management and others, or
3. a cross-section of people from different sectors and ranks, or
4. subgroups of all organization members.

Our considerations in deciding which forum is most suitable are these:

Top management. We would suggest a meeting with top management alone, if we had appropriate information: i.e., that all members of the management team wanted to work with us on their problems and had sufficient legitimacy and informal and formal power in the organization to get things moving.

Top management and others. If the problem described to us, or information from other sources, points to a rift or tension of some kind between management and other ranks in the organization, we would tend to include others in the problem-sensing session.* This generally allows the problems of the tension or rift to find expression in the combined meeting.

A cross-section of people from different ranks and sectors. If interviews with management and/or other information lead us to the conclusion that we are dealing with a weak management team trying to pull an organization through a difficult period, we would choose to hold the session with a cross-section of active and committed people, including members from the management team. We do this to get the widest possible assessment of the

---

* The "others" would include representatives of those segments of the organization where tension is felt by the top management.

situation and the problems and, also, to open the possibility of working through people other than management. We may need them as an internal-change-agent team, or some of them may have to replace members of the top team. Our premise is that if active and committed people diagnose their organization's problems and find that their help is needed, the meeting itself can be a first step in getting them involved.

Subgroups of all organization members. Sometimes in small organizations (not more than 300 people) the problem-sensing can be done with all the members. In this case, we would hold the meetings simultaneously (or on two dates) for all members broken up into subgroups of about 15 people per group. The advantages are that we are thus able to get information, viewpoints, and feelings from everyone involved, to lay the groundwork, and to ensure wider support for future change efforts.

There are disadvantages, too: the problem-sensing raises high expectations throughout the organization, and these expectations may be severely let down if there is not an immediate and effective confrontation of the problems; we would never use this forum in an organization under severe stress or crisis. The technical difficulties are also quite formidable. Preparing sufficient leaders for the subgroups, organizing the meetings, and summing up the material make this a difficult and time-consuming project.

When not to use

We generally would not use this process with work teams or with clients who are definite about what they want.

With *work teams* we prefer to use individual interviews when gathering information. Personal and interpersonal problems are often the core of a team's problems and these are generally gathered only by interviewing the team members personally. (See the section on "Individual interviews and group feedback," in this chapter.)

When clients are *definite about what they want* from us, we generally do not begin problem-sensing with groups. When a manager says he wants an effectiveness workshop within his top team, or job enrichment in a department of his factory, we usually do not say: "Stop! Let's first sense if this is what should be done?" Sometimes we do, if we have a good reason for it, but generally, when a client's requests are clear-cut and definite—and when it seems feasible by all our usual criteria—we acquiesce to their requests.

Who can use: 1. Managers
2. Consultants to organizations; facilitators

Purposes: 1. To "sense," pinpoint, and fix priorities on organization's problems

2. To "sense," pinpoint, and fix priorities on problems of part of an organization—e.g., a department, etc.

Participants: 8 to 15 people consisting of:
1. The top managers; or
2. The top managers and others; or
3. A cross-section from all ranks and all departments; or
4. All members of the organization divided into groups.

Materials:
1. Newsprint, felt pens, and tape
2. Writing paper and pen for each participant
3. Copies of Matrix page (Fig. 2.1)

Time: 2 to 4 hours.

STEPS IN PROCESS

1. Consultant gives introduction.
2. Participants write down two or three problems.
3. Consultant lists problems on newsprint.
4. Consultant makes classification, aided by group.
5. Participants write problems on Matrix sheet.
6. Participants divide 100 points between problems.
7. Consultant lists the points on newsprint.
8. Participants hold discussion to persuade one another to change priorities.
9. Participants change priorities.
10. Consultant notes final results.

Detailed process

1. *Introduction by consultant.* The content of the introduction depends on the purpose of the meeting. The following points may be included:

a. The "turbulent environment" of present times continuously creates new problems for the organization, problems which need to be dealt with in order to ensure healthy survival.

b. Problems are best dealt with in the first stages of their development. Later on, when and if they reach a critical stage, they are expressed in extreme feelings which create difficulties in finding constructive solutions.

c. Generally one is bombarded daily with everyday problems so that time is seldom found to deal with basic problems besetting the organization. This is the opportunity to begin dealing with them.

2. *Participants each write down two or three problems.*

a. The consultant asks the participants to write down, in full detail, two or three major problems of the organization that need to be dealt with.

Sometimes it is worthwhile for the consultant to add: "Include both basic problems that we never get down to dealing with, and new urgent problems that have recently cropped up."

b. Participants are requested not to talk or exchange opinions while others are still writing.

c. It sometimes helps to explain that a problem is "the gap between an existing state and a desired state." This helps to decrease the number of solutions given by participants under the guise of problems.

If the problem-sensing is done in a department or a team regarding their problems, the wording, of course, is changed to "problems of this department," etc.

If the problem-sensing is done with small groups covering the whole organization, it is worthwhile to print slips of paper which contain instructions followed by three lines for writing down the problems.

Note: The wording of the request is important. People list differently when asked for the "urgent problems," the "important problems," "problems we should deal with now," or even when "issues" or "concerns" are requested instead of "problems." The consultant must decide beforehand what the purpose of the problem-sensing is and word the request accordingly.

3. *Consultant lists problems on newsprint.*

a. Following the seating order, each participant reads out the problems he or she has listed, and the consultant writes the problems down on the sheet.

b. It is recommended that the wording of participants not be changed unless absolutely necessary for clarification.

c. Each problem is numbered in the order in which it is written down.

d. The consultant must take care that silence is maintained and no comments are made while the problems are being read out. Reactions may intimidate some of the participants.

4. *Consultant aided by group makes basic classification of the items.*

a. The consultant puts up a new sheet of newsprint and requests the participants to help him or her group similar items under the same headings. The consultant may even begin this grouping so that the participants understand what they are being asked to do. They generally catch the idea immediately and begin calling out something like: "Items 3, 8 and 16 can be put under the heading 'Lack of commitment.' "

b. The consultant puts down the new headings, preferably adding a few words that ensure that different aspects of the problem which appeared in various items find expression under the new heading; e.g., "Lack of commitment," (at work, volunteering, waste).

c. The new headings are listed alphabetically, a., b., c., d., etc. written one underneath the other. On the original newsprint with the original problems the consultant marks—preferably with a different-color marker—the alphabetical letter under which that particular problem is now listed. This allows participants to see which items have already been processed and which still need to be categorized under a new heading.

d. The consultant must take care not to categorize too widely, including under the same heading a wide variety of items that create a cumbersome complex problem difficult to analyze and solve. Again, if someone insists that an item cannot be subsumed under one of the suggested headings, it is not worthwhile to overrule him or her.

On the other hand, if the list of headings is too long it is difficult to process. A group of 12 people produces about 30 problems on the original newsprint and these can generally be condensed into a maximum of from 10 to 14 headings.

5. *Participants write problems on Matrix page.* Participants are now handed the Matrix pages (Fig. 2.1). The consultant slowly reads out a condensed version of the new headings and the participants write them down on the sheet one after the other in the places allocated to them.

6. *Participants divide 100 points among problems.* The participants are now requested to divide 100 points allocating to each heading by either or both of the following criteria: their importance or their urgency (or whichever criterion is decided on by the consultant and the group).

Participants are requested not to allocate all points to a few items but to try and spread them out among most of the items. Another possibility is to request them not to allocate more than 25 points to one item.

Participants often ask what is the use of the vertical columns in the Matrix. These can be used for either of two purposes: Some people need a number of trials in order to allocate the points; alternatively, many people —from our experience—like to copy out the allocation of points made by others when they are read out in the following stage.

Participants sometimes contend that the two criteria, "importance" and "urgency," are different and that one criterion would suit some problems and the other would suit others. Depending on the purpose of the meeting,

MATRIX PAGE – SUMMARY OF RESULTS														Problems of _____				

The form (Fig. 2.1):

Problems \ Names of group members													Totals		Priority	
													Raw	Average	Initial	Final
	100	100	100	100	100	100	100	100	100	100	100	100				

Fig. 2.1 Matrix page

the consultant should emphasize either one of the criteria or ask the participants to try and take both criteria into account.

7. *Consultant lists the points on newsprint.*

a. While the participants are engaged in step 6 (dividing points), the consultant prepares a newsprint copy in the form of the Matrix page.

The participants' names, in seating order, are listed along the top of the paper and the problem headings are listed from top to bottom. As shown in Fig. 2.1, columns at the right are allocated for Totals and for the Priority list.

b. The participants are requested, in seating order, to call out the points they have allocated to the first heading. The consultant writes them down on the newsprint. After completing one or two headings it is helpful to ask one of the participants who is quick at calculating to sum up on his or her sheet the total of each heading. The consultant writes down the points, then asks the helping participant for the line totals and puts them in their columns (preferably in a different color). This procedure is carried out for the rest of the headings until all are written up on the newsprint.

c. Calculate the average number of points assigned to each heading by dividing by the number in the group. Number the headings from "1" for the highest total until each heading has an initial priority or rank number.

8. *Participants discuss to persuade one another to change priorities.*

a. Generally the summing-up arouses greater interest and some minutes should be allocated for tension release.

b. The consultant explains that until now the procedure has been technical without discussion and persuasion. Now the time for discussion has arrived. "You can persuade one another to fix different priorities. If you are persuaded to make changes, then note them down and at the end of the discussion we will write up all the changes."

Some consultants prefer this discussion to be only one-sided; e.g., people can only speak for giving higher priority to some problem and may not argue with someone else about his or her opinion. Other consultants fix no rules and participants can speak about whatever they like either for or against a certain priority. The time allocated to this activity depends on how much time is at your disposal. If there are no time restrictions the discussion should not be limited until everyone has had his or her say. If circumstances demand, a maximum time for this discussion (e.g., from half an hour to an hour) can be fixed.

9. *Participants change priorities and consultant lists final results.* When the discussion is concluded, participants are asked how they wish to change the distribution of the 100 points among the headings. It must be clarified that adding points to one item means that points must be deducted from another item. It is sometimes worth limiting the number of points a person can allocate to one item. This limitation restricts some people from being too "clever" and distorting results by transferring all their points from items with very low priority to another that they especially wish to push ahead.

When all changes have been listed, the consultant writes down the new priority order of each item in the final column of the newsprint. It is worth reading aloud at least the first five items in their new order of priority.

10. *Closing the activity.* We generally terminate the activity with discussion among participants as to what will be done with the priority list. It could be the basis for another meeting of problem and action steps. "What to do with the list," may be the agenda of the next activity, etc.

Note: Problem-sensing should lead to action, change interventions, etc. The only circumstances in which it may not lead to action steps is when an explicit agreement is made beforehand to that effect between the clients and the consultant. This happens when as consultants we are not sure we will intervene and before coming to any agreement we wish to get an estimate of the problems in which we may be involved. The action plan would be limited to the one group. That is, under no circumstances would we do problem-sensing with many groups covering most of the members of the same organization unless we had a commitment from the client beforehand, and we ourselves were sure that we were ready to work with a large segment of the organization or even the entire organization.

Variation 1

After step 4, instead of proceeding with the matrix, members who wish to can: (a) explain the items listed, or (b) explain why an item is "important" or "urgent" or "needs to be dealt with." In such a case, Steps 8 and 9 would be eliminated and the results of the matrix accepted without discussion following allocation of points.

This is a slightly less structured procedure and some groups will find it a more natural way of fixing priorities.

Variation 2

After Step 4, all the rest of the steps are eliminated. No preference order is determined, but all items which received a sizable number of points are accepted as problems that need dealing with.

The team then proceeds to discuss the process by which each problem will be dealt with: what items will be delegated to other bodies, which need a special ad hoc committee to prepare proposals, etc. The detailed process of this stage is given in Chapter 10.

We use this variation when we are sure that both the team and we, the consultants, have sufficient time in the immediate future (preferably the following days) to begin working on all the problems.

If we know that after sensing the problem areas we will have only a day or two to begin working on them, we will not use this variation. Not fixing priorities might lead to dealing with secondary problems and postponing for a long period the confrontation of major problems.

INDIVIDUAL INTERVIEWS AND GROUP FEEDBACK

Use of interviews to identify concerns of members of a team so that these concerns can be fed back to the team as a whole. Helps pinpoint interferences with problem-solving and decision-making.

When to use

- This intervention can be used with a team of managers, a committee, or a work team of any kind.

- It is the initial intervention we use before beginning a team-development program with a managerial committee or any kind of team; it assists in determining the readiness for change in the unit or organization.

- It can be the basis for an intensive workshop with a committee lasting a few days, a week, or more, or it can be the beginning of a series of interventions with a work team.

- This intervention also serves as a final check before the consultant commits himself or herself to working with the team. For example, assume that all the information the consultant has received from the manager and others looks favorable, the unit seems ready, and the consultant believes that he or she can aid the team. Nevertheless, the consultant retains the option of backing out of the commitment if information derived during the interviews brings him or her to the conclusion that working with this team will not give the expected dividends or has little chance of being successful.

- The intervention in this form is *not* suitable for sensing problems of a department or organization in which the staff is so large that interviewing everyone becomes a formidable task.

Who can use:
1. Consultants and an outside facilitator with some experience.
2. Sensitive manager who can handle the first five steps, but *not* with his or her own team.

Purposes:
1. To sense the problem of a group on the individual, interpersonal, group, and intragroup levels.
2. To feed back the material to the group as a basis for:
   a. problem-solving sessions,
   b. a training course or workshop,
   c. a team-development intervention, or
   d. diagnosing the situation before making a contract between the consultant and client.

Participants: A team of any kind—a management committee, or a work team, but preferably with no more than 15 people.

Materials: Newsprint, felt pens, and tape.

Time: 1. The interviews: 30 to 60 minutes per person.
2. The feedback session may take from 2 to 4 hours, but serves as a basis for sessions that may take a few days or weeks, or many sessions with a team over a period of a year.

STEPS IN PROCESS

1. Arranging the interview schedule
2. The interviews
3. Preparing the feedback
4. The feedback session: absorbing the data
5. The feedback session: deciding in what order to deal with the problems
6. Working on the problem areas

Detailed process

1. *Arranging the interview schedule.* The consultant arranges the date and schedule of interviews with the client. Interviews should not be imposed as compulsory, and from our experience people generally welcome them. Nevertheless the consultant should make it quite clear to the client that nobody should be coerced to come to the interview against their will.

The number of people interviewed personally is limited only by the consultant's time and people's willingness. But when working with a team on its problems it is preferable that all members of the team be interviewed.

If during the interview it becomes apparent that interfaces with other groups are problematical, it may be worthwhile interviewing people personally or in subgroups from these other groups. We generally prefer to concentrate all the interviews in a day or two and not extend them over a long period. Concentrating the interviews allows us to compare notes and impressions and prepare the material while all is still fresh in memory. It also controls the level of tension associated with the expectations that are raised through the interviewing process. If we should decide to back out of the intervention, extending the interviews over a long period makes such a step more difficult.

When interviewing a work team or a managerial committee it is sometimes necessary to decide the length of the interviews beforehand, so that each person can be scheduled to come to the interview at a fixed time. A more flexible arrangement is possible if all interviewees are on the premises where the interviews are held. In such case, a room should be allocated at the work place for the interviews so that people can be flexible in the times they leave their work—no schedule being made—and each interviewee when finished goes to find and send to the interviewer another who has still to be interviewed.

When two consultants work as a team they can, of course, divide the interviews, and at the same time each interviews separately a different person. The advantage in this is that it is easier for a twosome to finish all interviews of a team in one day. Another advantage is the possibility of comparing impressions and notes, and defining the problems together.

The disadvantages of interviewing by two consultants is that when notes are compared and problems defined the consultants are not sure whether differences in their impressions stem from a chance division of different types of interviewees, or a distorted impression of one of the consultants. Interviewing by two consultants also creates difficulties and more work in summing up and categorizing the material. This will be explained in a later section of this intervention.

2. *The interviews.*

a. Firstly, the interviewee must be guaranteed anonymity and must know how the data will be handled and shared. Many consultants see the first interview as an intervention in its own right. Empathic listening and clarification of personal and group interpersonal problems often serves as a change activity. However, when team size and time limitations require that the interviews be restricted in time, their major purpose becomes the collecting of information. Then the interview's purpose is to gather as much information as possible and open the expression of feelings and attitudes of the team members to all relevant areas we wish to cover. Thus, while personal issues may be explored, the interviewee must be clear that the overriding purpose is data-gathering.

It must be kept in mind that the interviews also serve the purpose of creating ties and trust between the consultant and the members of the team he or she will later be working with.

b. *What will be made public?* At the beginning of the interview we explain that a great part of what is told us will be displayed before the entire team. However, we promise not to make public which of the team members expressed a particular attitude or feeling.

This procedure would seem to be "bad" modeling behavior for a team which later may have to begin to value openness, disclosure, feedback, and confrontation in interpersonal relations. Nevertheless, we prefer to suffer this disadvantage rather than receive less information at this stage.

c. *With whom to begin?* We generally begin the interview with the team leader or manager who directs the team. We leave open an option to reinterview him or her again after the rest of the team members. From the team leader we generally obtain all the formal details of the team composition: names, background, seniority, work, and responsibility of team members. We also ask the team leader the questions we ask other team members.

d. *What are the interviews about?* Among the questions generally asked in the interview are:

- What are your feelings and attitude about participating in the team-building sessions?
- What aspects of the team's functioning could be helped by the workshop?
- What major problems of the team should be dealt with?
- How do you feel about the division of tasks, responsibility, and power in the team?
- What do you find as barriers to your effectiveness, to getting the job done?
- What needs to be done to improve the team's effectiveness?
- How is the leadership in the team?
- What interpersonal problems are there in the team?
- How do you feel in the team?
- What are the relations and problems between the team and other bodies and individuals?

After interviewing two or three people we begin to get an idea of the major problem areas that need to be dealt with. Therefore, in the following interviews, we can get further information and attitudes relevant to these problems.

e. *Recording the interview.* The interviews may be recorded in writing or by tape recorders, or both. We tend to record the major points of the interview in writing and if possible also by tape. Some people have difficulty speaking freely in the presence of an operating tape recorder, so it is not always possible to tape the interview.

In any case we ask the interviewees' permission to take notes while they talk, and so far have not received a refusal. We promise them that: (a) the feedback will be anonymous; (b) anything they do not want displayed in the feedback will not be made public.

The advantages of taping as well as writing are that:

1) If anything is not clear in the notes it can always be examined later on the tape.
2) When processing the written material it is always possible to see if it truly expresses what was said.

3) Two consultants comparing notes and impressions can always revert back to the actual interviews in order to examine differences between them.

We do not tend to tape-record alone without taking notes because transcribing the contents of a tape recording onto paper involves a great deal of work, and this can be eliminated by taking notes during the interview.

f. *Organizing the material during the interview.* We usually keep a loose-leaf notebook for organizing the data. As mentioned in (d) above, after interviewing two to three people we begin to get an idea of the major problem areas that need to be dealt with. Processing the notes after the interviews is not an easy task. We therefore usually begin organizing the material for processing after the first two interviews. Such organizing is done by making a preliminary breakdown of the material into categories of problem areas and in the following interviews grouping the different problems on separate pages in our notebook, one section of the notebook for each problem. For example: Say we are interviewing a committee and have already interviewed two or three people. We read our notes and see that most of the problems revolve around four headings:

1) Relations between the team's chairman and the team members are problematical.

2) Problem-solving discussions are generally ineffective.

3) Many decisions are not implemented.

4) Relations between the subcommittee and the budgeting committee are strained.

In the subsequent interviews, when interviewing each person, we devote a separate page in our notebook to each of these headings. We use notebooks with detachable pages, so that later we may collect (and keep) the different pages in separate groupings showing what each of the interviewees said about the same subject. We are aware that some consultants find it difficult to take notes this way. So if you find this inconvenient, then just write down everything a person says and later categorize it. In this case, it will make things easier for you later if you write each statement a person makes on a new line in your notebook.

Note: We are careful not to be too biased in our first categorization. We are aware of the possibility that the first people interviewed may not be a representative sample of the entire team. We therefore keep open ears in the subsequent interviews and are ready to add categories, if we feel they are needed, or reorganize the categories if the subject matter demands it.

3. *Preparing the feedback.*

a. *Organizing the comments into problem areas.* Categorizing the material during the interviews will save the consultant a great deal of work. Nevertheless, he or she will have to do the following:

- The remarks of each interviewee that relate to a specific heading must be separated from the rest of his or her comments and put into its appropriate pile. For possible use in the future, the consultant should identify each page of comments with the name of the interviewee who made them.

- The comments of the first two or three people interviewed, which were not categorized, must be broken up and rewritten, if necessary, under the new headings.

- The piles must be reread by the consultant and illegible passages made readable for typing.

- Material categorized under the wrong heading under pressure of the interview must be placed under its correct category.

- Comments not categorized under a heading during the interview should be categorized under one of the existing headings or, if necessary, under a new heading.

- Each pile must be reread and the categorization re-examined. Perhaps one heading contains within itself two major problem areas and it is worth separating them for specific attention and treatment. On the other hand, maybe a pile has very little and should be combined with another pile, under that pile's heading. Another possibility is to combine it with part of another pile under a new category.

- The material is now prepared in typing.

b. *Comparing notes between two consultants.* If the interviews are carried out by two consultants they should, if possible, meet after each has interviewed two people. At this stage they should try to agree on a common categorization that they will try to maintain during the rest of the interviews. When for various reasons a meeting of this kind does not take place, categorizing the interviews is a much more difficult task. If one consultant begins interviewing before the second, it is worthwhile for him or her to suggest the categories to the second consultant before the latter commences interviewing.

If the two consultants have collected the comments under the same headings, the process at this stage is similar to that described under (a) *Organizing the comments into problem areas.*

If common categories were not agreed upon during the interview, the consultants will now have to decide what they will be and reorganize and possibly rewrite all their material accordingly. If the consultants received very different impressions from the interviews as to what the problem areas were, they may have to refer back to the tape recordings (if any were made) or find some other way to organize the material.

c. *Deciding whether to go ahead.* With the typewritten categorized material available, this is the best point for the consultant to reconsider whether he or she wishes to go ahead with the intervention, training, or workshop. The written material and the impressions of individual personalities and their willingness to cooperate with the consultant constitute sufficient information for the consultant to decide whether to go ahead or to back out of the particular intervention.

The considerations which must be taken into account when making this decision are detailed in the introduction to this chapter.

It has sometimes happened that we did not even have to begin preparing the feedback, and that immediately after the interviews it was clear to us that we would not accept this particular request for help. When we were in doubt, we found it worthwhile to categorize and prepare the material, typewritten, and then discuss the matter with other consultants in our team.

d. *Choosing what to display in the feedback session.* There are no clear-cut rules in deciding what to display at the feedback session, but the following considerations should be taken into account:

- The material displayed should give a not too disproportionate share to every interviewee's comments.

- The total display should not be too large for people to read and understand. We generally condense the material to about five to eight problem areas, devoting one newsprint (more or less) to each area.

- It is more effective to give comments in the interviewees' own words than to use those of the consultant.

- When two interviewees have made exactly the same comments we choose the one worded more expressly and put an asterisk (*) next to it to show that another person has made the same remark.

- When most of the people have spoken a great deal in the same way about the same problem we will write their comments (although repetitive) to give this problem the weight it deserves.

- We do not display material the interviewees have asked not be made public.

- We generally do not write names in the feedback display that have been mentioned only once in the interview, for at this stage we are not yet sure whether the problem that mentions a specific individual is that of the person interviewed or of the person spoken about. Sometimes we word a comment of this kind anonymously to express the point of interpersonal tensions or whatever else the problem may be.

For example: "I feel there is rivalry and much tension between X and myself which is disrupting the team's work."

When most members of a team have spoken about specific problems with a team member (most often the leader or chairman) and the problem seems manageable by open confrontation, we will put the person's name on the feedback display. We will consider the person's ability to receive the feedback and we may censor out extreme expressions, but if we feel that the matter is important, not too disruptive for beginning the session, and manageable under our guidance, we will display the name in the feedback.

■ We edit the typewritten material technically, erasing some comments and changing others, and then give them to our secretary to prepare in clear bold writing on newsprint. Each newsprint page is headed by the name of the problem area it deals with, e.g., "Interpersonal Tension in the Team," "Ineffective Distribution of Responsibility," etc. We generally also prepare one newsprint with only the names of these problem areas listed on it.

4. *The feedback session: absorbing the data.*

a. *Introduction and display of feedback.* The consultant is advised not to put up the interview feedback for display at the beginning of the session. Anything said while the feedback data is on the wall is wasted because people will be reading the material. If the feedback session is at the beginning of a workshop, it is better to get done with all announcements and agenda arrangements before dealing with feedback.

We generally spend a few minutes explaining how the material was organized and categorized. At this point we can display the newsprint with the names of the problem areas listed one beneath the other. We generally say some words about the relative stress put on each item by the team members as a whole during the interviews.

The newsprint can now be put up and the team members are invited to read them. People generally get up and read each newsprint one by one. We do not begin the next activity before the last person has finished reading. Inevitably some finish reading before the others and lively discussions break out among twosomes or threesomes. As long as these do not interfere with the people who are still reading, we do not intervene.

b. *Comment on the material.* When all have finished reading we begin an open discussion. All participants can say whatever they want to about the data, about their reactions to the feedback, about specific items in the feedback or whatever they wish.

We prefer this open discussion at this point in order to allow people to let off steam and relax tension before beginning the more structured, decision-oriented session which will soon follow. We intervene as little as possible in this discussion and when all who wish have had their say, we suggest that we move on to the next stage of discussion of the problem areas and how we will deal with them.

5. *The feedback session: deciding in what order to deal with the problems.* The question is put to the team: What is their order of priority in dealing with the problems? Sometimes there are no difficulties and the team soon arrives at a decision about priority. If we do find extreme differences of opinion, then at a suitable point we suggest that the team use a matrix to settle the differences. (See Chapter 10.)

The importance of fixing priorities depends on what plans have been made to continue working with the consultant. If the problem areas are to become the basis for a five- to seven-day workshop with the consultant, the order of dealing with them can be left to the consultant's decision. It is important that the consultant know the team's priorities, but since he or she can begin dealing with most of them during the workshop, their order is not crucial at this point.

On the other hand, if the team is meeting for only two or three days and further meetings with the consultant will only take place periodically after some time, the priority order is given much weight by the team members. In this case we generally tend to hold a short discussion and then use the matrix to help establish priorities. Our consideration is not to spend too much time on this stage but to get down to work on the problems themselves.

In both cases we tell the team that the priority they decide on will guide us, but that it will not be the only factor in deciding in what order we work with the group on the problems it has defined.

We often meet situations in which a team which is seriously disrupted by interpersonal conflicts prefers to get down to business with problems like "improving our decision-making abilities." In cases of this kind we try to clarify with them how the hidden agendas are disrupting decision-making. We may ask them to trust us to respect their priorities, but explain that our professional experience may indicate some changes in their order so as to maximize effectiveness in dealing with them.

In all cases we end this part of the session with a newsprint on the wall (or board) on which the problem areas are listed from top to bottom in the order of preference decided upon by the team.

6. *Working on the problem areas.* How to work with the team on its problem areas is the subject of many chapters in this book. Generally the problems a team defines are those covered by the processes and interventions detailed in this book. We therefore plan a series of sessions with the team, using these processes to help the team deal with the problems and learn ways of confronting similar problems in the future without our assistance.

QUESTIONNAIRES AND FEEDBACK

Using standard or specifically developed questionnaires to analyze and determine the central problems or concerns of a group, team or organization. Following the collecting and organizing of the data, feeding back the results to the organizational unit.

When to use

There often is an almost automatic attraction to questionnaires in a society which emphasizes the scientific method. Thus it is essential to think through the specific usefulness of the questionnaire method as compared with the method we have described under "Problem sensing with groups." To that end we offer you a number of positive and negative points regarding the application of the questionnaire approach: These positives and negatives refer especially to the kind of questionnaires described later as Types 2, 3, and 4.

   1. *Positive aspects of the questionnaire approach.*

   a. An "objective" research questionnaire is considered by some consultants as *more reliable* than data gathered by asking people what the problems of the organization are.

   b. Many clients are of this opinion as well; they want an "objective, scientifically based" report. In fact some clients want just this alone —a scientific report, which they will consider before deciding to do anything else.

   c. The population covered by a research questionnaire is generally *larger* and more representative than that covered by group problem-sensing. In small organizations of a few hundred people the questionnaire can even be answered by the entire population.

   d. Questionnaires make it possible to *compare subgroups,* different departments, different teams, different age groups, etc. This is an advantage that allows the consultant to pinpoint particular problems in different parts of the organization.

   e. Often the questionnaire is more comprehensive and covers *more aspects of the organization's life* than those brought up in problem-sensing with groups.

   f. The *relations* between various important factors can be found and their causes analyzed. Correlations and various forms of statistical analysis can bring scientific proof of the relationship existing between factors.

   g. *More exact* information can be derived. There is a difference between saying that "quite a number of people are dissatisfied with their work" (which is generally the maximum we can derive from problem-sensing) and the statement that 40% of the people expressed dissatisfaction or extreme dissatisfaction with their work and 60% expressed different degrees of satisfaction ("satisfied," "very satisfied").

h. If the questionnaire is a standard one, the data of the organization can possibly be *compared* with that of similar organizations which have made the same research. This gives one a yardstick with which to compare and evaluate the findings.

2. *Negative aspects of the questionnaire approach.*

a. Giving research reports does not *of itself* bring either the necessary or sufficient change. People do not usually change their organization or their team behavior just because they received a scientific report of their problems and the causes of these problems. Even when a work team is confronted with its own data, change does not come of its own unless planned and implemented. Let there be nothing unclear about this statement! Research feedback can be the first stage in a change effort, but it must be followed by other appropriate intervention methods if actual development is to take place.

b. In using a questionnaire there is possibly a *huge disproportion* between the assessment stage and the intervention stages. Quite often, so much energy, time, and money are put into preparing the questionnaire, applying it, processing it, analyzing it, writing it up, and reporting it as feedback, that all the effort ends there. That means that after all these activities and costs, little energy and few resources remain for the actual interventions of dealing with the problems.

c. Research is *time consuming.* Even with a standard questionnaire, preparing, applying, and reporting take at least a few months. With a research questionnaire specifically prepared for an organization the whole process can take a year or more.

d. This leads to another weakness of questionnaire material—that by the time the data is fed back it may be *outdated.* The speed of change is so great in our times that research data collected a year or two previously may possibly be history today.

e. The questionnaire approach is *costly.* The whole process of preparing, applying, and reporting such research is very expensive, and that must be weighed against its results.

f. The questionnaire approach often brings up far *more problems* than can ever be expected to be dealt with. If the instrument is a good, sensitive one and includes comparative data of subgroups, the manager/consultant is going to be faced with a mountain of unearthed problems, many of which need confrontation. People ask themselves: "Why do we need so much information when it is probable that only a small part of it can be dealt with in the immediate future?" If priorities are then fixed and three or four problems chosen for confrontation, the question arises, "Why did we need the research? We could have told you these are the major problems without the costly, time-consuming research."

g. *Research raises high expectations.* If many people in an organization are asked many questions about the organization's problems and their own, it is natural that they will develop high expectations for important changes in the near future. In any case, until the data are finally ready for feedback, people feel let down because nothing has happened. After the data have been fed back, it generally happens that the change efforts made in one area or another may not directly affect many people. Even when changes do take place in some areas of the organization, it may be from six months to a year after the questionnaires were filled in before the effects can be felt. People feel let down.

h. People often resist and *do not accept* research data. It quite often happens that the research questionnaire is a standard one that the members of the organization had no part in preparing. In such cases it is quite usual for people not to accept the findings. They see them as not belonging to them—something from outside and alien. They had no part in it and want no part in it, the more so if it throws light on negative aspects of their functioning.

Who can use:	1. For extensive use of the questionnaire throughout an organization, only a consultant experienced in organizational research, feedback and interventions.
	2. For more limited use, the manager experienced in evaluation research who has some experience as a facilitator can use the method described here as Type 1.
Purposes:	1. To determine an organization's problems, discover causes, and determine relationships between problems and causes.
	2. To determine problems of subgroups in the organization.
	3. To use the results of the questionnaire as feedback to the organization, its management, subgroups, etc.
	4. To use questionnaire results as a basis for change efforts and activities in the organization.
Participants:	1. Total sampling of organizational or subgroup members.
	2. Random or representative sample of organization.
Materials:	1. Different types of questionnaires:
	a. Problem-identification questionnaire
	b. Standard questionnaire

c. Standard research questionnaire

d. Special research project

2. Forms for organizing questionnaire data:

   a. Forms for categorizing responses

   b. Forms for coding data

3. System for comparing different results:

   a. Use of computer

   b. Hand-sorting method (e.g., McBee sorting system)

4. System of displaying the results for feedback:

   a. Mimeographed tables

   b. Newsprint, felt pens, and tape

   c. Slides

Time: From six to twelve months: For the simplest of questionnaire methods about one month is required; for the more complicated about six months to a year.

STEPS IN PROCESS

1. Initial contacts with client or change team

2. Selecting the questionnaire method

3. Preparing the questionnaire and gathering hard data

4. If such a team has not been previously identified, choosing the change team and providing necessary training

5. Administering the questionnaire

6. Analyzing and displaying the data and results

7. Feedback of major results

8. Fixing priorities for action program

Detailed process

1. *Initial contacts with client or change team.* We have found that an essential ingredient for success in this type of intervention is high client involvement at all stages of the process. Such involvement is the key factor in increasing and acceptance of the results and commitment to work on them in a change program. Thus, in the initial contact with the client, it is useful to examine the various alternatives in the questionnaire approach which offer the client the positives and negatives of options. In so doing, more data and an even clearer picture of the organizational climate often emerge.

It has been our general experience that at the stage of reviewing questionnaire alternatives, the procedure should be carried out with a change team rather than just one or two key people from the organization. It is essential to have a spectrum of opinions at this early stage since the questionnaire will have wide distribution and the results of the questionnaire are likely to affect many members of the organization. The change team can be involved in a number of different ways during the entire process. For example:

a. In preparing the questionnaire, it can add and delete questions based on the members' awareness of the organization.

b. It can decide what aspects of the organization's life should be covered and in what ways the data might be subgrouped; e.g., by departments, by level of work within the organizations, by age groups.

c. It can handle the entire administration of the questionnaires under the guidance of the facilitator.

d. Its members may do the final analysis and determine conclusions if the consultant has organized and displayed the results to facilitate such independence in the use of the results.

e. It can be trained to help other units within the organization analyze their own data for application within their own department or unit.

f. It can reach out to other members of the organization so that as many people as possible will be involved in the process.

2. *Selecting the questionnaire method.* Assuming that the organization has decided that a questionnaire method is the desired approach, the following criteria are suggested in choosing the optimal method:

a. How immediate is the need for the results?

b. How extensively can the results be applied to the organization? How relevant are the results to different groups or units in the organization?

c. Do you want all aspects of the organization's life covered or only a particular field, such as work satisfaction or the organizational structure?

d. What is the desirable level of refinement of the results? Do you need general problems identified or *very specifically related to each unit* of the organization?

e. Do you only want to identify problems or are you also interested in data on *relationships and causes*?

f. What are the available resources? People resources? Money resources? Time availability?

g. How interested are you and others in carrying out such a study of the organization?

h. Thinking of the respondents to the questionnaire, what type of questions and approach would fit their level of understanding; their needs?

We suggest that the facilitator and change team consider the following types of questionnaire methods:

Type 1 *Problem-identification questionnaire:* This approach is problem-sensing with a representative group of the organization; organizing the problem statements on a questionnaire with space for respondent to add problems or concerns; and distributing the questionnaires to all or a sample of the members of the organization for their responses.

Characteristics: Easy to apply; results in two weeks to a month; low level of refinement; limited need for resources; low level of interest needed; items on questionnaire can fit the understanding of the respondents; data on relationships and causes *cannot* be arrived at directly through questionnaire; data *cannot* be compared to studies of other organizations.

Type 2 *Standard questionnaires:* These are standardized questionnaires developed by individual consultants or consulting firms. In some instances they can be acquired from these firms and applied by a member of the organization interested in the study. Many consulting firms require that they carry out the entire procedure.

Characteristics: Moderately easy to apply; results within a short period of time; high level of refinement; moderate need for resources; moderate level of interest necessary; items on questionnaire *cannot* be modified; data on relationships and causes may or may not be arrived at through the questionnaire; results *can* be compared to those of other organizations.

An example: Organization Health Survey by W. J. Reddin, Organizational Tests Ltd., 1973. Practical information about these kinds of questionnaires can be found in *Instrumentation in Human Relations* by Pfeiffer and Heslin.

Type 3 *Standard research questionnaires:* These are methods often developed by faculty members at universities. The questionnaires are preplanned for computer analysis.

Characteristics: More difficult to apply; results within a few months; high level of refinement; higher need for resources; higher level of interest necessary; items on questionnaire *cannot* be modified; data on relationships and causes *can* be arrived at; depending on source, items sometimes can and sometimes cannot be compared to those of other organizations.

An example: Survey of Organizations, from Taylor, J. C., and D. C. Bower, *Survey of Organizations.* Ann Arbor: Institute of Social Research, 1972.

Type 4 *Special research project* (using a questionnaire): Such an approach builds a research study around the questionnaire method. The research is tailor-made to the organization's particular needs.

Characteristics: Often difficult to apply; results within six months to a year; high level of refinement; very high need for resources; very high level of interest necessary; selection of items on questionnaire *can* be influenced by client; data on relationships and causes *can* be arrived at; items *cannot* be compared with other organizations.

3. *Preparing the questionnaire and gathering hard data.* (In this section we will deal specifically with questionnaire Type 1. For Types 2, 3, and 4 the consultant must either utilize the approaches of researchers who have developed standard methods or develop his or her own modifications.) For questionnaire Type 1, we suggest that the experienced manager or consultant take the following steps:

a. Review the organizational structure and select a group of between 10 and 20 who represent the organization in terms of worker-manager levels; departments or subgroups; length of service with organization; sex, ethnic background (when appropriate); other factors that might be relevant to your organization.

b. Invite the attention of the members of the group through a letter from the organization's highest executive or managing group which explains the purposes and goals of the process.

c. Ideally, invite the group to a problem-sensing meeting to identify the central concerns/problems that they are aware of. (In case of time constraints, send a memo to the group members requesting that they list the five problems that most interfere with the operation or development of the organization. Follow up the memo with personal phone calls to each of the group members.)

d. After receiving responses from all of the members of the group, organize the questionnaire as suggested in Fig. 2.2. The responses should be grouped so that all are included in the section entitled "Problem statement," using language as similar to that of the respondents as possible. After all the problems are listed, leave sufficient space under that section of the questionnaire for additional problems or concerns.

Problem Statement	See as problem; I can do something about it	See as problem; I cannot do something about it	Do not see as problem
1. Cannot get my ideas to be heard by top management			
2. Seems to be no direction from top management			
3. Need more training in basics of managing people			
4. Etc. (for additional problems identified by respondent)			

Fig. 2.2 Problem-statement record sheet

We cannot stress enough the importance of gathering *"hard" data* together with the "soft" data of the questionnaires. By "hard" data we mean numbers and indices such as: the number of employees (members); manpower turnover rate; absentee rate; age of managers; annual profit rate over the past five years; percentage expenditure in research and development; other economic indices that are readily available; etc. Such data will be very useful in the analysis of the results.

4. *Selecting and developing a change team.* As indicated under Section 1 of "Detailed process," it is most desirable to have a change team throughout the intervention; however, if such a team has not been identified by this time, it is essential to select the members now. They may well come from the 10 to 20 people who have already been involved in the developing of items for the questionnaire. However, the change team should have both formal and informal power within the organization. Further, they should be people who can see "the larger picture" and who are not just caught up in the details of getting the immediate job done. The change team should include from 6 to 8 people.

The training and development of the change team requires basic experiences in building a team (see Chapter 6) as well as some specific skill training for the different phases in developing, handling, and interpreting the results of the questionnaire. Again, the particular skills required for the completion of the questionnaire method are related to the initial choice of procedure. In the procedure we are detailing, the skills should include:

a. Narrowing down the items to be included under the problem-statement section of the questionnaire.

b. Stating the problem statements clearly while using the words of the respondents as much as possible.

c. Brainstorming about ways to gain interest and participation among all members of the organization.

d. Interpreting the results so that they *can* be readily used by the organization.

e. Presenting results so that they *will* be readily used by the organization.

f. Feedback of major results to other members of organization.

5. *Administering the questionnaire.*

a. *Selecting the sample.* Selecting the people who will fill out the questionnaire is an important decision. The three factors to be considered are: optimal results; raising expectations; and future involvement and impact. If the questionnaire method is being used with a small organization or a department, it is usually advantageous to include all available members in the sample. Thus the results reflect all elements of the unit. When the future interventions take place, all participants will have some idea about the beginnings of the process.

In a larger organization and when the plan is to understand and work on total organizational problems, some method of sampling must be applied. One approach is to develop a sample by selecting more people, like the original 10 to 20, who represent the organization and were used to develop the questionnaire. Sampling can also be accomplished by taking a percentage of the people in the organization to make it a representative approach. The percentage is applied to each of the units of the organization. For organizations of 5,000 people or more a 10 percent sample generally is sufficient. As the numbers in the organization decrease, the percentage should increase so that you would not have less than 200 respondents in the sample except for organizations whose total membership is less than 200.

b. *Administering the questionnaire.* The units of the organization should be divided among the members of the change team. From the standpoint of dividing up the organization, the change-team members have full responsibility for distributing and collecting the completed questionnaires. The following steps are suggested:

▪ A letter from the executive officer or executive committee should accompany each questionnaire, indicating the importance of the survey to the organization and urging each person to reply.

▪ Using the questionnaire form (see Fig. 2.2), the change-team member can allow each respondent to be anonymous, yet the department or unit can be identified for future analysis. (*Note:* Generally we have found that respondents are more open when their names are not required; however, it is possible to ask for some identifying data such as: age to the nearest decade; position in organization or unit; or other factors that will not easily identify the person yet may be useful in the analysis of the data.)

■ When possible the change-team member and the leader or department manager might have a short meeting with the respondents to explain the procedure, including the sampling method. If only a select group has been chosen, there usually is some feeling of competition, and it is useful to give as accurate and uncomplicated an explanation as possible about the way people were chosen as respondents. The respondents must be given a date by which the questionnaire should be returned. If questionnaires have not all been returned by the date, the change-team member will send out reminders, and then set another deadline, indicating that questionnaires received after the new date will not be used in the study.

6. *Analyzing and displaying the data and results.* The change-team member can organize the data from the questionnaires he or she has collected by taking a blank questionnaire and tabulating the responses on that sheet. When there are more additions to the problem statements than there is space available, the team member can draw another questionnaire on a blank piece of paper and (using the same headings) write in the additional problems. Repeat problems with slightly different wording should not be eliminated but tabulated next to the appropriate problem statement. The next steps are best taken with the total change team:

a. Newsprint should be set up with the headings of the questionnaire at the top, and the original and additional problem statements should be recorded in the "Problem Statement" column.

b. Each change-team member calls off the tabulations from the units he or she was responsible for.

c. The first set of results to be discussed by the change team is under the first column, headed "See as problem; I can do something about it." These results are likely to have the earliest and best payoff when future interventions are being considered. The second column; i.e., "See as problem; I cannot do something about it," very often reflects the respondents' views of the managers and executives.

d. The change team can organize the results in many different ways such as:

■ For report to the total organization, the problems can be ranked according to the number and kind of votes given by all the respondents. Bringing these results together with the "hard" data (see Section 3 of "Detailed process") may help focus attention on some central issues of the organization. In some instances, the change team may suggest some alternative action steps. Report form: typed and duplicated.

■ For report to units of the organization, the data can be ranked according to the votes of respondents from that unit. Comparisons can be made between the overall organizational results and the results collected from each department. Within a unit, the results might be displayed on newsprint rather than typed in a written report form.

■ We suggest that the change team think about the best ways of displaying the results for different organizational groups.

7. *Feedback of major results.* The change team must determine the most desirable process for feeding back the major results. In our experience, it is essential to select from the report some overriding issues or *themes.* A theme might be: Performance evaluations are not presented in a clear, direct manner so workers are not sure where they stand or what they must do to perform better or be promoted; or top management is not listening to the ideas suggested by managers and workers below them. It must be shown that each theme is supported by the problem statements that were identified through the survey. The major themes should be presented to top management in a form and process that fits the organization. An effective approach has been:

a. Meeting with the executive officer to discuss the major themes and ways of feeding back the results to the executive committee and other parts of the organization.

b. Organizing a meeting of the executive committee to review the major themes and consider recommendations. The major themes might be presented on newsprint with reference to questionnaire results. Each member of the committee would have previously received the total report of the questionnaire. During such a meeting members of the change team might share their recommendations with the executive committee and through this sharing help build with the executive committee a group of tentative recommendations for approaching some of the problems. We have found that many top executives who have not experienced this approach need assistance in getting started, and the change-team members can be of much help in this process. The executive committee must help decide the action steps, including how the report would be used with different units of the organization.

c. In deciding on what to display during the feedback session or sessions, see "Individual Interviews and Group Feedback," particularly "Preparing the feedback."

8. *Fixing priorities for action program.* The priorities for an action program must be determined by the decision-making body that will be closest to the specific action. If we are referring to total organizational matters, then the top executive or executive committee must deal with such priority-setting. We suggest that you review the procedure outlined under "Problem-

Sensing with Groups," particularly Sections 5 through 9 of the "Detailed process."

When the action program is within a unit of the organization, particular attention should be given to the problem statements that the members of that unit saw as problems they could work on.

Note: The reader is referred to Chapter 5, "How to Begin Dealing with Problems," for a procedure by which to decide how to process the problems in the decision-making body.

ASSESSMENT OF THE ORGANIZATION AS A SYSTEM

Assessing the total organization or a department as an operating unit or system. Can give you a sense of the sources of problems as well as identifying the people who can help deal with the problems.

When to use

We have found that the application of this type of assessment is useful *anytime.* A manager may use such an approach when she or he:

- Has the time.
- Is interested in *the source of a nagging problem* either within his or her own department or in a department that has a functional connection with it.
- Is planning a new approach, such as a job enrichment program or the use of new equipment, and wants to *assess the available resources for or potential interferences with* establishment of the new program.
- Is interested in career development in the organization and wishes to assess his or her *chances of success or to identify the best career development options.*

Who can use:
1. Any person in the organization who has access to people in other departments of the organization.
2. Consultants to organizations.

Purposes:
1. To gain a broader perspective about the way an organization operates.
2. To determine sources of help or interference within the organization or unit of the organization.
3. To locate the source of problems within the organization.

Participants:
1. Just the manager in any department.
2. A manager and a selected group of other managers.
3. Top management of the organization.

Materials: 1. Paper and pencil.
2. System-as-an-Organism recording sheet (Fig. 2.3).

Time: 1. 9 to 10 hours for total assessment.
2. 4 to 5 hours for initial or baseline assessment.

STEPS IN PROCESS

1. Looking at system as an organism (initial or baseline)
2. Leadership/decision-making system
3. Communication/information system
4. Resource system
5. Interpersonal relationships system
6. Review/evaluation system
7. Communicating results of assessment

Detailed process

1. *Looking at system as an organism (initial or baseline).* We have found that you can gain a very useful picture of your department or team or total organization by thinking of the unit as though it were a living organism. After all, a human invention, comprised of a group of people, carrying out a specific function should have all the elements of an operating organism— if it is functioning effectively. What we are asking you to do is to test for the *presence* and the *level* of *effectiveness* in each part of this organism. Choose anyone in your organization—*including yourself.*

a. The *thinking source:* Who does the planning? Who has the long range and broad perspective? Who does the problem-solving? Who has a head on his or her shoulders?

b. The *feeling source:* Who responds emotionally to the human issues? Who makes the comment: "It feels right so why not?" Who might say, "Why don't you give him a break?" Who gets a tear in his or her eye during the five- or ten-year service awards?

c. The *listening source:* Who focuses on what the other person is saying? Who seems to bring up another person's view when a topic or problem is being reviewed?

d. The *digesting source:* Who not only listens to others but brings together varied views on a subject? Who integrates what may be learned from within the organization and from outside sources? Who puts together a good summary of the thinking on a subject?

e. The *action source:* Who comes through with: "Well, let's get going"? Who comes back to the next meeting reporting the action steps he or she has taken? Who gets into trouble for having acted without total agreement?

f. The *blocking source:* Who always comes up with: "Well, I think we need more information"? Who questions making any changes in the organization?

g. *Source of expending energy:* Who is always free with the money of the organization? Who comes up with ideas but never thinks of how much time and money they will cost?

h. *Source of conserving energy:* Who is always turning off the lights and talks about the wasting of time and money? Who tries to cut corners in implementing the marketing program?

i. Now, think of other parts of any living organism. Are there *any other functions* of that organism that you feel are or should be a part of your organization? For example, protective covering. If you think of another source, list that source on the System-as-an-Organism recording sheet (Fig. 2.3).

j. Think about the people in your organization or unit and try to *identify the person(s) who could be the source of all the different functions*

		Names of People					
Source	Self	Respondent 1	Respondent 2	Respondent 3	Respondent 4	G.A.	N.C.
Thinking							
Feeling							
Listening							
Digesting							
Acting							
Blocking							
Expending energy							
Conserving energy							

Fig. 2.3 System-as-an-Organism recording sheet

G.A.: general agreement on people who fulfill this function.
N.C.: no consistent source in the organization.

suggested above. You may well find that the same person assumes more than one function. Record the names of the people on the recording sheet, in the column labeled "Self."

k. The next step requires determining who in the organization *can give you additional input* about the way the system operates. Identify three or four people whom you respect and trust, who are in different departments, and who may see the organization from a different vantage point than you do. Interview them, using the same procedure that you followed in assessing the organization. Record their responses on the recording sheet by listing the names they give you in the appropriate rows of the various "Respondent" columns.

l. Review the Recording Sheet and place the names of those whom your respondents most consistently suggest as source people in the column headed "G.A." If there are no source people—or no consistent source people—in a given area, record an X in the appropriate row of the "N.C." column. We have found that identifying a lack of consistent source people, or people fulfilling some essential functions of the organization, will help with reaching into the core problems of the organization.

m. With this information in front of you, think about the question or problem you had in mind when you started this intervention. What have you learned about *your own role in the organization?* Can you see *what additional functions you might assume?* Have you gotten some *insights about certain people* in your organization? We have found that after such an exercise, some managers became unlocked from a rather stagnant position and either achieved recognition and thus promotion or created some additional position which was helpful to themselves and the organization. For example, a young manager of a technical department was feeling very limited in his position and was seeking some broader responsibilities. He applied the baseline approach to a number of departments in the organization, including the group of top executives. The results allowed him to be clearer about how different managers could be helpful to him in reaching his goal. He knew that initially he must avoid the "blocking" source. He could see that discussing his future with the "listening" sources might assist him in clarifying his objectives. After such clarification, further discussions with the "thinking" sources might assist him in fitting his objectives into the long-term objectives—needs of the organization. He followed these steps and they helped him gain a general manager's job.

n. As indicated earlier, this sequence of steps can be used to gather an initial or baseline view of the organization. It may be sufficient for your needs. However, if you require a more detailed approach, follow the next steps.

We offer these next steps for managers or consultants who are trying to gain a clear description of the entire organization. They provide a series of questions which will ensure tapping into all the important systems within the organization. It is also possible to examine any one system as a separate entity, if you happen to be particularly concerned with that subsystem. We find it important that you inform the appropriate people that you are *undertaking such an assessment.* We suggest that you start a loose-leaf notebook for recording the data you collect. The notebook might be divided into the five systems and the last section can be used for writing up the assessment.

2. *Leadership/decision-making system.*

a. *How are decisions made in your organization, your department, etc.?* There are two distinct mechanisms—the formal and the informal decision-making processes. You should observe carefully at least one problem or issue and attempt to determine how the decision was made. What were the formal steps? What happened after the meetings? You may have to ask a few questions about some conversations held during coffee breaks or over the telephone.

b. *How do decisions get implemented?* Does the individual or group who made the decisions clearly give the authority and responsibility to the implementers? Do certain people get piled up with the implementation? Do certain people offer their services all of the time? Does the implementation start with a blast after which people gradually lose interest? Are certain kinds of decisions implemented more readily than others?

c. *How do the power groups in the organization operate?* Are some groups always supportive of one another whatever the decision? And are other groups always antagonistic? Are some individuals or people always trying to bridge between groups, functioning as bridges or linking pins between individuals or groups? Is power used mainly to further the objectives of the organization or for personal reasons?

3. *Communication/information system.*

a. *Who are the collectors of information?* There are certain people in the organization who seek out information, whether it is formal memos or just rumors. Who are these people? Are they located in any special places in the system? Are they mainly secretaries? Administrative assistants? Top-level managers?

b. *Who has what information?* There usually are some people who have the more powerful information, the inside dope. Who are they? Other people just collect it all. Who are they? Still others collect the gossip. They will know who is getting married or divorced—all the special relationships among members of the organization.

c. *What kind of information is special for your organization?* It is always useful to understand what is the more powerful information for that organization. Some organizations place the emphasis on finances; others on acquisitions, or job opportunities, or personal gossip, and so on. You can get special understanding of the nature of the organization by just ranking the importance of information as you see it. It is also useful to get some other opinions.

d. *What are the patterns of flow of information?* Who seems to talk with whom? When people take coffee breaks, how do they cluster? Do the people with a lot of information meet together? Do people from different departments seem to mix and exchange information? What are the usual ways of passing information—memos, bulletin boards, meetings, etc? Who are blocks to the passing of information? Does someone just let it pile up? Any consistent complaints about not getting messages?

4. *Resource system.*

a. *What are the available resources for getting the job done?* Who has the special skills for particular kinds of decision-making? Who would you ask to evaluate someone's competence to do a job? Who is the person with that special mechanical know-how? Who can really push something along? Who seems to have the really high motivation? Who has that special dedication? Who do you turn to if you need money to get the job done?

b. *What are the available resources for fulfillment, growth, or fun?* Who has that special way of making you feel good? Who seems to always have the group around him or her just having a good time? Who gives you that sense of good spirits, a feeling that you just want to do more?

c. *What is the best way to pull the resources together?* Is it best to go to each person individually? Is it best to bring together a group of the resources and work on the problem? Is it better to do the whole job at one sitting, to work on it until the group is finished? Or is it better to go at it piece by piece? What seems to be the optimal way for your organization?

5. *Interpersonal relationships system.*

a. *What is the past history of mutual support?* Who seems to easily help whom within the organization? Has such support been shown for a long period of time? If such support has stopped after a time, what seemed to cause the ending of support?

b. *What is the past history of conflict?* Who has seemed in conflict with the organization over time? Has anyone showed a pattern of conflict with organizational objectives? Has it come to an end? How did that happen? Anyone show a pattern of conflict with a particular group or department?

c. *Who is open with his or her views?* Some people have a way of just sharing their thoughts. Who shares openly about decisions? Who is willing to tell you how to bring about change? Who seems straight about their attitude toward others—just tells it like it is?

d. *Who is resistant to change?* Some people just have a lot of trouble with change; who are these people in your organization? Who seems to block some seemingly good moves? Who just sits on things?

e. *Who makes you feel uncomfortable?* Some people just give you that feeling of: "I don't want to stay with her or him very long." Any of those types around? What seems to make such uncomfortable feelings happen? Under what circumstances? Do these bad feelings seem justified?

6. *Review/evaluation system.*

a. *Who in the organization carries out evaluation?* When someone remembers that we must evaluate some work of ours, who is that someone? Who has the evaluation function as a formal part of his or her job? What departments or groups of the organization include periodic evaluation? Who seems to take the initiative for such evaluations? Is the purpose different for different evaluators?

b. *How often is evaluation carried out within the organization?* Is it carried out periodically, at fixed intervals, or just whenever someone thinks of it? Does the period vary in different parts of the organization?

c. *Does evaluation have a useful and creative impact on the organization?* Do you find that people are motivated to produce more after such evaluations? Do you see that a particular program is appropriately changed because of the evaluative process?

7. *Communicating results of assessment.*

a. We strongly recommend that you check your information with some trusted co-workers in the organization before organizing it into a report for yourself or for more general display. As indicated in establishing the baseline assessment, you should identify some people who may give you additional data because of their way of viewing the organization. Of course, this type of additional data is most critical when you feel unsure of the data you have already collected. Or if you feel you have identified a very disturbing situation, then getting additional views is essential. Further observations should be recorded in the appropriate section of your notebook.

b. At the end of each section of your notebook, a summary statement is useful. You should select the five-to-ten most critical facts about each subsystem, judging for yourself what is critical and what is not. Some managers focus on problems; others on the most surprising findings; others on the insights about the subsystem that are suggested by the study.

c. The summary statements can be used as the body of the assessment write-up. It is often useful to have some introductory remarks about the purpose of the assessment and a statement of the method used to collect data. Finally, a section on conclusions and, if appropriate, the recommendations for next steps.

d. You must think through how your work will be communicated or displayed. Such an assessment can raise expectations and anxieties. As was indicated at the outset, appropriate people should be warned of the assessment effort. It usually follows that at least these same people would share the results of your work. Often, these people are helpful in deciding in what other ways the results of the assessment might be used.

Variation 1

In the baseline study (Step 1) you can save considerable time if you do not seek additional observations from other people. Such a variation has been found acceptable when you just want to get a better understanding of your own department.

Variation 2

The entire assessment procedure or just the baseline (Step 1) can be included in a workshop of managers from different organizations. We have found that sharing assessments in groups of four has provided each participant with some additional insights into their own organizations.

> *Note:* This intervention, Assessment of the Organization as a System, is a modification of an assessment procedure developed by Drs. Joseph H. Handlon and Melvin E. Allerhand.

Improving
your managerial
style

3

For managers: to offer a series of interventions that will increase your awareness of different learning and managerial styles so that you are clearer about your approach to working with people and can suit your style to the work situation.

For facilitators and consultants: to offer you a number of processes for groups of managers.

GUIDE TO APPLYING INTERVENTIONS

What is improving your managerial style?

- Managerial *style* improvement may be approached by working on three elements that have a major effect on: (1) the manager's emphasis on "task" or on "people" in different situations; (2) the manager's learning style and its affect on his or her managerial style and ways of communicating with others; (3) the manager's basic attitude toward people and his or her theories about what motivates them at work.

- A person's managerial style finds expression in the way he or she handles people and tasks in different situations. The balance a manager finds between satisfying the demands of these two factors is of major importance in determining his or her style.

- Different work situations demand different emphasis on the "people" and "task" aspects of management. The ability to adjust to suit the conditions of different work situations is an important factor in determining the effectiveness of the manager's style.

- By receiving feedback from others on how these aspects of his or her functioning affect them, a manager can reevaluate the effects of his or her style and take steps to improve it.

- Managerial style is closely connected with a person's learning style. Learning style is the specific way a person best absorbs information and knowledge; it influences what the manager receives as communications from others and how he or she communicates with them.

- Awareness of one's own learning style and the different learning styles of others helps a manager adjust his or her modes of communication with others to the medium that best reaches them.

- The way a manager treats people at the workplace is influenced by his or her basic attitudes and theories about people and what motivates them at work—e.g., one who believes that most people prefer not to make an effort at work will probably try to enforce close control.

- Becoming aware of his or her basic theories about people and what motivates them at work can bring a manager to reexamine these beliefs and reevaluate them.

- Changes in a person's basic theories about what makes people work effectively can bring about parallel change in that person's management methods and style.

- Changes in the three elements affecting managerial style are enhanced when one becomes more aware of them, receives feedback on them and discusses them with others.

About the interventions in this chapter

For individual managers. We have found that individual managers may gain self awareness through application of these interventions on their own. But since these processes require much personal searching, managers who are attending workshops with other managers seem to benefit more than those who apply the processes by working on them alone. Feedback from others helps. We suggest that you think about these interventions as a more *personal* help to yourself as a manager and an individual. Working on your personal effectiveness and examining your managerial style might have payoffs for you—and your organization.

For work teams. Work teams that have close and long-term relationships can benefit from the interventions in this chapter. The facilitator should take into account that some of the sharing requires a high level of trust to get the best benefits from these processes.

The interventions

1. *Confronting your learning style.* This was developed as a way of look-ing at the basic way that you operate as a learning person. You are asked to look over some aspects of the way you learn that previously you may not have paid attention to. The process may get you to think about changes in how you communicate or how you might organize your work differently. This intervention relates to the work of Kolb, Rubin, and McIntyre.

2. *Balancing your managerial style.* You are asked to examine your orien-tation to tasks and persons as it relates to handling your job. In the process you try to build the best fit between your style and the de-mands of your specific job situation.

3. *Examining your basic attitude toward people.* You are asked to re-view your assumptions about people and to check on how these as-sumptions are reflected in your approach to team members. You exam-ine whether changing your assumptions will cause team members to become more motivated and take more initiatives. This intervention is based on the theories of Douglas McGregor.

MATRIX OF INTERVENTIONS

Intervention	Use	Who can use	Time demand
Confronting your learning style	Communication problems; not being understood; not understanding	Manager with practice	About 3 hrs
Balancing your managerial style	Understanding and recognizing impact of style	Consultant; facilitator; manager not with own team	3–10 hrs
Examining your basic attitude toward people	Getting at your attitudes toward people and how to increase motivation	Consultant; facilitator; manager	3–10 hrs

Possible outcomes

1. More clarity about how you learn.
2. Increased sensitivity to how others learn.
3. Better use of your skills in teaching people.
4. Sharpening your ways of dealing and communicating with people who have different styles.
5. Using more of the talents of other members of the team to complement your way of doing things.

6. Being clearer about your view of why people function as they do.

7. Increased motivation and initiative-taking by team members.

8. Change in control method as a result of reexamination of basic theory of what motivates people.

9. Taking the "people" factor more into account in work situations.

10. Better atmosphere in team as a result of more consideration for people.

11. Greater ability to suit managerial style to the demands of the situation.

Recommended readings

1. Blake, R. R., and J. S. Mouton, *Building a Dynamic Corporation Through Grid Organization Development* (Reading, Mass.: Addison-Wesley, 1969).

2. ————, *The Managerial Grid* (Houston: Gulf Publishing, 1964).

3. Kolb, D. A., I. M. Rubin, and J. M. McIntyre, *Organizational Psychology: An Experimental Approach*, 2d ed. (Englewood Cliffs, N. J.: Prentice-Hall, 1974).

4. Kolb, D. A., et al., *Organizational Psychology: A Book of Readings*, 2d ed. (Englewood Cliffs, N. J.: Prentice-Hall, 1974).

5. McGregor, D., *Human Side of Enterprise* (New York: McGraw-Hill, 1958).

6. Reddin, W. J., *Managerial Effectiveness* (New York: McGraw-Hill, 1970).

7. Hersey, P., and K. H. Blanchard, "Leader Effectiveness and Adaptability Description," in J. W. Pfeiffer and J. E. Jones (eds.) *1976 Annual Handbook for Group Facilitators* (San Diego: University Associates, 1976).

CONFRONTING YOUR LEARNING STYLE

Understanding how your way of learning influences your communication, relationships with other people, and, in general, your managerial approach.

When to use

We have found that *one* reason for the presence of a "communication problem" is the confusion that results from different learning styles. The following circumstances might therefore suggest either confronting your style or a more general examination of the learning styles in an organization or as they show up in a team.

- Memos and reports keep piling up on your desk and you get that sense of "How am I going to get through all of these papers."

- Two people in your department just seem to talk past each other, as though they are talking different languages. They either do not seem to understand each other or, when they seem to agree on an action, future behavior suggests they really had not reached an agreement.

- You keep listening to discussions at meetings and can't seem to follow what's going on. You feel you understand all the words, but the meaning of what is happening often escapes you.

- A department in your organization just seems to be in trouble with the rest of the organization much of the time. The members of that department do not seem to be understood even though they seem to be trying to get their message across. Such specific complaints often are reported about accounting or engineering departments in general manufacturing businesses. Members of those departments also complain about personnel or production departments.

- You and your spouse may get into some angry exchanges after you explain something that seems so simple to you. You just don't understand why he or she cannot get what you mean, then one thing leads to another and builds up to an argument.

Of course, the above-mentioned problems may arise from reasons other than differences in learning styles. Nevertheless it is worthwhile to determine whether or not working on learning-style differences might help.

Who can use:
1. Manager by him- or herself
2. Top executive
3. Any level manager and his or her team

Purposes:
1. To gain a clearer picture of your learning style
2. To recognize the connection between how you learn and the way you manage
3. To become more aware of the influence of your learning and managerial styles on co-workers
4. To attempt to institute change in the pattern and methods of information flow on the basis of your greater awareness of your learning style and how the learning style relates to your management approach

Participants:
1. One individual
2. Up to 15 in a team or workshop setting

Materials:
1. Felt pen and newsprint (if using with a group), tape, paper, and pens
2. Learning-Style Inventory (from Kolb, Rubin, and McIntyre)
3. Learning Comparisons Process (Figs. 3.1, 3.2, 3.3)

Time: About 3 hours

Detailed process

1. *Lecturette discussion of what is learning style and how it relates to managerial approach.*

a. We strongly agree with the position that the effective manager is the one who can learn to adapt, to be aware of problems and methods of solving those problems. We have found that as managers learn more about the way they learn:

1) problems are solved faster,

2) communications with co-workers become more accurate,

3) unnecessary paperwork tends to decrease, and

4) people within a department increase the degree to which they work with each other in solving complicated problems.

b. Kolb et al. have identified an experiential learning model which suggests that all of us go through a series of steps in learning; i.e., from concrete experiences to observation and reflection to the formation of abstract concepts and generalizations to testing implications of concepts in new situations. Further, they suggest that people have different learning emphases or different styles in learning.* Some people tend to be "focusers"—they are practical and use a set of tried and true rules in learning something new. Other people stand back and just observe something and come up with many different ways to solve problems ("brainstormers"). Still others learn best as they put together different parts of a situation and come up with another possibility—the people in your plant who always suggest a theory about declining sales or

---

*   Kolb reported four learning styles, namely, the converger, the diverger, the assimilator and the accommodator (in Kolb, et al.). We have expanded on some of these styles based on our own observations and relabeled the styles in the following way:

Kolb's terms:	Converger	Diverger	Assimilator	Accommodator
Our terms:	Focuser	Brainstormer	Theorizer	Doer

turnover (the "theorizers"). Finally, there are the "doers," the co-workers who are always coming to you with that new idea they've just read about, want to try it out right away in the plant, and do. You probably have seen them all around the organization. We want to emphasize that all of us use all the learning styles; however, we tend to emphasize one style over another.

c. In general we see a match between the learning style and the managerial approaches in the following way:

Learning Style	Managerial Approach
1. "Focuser"	Manager who is technically very sound; knows the rules of the situation and can reach good solutions by following the "facts"; has limited allowance for people errors; expects task to be completed within a short time frame; once a decision is reached, action is Go.
2. "Brainstormer"	Manager who comes up with all those ideas; can amaze you with how his or her mind goes in so many different directions; seems to know where everything is even though it looks like a clutter; can handle unclear or ambiguous situations; does not seem to be aware of the small steps in getting a job done.
3. "Theorizer"	Manager who listens or watches and does a lot of thinking about what he or she hears and sees; expects that things will be orderly and follow a certain sequence; considers many possibilities before a decision is made; thinks a lot about a decision and once the decision is reached, action is—Maybe.
4. "Doer"	Manager who likes to go into the plant and make the machine work; demonstrates how to do something when teaching someone else; uses few words; has a lot of feeling but may or may not show it; takes risks; moves around a lot.

d. Just as with learning styles, we all use the different managerial approaches to varying degrees. We have found it most useful to have a good discussion about the relationship between learning styles and managerial approaches. Often we will write a comparison of these two sets of styles on newsprint so that the individual or group can better focus. The discussions lead to thoughts about specific people in the organization. Usually, each individual starts to think and comment about his or her style.

2. *Determining your learning style.*

a. One method we have used is the application of the *Learning Style Inventory* (LSI) presented by Kolb, Rubin, and McIntyre. If you choose to follow this approach, you must get copies of the inventory and the method of scoring, which is all contained in their manual. Also, you can learn more about the relationship between the different ways to learn and managerial approaches by reading: Kolb's "On Management and Learning Process," from Kolb et al.

b. We have developed a process which in part builds on the work of Kolb et al. We call it the *Learning Comparisons Process,* and its objective is to help you gain an understanding of your learning style.

1) Before starting the process, you must copy the items in Fig. 3.1 onto 3 × 5 cards—each item, with its number, on a separate card. Next, shuffle the cards so that you have a good mix. Then do the following:

a) Take the first two cards and compare the statements on them. Ask yourself, "Which of these two statements best describes my way of learning or understanding something new?" When you have answered that question, go on to step (b).

b) Referring to the LCP recording sheet (Fig. 3.2) find the one box that can be identified by the numbers of *both* the statements you compared. For example, suppose that you were comparing

---

1. Listening to a lecture on new ways to organize a department.
2. Discussing with the maintenance engineer differences between new and old equipment.
3. Taking a new car for a drive.
4. Reading about the changes in a new car line.
5. Learning a different language by starting with reading about the culture of the country in which the language is spoken.
6. When you get one of those new gadgets, you try to use it in ways *not* explained in the directions.
7. When you come into a room, you get your bearings by checking whether the pictures are hanging straight and the room is in order.
8. When you drive into a new location, you can immediately sense the way the area is laid out. For example, which way is North, South, etc.
9. You aren't really clear about what happened at a meeting until you reread your notes or got the minutes.
10. You really get to know someone by doing something with that person.
11. You have a dozen different interests and you never feel you get involved in any of them.
12. When you hear or read an interesting thought your mind takes off in many different directions with related ideas.

Fig. 3.1 Learning comparisons process (LCP) items

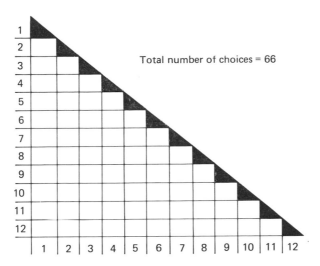

Fig. 3.2 LCP recording sheet

statements 1 and 4; the *only* box that bears both those numbers is in column 1, row 4. Now, in that box write the number of the statement you chose in step (a). That is, if you decided that statement 1 best described your way of learning or understanding something new, then you would enter a number 1 in the box in column 1, row 4.

c) When you compared statements 1 and 4, you selected 1; therefore set statement 4 off to one side. Now take a new card from the statement pile and compare it with statement 1. Let's say that the new card contains statement 11, and that in making your comparison you choose statement 11 over statement 1. The only box with those coordinates is in column 1, row 11—and that is where you enter your new choice, 11.

d) You now set aside statement 1, draw a new card, and compare that with statement 11, entering your preference in the box with the proper coordinates on your LCP recording sheet. Continue this until you have gone through the statements.

Once through the statements you may, if you wish, reshuffle the cards and go through them again, ignoring the accidentally repeated comparisons. Or you may prefer to consult the LCP recording sheet itself; the coordinates of the empty boxes show clearly which statements have not yet been compared. In all, there are 66 comparisons.

If the LCP is being used in a group, then the items should be listed on larger cards or on two flip charts with newsprint—one item per card or sheet. The facilitator holds the set of cards in front of the group. Each person has an LCP recording sheet to record the numbers associated with the statements.

2) As indicated earlier, every person uses all styles of learning to different degrees. The next step will help you to see to what degree you use the different learning styles. Count the number of times you selected each of the statements, then enter the total for each statement beside the appropriate statement number in Fig. 3.3 (in the column headed "Number of times chosen"). When all the statement-number totals have been entered, add up the number of times statements were chosen for a given style. For example: Suppose you

Style	Statement numbers	Number of times chosen	Total for style-related choices	Weighted score for style
"Focuser"	5			
	7			
	9			
"Brainstormer"	6			
	11			
	12			
"Theorizer"	1			
	2			
	4			
"Doer"	3			
	8			
	10			

Your learning pattern:
List styles from highest to lowest total weighted score

A. _____

B. _____

C. _____

D. _____

$$\text{Weighted score for style} = \frac{\text{Total for style-related choices}}{66}$$

Fig. 3.3 LCP ranking sheet

chose Statement 4 five times, Statement 5 seven times, and Statement 7 eight times. Those three statements (and only those three) reflect the style of the "Focuser," so you have chosen "Focuser" statements 20 times. Enter that total in Fig. 3.3, in the column headed "Total for style-related choices," in the "Focuser" style row.

To get the weighted score for style, divide the total for style-related choices (20 for the "Focuser" style) by the number of choices made (66). The result is .30, and that is what you enter in the first ("Focuser") row of the column headed "Weighted score for style."

Repeat this process to get your weighted score for each of the other three styles—"Brainstormer," "Theorizer," and "Doer." When you have finished, enter the style with the highest weighted score on line A, at the bottom of Fig. 3.3, the style with the next-highest weighted score on line B, and so on. (For example, if the "Doer" style had the highest weighted score, you would enter "Doer" on line A, etc.)

If your highest weight is in the "Doer" cluster, then you tend to be a "doer" learner; however, look carefully at the level of the other types. You may find that there is an almost equal distribution of choices. Of course, this result would suggest that you are using equal amounts of the different ways of learning.

3) We want to strongly caution you that this method or any other approach is useful *only* as a help to understanding your style. We find that people can get *some direction* in discovering more about the way they learn and manage through such processes.

3. *Examining the influence of learning style on co-workers.*

a. Discovering things about your style usually requires some time for reflection. We like to give both individuals and groups a chance to think over what this additional information means to them; we invite them to see how the data fit with their own experience. We ask such things as: Do you have any other evidence to support or reject these results? If you accept the results, in what ways did your style show up in the last few days at work or at home?" Most participants are able to report such experiences with little assistance. They are asked to record their thoughts on paper. If a journal of learnings has been introduced, then the participants are asked to record these thoughts in their journals.

b. In a workshop with a team, each person carries out the process from the beginning of the intervention through Step 3a. It is then useful to form the team members into groups of four to discuss events that can be identified as evidence that they are using the learning style as explained in Step 3a. Such discussions will usually sharpen the picture for most people. They will also help people recall additional events from the previous days. Sometimes we find people in such groups remarking on how a member is demonstrating his or her style during the subgroup discussion. If the facilitator observes such demonstration of learning style, and it is not picked up by other group members, he or she should point it out. Nothing seems to raise awareness more than giving immediate feedback to a person who has shown an example of his or her learning style while in such a learning subgroup.

c. In a workshop setting, we might sometimes try to help emphasize the differences in style, and some of the advantages and disadvantages of those differences, by organizing the workshop or team into subgroups of from four to six people, each group having at least one person with each different style. That is, each group ideally has at least one person who has primarily a "doer" pattern, another person with primarily a "focuser" pattern, and so on. We have used different ways of getting the groups going. For example, at times we have:

1) Told them to decide on an activity by themselves and then carry it out.

2) Invented a problem related to their work and requested that they find the best solution to it that they could.

3) Given them a box of Tinkertoys or Lego and told them that they could make what they wanted, but they must use all of the pieces and then present the work to the entire group or team.

4) Presented them with a topic for discussion (e.g., What do you think of the government's approach to energy usage?), then had the group form a circle within the larger circle (fishbowl) and discuss the topic. (When there is time, all subgroups have the fishbowl experience.)

After one of the above experiences, we invite all the participants to think and then write the answers to the following questions:

1) Who in the subgroup did you feel understood you? Did not understand you?

2) With whom did you get most frustrated?

3) With whom did you feel most comfortable?

4) If you had a very difficult problem to solve, which two other people would you choose to have work with you?

5) (If it is a workshop) Who in your work group back home reminds you of the person you had the most difficulty with in this subgroup? The least difficulty with?

6) Can you see any connection between your answers to these questions and differences in learning style?

Before the end of a workshop, we might give participants time to design a project in which they will try to become more effective in working with one or more members of their team or department. The specifics will be discussed in the next section.

4. *Increasing the understanding and use of information with co-workers.*

As suggested earlier, we sometimes find that problems of communicating with and understanding each other are related to unclarity about differences in learning style and insufficient skill in making optimal use of different learning styles. Thus we suggest to the individual manager or the team that they focus on solving any issue that appears connected to differences in styles. We would suggest doing this if there is some indication that the problems arise from differences in learning style and the team is open enough to go through such an experience. It is more likely to be accepted by a team that has been through a workshop.

Let us look at the steps for a single manager, assuming that he has gone through the previous parts of this intervention. (*Note:* In our experience most managers require the assistance of a consultant or facilitator.)

a. Call a meeting of all the members of the team.

b. Explain that you have learned some things about the way you learn and manage and you want to apply these learnings to the team.

c. First, you would like to explain a little about learning and managing styles; then you want each person on the team to go through the exercise on learning about their own learning styles; and finally, have a discussion on the connection between learning and managerial styles.

d. Now, you would like to brainstorm (see Chapter 5) some problems in the working relationships of the team that might be connected with differences in learning style. For example, at the end of team meetings frequently the decisions of who is responsible for the action are unclear. Such unclarity may be the result of different styles. We could look at the way those issues are dealt with and who seems to have difficulty in the style with which they are handled. Or, another problem that might be connected to differences in style is the road block in getting action because of the slowness of one or two team members. Let us look into those blocks and see if they have something to do with not paying attention to different styles of learning.

e. After the listed ideas have been identified, work on selecting and working on the problem as suggested in Chapter 5.

Variation 1

When there is limited time, it is possible to exclude Step 3c. The major purpose of this step is to increase awareness of the differences in learning style. Some people have gained a better perspective by just going through the first two parts of Step 3.

Variation 2

While we have found that using more than one way of determining learning style has a number of advantages, you can reduce time and expense by eliminating Step 2a and going right into 2b.

BALANCING YOUR MANAGERIAL STYLE

When to use

This process should be used about *midway* during an intervention session or workshop lasting at least two days. It is advisable not to use it before the groundwork has been laid, because, in order to be effective, this intervention requires that the workshop participants be basically willing to give and receive possibly painful feedback. The earliest we would use it would be in the evening after a full day's training intervention that dealt with openness and feedback (preferably after the team has accepted the "Johari Window" terms and ideas).

On the other hand, it would be a bit reckless to use this process as the last in a series of interventions or training experiences, without being sure that the time remaining to the team will suffice for dealing with all problems that may arise. The latest we would use this process would be in the morning of the last day of training/intervention, provided we still had the whole day at our disposal for dealing with tensions that might surface.

We generally use this process with either: (1) a manager's or work superintendent's workshop; or (2) a work team.

1. *With managers.* Within a workshop for managers (or superintendents), this process can be used only if the participants are sufficiently familiar with one another's work style to be able to give each other feedback. This is possible only with managers who interact with one another sufficiently at their place of work. Another possibility is that the managers have been together long enough in the workshop to be able to give each other feedback on their behavioral style.

We generally use this process in most of the managers' workshops we hold because we have seen that it is one of the basic processes that can be helpful to most managers. The terms are simple to grasp and the feedback makes the participants aware of two of the most important dimensions of a person's behavior in a team.

2. *With a workteam.* We do not use this process in every work team, but only when we find (in the individual interview and feedback, or during the period of working with the team) that it is needed. Generally, most teams we have worked with needed the experience of this process. We have found it useful and effective in dealing with the following circumstances:

a. *Tension in the team about getting work done.* We use the intervention when we encounter a team in which there is much tension, either on or beneath the surface, about how to get work done, the pace of work, or effectiveness and productivity. When people in the team have different attitudes about the stress they put on getting tasks done, or about attending to individual needs, this often leads to tension. Sometimes people feel they are carrying more than their fair share of the burden for others who care less about results and productivity. Often the person in charge of the team sees it as his or her responsibility to get the team's tasks accomplished. This sometimes causes the leader to develop an authoritarian, criticizing, distrustful style of supervising and interacting with other team members. They, on their part, may do just as the leader expects: may shirk responsibility for task accomplishment. This situation is loaded with tension. The team may be producing the output demanded of it, but in the long run people will find ways of "doing in the system" and finally productivity will be adversely affected.

b. *Laxity: All good friends, but no work done.* In this situation, all individuals in the team (including the person in charge) have reached a stable, easy relationship—but work is suffering. Essential decisions are not made, and effectiveness is relatively low. Above the surface all is fine, but the payoff must come—either in the form of pointlessness and lack of satisfaction in working with little results, or in the form of demands from outside the team to show results. In a situation of this kind the intervention is useful.

c. *Bureaucratic leadership and culture.* When we find a team working "according to the book," with low commitment, little creativity, and negligible interest either in their task or in each other, we have met a bureaucratic culture. People treat one another impersonally, and regard their work with relative indifference. They do what must be done, but that's all. The intervention can help in bringing this situation to awareness and confronting it.

Who can use:
1. Consultant
2. Outside facilitator with A.B.S. experience
3. A sensitive manager *not* with his or her own team of subordinates *nor* with his or her peers managers' team.

Participants:
1. A team of not more than 14 people
2. A managers' or superintendents' workshop of not more than 14 people who know each other
3. In both cases, preferably not less than six people (though possible)

Purposes: 1. To help a team overcome difficulties or ineffectiveness stemming from an unbalanced managerial style or work culture
2. To assist managers in becoming more aware of their managerial style, its effect on team effectivity, and alternate ways of behavior.

Materials: 1. Newsprint, felt pens and tape
2. Pens or pencils
3. Slips of blank paper
4. Newsprint: Different Managerial Styles (Fig. 3.4)

Time: 4 to 8 hours

STEPS IN PROCESS

1. Consultant's introduction and explanation of the two dimensions
2. Participants score themselves
3. Participants score others
4. Participants' scores are noted on newsprint
5. Consultant explains different managerial styles
6. Participants discuss their scores
7. Consultant explains effective/ineffective styles
8. Participants' discussion and decisions

Detailed process

1. Consultant's introduction and explanation of the two dimensions

a. *Introduction.* We tend to introduce this experience both by connecting it to previous experiences and by explaining its purpose. Connecting it to previous experience might be done by mentioning what problem areas in the individual interviews led us to decide the experience was necessary for the team.

To explain the purpose one might remark about the difficulty of balancing relationships in a task group that has to show results and be effective, and at the same time maintain some standard of cohesive relations, mutual aid, and understanding between its members (that is, take care of "maintenance").

b. *Explanation of the two dimensions.* The consultant explains that:

■ There are two major dimensions by which our behavior in our team (or with our subordinates) can be evaluated: as "task," or as "maintenance."

- A person with a task orientation stresses getting the job done, being effective, showing results, being productive, and turning out products.

- A person with a maintenance orientation stresses and cares about maintaining good relationships, having people find satisfaction in the team and in the work, satisfying different individual needs, interests, and capabilities, and showing thoughtfulness for people.

- Each of us, in dealing with our team, stresses these two dimensions in varying degrees. (We will evaluate our attention and stress on both these dimensions, on a scale from 1 to 10. Those who consider themselves high in task orientation should give themselves from 8 to 10 points on that scale; those high in maintenance orientation would give themselves 8 to 10 points on that scale. An individual might, for example, be low on task—say 2 points—and medium on maintenance—say 4 or 5 points.)

- Some people quite often have difficulty grasping the fact that a person can be high in both task and maintenance orientation. Generally, other team members help clarify this issue.

2. *Participants score themselves.* The consultant explains that each person will soon be requested to grade his or her score on both dimensions. At this point we have found it worthwhile to promise that people will not be expected to reveal their self-evaluation scores to others unless they wish to do so. Those scores are only for their personal use, and after writing them, participants can put them away in their pockets.

The consultant now hands out to each participant a bundle with slips of paper equal to the number of people participating. Each slip has on it the name of a different participant and two words: "task," and "maintenance," as shown here.

Name_____

Task_____

Maintenance_____

Participants are requested to take out the slip of paper with their own name, and give themselves the scores they think they deserve in the two dimensions. When finished, they may put the paper away in their pocket.

3. *Participants score others.* Participants are then requested to take the slips of paper bearing the names of the others, and score each participant according to their experience of that person in their everyday interaction with the team. (It should be stressed that participants should *not* put their own names on the slips—they remain anonymous.)

Tension becomes quite high, often broken by jokes and quips. As much as is reasonably possible, people should be allowed to concentrate without interference. Those who have finished are requested to retain their slips and not interfere with others still writing.

Inevitably some will say that they are unable to score someone else on the team because they have not interacted with that person sufficiently. We suggest that, nevertheless, everyone make a try on the basis of whatever experience they have had with the other team members—even if it is only in the training and interventions up to this point.

Anyone who is genuinely a new member of the team and has never worked or interacted with the other members before may have to be left out of the process. He or she can serve as an observer, who may later be requested to give the team feedback on other people's behavior throughout the whole process.

People are requested to hand in their slips of notes to the consultant after they have finished scoring everybody. The consultant then arranges the notes in piles according to the name of the participant being scored. When this has been done, each person receives the pile concerning himself or herself. Time should now be allowed for people to read their notes, absorb them, and let off tension each in his or her own way. Some may be silent, others noisy, some angry, some thoughtful, others pleased.

4. *Participants' scores are noted on newsprint.* The consultant puts up a sheet of newsprint and draws two columns on it. At the head of one column the consultant writes "Task," and at the head of the second column: "Maintenance."

Participants are now requested to calculate and call out their average scores on each dimension. That is, each person adds the sum of the "task" scores and divides by the number of slips he or she received (excluding his or her own). A similar calculation is done with the "Maintenance" scores.

As the participants call out their two scores, the consultant notes them down in the appropriate columns and adds the person's name. When this procedure is finished, the result is two columns of numbers with each person's scores on the two dimensions.

5. *Consultant explains different managerial styles.* Now is the time we find suitable to give a more detailed understanding of managerial styles.

We put up a sheet of newsprint showing the different managerial styles (Fig. 3.4) and explain the mode and characteristics of each style.

We now read out the script in the newsprint and enlarge somewhat on each style. We point out that of course these are only five of the many ways of behaving as a manager.

We ask for and give examples of behavior under each of the five styles in the form of supervision and control, communication, relationships, decision-making, dealing with conflicts, etc. We point out that a person may act differently in different teams and groups of which he or she is a

Indifferent management has little concern for either management or tasks. Often the work doesn't get done and morale is low.

Task management has maximum concern for the task and very little for maintenance. It is often autocratic and indifferent to people's feelings. It may lead to discontent and conflict.

Maintenance management has maximum concern for maintenance and little for the task. Relations may be fine, but is the work being done?

Average management has an intermediate concern for both maintenance and the task. Many managers may find themselves in this category.

Problem-solving management has maximum concern for both maintenance and task. This is generally the most effective style.

Fig. 3.4 Different managerial styles

member. What was requested was the style used most often by each person in this team.

6. *Participants discuss their scores.* The team members are now invited to give their reactions to their scores and discuss them freely among themselves.

Throughout the discussion, wherever suitable, we draw people's attention to the following:

a. A gap between the self-evaluation score and the feedback score should be food for thought and comment.

b. The spread of scores received by one individual deserves attention. What does this mean? Do some people react to that person differently than do others? What conclusions does he or she draw?

c. If a person received a high score in one dimension and a low score in the other dimension, does he or she know why—or want people to give concrete reasons why they gave him or her a low score?

d. In general, does anybody want to hear more about why they were given their score? If so, the consultant can ask the team members to explain the ratings they gave the person making the request—but only on the condition that he or she merely ask for information or illustration, and *make no argument or defense.*

The consultant must be very attentive and sensitive during this working-out part. He or she should encourage open expression of feelings, and should bring out into open confrontation any hidden agendas and under-the-table interpersonal tensions.

Sometimes we may prepare the team leader or manager for an unexpected shock by making the remark (quite truthfully) that, from our experience, generally the most active people in a team get the hardest feedback.

This part of the process should be allowed to continue as long as needed and until the consultant feels that all feelings and reactions have been expressed, ventilated, and clarified.

7. *Consultant explains effective/ineffective styles.* The consultant now brings up the matter of contingency. We ask the participants if they think they would have received the same scores from other groups in which they participate, e.g., family, peer group, etc.

When some say they would not get the same score, we point out the following:

a. A person often has different styles in different groups.

b. In the same team, a style which is suitable under one set of circumstances may be ineffective under different circumstances;

c. There is no "good" or "bad" style, but only an effective style, which is the style most suitable under the particular circumstances and with the particular team. (We can ask the members of the team to give us examples to illustrate points b. and c.)

d. It is important to be flexible enough to suit your managerial style or the team's style to the different circumstances. (We ask for illustrations of this from the team's work.)

We ask the team members to try and list the kind of work team, organization, technology, or other circumstances under which each particular style is more effective. Then we put their suggestions on newsprint under the heading of the appropriate style. If necessary we add these comments:

a. Working with a group of relatively autonomous professionals and specialists generally demands a high concern for maintenance.

b. A team with established procedures, in which the work is intrinsically interesting and relatively simple, can probably manage with a midway managerial style.

c. An emergency solution probably demands greater task orientation. Things have to be accomplished quickly.

d. Commitment and motivation from people generally demand strong emphasis on both maintenance and task.

e. Monotonous, repetitive factory work probably cannot be controlled without a high task orientation. However, the problem remains to determine how long this maintains effectiveness and what can be done to enrich the jobs.

f. The trend seems to be for people to look for more satisfying, enriching, and fulfilling work. This trend means that there is an almost continuous need for high concern both for maintenance and for task.

g. Even when there is a high concern for both maintenance and task in an organization, one must always be aware of circumstances which demand, temporarily, that there be greater concern for one of the two dimensions than for the other. That is, at a time when fast decisions must be made, it is impractical and ineffective—and in the long run causes dissatisfaction among the people—to try to ensure that everybody has expressed all their feelings and attitudes, and all has been taken into account.

The consultant who wishes to attain a better understanding of the relationship between managerial style and organizational conditions is advised to read W. J. Reddin's *Managerial Effectiveness* (see recommended readings). For details on the relationship between style and the maturity of group members, see P. Hersey and K. H. Blanchard's *Leader Effectiveness and Adaptability Description* (also in recommended readings).

8. *Participants' discussion and decisions.* We ask the team what should be the dominant style and the secondary style under their particular circumstances. When this has been settled, we request members to throw in ideas and suggestions on how to enhance these styles in the team life.

If possible, appropriate decisions are made on structural, procedural, and normative aspects of the team's life that will assist it in maintaining a more appropriate style.

Sometimes, if the situation of individuals in the group is such that they may need further help in balancing their managerial style, we divide the team into couples who try to aid each other.

The process can be terminated by giving each participant a handout of Fig. 3.4, "Different managerial styles."

Variation 1

In a workshop for managers not familiar with one another's style, it is advised not to do this process until people have become sufficiently acquainted with each other in task-oriented exercises and simulations.

Part 8 of this process needs also to be changed as appropriate for the team.

Individual managers from different teams will be requested to think out what managerial style suits their particular set of circumstances, and explain why. After this they may comment on how they intend in future to balance their style to suit the circumstances.

Variation 2

For consultants and teams who prefer a less structured process, after step 4, in which participants' scores are marked on the newsprint, the rest of the process need not be in sequential steps.

People can be asked to give their reactions, and at appropriate points the consultant can intervene with an explanation of effective/ineffective styles, with couples helping each other, with identifying the style suitable for the team, and so on.

EXAMINING YOUR BASIC ATTITUDE TOWARD PEOPLE

Reviewing your assumptions and attitudes about people and how such attitudes influence your working relationships.

When to use

We would use this process with a work team, with a managers' committee, or in a managers' or supervisors' workshop.

After problem-sensing (see Chapter 3) with a group (a work team or managers' committee), or after individual interviews and feedback, or during process-observing, the following problems may be identified:

1. There is much mistrust among the people; they do not rely on one another.
2. There is a general feeling of close supervision and extreme centralization of authority and responsibility.
3. Motivation and initiative are low among team members, and this is connected with the lack of independence and authority in the areas of their responsibility.

If any of the above were the problems identified, we would use this process. Since the level of confrontation is not high, the process can be used with a team toward the beginning of an intervention or workshop.

We would use the process with a managers' or supervisors' workshop if we thought that the previously identified problems were likely to arise. It can be generalized that there is a place for this process in most workshops for people in positions of authority.

Who can use:
1. Consultants
2. Managers in their own team or another team

Purposes:
1. To help people become aware of and identify their basic assumptions about people they work with
2. To allow people to reexamine and assess their basic assumptions about people
3. To help people to discover whether there is a gap between their assumptions about people and the actual behavior of those people
4. To enable any participant who is interested to begin changing his or her assumptions and/or the behavior based on those assumptions

Materials:
1. Newsprint, felt pens and tape
2. Newsprint with X and Y theories (Fig. 3.6)
3. Handout of X and Y theories

Time: 3 to 10 hours

Detailed process

1. *Relationship between values and behavior.* This part can be done in either of two ways:

a. One can have a free discussion of the relationship between our basic values and assumptions regarding people and the character of our everyday relations with them. The consultant can, at a suitable point, draw an illustration of this relationship (see Fig. 3.5).

b. A second way of doing this part is to display a newsprint on which Fig. 3.6 has been copied and ask for people's comments and opinions about it.

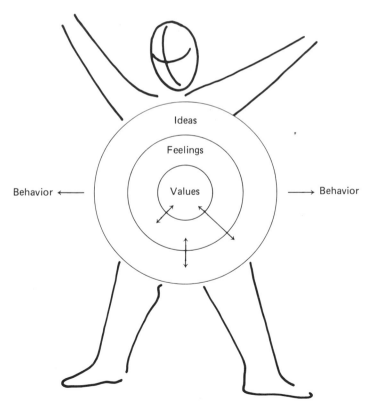

Fig. 3.5 Relationship between values and behavior

Theory X	Theory Y
People by nature generally:	People by nature generally:
1. Do not like to exert themselves and try to work as little as possible	1. Work hard toward objectives to which they are comitted
2. Avoid responsibility	2. Assume responsibility within these commitments
3. Are not interested in achievement and outputs	3. Desire to achieve and attain outputs
4. Are incapable of directing their own behavior	4. Are capable of directing their own behavior
5. Are indifferent to organizational needs	5 Want their organization to succeed
6. Prefer to be directed by others.	6. Are not passive and submissive and prefer making the decisions about their own work
7. Avoid making decisions whenever possible	7. Will make decisions within their commitments
8. Cannot be trusted or depended on	8. If trusted and depended on, do not disappoint
9. Need to be supervised and controlled	9. Need support and help
10. Are motivated at work by money and other gains given them	10. Are motivated at work by interesting and challenging tasks
11. When they mature—do not change	11. Are able to change and develop

Fig. 3.6 Assumptions of Theories X and Y

It might be worthwhile to mention the difference that sometimes exists between declared and true values: *Declared values* are what people say their values are in order to fit into the ways or norms of most people.

True values are those a person really holds and believes in, and which in everyday life guide his or her behavior, whether or not he or she is being observed by others.

2. *Theories X and Y displayed.* Two newsprints are now displayed before the team. One has on it a suitable version of Theory X; the other illustrates the main ideas of Theory Y. There are many different versions of these two theories which are all elaborations or modifications of Douglas McGregor's *The Human Side of Enterprise.*

The one we prefer is: Fig. 3.6.

The consultant is advised to think through the list of assumptions and choose the elements or list most suitable for the people he or she is working with as well as himself or herself.

3. *Theories X and Y discussed.* Participants are asked for their comments on these two theories and how they personally stand in regard to them.

The following comments can be made either at the beginning or at appropriate points throughout the discussion.

a. These two theories represent two completely different basic values and assumptions regarding people you work with.

b. These different basic attitudes affect a person's managerial style, his or her relationship with peers and subordinates, the level of trust in a team, an organization's formal and informal structure, etc.

c. The two theories can be regarded as two extremes on a line (this can be illustrated on a newsprint), and a person or team can be at any point on this line.

d. Sometimes people find themselves in complete agreement with almost all the statements in one Theory except one or two.

e. Belief in either theory will help create the conditions that support that theory. That is, if we do not trust people, supervise them too closely, and treat them as if they do not have personal motivation, then we will soon find that we cannot trust them, must supervise them closely, and cannot expect to see any signs of personal motivation. And vice versa: when we trust them, give them autonomy, and help to create conditions for personal satisfaction, we are seldom disappointed. In other words, people in groups tend to behave as they are expected to behave.

f. Some kinds of work are still repetitive, boring, physically tiring, and provide little satisfaction. Under these circumstances people may want to work less and shirk their duties. The problem here is not whether Theory X or Theory Y is true; probably under these conditions the only way to supervise is still by the assumptions of Theory Y. But the genuine problem in these circumstances is to determine what can be done to change the working conditions so that each person will gain more from the experience and feel more like a person.

How this discussion will develop is hard to foretell. Sometimes people do not get very involved and the whole discussion may last not more than an hour. On other occasions we have seen this discussion become the most enriching and effective part of a week's workshop, lasting a day and more.

4. *Individual feedback.* If the discussion in the preceding stage was intensive and personal, with some people stating their assumptions and

others giving their feedback on what assumptions their actual behavior reflected, this stage in the process may be superfluous. In such a case the process can end after Stage 3.

But if, as sometimes happens, people tend to speak in more general terms, do not connect the theories to themselves personally or to their own behavior, and do not give each other feedback, then we prefer to continue the process.

We again draw a continuous line on a newsprint, with Theory X marked at the left and Theory Y at the right pole. Then we number the scale from 1 to 9, as shown here. We then go "round the circle" with each person in turn being the object of feedback.

Theory X ———————————————————————— Theory Y
        1   2   3   4   5   6   7   8   9

This step, in which participants receive feedback, may be one of the first activities in a workshop or intervention. Thus we tell the group members that they can choose whether or not to receive feedback. However, if this process is done later in a workshop, we do not offer this option unless someone requests it.

As each person is dealt with in turn, people are asked to state what score they would give him or her on the X/Y line. They should also try to give concrete examples of behavior exemplifying the particular theory.

Those receiving feedback are requested not to argue and answer back, but only to listen. If they wish, they can ask for clarification. When everyone has commented about a particular person, that person can then say whatever he or she feels. Such rules are essential to help each person to focus on what he or she is hearing instead of just developing a defense.

When all team members have received feedback, they may express themselves freely about what has taken place, their feelings, etc.

5. *Helping pairs.* If the consultant gets the impression that some people have received feedback which disturbed them, or that they are very pensive and immersed in themselves and their feelings, we suggest that the team be divided into "helping pairs."

Each person in the "pair" expresses his or her feelings after the experience, while the partner tries to help as much as possible. It is generally worth reminding everyone of the "conditions of giving help." (See Appendix II, Some Basic and Standard Methods.) After the first person in each pair has finished, they change roles—the helper now becoming the helped.

Handouts: At the end of the process—whether after Stage 3, 4, or 5— we complete it by giving to each participant handouts of Theory X and Theory Y, to serve them for later thought and use.

Variation 1

If a less structured process is preferred, it is possible just to display the newsprints of Theory X and Y and have the participants discuss them and their relevance to personal assumptions and behavior. Usually when people do this and state their position, others are encouraged and give them feedback.

Variation 2

If time is short, Steps 1 and 5 may be skipped.

Variation 3

If this is a workshop in which people have not worked together, Steps 4 and 5 will have to be skipped.

Variation 4

In a workshop of strangers, instead of having people place themselves on a line between Theory X and Theory Y, they can divide 10 points between each two parallel statements. Then they allocate most, or all, of the 10 points to the statements they agree with. When all statements have been completed, they sum up how many points they gave to each theory. Each pair of statements is taken in turn. Participants explain and discuss with each other how they have allocated their points and the reasons why.

If this variation is chosen, then each participant should receive a handout of the two theories at the beginning of the process.

If we choose this variation we will not give comments e and f (mentioned in Step 3) *before* the discussion but only if needed, at an appropriate point *during* the discussion.

Increasing your effectiveness as a manager

4

CHAPTER OBJECTIVE

For managers: to review your way of organizing time, space, values, priorities, decision-making, and goal attainment so that you might become more effective in working with and managing people and organizations.

For facilitators and consultants: to offer you a number of processes to introduce these to groups of managers.

GUIDE TO APPLYING INTERVENTIONS

What is increasing your effectiveness as a manager?

Among other things:

- It is a way of looking at how you handle things and events around you so that you are more in control.

- It is examining the way you organize time so you are using it, rather than it (time) using or leading you.

- It is being clearer about what you want as a manager and how you will act to achieve these goals within your organization.

- It is becoming clearer about your needs and which of them you want to act on to become more effective as a manager.

- It is being clearer about what you value and finding ways to change your behavior to be more consistent with such values.

- It is looking into the past and present to see what plans for the future can be identified, so that you will have as full a life as possible.

- It is examining your current approach to decision-making and becoming clearer about the types of decisions to be made and the appropriateness of including team members in making those decisions.

- It is recognizing how you use the space around you so that your use of that space will be more supportive of you as a manager.

- It is defining your managerial goals and finding ways to attain them with the help of others in the organization.

About the interventions in this chapter

The interventions in this chapter, like those in the preceding chapter, deal with the more *personal* aspects of managerial effectiveness. There are other aspects of managerial effectiveness—such as improving decision-making ability, enhancing team-building skills, learning to define objectivity, etc., but we will deal with these in other chapters of this book.

When these interventions are included in workshops, their major thrust is toward assisting managers to use themselves and their environment more effectively. In each case, the managers review their behavior and think through ways of spending their time more effectively and constructively. They do this by attaining better knowledge of themselves and their needs. The increased self-knowledge is directed toward more effective use of the work environment and the resources of others.

The interventions

1. *How are you using your time?* This is directed at going over the weekly schedule item-by-item so that the managers learn how they are using time. They examine different ways of "slicing the time pie" so that they are doing what they should be doing and appropriately delegating nonessentials to others. The intervention has built on many of the ideas of Peter Drucker and Alan Lakein (see recommended readings).

2. *Organizing your space in your organization.* This requires managers to become more acquainted with their attitudes and feeling about space, the way their learning style influences use of that space, etc. With such information in mind, we suggest that managers make some changes in their immediate office space and the ways in which they use it to better achieve their goals as managers.

3. *How do your values fit your priorities at work and home?* This intervention is a method for closely reviewing personal values. After such awareness-raising, the managers examine whether or not their values are consistent with their behavior. There is an opportunity to reorient behavior to gain more consistency.

4. *Your personal life planning and action steps.* People review their past experiences so that they can apply what they have enjoyed to future plans. The intent is to build such planning into life on a regular basis so that work life and life in general can become fuller and life crises less overwhelming.

5. *With whom do you make decisions?* This focuses on how managers determine what kinds of decisions must be made by themselves alone and which decisions require the participation of others in the team. It emphasizes the importance of team decision-making but clarifies which types of decisions are best dealt with in other ways. We built on the ideas of Tannenbaum and Schmidt and of Vroom and Yetton (see recommended readings).

6. *How do you attain your goals in your organization?* This is a process of strengthening one's ability to move things in the organization through clarification of his or her managerial goals and how those goals meet the needs of others in the organization. The intervention is a personalized application of open-systems planning, that is, having different people and parts of an organization recognize their needs and objectives and, through appropriate sharing, arrive at more realistic and effective planning. The idea comes from some working papers by James Clark and a variation developed by G. Epstein.

MATRIX OF INTERVENTIONS

Intervention	Use	Who can use	Time demand
How are you using your time?	Better control and use of time	Manager or facilitator with team; possibly manager alone	4–7 hrs
Organizing your space in your organization	Knowing your "space" needs; reorganizing to fit those needs	Manager with practice; facilitator with managers	2–3 hrs
How do your values fit your priorities at work and at home?	Becoming more aware of your values and seeking more consistency between values and action	Manager with practice; facilitator with managers	6–7 hrs

Intervention	Use	Who can use	Time demand
Your personal life planning and action steps	Reviewing past to help identify goals for future; developing action steps	Consultant with group; possibly manager alone	6 hrs
With whom should you make decisions?	Looking at types of decisions and who should share in making them	Manager with another team— not his or her own; facilitator with a team; possibly manager alone	2–4 hrs
How do you attain your goals in organization?	Defining goals and getting help to attain them through others	Manager for self; or facilitator with a group	8–16 hrs

Possible outcomes

1. More awareness of actual use of time.
2. More control of use of time.
3. Increased effectiveness in delegating work and responsibility.
4. Increased effectiveness in personal organizing.
5. Feeling more on top of things, more in control.
6. Feeling good when working in the office environment.
7. Having more of the "just what I need" materials and machines at finger tips.
8. Feeling more that one is going in the "right" direction.
9. Feeling better about what one is doing.
10. Having a clearer idea about where one is going.
11. Being able to do more of the things that one wants to do.
12. Feeling surer about decisions.
13. Knowing more clearly when one needs and wants help in decisions.
14. Being clearer about who to include when making different kinds of decisions.
15. More sensitivity to what others are expecting from you.
16. Greater satisfaction in directing personal needs and work goals in a compatible direction.
17. Greater ability to move things in the organization.
18. More sensitivity to using the help of others to attain managerial goals.

Recommended readings

1. Drucker, P. F., *Management: Tasks, Responsibilities, Practices* (New York: Harper & Row, 1973).

2. Hall, E. T., *The Hidden Dimension* (Garden City, N.Y.: Doubleday, 1966).

3. Kirn, A. B., *Lifework Planning* (Hartford, Conn.: Arthur Kirn & Associates, 1974).

4. Lakein, A., *How To Get Control of Your Time and Your Life* (New York: Signet, 1974).

5. Tannenbaum, R., and W. H. Schmidt, "How to Choose a Leadership Pattern," *Harvard Business Review*, Mar.–Apr. 1958, pp. 95–101.

6. Vroom, V. H., and P. W. Yetton, *Leadership and Decision Making* (Pittsburgh: University of Pittsburgh Press, 1973).

HOW ARE YOU USING TIME?

Approach to better use and control of time within the work situation through learning to be more aware of what you are doing with your time, categorizing your work activities, and setting different priorities in time usage.

When to use

We use this process when problem-sensing or observation causes us to doubt that individual managers use their time effectively.

It may be a question of: "Are the managers spending their time on what they should really be doing?" It may be an awareness that much time seems to be wasted without an accounting. It may be that managers are worrying why they can't ever find time to deal with major problems in their sphere of responsibility. Or, maybe, it is a general vague feeling of the managers that they could improve the use of their time if only they knew how.

We use this process either in a workshop or a training course with managers of various levels or with management committees. It can be modified to present to one individual. The basic criterion for determining who can be helped by this intervention is: "Has the person some control of his or her time at work?" This criterion excludes all ranks whose work gives them little control of their own time and its use. A machine or a supervisor determines what they will be doing with their time.

We would not use this intervention for the group level. It is geared to individual use. That is, it would not be suitable when, for example, a committee complains of ineffective use of its time during meetings (see Chapter 6).

This process is not geared to the problem of a person's general use of time during and *after* work (at home, etc.) in order to serve his or her life goals. That kind of process is more for personal growth and self actualization, while the process described here is aimed at effective use of time at *work* only.

Who can use: This process can be used by anybody helping a group of people by following the steps described. You can also go through the process yourself, for your own individual effectiveness, without outside aid. Do this by just following the instructions, and skipping the steps that are specifically for group use.

Purposes: 1. To help managers become aware of and examine what they do with their time
2. To help them find ways of using their time more effectively

Materials: 1. Newsprint, felt pens, and tape
2. Pens and paper for each participant
3. Time-keeping booklet per participant (optional)
4. Time-use questionnaire per participant

Time: 1. Individual prework: A half-hour to an hour a day prior to the meeting, for one week
2. Group process: 4 to 7 hours

STEPS IN PROCESS

1. Individual prework: Writing daily all work activities and categorizing them

During the meeting:

2. Short lecturette on use of time
3. Participants estimate lecturette time
4. Participants answer Time-use questionnaire
5. Discussion in threesomes
6. Planning implementation of changes
7. Participants' suggestions on planning and controlling time

---

Note: Variation 1 (at the end of this process) will suggest an alternative process for use if prework cannot be done.

Detailed process

1. *Individual prework: Writing daily all work activities and categorizing them.* The purpose of this and the following step is to help the participants become aware of what they really do with their time at work. That's an eye-opener in its own right, and is worth doing even if it cannot be followed by the rest of the steps in the process. It gives the succeeding steps a healthy grip in reality by dealing with everyday chores and activities as they actually are and not as might be estimated. Therefore, an effort should be made to have the participants complete this prework before coming to the meeting. If there is some reason why this positively cannot be done, then the process can be carried on without the prework (see Variation 1). But it is much better to have the prework done if it is at all possible.

If we have an opportunity of meeting the participants a week or more before the workshop, we will give each person a Time-keeping booklet and explain what to do. If this is impossible, and we are working with a management team, we will hand the booklets to the person in charge, explain their use, and request him or her to meet the team and explain what to do. It will be that person's responsibility to see that everyone does their prework.

If we are dealing with individual managers who do not work in the same place, we send the booklets and instructions by mail.

The Time-keeping booklet is simply a seven-page booklet (with a page for each workday) in which people write down what they do during all of the hours they spend at work. Figure 4.1 shows an example of a page from the booklet.

The instructions to be given are as follows:

a. For every day in a typical work week write down at the end of *each* day what you did in each hour of your work time.

Activity	Time (minutes)	Category

Fig. 4.1 Page from time-keeping booklet

Activity	Time (minutes)	Category
Going over mail	60	
Consultation with . . .	120	
Board committee meeting	180	
Unaccounted for	40	
etc., etc.		

Fig. 4.2 Example of activities

b. The left column, "Activity," is for what you did during a specific period. The column "Time" is for how much time (in minutes) you spent on that particular activity (see Fig. 4.2).

c. At completion of work week, go through your activities and decide into what categories they can be broken down—for example: answering phone calls; committee meetings; receiving requests and being bothered; planning ahead; going over mail; meeting customers; etc.

d. After you have decided what categories to use, then categorize each activity and write the category in the column on the right.

e. On the last page sum up how much of the week's time was devoted to each category of activities.

f. Work out for each category what percentage it was of the total week's time.

g. Copy your summary in percentages with a felt pen on half a newsprint. The summary should look like this:

Name

Category	Percentage
Committee meetings	15%
Being bothered	7%
Answering mail	10%
etc. etc.	%
Unaccounted for	5%

h. Bring the summary and booklet with you to the workshop.

Note: If the booklet cannot be supplied, participants should use their daily calendars or a blank notebook to carry out process.

2. *Short lecturette on time.* The meeting begins with a short lecture to introduce the concept of "time" and its control. The lecturette also has a second purpose, to demonstrate the difficulty we have in estimating time (this will be explained later). The main points in the lecturette are these:

a. Of the three resources—money, labor, and time—time has special characteristics not found in the others:

- Time is not flexible. Increasing demand does not increase supply.
- Time cannot be substituted by other resources.
- Time is finite.
- Everything demands time.*

Alternatively, these points can be written on newsprint and people asked to comment.

b. In dealing with the use of our time it is worthwhile to ask these questions and follow these steps:

- How do you really spend your time?
- In what activities?
- Are there any time blocks which are controlled by others—your superiors?
- What changes need to be made?
- What is the best time planning period for you: monthly, weekly, daily?
- What better controls can you exert in the use of your time?
- How can you create concentrated chunks of time to do what you really should be doing?

This last point should be elaborated: Most managers spend too much of their time *reacting* to things that come to them: small crises, people walking in, answering mail, phones, etc. All this often leaves managers with no time for taking initiatives and doing what they really should be doing—taking new initiatives, forecasting, planning ahead, strategic thought and planning, advancing their own professional and managerial capabilities and skills, examining problems of organizational structure, initiating efforts of productivity and development, dealing with basic problems and assessing organizational (or departmental) goals and ways to achieve them. All these activities demand chunks of time alone and undisturbed, to work on them and plan their implementation.

---

*   We have used the ideas of Peter Drucker (see recommended readings). We urge those who wish a wider understanding of these points to examine his writings.

3. *Participants estimate lecturette time.* The lecturette lasts about 11 to 14 minutes. Before beginning, the consultant checks the time, being careful that the participants do not notice him or her doing so. When the lecturette is over, the consultant again checks the time and records the length of the lecturette.

The consultant now asks the people to estimate how long the talk lasted.

People give various estimates—5 minutes, 15, 20, etc., and the consultant notes them down on the newsprint.

When all have finished, the consultant writes on the newsprint the actual time he or she spoke, pointing out the difference between the minimum estimates and the maximum estimates, and the true time. The consultant then discusses how the difficulty of estimating time correctly is connected with the fact that people see things differently and experience time differently depending on how interested they are in a subject or activity. The group should be helped to conclude that time slips away and must be better controlled or there is a considerable decrease in effectiveness.

4. *Participants answer Time-use questionnaire.* Participants are now handed the Time-use questionnaire (Fig. 4.3) and requested to take out the summary of their prework Time-keeping booklet. They are then requested to work individually on the questionnaire, referring always to the facts of their use of time as summarized by them in the booklet. Participants who finish before the others are requested to go over the questionnaire a second time and try to think of more ideas and possibilities.

5. *Discussion in threesomes.* Participants are divided into subgroups of three people each. Each person in turn hangs up the newsprint with the summary in percentages of his or her categorized weekly activities. After giving the other two time to read the newsprint, he or she reads out to them his or her answers to the questions and decisions regarding changes.

When that person has finished, the others may ask questions to clarify unclear points. They then voice their opinions about his or her use of time and possible changes. The person on the receiving end is *not* allowed to argue, but only to ask for clarification. He or she is requested to write down for later use the main points of what was said.

When one person is finished, the next in turn carries through the same procedure. At least half an hour is needed for each person, so that the whole procedure, in threesomes, should take about 90 minutes.

6. *Planning implementation of changes.* Participants are now requested to return to individual work. They are to consider their former thoughts about what to change and the remarks they received in the threesome. They should now decide what changes they will implement and how they will go

1. What percentage of your time are you reacting to others and doing everyday chores?

2. What percentage of your time are you taking the initiative (initiating projects, thinking things out, confronting basic problems, planning ahead, implementing, etc.)? Think about your actual use of time. Does your use of time express proportionately the things you should really be doing to attain your work objectives?

3. To what should you be devoting more time?

4. To what should you be devoting less time?

5. Who are the people to whom you should be devoting more time?

6. Who are the people to whom you should be devoting less time?

7. Do you let others (telephones, visitors, requests, etc.) dictate too much your use of time? What can be changed and how?

8. Examine each activity in your list of activities and ask yourself: "If this was not done at all what would happen?" If the answer is "nothing," how are you going to stop doing it?

9. Which of the activities on the list could be successfully done by another person? How can you go about arranging that?

10. Do you make too many last minute decisions and thus close options of making better use of your time? If so, can you fix a weekly time-planning hour?

11. Can you decide on a regular day of the week (hours and place) when you can take a "chunk of time" to do your thinking, initiating, planning, etc., without outside interference?

12. Do you participate in too many committee meetings? If so, which can you arrange not to attend? For which of them can you invite some other person to represent your department?

13. Do you use the hours of the day in which you are most effective to do the things that are most important? If not, what can you do about this?

14. Think about the ways you send and receive information, your secretarial arrangements and the physical layout of your office, etc. Are these arrangements organized to save your time or to waste it? What can be improved, and how?

When you have finished answering the questionnaire, sum up below the changes you intend to make or will examine the possibility of making:

1.

2.

3.

etc.

Fig. 4.3 Time-use questionnaire

about it. The decisions should be put down in writing with short notes about ways of implementation.

From 15 to 20 minutes is sufficient for this stage. People who finish before the others are requested to read their questionnaire again and see if they can add anything more to be changed.

7. Participants' suggestions on planning and controlling time. The consultant now raises the question of practical ways to plan the use of time and maintain control of it.

As examples, he or she can give: keeping a list of things that have to be done; planning weekly and daily; considering what blocks of time in a week or month are out of my control; e.g., meetings determined by my supervisor.

The consultant requests the participants to write down a list of any ideas or techniques they may have for planning and controlling time.

People are requested not to be critical and not to write only tested ideas, but to put forward any idea that comes to mind.

When all have finished, each in turn reads out his or her list and the consultant writes them down on newsprint.

A typewritten copy of the ideas is handed to each participant after the workshop.

Variation 1

If people were unable to do the prework the consultant begins with Step 2. After Step 3 and before Step 4, the following can be done:

The participants are requested to try and reconstruct what each does with his or her work time on a typical day. When the reconstruction is finished, each draws a circle on a newsprint and divides the circle into segments according to the estimated percentage of each kind of activity (see Fig. 4.4).

The rest of the process can continue from Step 5 onward along the lines described in the previous section.

Variation 2

If the consultant or participants are very pressed for time and the process has to be shortened, Steps 2 and 3 can be eliminated. If further cuts are

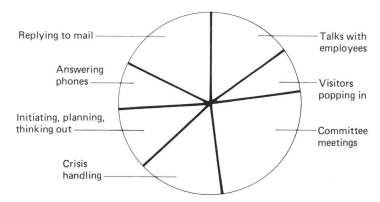

Fig. 4.4 Use of time at work

needed, Steps 5 and 7 can be eliminated. The shortest version possible is: Steps 1, 4, and 6.

ORGANIZING YOUR SPACE IN YOUR ORGANIZATION

A method of looking at yourself and your surroundings in terms of "space" and taking steps to change things to suit your needs and wants.

When to use

Individuals in work situations sometimes feel crowded or feel as though they can't carry out their work effectively. Under these circumstances, employees may have not organized the space around them to enhance their effectiveness. We find that the color of a room, the arrangement of furniture, and the manner in which the necessary tools are placed, can help or interfere with an individual's effectiveness as a worker.

We have found at times that people cramped in a corner have considerably increased their level of effectiveness and creativity when they were given a sense of openness.

We have also observed that the decision about where a person is located can be seen as reflecting that person's competence. We have noted that giving people more freedom in organizing their space or in choosing their location seems to increase their willingness to work and produce for the organization

Finally, we have seen that as individuals become more aware of their style, and able to express that style in organizing the space around them, they can become more effective in their work.

Who can use:	1. Any manager by him- or herself
	2. Consultants to organizations in a workshop with managers
Purposes:	1. To become more aware of your attitudes and feelings about space
	2. To change things around so that they suit your needs and wants from space
Participants:	1. A manager by him- or herself
	2. In a workshop setting for managers
Materials:	1. Newsprint, pens, tape, paper and pencil
	2. Materials used for "Confronting your learning style," Chapter 3
Time:	3 to 4 hours

Detailed process

1. *Assessing elements of your space.*

   a. We see personal space as having three major elements of the following list:

   1. Physical makeup and space
      a. the way you look
      b. the way you move
      c. the way you perform
      d. the boundaries of your personal space

   2. Physical environment and space
      a. the way you organize things around you
      b. the way you furnish your personal areas

   3. Learning style and space
      a. the way you take in information and events
      b. the way you use people to help you learn

During a workshop, the list is written on newsprint and discussed with the participants. When an individual is doing this process alone, we suggest reading through the characteristics to get a clear idea of each. If you are keeping a notebook or journal for yourself, or in a workshop, it is useful to record your thoughts as you read through the different aspects of space. We find that this type of recording increases your focus on the task at hand.

   b. *Physical makeup and space.* When you walk into a room, what can happen to you and to those who are in the room? If you are a very tall person, you may feel that you want to crouch down, and the people observing you may feel a little overwhelmed by your size. If you are a very small person, both you and they will react another way. We have seen meaningful workshops come to a halt when either type of person enters the room. You may also have noticed that in some organizations there are more people who are tall and strong-appearing than there are other types. Other organizations might be made up of people who are predominantly burly and sinister, while others may consist primarily of round and soft types of people. In dealing with an organization we often find it interesting to look around and see whether there may be a selective factor which determines who is included in such an organization, just on the basis of their physical appearance.

What type are you? How would you describe yourself? Write it down in your journal or notebook. Ask some other people to describe you physically. If there is someone in the workshop with whom you feel comfortable, or someone in your office, ask them to describe you and then write that down in your notebook. If you can ask two people to do so, better yet.

Now, think of the way you fill your space. Do you keep your hands close to your body? Behind your back? In your pockets? Do you walk briskly or move along at an even, slow rate? Do you use a lot of hand movements when you speak? You probably could think of a lot of things that you do with your body in filling your space. Write those down in the journal or notebook. How far does your physical space extend? How close can you sit to people? When do you feel someone is intruding into your physical privacy? Add these notes to your notebook as well.

c. *Physical environment and space.* This refers to what you have around you and the way you organize it. Some people have their desks piled with paper and things; others have nothing on the top of their desks. Still others have papers in neat piles, organized by their own hands or the hands of an assistant. Some offices have walls filled with photos, posters, or paintings. Others have nothing on the walls. Still others have one or two well-placed paintings or a favorite saying. Some persons have photos of the family; others have trophies. Some people like one fresh flower each day; others will enjoy a plant. Still others prefer some attractive plastic plant or flower arrangement. What about you? Some people prefer everything around them to be functional; others place more weight on things being aesthetic; still others prefer comfort. Some think of the social implications of physical layouts; others only of efficiency or simplicity.

We ask participants in this process to do a thorough observation of their personal spaces, including their office, special rooms at home, personal areas. Record what you have observed in each of these spaces. What patterns do you notice? Ask some others what they notice about the way you handle your personal environment. Record those observations also. If at a workshop, try to record the back-home spaces.

d. *Learning style and space.* This concerns the way you take in events around you and how you use people and things to help you in learning. If you learn through doing, you will probably use a lot more space and want more open space around you than if you learn more through reflection. If you are more of a reflective kind of learner, then you probably will *not* want many busy things on the walls or on the desk. Your particular learning style has a great influence on the way you manage. Developing your space to be more consistent with your learning style can make it either more supportive or less supportive to your particular style of managing. We have found that people who are aware of their learning style and organize the space around them to fit that style, can apply themselves more effectively to many of their management activities.

We suggest that you refer to the intervention in Chapter 3 entitled "Confronting your learning style," and follow the steps of that intervention through Step 3 b. As with the other elements in this intervention, we suggest that you record what you discover about your learning style in the journal or notebook.

2. *Developing a picture of your space.* The previous steps have probably heightened your awareness of your relationship to your space—that is, the space you want for yourself. We expect that through such a process you might be able to be clearer about your needs and wants as related to space. To be more explicit, a *need* is something to be satisfied.

A *want* is the choice of the particular need you wish to act on. Thus, a need is a potential state, and a want is something that will move you from potential to action. We have found different steps that will help you to form a more precise picture of your space. Some people prefer one kind to another, so please choose:

> *Possibility A:* At the top of a separate piece of paper, place the phrase "I need . . . ." At the top of another piece of paper, write "I want . . . ." Keep both papers in front of you while you read your recordings about the three elements of your space.

As you read the material think of the things that you need connected with space. In other words, think of the space around you, and what you think would make you feel satisfied and fulfilled if that space was used in certain ways. For example, would you feel more satisfied if you had many more chairs or books in your room or office? Would you feel more satisfied if you had lights on the wall rather than on the desk? Would you feel more satisfied if you had a window in your office? Would you feel more satisfied if things felt more comfortable? Would you feel more satisfied if the room felt more friendly? Would you feel more satisfied if more people wanted to come into your office?

Now think of the things that you *want* that will result in getting you what you *need*. For example, do you want to pay for putting a window in your wall? Would you want to think about the different kinds of photographs you could put on your wall to make it look more the way you would like it? Would you want to talk with the manager of purchasing about buying some chairs or some additional equipment to satisfy your need? Would you want to suggest at your next department meeting that everybody should look over their lighting needs to see how they can be changed to increase efficiency?

As you allow yourself to think about your needs, then list those needs on the paper titled "I need. . . ." The wants are recorded on the sheet headed by "I want . . . ." Most people seem to have a much longer "I need" list than an "I want" list.

When you have finished making out your two lists, read through them again and try to get a picture of how you might reorganize your space and how your office might look after you have reorganized it. You might also think about reactions to this newly organized space. For example, what might be the reaction of a group of strangers who come in to this space? How would it feel to have a meeting in your newly organized office space? As you think about this, record your thoughts and feelings under these two different situations. Through these processes, you're forming a picture of you in your space.

Possibility B: Another approach involves setting up three sheets of paper, each headed by an element in your space: that is, (1) physical makeup, (2) physical environment, and (3) learning style. While reading through the observations about each element, record on an appropriate sheet the main themes that come to your mind. These might include wide-open space, much movement felt when you're in the space, clutter, orderliness, etc. Follow these main themes with a list of "I need" items connected with the theme. For example, you may say "I need things to be functional," or "I need things to be aesthetic." Then make a separate list headed by "I want" items connected with the themes. For example, "I want a different filing system," "I want a different intercom system," "I want a different wall covering in my office." The end result is that there would be a set of need and want statements on each of the three elements that take up your space; that is, physical makeup, physical environment, and learning style.

By reviewing each of these lists, you will be able to get a clear idea of the kind of space you would like to create. Then, following the procedure at the end of Possibility A, you can get some greater sense of how you would feel with this new space. Again, consider how it might feel to have a group of strangers walk into your reorganized space, or how it might feel to have a meeting take place in your reorganized space.

By this time, you will be much more aware of the manner in which you might want to start changing your space.

3. *Applying your space picture to your surroundings and organization.*

a. You can now go to your office and start moving things around, putting them in a different order, etc. Spend an hour or so (in private) and use this area as an experimental ground. You might want to put pictures on the wall, look at what you've done for awhile, then take them down and put something else up. You might want to shift furniture around. You might want to get the sense of having things piled in different ways. Some people get elaborate and take photographs of the space organized in different ways, and then study the set of photographs to see how they might feel under different conditions. Through this experimentation, some managers have taken the step of making their space (their office, their work area) really reflect their own needs and wants. You may simply want to select the arrangement of your space that is most reflective of your space characteristics. The end result of such rearrangement may make you feel more comfortable in your office; the right equipment and material are at your fingertips; you can move around the room more fitting to your style, etc.

b. We have found that if you wish to go beyond your own office, three things must be considered: (1) you begin by working on your own office anyway; (2) you must decide what changes you want to make outside of your office; (3) you must decide which people are likely to be affected by changes you are likely to make.

Working on your office might pinpoint some of the larger changes you may make connected with your space needs. We sometimes get comments that "As I was moving things around, a thought came to my mind. I knew what I wanted to do." So keep the notebook or journal handy for recordings of additional thoughts.

Spend some time by yourself, then, with a trusted person with you, think about the changes you would like to make. Ask yourself different kinds of questions. For example, "Now I know that I am a more organized person, or a person who needs a lot of open space. How would I like to set up my appointment schedule? What type of information flow do I want? In what form do I want to receive information? Do I want information in longer form or shorter form?"

Make a list of changes you want to satisfy your space needs and wants. Be as specific as you can be. As you go over the list, think about each one happening. Do you get a sense that it is helping you to be more effective and satisfied? Examples of changes you may decide on are: different layout of the offices; different equipment in the offices; different information systems. Think of the people affected by each of these changes. Make a list of their names next to the changes you have listed. How will these persons be affected by the changes? Select from the list two to three of the people who will be most comfortable about accepting the changes you wish to make.

You have now reached the step before the move into changing these things around you on a more extensive basis. Your success in implementing these changes will depend on such things as the preparation of the critical people, the level of threat felt by the changes you have identified, and the "ripple" effect—how many people at what different levels will experience the changes that you're suggesting.

The following steps have been effective in the process:

1) Meet with the two to three of the people identified above and explain your plan. You can meet with them individually if you feel better that way. Get their thoughts and reactions. But remember that you are creating *your* space. They should know that your effort at this time is focused on your needs. Maybe they can work on their needs at another time.

2) Ask the people if they can identify all of the other people who will be affected by the changes you're planning. Can they add any other names?

3) Privately, look at each change and list the people most affected by the change.

4) Meet these people and discuss the changes you are planning, with a rough idea of the steps you wish to take. Get their reactions and think them out.

5) Take any action steps upon these changes that seem feasible after this consultation.

Many people find it useful to have a visible reminder of the changes they are planning. Such a reminder could take the form of a flow chart on the wall and a list of the changes with the people involved. If the changes are more in the physical arrangements of the space, then some kind of a "before-and-after" sketch might be a useful reminder.

Variation 1

When using this intervention during a workshop, you can use all the steps up to Step 3a. Then we have to role-play with each participant instead of taking Step 3b to prepare for the application beyond the office. The participant selects from three to five people from the workshop who assume the roles of the trusted persons in the organization. We have found this role-playing to be useful as preparation for the back-home implementation. Also, role-playing has been helpful when the participant selects someone from the workshop who represents a block to implementation. Talking about the changed plan has also provided good prework before returning home.

HOW DO YOUR VALUES FIT YOUR PRIORITIES AT WORK AND AT HOME?

A way of achieving consistency among your values and among your values and actions.

When to use

Although values are not frequently brought out into the open, we do lose a lot of sleep when we just skip over them. At best, we seem to wait to examine them at some religious service or education program. We have learned that the following are examples of the kinds of problems or issues that are often associated with value conflict or unclarity about values:

- A manager is required to fire a worker who has had high absenteeism because of many problems in the worker's family.

- Polluting the air and water is recognized as a danger to our health, yet the manager knows the manufacturing process is polluting the air every day.

- A manager is required to conceal some information from the government inspectors which, if disclosed, may get the company in trouble or at least delay some shipments.

- A manager feels compelled to hire minority people because of the company's affirmative action program to increase the number of minority people in the organization.

- A co-manager and friend confides in the manager that he will be leaving his job in the next three months and urges the manager to keep it secret since the information would stop his imminent promotion.

- The company has a policy of open and honest communication with all employees. As a manager, you are told to handle contacts with all employees using such communication. You feel deeply that only the better-educated and higher-level employees can use and understand this form of communication.

When you may be feeling confusion or anger over such issues, it can be very useful to take some time and review where you stand on things that are important to you as a person (your values); actually determine what your values are; how they are seen by others close to you; how you can become more consistent in acting on your values; or, if appropriate, change the values on the basis of your greater awareness that what you had previously valued is no longer as desirable to you as before.

Who can use: This intervention can be used by any managers who are aware of some stress between their values and their behavior within the organization or in their families. Managers who have applied the process to themselves may become interested in working with their co-workers on the same intervention.

Purposes: 1. To become more aware of the values with which you operate

2. To determine the agreement between your view of your values and how others close to you perceive your values

3. To increase the consistency between your values and your actions within your work organization and your family life

Participants:
1. Any individual manager
2. Any manager and his or her team
3. All participants in an advanced workshop on increasing management skills

Materials:
1. Newsprint, felt pens, tape, paper and pencils
2. Copies of Value rating sheet (Fig. 4.5)
3. Notebook or journal

Time: 6 to 7 hours

STEPS IN PROCESS

1. Listing and rating value words or phrases
2. Dealing with value-oriented situations
3. Recording of decisions and significant actions
4. Comparing actions and values
5. Reviewing gap between actions and values
6. Action steps toward reducing gap between actions and values

---

Detailed process

1. *Listing and rating value words.*

a. Take about five or ten minutes to think of *different situations that are important to you*—at work, at home, in any social situation, or just when you are alone. Jot down enough about each situation so you can be easily reminded of it. It may take you a while to get into the mood of thinking about such events. Some people are helped by closing their eyes and thinking of *people who are important* to them. Others find it more useful to think of things and places that are important to them.

b. On the same sheet of paper, write down the *words or phrases that indicate things you value* that are associated with those situations. The phrases must express some action or some sense of being. For example, if you think of the last football game in which you played, then you might value competition. If you think of a quiet walk in the woods, then you might value quietness or the beauty of the outdoors. If you think of your brand new sports car, you might value making money, or making a good impression, or competition. If you think of an intimate talk with your friend or spouse, then you might value being close to people or being open with people. Be sure to write as long a list as you can. You may have to push yourself after you have recorded a few. Also, you don't have to limit yourself to just the phrases connected to situations that you have recorded. Really try to get at everything that you value, using some action toward others or connection to your own feelings or sense of being.

c. The next step requires that you *record the value words or phrases* on the handout entitled, "Value-rating sheet" (Fig. 4.5). List all the phrases in the first column. Use two sheets if necessary. Now, go over each phrase and decide whether you associate the value only with your *work,* or only with your *home life* or do you associate it with *both.* This phase of the intervention is designed to help you become aware of whether you tend to keep your values in certain compartments or whether you are connecting the different parts of your life. If you are doing this exercise alone, then take some time to think about the different values and how they fit, or *might* fit, into the different parts of your life. Do you find that you value being alone in your home life and do *not* value being alone at work? Or did you think that you take time for yourself at home, but you are always surrounded by people at work? Or maybe it's the other way around; i.e., you operate in privacy most of the time at work and then you are always surrounded by family when you are at home.

d. If you are doing this exercise in a group, after each participant has completed the Value-rating sheet, pairs should be formed to share with

	Value phrase	Associated with work only	Associated with home only	Associated with both
1.				
2.				
3.				
4.				
5.				
6.				
7.				
8.				
9.				
10.				
etc.				

Fig. 4.5 Value-rating sheet

How do your values fit your priorities at work and at home?   95 each other how the values fit into the different parts of their lives. Such a discussion will often help to clarify values, help you recognize other values, and increase your awareness about connections between the parts of your life.

2. *Dealing with value-oriented situations.*

   a. Now, think of a work or a home situation, *where you felt the strong presence of one of your values.* It could be a situation which you felt you were being very good about how you handled your values or one in which you felt under a strain. Record the situation in as much detail as you can remember it. On the first part of a page from your notebook or journal:

   1) *Describe the circumstances* leading up to the situation.

   2) *Describe how you handled* the actual situation.

   3) *Record your feelings* after the situation was over. Now that you have written this description, do you think you would handle the situation the same way? If you think that you would change the way you would deal with the situation, also record on the same sheet of paper.

   4) *The modifications in your behavior.*

   b. If you are doing this exercise alone, seek out a colleague, your spouse, or a friend, and read to him or her everything about the situation, leaving out how you handled or felt about it. Then ask the person how he or she thought you would have handled it. Record the responses on the same sheet of paper, making sure that you have an accurate recording by reading back to the person what you have written. *Discuss the similarities and differences between what you did and what the other person thought you would do.*

   c. Sometimes we find it worthwhile to try this same procedure *with more than one person.* When this intervention is used in a group, subgroups of four benefit from carrying out this procedure with each other. After each individual has reflected on the feedback from the other three, the subgroup may wish to discuss some general learnings they have gotten from the experience.

3. *Recording of decisions and significant actions.* This aspect of the intervention can be carried out in at least two ways; i.e., keeping a daily record of decisions and significant actions, or reviewing the previous week and writing down such acts. Sometimes we have found it useful to divide the recording between work and homelife. At the conclusion of the recording, organize the decisions or acts on a sheet of paper as shown in Fig. 4.6.

Record the acts in a chronological order. Think about the values that are associated with each act and record them in the second column. Then decide

	Act/decision	Value(s) associated with act/decision	Consistent (C) or Inconsistent (I)
1.			
2.			
3.			
4.			
5.			
6.			
7.			
8.			
9.			
10.			

Fig. 4.6 Record of decisions and acts

whether or not there is an inconsistency between your acts and your values. Place a "C" for consistent or an "I" for inconsistent in the third column.

4. *Comparing actions and values.*

a. Look over your list and see whether *any patterns* are suggested. Do you find that you are regularly inconsistent about certain values? Are there any differences in consistency between your home acts and work acts? Do you notice yourself avoiding any life issues? Sometimes we find that as a person reviews the list of acts, whole sections of life are not recorded. For example, one person left out all acts and decisions associated with his children; another person omitted all money-related situations.

b. We find that *discussing these findings* is useful. Again, the use of a person close to you can enhance the process. If in a group situation, select someone whom you have gotten to know fairly well.

c. Another way of utilizing the information from your Record of Decisions and Acts is to *make two lists,* one a list of all the consistent (C) items and another list of the inconsistent (I) items. A second step is to consider the list of consistent items as a group and determine *how important this group of values is to you.* Then follow that phase with a review of the inconsistent items as a group. As you review these groups, do you find that your most important values cluster in the (I) group or the (C) group? As you look at each group, which items can you easily set aside and which items do you feel you just could not discard?

d. At times some people have difficulty in determining the most important value clusters. All the values seem to be so important. One technique we have found useful is technically called *paired comparisons*. In simple action steps, you write all your value phrases on separate sheets and assign consecutive numbers to each sheet. Then you compare every combination of the value phrases according to their importance to you and record the choice for each comparison on a piece of paper. So you end up with how frequently you chose each value phrase. From these results you can determine a ranking which shows the level of importance of each value. Then you can go back to the two lists of (I) items and (C) items and see whether your most important values cluster in one list more than in the other. (See similar process described on pp. 54 and 55.)

5. *Reviewing gap between actions and values.*

a. At this point, most people are aware of how much of a gap they feel between actions and significant values. You may want to select from the list of (I) items the values that are *not only important but also easier to work on*. We find that practicing reducing such a gap is more successful when you start with changes that are more readily achievable. For example, you may have discovered that you value honest and open communication with all important people in your life and that your actions show that you have been inconsistent in carrying out such communication; i.e., you can be open with your spouse and a close friend, but not with co-workers, your boss, your parents, and your older children. In choosing a first step in becoming more consistent, you should select the person who would be the easiest to work with.

b. If you are satisfied with the relationship between your values and your actions, then the intervention is over for you. If you feel there is more work to be done, then you should review the next step.

6. *Action steps toward reducing the gap between actions and values.*

a. Select the value area that you wish to work on.

b. Determine whether it is best to initiate the work on the value at home or at work, and also select the best person for you to work with

c. Meet with the person and explain the process you have just completed, and indicate to him or her that you wish to establish a learning contract. The contract should include the following elements:

1) General purposes

2) Specific purposes which include very concrete objectives; e.g., to be more open with you when I am uncertain about or disagree with your approach to other personnel.

3) The learning activities; e.g., after each encounter between us in the next four weeks, we will spend at least 15 minutes before the end of the day discussing my degree of openness.

4) Periodic evaluation; e.g., at the end of two weeks we will have an hour to review what has occurred in the past two weeks and make any necessary corrections in the contract.

Variation 1

As indicated in certain steps in the process, this intervention can be used in its entirety in an advanced workshop for managers who are interested in changing their relationships with significant people at work or at home. It can also be used with a manager and his or her work team, but usually would require an external consultant.

Variation 2

Step 1 *or* Step 2 can be deleted if there is some time limitation. As suggested, those steps are warmup steps for Step 3. However, it is essential to include at least one of these steps.

YOUR PERSONAL LIFE PLANNING AND ACTION STEPS

Method of reviewing some past and present parts of your life to assist you in planning and taking action steps to implement your goals in the future.

When to use

We have noticed that there are periods in each person's life when things just do not seem to hold together. Such periods have been called crises. Crises occur from the early stages in life (probably as early as three years) to very late in life. In our experience, such crises can take less of a toll when the individual sets some time for planning.

There is always resistance to planning for the future. First of all, there are so many things to do now and the future seems so far away. Secondly, as soon as you get started some emergency arises that needs your immediate attention. Finally, planning begins and things change and all the plans you have made do not seem to fit. We are sure that you can come up with more reasons *not* to plan.

We have concluded that with all of the potential resistance, there is no *good* time. Thus we are left with the question: Do we wait for the emergency and then have to take the time out or do we make ourselves just do it? Either way forces you to set the time aside. Of course, we feel that planning under pressure results in much poorer plans. So we conclude that you should take the time and set up the type of supports that will help you continue the process to its end. These, together with the help you'll get back home, make it more likely that you will continue the action steps.

Although we know some people who have been able to do such planning independently, we are now convinced that the vast majority of people require some group setting. So we will present this intervention as part of a workshop. However, it is quite possible that a work team or other groups can use this process. If you find that you are able to do this alone and implement what you have planned, you are advised to do it periodically. We have found that going through this process on one's own every six months has significant payoffs.

Who can use:
1. Any manager, but to be effective we suggest a group setting
2. Consultant in a group or workshop setting

Purposes:
1. To assist in the identifying of life themes that have been dropped from current life experiences
2. To assist in building a future life plan on strengths and positive experiences
3. To establish the necessary supports to ensure the implementation of the life planning

Participants: Group or workshop setting, including from a minimum of three people to a maximum of 15

Materials:
1. Newsprint, felt pens, tape, pencils and paper
2. Notebook or journal
3. Life goals/values list (Fig. 4.8)
4. Tape recorder(s)
5. *Lifework Planning* (manual and workbook) by Arthur G. Kirn. These materials can be obtained by writing to: Arthur G. Kirn and Associates, 106 N. Beacon, Hartford, Connecticut 06105. (*Note:* Kirn's manual can be used for alternatives to this intervention and for a more extensive process.)

Time: About 6 hours

STEPS IN PROCESS

1. Self-assessment through looking into your past
2. Organizing your self-view into themes
3. Ranking your life goals and values
4. Defining the selected life goals
5. Deciding on action steps
6. Setting up a system for implementing changes

Detailed process

1. *Self assessment through looking into your past.*

   a. *Who are you?* This is a question that many people wonder about, and they answer it in a variety of ways. Most often the answer is worked on in the dead of night with high anxiety over some complicated problem. We find that asking this question in a workshop format produces some important insights. We can ask it in the following way: Think of all the ways you can answer the question *Who am I?* Write down on a piece of paper or in your journal as long a list of answers as you can make. You can use any kind of words to answer—nouns like "woman"; adjectives like "handsome"; verb forms like "developing." Try to list more than 20 items. After you have finished your lists, form the group into subgroups of three and discuss what you learned about yourself. If you think of any more ways of answering, record those responses also. Spend about 20 minutes in the group. We find that it is important to keep the process *moving along* so that the planning activity does not feel weighty. Record your learnings in your notebook. For example, what ideas about yourself were new—or at least not recently thought about? Did you have any special recollections as you were discussing your list?

   b. *Where did you come from?* Everyone in the group is asked to draw a line or lines that will best describe his or her life. We find that spending some time discussing what we mean by a life line usually produces much better results. Thus, any questions to help clarify will be accepted. Sometimes it is necessary to draw some typical lines showing the ups and downs of life (Fig. 4.7). However, we try not to give an example since the example is often limiting.

   After everyone has completed their lifeline, we ask the participants to draw a vertical line at the point which would represent *Now.* Then ask the group to form into the same subgroups of three and discuss the events of their past (from the left of the vertical line) that are represented by the line. Again, just take about 20 minutes. After the discussion in subgroup, have the members record some of the highlights in their notebooks. For example, did anyone change the shape of their lifeline and why?

   c. *What did you enjoy doing in the past?* This question is another search into the past for experiences that might prove useful for future planning. All the members of the group are asked to think about their past life in five-year segments. That is, think about the periods from 0 to 5 years, from 5 to 10 years, etc., to the present. Now, what do they recall that they did during those periods that was great fun? Be sure to have them go through each period two or three times to get it into the foreground, then write down all their recollections. Then have them

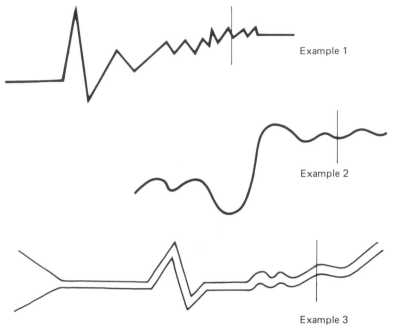

Example 1

Example 2

Example 3

Fig. 4.7 Examples of lifelines

rejoin their group of three and try to help each other recall more of these enjoyable activities. Have them spend about 45 minutes in the subgroups, recording what they learned. For example, what kinds of things bring them enjoyment?

d. *What were some of your peak experiences?* We recognize that most enjoyable activities and peak experiences might coincide. But we are looking for the powerful positives. So we ask the group members to write down from three to five of their peak experiences. We understand a peak experience to be an event that makes one feel that everything seems to fit together; a feeling of being in tune with everything inside and outside of oneself. Some people have felt such experiences when alone watching the sea, or when sharing with a special group of family or friends some moment of creation or triumph or even sadness, or at the birth of a baby, or when seeing the results of their work, and so on. We tell the group members: Review your peak experiences privately for a while. What more have you learned about your strengths? Write those down in the journal. What kinds of situations lead you to peak experiences? Remember the next step will involve building your future plans through a process of emphasizing the positives.

2. *Organizing your self view into themes.* The next step puts each member of the group into the position of a detective who is trying to locate positive threads or themes. A theme is an event or experience that repeats itself, for example an interest in music or meeting certain kinds of people. It does not matter how small or large—how significant or insignificant—a given thread is; they should all be written down on a separate sheet of paper. Participants may write down the major themes from their notes. Sometimes people find it more effective to dictate themes while another person writes them down. Such a person should make a contract for mutual help with another person who prefers the same technique. Whichever system they use, everyone should have a list of these themes in their notebook or journal *and* written with felt tip pens on a large sheet of newsprint. The completed lists of themes on the newsprint should be placed on one of the walls of the room, so that everyone may walk around the room reading the different sets of themes. Individuals may get ideas from the lists of other participants that they can add to their own—and they should not hesitate to make such additions.

3. *Ranking your life goals and values.* At this time, we find that thinking of ways of fitting these themes into a larger perspective has positive effects. Thus, we have the group look over the handout entitled "Life goals/values list" (Fig. 4.8). As you can see, there are 11 items on the list and room at the bottom of the page to add more items. Then, although the words will vary with each group leader, we give the group members the following instructions: With the major themes on the newsprint in front of you, think about the past and decide which of these life goals/values were really important for you. Check back and forth from the list to the themes, looking first for values or goals that were important in your past. Each time you find one, mark an × opposite that goal or value in the column labeled *Then.* After you have identified all the goals and values listed that were once important to you, write them in your journal, ranking them numerically from the most important (number 1) down to whatever is your last item. Also, mark those numbers on the *Life goals/values list* beside the × marks in the column labeled *Then.*

Look over the list of your goals/values again. How do you see those goals and values fitting into your life in the future. What really will be important to you? Identify these items with an × in the *Now* column. Write this list in your journal and think about how deeply each item may touch your life. Rank these items using the same system as you used for the *Then* ranking. Under the *Now* column, record the results on the handout (Fig. 4.8). (Note that you may have marked some items as important both *Then* and *Now.* Others may not have been marked in either category.)

Now the groups of three should reform and discuss the comparison of the *Then* and *Now* rankings. What are the differences you see as you com-

Then	Now	
————	————	a) *Leadership:* To influence others; to organize and direct others toward identified group goals.
————	————	b) *Expertness:* To become an authority in a certain area; to develop an expert level of skill and accomplishment.
————	————	c) *Prestige:* To become well known; to obtain recognition, awards, and high social status.
————	————	d) *Service:* To contribute to the needs of others; to be helpful to others.
————	————	e) *Wealth:* To earn a great deal of money; to build up a large financial estate.
————	————	f) *Independence:* To have the opportunity for freedom of thought and action; to be in control of my own life at work and at home.
————	————	g) *Affection:* To gain affection and companionship from others; to have a close relationship with others.
————	————	h) *Security:* To achieve a strong sense of having what I need —a secure and stable position; to know that I will be secure in later life, etc.
————	————	i) *Self-realization:* To realize or approach a feeling of using myself to the utmost; to be creative in what I do.
————	————	j) *Duty:* To dedicate myself to the total pursuit of high goals, values and principles; a very strong mission.
————	————	k) *Pleasure:* To just enjoy life; to be happy and content with all the good things in life.
————	————	l) ————————
————	————	m) ————————
————	————	n) ————————
————	————	o) ————————
————	————	p) ————————

Fig. 4.8 Life goals/values list

pare the rankings? What does this tell you about yourself? See if you can give and get help from each other in the trios. Do you see some important differences that you seek in your future life? If you do, record those thoughts in your journal.

4. *Defining the selected life goals.* We see this phase as the payoff step. All the preceding efforts are looking at events, awareness-raising, etc. The payoff is connected to working on the differences between what the individual's goals were and what they are, and, as part of this thinking, what they want to reestablish in their lines that was enjoyable and productive.

In the total group, we ask each participant the following: Describe the Perfect Day—three to five years from now. Think of the total day—work and home. What are you doing? Who are you doing it with? What are your feelings? It is expected that the future goals will be built into such a day. Record the day in your journal.

Now, look at that day, review your goal rankings in Step 3, and specify the goals you want to work on to achieve all the elements of that day. List as many as you can.

Reform the subgroups of three and clarify the goals. Make them very *specific*. Be sure that they are *realistic*. Be sure that *your involvement* is included—what you will be doing to accomplish the goal. Be sure that what you will be doing will be *observable*, at least to you. After you have worked over those goal statements as a group, separate so that each of you can rank the goal statements numerically, with the highest priority statement ranking as number 1, and so on.

List the goal statements on a sheet copied after Fig. 4.9, Goals and action steps.

After you have recorded all the goal statements, compare the ranking of those statements with the *Now* column of the Handout. Do the rankings generally agree? As you review and compare these lists, do you think you should change the rankings?

5. *Deciding on action steps.* After participants have worked on the comparison of their goal statements and the "Now" rankings and feel that the rankings are valid, they should begin to brainstorm action steps for each goal. (See Chapter 5.) Some may find it helpful to pair with another person, each in turn to record the action steps while the other brainstorms. Other participants have found that identifying the action steps privately is more fruitful. We have observed that some people prefer to *write* these down and others do better at first by *tape recording* their thoughts.

Goal Statement	Action Steps
Goal 1:	Goal 1 action plan:
Goal 2:	Goal 2 action plan:
Goal *n*: (Your last goal)	Goal *n* action plan:

Fig. 4.9 Goals and action steps

When done, each participant should look through his or her action steps and give each one an identifying phrase or label, then list all the steps on the Goals-and-action-steps sheet.

6. *Setting up a system for implementing changes.* When the preceding has been accomplished, we give the group members the following information and directions:

a. Your list of action steps could be stretched out over a three to five-year period. It is likely that there are some very difficult steps and others that are simpler. It is also likely that some steps will take a lot of time to accomplish and others will take less. Your next step is to divide the action steps associated with each goal into those steps accomplishable in one year or less, and those steps that will take more than a year. To complete this phase, take a sheet of journal paper and divide it into two columns by drawing a line down the middle. At the upper edge of the sheet, write the goal statement. At the top of one column put "First Year" and at the top of the second, write "Beyond First Year." Now, record the action steps for Goal 1 under the appropriate column.

As you are recording the action steps, particularly the long-term ones, you are likely to think of shorter-term actions that must precede the longer-term steps. Record those steps under the appropriate column. Often we find participants adding many more steps to the "First Year" column.

Now just look at the "First Year" column and try to rank the items, keeping in mind just one thought—which steps must I take before the step I am now considering? We suggest looking at the first step and then checking the whole list to see which steps seem to precede the one you are now considering, and which follow. Use your own system of recording this ranking. (Some people may want to follow a modified form of the comparison process explained in the intervention entitled "Confronting your learning style," Step 2b, which appears in Chapter 3.) However you do it, you should follow the same system with each of your goals.

b. You have now identified a group of steps you must take during the first year of implementing your action plan. We have found it useful to write all of those steps on a piece of newsprint, giving plenty of room for each step. Specifically, divide the newsprint into three columns. At the top of one column put "Action Steps for First Year." The second column should be labeled "Time Frame" and the third column should be labeled "Responsible Parties." You may well need more than one sheet for all of the goals, but try to fit them on as few sheets as possible.

Looking over the "Action Steps" list, do you see any steps that are either identical or at least related. If so, draw a line connecting those steps. If a connectable step is on another sheet, show the connection near both items.

Now look at your first action step and think about when you must get started in order to accomplish this step. Also estimate how far into the year you must go to accomplish that step. Record both beginning and ending dates beside the goal. Do the same for all goals.

The next step is to think through which people in your life are connected with the particular goal. Try to think of all people—people who could help you achieve the goal and others whom you feel might hinder you. Record the names under the third column, entitled "Responsible Parties." Various systems are used to organize the action steps for the first year. We feel that you must choose the system that will be most supportive for you. Most people choose to keep the action plan in their notebook or journal. We suggest that you section the notebook into the twelve months. For the first month of implementation, you would list all the action steps that need to be taken for that month for all of the goals. Be sure to use some way of identifying which goal and action step are related. After you have listed all the action steps for a given month, look them over to see what is the natural flow in the month. For example, if one action step is to meet with all the people related to achieving the goal, then you must decide which one to meet first, and so on. Or if it is a group meeting, what are the preparations you must make for that meeting. Another example: Suppose you want more music in your life, and as part of the action plan you must purchase a stereo and also look over various consumer reports and suggestions about stereos—then looking over the information must precede the purchasing, and so on. After you have worked over the first month, we are sure you will find it necessary to rewrite the page into the actual sequence or steps.

Yes, participants find this a long and tedious process. But, if you can complete the entire first year—or at least the first six months—*before* the end of the workshop, the chances of staying with the action plan are much greater.

A second part of the support for working on the plan is—people. The third column of your newsprint chart, entitled "Responsible Parties," should include the people who are likely to support you in working on the action plan. Look over the names listed for each goal. Does one person stand out as most likely to be supportive to you in achieving this goal? Circle that person's name. Now look over the names associated with each goal and do the same thing.

The outcome of this phase of the exercise is a support group—the group of people in your life who you feel might want to help you act on your plan. As you look over this group of names, do you think of anyone else in your life who just must be included? The group should not be much more than five or six people. We have found that the first step after the workshop should be the convening of this support group, or at least meeting individually with one or two members of the group. These people must have a clear idea of your plan and the related actions.

Some additional words about support. Your style will dictate the usefulness of different kinds of support. For example, some people do not find it useful to meet with their support group as a group. They just keep the five or six people in mind as a "mental" support group. However, they usually find it more advantageous to meet with the members individually. Some others find it important to set up personal contracts with support group members. For ideas about setting up personal contracts, see Chapter 7. The contracts directly involve the implementation of one or more goals.

Still another useful trick is the making of a flow chart or time line. Figure 4.10 shows the basic structure of a simple flow chart. Sometimes drawing such a time line and posting it near your desk has a great KITA (Kick in the . . .) value. At least it is a reminder that your life

Goals	Years 1977 to 1978												79–80	80–81
	Months													
	J	F	M	A	M	J	Ju	A	S	O	N	D		
Goal 1:		⊢———————————→												
Goal 2:			⊢—————————→											
Goal 3:	⊢————————————————————————————→													
Goal 4:							⊢———————→							
Goal n:								⊢——————————————————→						

Fig. 4.10 Sample time line

goes on and may get you thinking about taking time to implement the plan.

A final word on replanning. All plans must be reviewed and revised as you get more data from the experience of trying out what you have planned. We know that you will be reviewing and changing them as you face the real world. Fixing a regular date helps. We have found it convenient to do this on the first day of every month. An hour on each weekend reviewing action steps gives good results.

Variation 1

We indicated that the ideal approach to using this intervention is in a group or workshop setting. It is possible to work on all of these steps privately, but of course the discussions in groups of three will then be eliminated as well as the pairing with another person. We strongly suggest that anyone doing this intervention privately attempt to discuss some of the steps with another person. Such involvement can build toward a support system.

WITH WHOM SHOULD YOU MAKE DECISIONS?

Examining who actually makes different kinds of decisions in a team and considering who should make them in the future.

When to use

We use this intervention when we find, in problem-sensing with individuals or with groups, or through observation, that something is not going well with the decision-making process in a team. "Not going well" refers to the person(s) responsible for the decisions.

We often become aware of this from complaints of team members. Some will say that the decision-making process is ineffective. They may complain that the person directing the team makes too many *decisions on his or her own* without consulting the team. They feel "out of it" and not involved in major decisions. Quite often this is brought to our awareness by the top manager, who will not complain that he or she makes too many major decisions, but will probably speak about *lack of commitment* on the part of team members toward the team and its goals and policies. The manager may speak of team members not *backing team policy;* of *difficulties in implementing* decisions through members, or of *lack of involvement and interest* of people in the team.

In cases like this we usually make a close scrutiny of the decision-making process. We interview the top person and others to find out who makes what decisions. We try by observation and questioning to get a picture of the major trends in the "who makes it" aspect of the decision-making process.

Sometimes team members will complain that decisions are brought to them *ready made*. Someone has come to a previous conclusion and all they are requested to do is to give the rubber stamp. People feel they are being used and not genuinely consulted. They feel they have little sway over the team's major decisions. If they oppose a policy decision of the top manager and his or her colleagues, this will have little effect. If the top manager meets opposition, he or she will find a way to overrule or circumvent the team. People feel they are only consulted on *minor* matters, and that all major matters and important decisions affecting them are beyond their control. Often members talk about a *clique* that in fact *makes all major decisions*. People may say that the top person consults one or two people and they are the ones who decide things.

We may meet this situation from a different angle. We may discover tension in a team between two subgroups, and when we begin looking for the causes of the tension we find that one of the subgroups is "in" and the other is "out." In other words, one small subgroup makes all major decisions and the other people in the group are aware of this and resent it. There is another completely different set of circumstances in which we would use this process: we quite often observe a committee or team working very ineffectively because its agenda includes many items that should *not be discussed in the forum of the committee*. These may be items that the manager—alone or with consultation—should have settled, and not brought before the entire team. Sometimes there are decisions which should have been made by a subgroup of involved members alone. Sometimes there are problems which are of no interest to team members or in which they have no expertise, and these should have been settled outside the team.

We have often come across managers who have participated in T Groups or similar training and have translated such an experience into a policy of *consulting everybody about everything*, making all decisions within a team framework. We have also met managers and consultants who, as a result of T Group training, forget the task aspect of making committee decisions and spend a disproportionate part of the team's time on having each person express his or her feelings on the matter to be discussed. This sometimes results in having all members of the team state how they personally stand on the issue, their feelings about it, how it affects them, etc. Discussions drag on endlessly; the team members express themselves, but few decisions are made. People get bored and tired of this ineffective ceremony and the lack of results soon leads to feelings of futility and lack of commitment—and attendance at meetings drops off. We often use the "with whom shall I make decisions" process as a regular part of workshops with managers coming from different organizations. We have come to the conclusion that most managers have never seriously considered who they make decisions with. Few managers have experimented with trying out alternative processes for making decisions on different kinds of problems. Very few managers have given thought to the considerations and factors related to decision-making.

Who can use:
1. Anyone who has become acquainted with the process
2. A manager or facilitator with any team, except his or her own team
   A manager is advised not to lead this process with his or her own team but to get the help of an outsider to lead the process
3. For one's own edification, a manager can use this process alone in the form described in Variation 1

Purposes:
1. To increase awareness of considerations in deciding with whom to make a decision
2. To increase awareness of how you make decisions and how they are made in your team
3. To increase awareness of changes the team wishes to make in the process of decision-making

Participants:
1. A team of any kind
2. Groups that meet regularly
3. Individual managers in a workshop

Materials:
1. Newsprint, felt pens and tape
2. Placards: "Ways of making a decision" (Fig. 4.11)
3. Handout: "Considerations in deciding with whom to make decisions" (Fig. 4.12)

Time: 2 to 4 hours

STEPS IN PROCESS

1. Display and explain model of "Ways to make decisions"
2. Team scores ways its decisions are made
3. Discussion of considerations in deciding with whom to make decisions
4. Team scores the way it wants decisions to be made
5. Feedback to leader of team

Detailed process

1. *Display and explain model of "Ways to make decisions."* We introduce the process by referring to our observations and/or the feedback we received which led us to believe that it was necessary to work on this area of decision-making (see the section on Individual Interviews and Group Feedback, in Chapter 2). We may display or repeat quotations from members' interviews or we may give specific instances from our observation which have indicated to us that the decision-making process in the team needs clarification.

We differentiate between other interventions, the purpose of which was to improve the problem-solving ability of the team (see Chapter 5), and this process, the purpose of which is to examine *who* makes decisions and who should make the decisions. At this point we may detail the objectives of the process as described in "Purposes" above.

We now display the placard, "Ways of making a decision," as shown in Fig. 4.11.

1. *Manager only:* The manager solves the problem or makes the decision without asking for information or opinion of others.

2. *Manager consults:* The manager asks for opinions and hears considerations of *individuals* from the team, and afterwards makes the decision on his or her own.

3. *Subgroup decision:* The manager discusses the problem with one or more of the team members and makes the decision *together* with them.

4. *Team decision:* The manager brings the problem before the entire team. The team discusses it and makes a decision by vote or consensus.

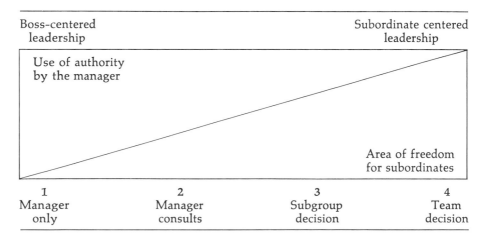

Fig. 4.11 Ways of making a decision

Note: It will be noticed that we use four categories in our Fig. 4.11, Ways of Making a Decision." The original model used by R. Tannenbaum and W. H. Schmidt (see Recommended readings) contained seven categories. V. H. Vroom and P. W. Yetton (see recommended readings) use a five category model.

We started with the seven category model; later changing the number and also definitions of categories. Finally, we settled on the form described here as the one we found suitable for the kind of organizations with which *we* worked.

It seems reasonable to us that a manager or consultant should *suit the categories to the reality of the organization/team he or she is working with.* In other words, if the team you work with uses other ways—or more ways—than the four described, you should modify your model to include them. Do not feel that the model we suggest is the only model. Readers who are interested to go more deeply into this subject are advised to read both the article and the book previously mentioned. Vroom and Yetton have developed a "decision tree" to help the manager decide how and with whom to make decisions. At the time of this writing we have not yet tried it out, but it looks promising. In their book the authors also describe a course for training managers in the use of their model and "decision tree."

One of the team members reads out the placard and we try to make sure that all members of the team thoroughly understand what we are talking about. We sometimes ask people to give practical examples from the team experience of each of the four categories above.

2. *Team scores ways its decisions are made.* We now wish to examine how in practice decisions are made in the team. We do this by either of two methods: by (a) team consensus or (b) scoring.

a. *Team consensus.* Each of the four ways of making decisions is considered in turn and the team tries to reach a consensus on how many decisions are made in each way. This can be done along a scale of: "very few," "few," "some," "quite a lot," "many," "most," "all."

The team should try to come to an agreement about which of the categories on this scale from "very few" to "all" best describes the frequency of using each of the four ways of making decisions. The results of this process gives the team a clear sense of who is responsible for decision-making.

b. *Scoring.* Each member allocates 10 points among the four ways of making decisions. The points are allocated proportionately to the member's view of how many decisions are made in each way. For example, if most decisions are made by "Manager only" and the rest of the decisions are "Team decisions" a person may allocate 8 points to "Manager only" and 2 points to "Team decisions."

Members score *individually* on a sheet of paper. The report of each member's scoring is charted on some newsprint. The sum total of the points that all team members gave to that category, divided by the number of people participating in the scoring, indicates the way the team uses the different methods of decision-making.

3. *Discussion of considerations in deciding with whom to make decisions.* We open a discussion by making the following points:

a. There is no "good" or "bad" way among the four ways of making decisions. *Each way can and should be used* depending on circumstances and the kind of problem being dealt with.

b. *Using one way disproportionately*, or not using another way which might better fit the circumstances, will create problems. We now ask the team members to try to suggest what considerations should be taken into account when deciding with whom to make decisions.

All such suggestions are written up on newsprint and discussed. We sum up along the lines of the handout: "Considerations in deciding with whom to make decisions (Fig. 4.12). At the end of the process this handout remains with the participants. Someone reads the Handout aloud and time is taken for clarification and discussion. We sometimes add the following points:

a. Too much use of (1) "Manager only" and (2) "Manager consults" may create problems of commitment, implementation, and quality.
b. Too much use of (3) "Subgroup" may create problems of cohesion, commitment and implementation.
c. Using (4) "Team" too much may create problems of time, pressure, tedious, and ineffective meetings.

4. *Team scores the way it wants decisions to be made.* In Step 2 the team scored how it saw decisions were actually made. We now focus on how the team would prefer decisions to be made.

Step 4 is an attempt to agree on the desired way of making decisions within the particular set of circumstances and the problems of the team itself.

If we used "Team Consensus" as our scoring method in Step 2, we use it again in this stage. People are requested to use the same categories to designate how they would prefer decisions to be made in their team. An attempt will be made to reach consensus on the desired ratio for use of each of the four ways of decision. If we used a scoring system of allocating 10 points, we repeat it, but this time, people will be requested to allocate the points so as to express the way they desire decisions to be made.

When scoring is complete the scores are written up on the newsprint on which were written the scores of Step 2 (preferably with a different colored marker). The team then discusses the *differences and gaps between the existing situation and the desired one.*

1. Time	4. Team cohesion
2. The quality of the decision	5. The quality of the problem
3. Commitment and implementation	6. Some rules of thumb

1. *Time:* Some decisions are *urgent and cannot wait* until a large group is convened. Of necessity the manager must make such decisions alone or with some select people.

Burdening meetings with problems that are not relevant to the entire team creates tedious and ineffective sessions.

Managers can and should make some decisions on their own, with consultation, and with subgroups.

2. *The quality of the decision:* Decisions should be made *with all the relevant information and expertise available* to the decision makers. Decisions made without the necessary information and expertise are low-quality decisions. We must ensure that people having the relevant information and expertise are involved in some way in the decision-making process.

3. *Commitment and implementation:* People are generally more committed to a decision if they are *meaningfully involved in making the decision.* People may not implement a controversial decision when they were not involved in making it. Commitment and implementation are strong considerations for involving in the decision-making process as many persons as possible *who will be affected by the outcome* of the decision.

4. *Team cohesion:* Differences of opinion within a team are best thrashed out *in open discussion and confrontation* within the framework of the team's meetings. Disproportionate use of "clique" decisions may break up team cohesion.

5. *The quality of the problem:* The quality of a problem should be a major factor in deciding on what level a decision should be made.

Some of the considerations determining the quality of a problem are:
   a. The amount of *resources* (manpower, money, expertise) involved.
   b. Values and/or basic social, political, moral, or ethical factors involved.
   c. How long the decision will commit the organization.
   d. How many important *areas of organizational life* will be affected by the decision.
   e. Whether the decision will set *precedents.*

6. Some rules of thumb:
   a. As often as possible a decision should be made by *those who* will implement it.
   b. Try to *involve* in the decision process all *those who will be meaningfully affected* by it.
   c. Be sure you have *all necessary information and expertise.*
   d. *Don't overburden total team meetings* with problems that can be solved effectively by some smaller group or person.

Fig. 4.12 Considerations in deciding with whom to make decisions

It is preferable to lead this discussion along a constructive problem-solving form, and to obtain suggestions for closing the gap between reality and what is desired. (See Chapter 5 for ideas on how to lead such discussions.)

5. *Feedback to leader of team.* The scoring and discussion in Step 4 has already given the manager (or chairman) feedback on how the team members see things. He or she knows that they want more decisions made in one way and less in another way. Nevertheless, it is often worthwhile to devote a discussion to the subject of giving feedback to the manager on specific items.

We suggest that team members tell the manager what *kinds* of decisions they want to have made more (or less) often *in team meetings;* what *kinds* of decisions the manager makes *on his or her own* that the team members are happy with (or unhappy about); what *kinds* of decisions the manager makes with a subgroup that the team members can (or cannot) wholeheartedly accept; and so on.

The manager is requested *only* to listen and *not* give answers. He or she may request clarification, but should not argue back. When all have finished, the manager is requested to give his or her reactions and conclusions. If possible, *formal resolutions should be made* as to the future conduct of making decisions.

Variation 1

As an individual manager reading this book, you may want to consider two alternatives. You can invite another manager or facilitator to lead the process with your team. Or, alternatively, but probably less effectively, you might apply the process and try to analyze your way of working. You would examine concretely what decisions you have made lately and consider whether or not you are taking into account all the considerations detailed here. Have you been using certain ways of making decisions disproportionately—either too much or too little? Then, consider whether you wish to make any changes in the future.

Variation 2

Individual managers in a workshop who do not generally work together will need a different process.

Steps 1 and 2 can remain unchanged. The feedback processes in Steps 3 and 4 will have to be replaced by individual estimates both as to the present situation and the desired situation.

Another possibility is that in Step 3 the manager makes an estimate of how much he or she uses each of the different ways.

In Step 4 the workshop breaks up into subgroups of three or four people and each manager in turn displays his or her estimate. The others in the subgroup question the manager, comment on what they have been told, and try to help the manager improve his or her effectiveness in this area.

HOW DO YOU ATTAIN YOUR GOALS IN THE ORGANIZATION?
(Open-System Planning)

Helping managers to determine their influence in the organization, to define their goals, examine them, and plan how to attain them with the help of others in their organization.

When to use

We use this process in a workshop of managers who do *not* work together but perform similar managerial functions. This can be used with sales managers, personnel managers, production managers, or any other kinds of managers so long as we have at least a group of four people who *fill similar managerial capacities.*

The managers should *not* be people working together in one organization. For example, it is better to work with personnel managers from different organizations and companies. However, the process can also be useful in a *large* organization in which sales managers are from different areas of the country.

Preferably, this process should be introduced toward the end of a two-to-four day workshop. Under such circumstances, the managers have already become acquainted with each other.

If a large organization is holding a managers' seminar or workshop including different subjects, this process might be used as a preparation for the "return home." For instance, we have chosen to use this intervention when an organization is running its own managerial seminar or workshop and has asked us to work with the group for a segment of the workshop.

We would use this workshop only with managers who already *have experience in their particular job,* and not with a group of managers who are training to enter a new function. The whole process is vital only if people have actually experienced what they are talking about.

Managers can go through the process by themselves. However, the benefit is enhanced when they can periodically discuss their learnings with someone they trust.

Who can use: 1. A facilitator with from four to six people (one facilitator for each group of from four to six)
2. A manager by himself or herself

Purposes: 1. To help managers define their goals
2. To help them examine their influence on the subsystems they work with

3. To help them clarify their strengths and weaknesses in their particular managerial functions
4. To help them clarify what others expect of them
5. To help them plan steps of action to attain their goals

Participants: Any number of subgroups of from four to six managers in similar positions. The size of the subgroup is important. During certain parts of the process each manager's work is examined individually. Therefore, the larger the subgroup, the longer the process takes. It can be done with a subgroup of eight people but would then take longer than two days and might tax people's patience.

Materials: 1. Newsprint, felt pens, tape, paper and pencil
2. Placard "What you will be doing" (Fig. 4.13)
3. List of people in your organization arranged by units or departments

Time: About 16 hours

STEPS IN PROCESS

1. Explaining purposes and dividing into subgroups
2. Defining and clarifying goals
3. Self and systems: examining your influence in the organization:
   a. listing people you can influence
   b. listing people you have ties with
   c. examining your influence on subsystems
4. Examining what strengths are needed and which you have
5. Self and systems: examining what others expect from you
6. Redefining goals and ranking them
7. Planning action steps

Detailed process

1. *Explaining purpose and dividing into subgroups.* We put up the placard shown in Fig. 4.13 ("What you will be doing") and briefly explain the various steps we will go through. The rationale of each step is explained by referring to its purpose as detailed in "Purposes" above. The purpose of the total process is also explained.

The placard "What you will be doing" remains on the wall during the two days we work with the group. People can always refer to it to see where they are and how they have progressed.

1. Defining your goals
2. Self and system—examining your influence in the system
3. Examining what strengths are needed and which you have
4. Self and system—examining what others expect of you
5. Redefining goals and ranking them
6. Planning action steps

Fig. 4.13 What you will be doing

Participants are now divided into subgroups of from four to six people. We try to let people choose whom they wish to work with in the subgroup since we know it will be easier to express themselves more openly with people of their choice.

It is better to have subgroups of four people each, if the number of facilitators allows. Six people in a subgroup is feasible but as many as eight in a subgroup is often tiring for the participants.

Note: All the work from this point on is in the subgroups.

2. *Defining and clarifying goals.* The participants, separately, write from four to six specific goals they wish to achieve as managers in the organization. They should each write the most important goals that they will try to attain, as part of their managerial function, on returning home. The goals should be specific and not wide and vague. We give examples: "Raising productivity" is wide and vague. "Decreasing absenteeism in Department X" is more specific.

The group members are given time to think and write down their goals in their notebooks. We ask that each goal be written in short sentences; i.e., not more than 10 words per goal.

When the members of the subgroup are finished, they read out, in turn, the goals they have decided on. We have prepared for each person a newsprint which is headed with his or her name and the word "Goals." As each one reads out his or her goals we write them up on the appropriate newsprint. Many people need help in concisely defining goals, so we make ourselves very available during this phase of the process.

When all the goals are up on newsprint, each person in turn explains them to the other members of the group. The group members try to understand, and to help clarify and specify the goals if necessary. This discussion helps each person become more clear about what his or her goals really are. If desired the person can make corrections on the newsprint.

Note: At this stage people often tend to start trying to give advice and solutions to the persons explaining their goals. Should this happen, we intervene and explain that we shall do this at a later stage when it will be more effective.

How do you attain your goals in the organization? 119

3. *Self and systems: Examining your influence in the organization.* This step contains a number of substeps: (a) listing people you can influence; (b) listing people you have ties with; (c) examining your influence on subsystems.

a. *Listing people you can influence.* The group members each have to write down the names of about ten people on whom they have influence, and who, in turn, have influence in the organization. If we are dealing with managers of a specific department (sales, production, etc.) they will refer to that department only when we speak of organization. General managers of smaller companies will have to try and refer to the organization as a whole. In a smaller company, managers with a specific function throughout the organization—e.g., personnel managers—should also try to refer to the organization as a whole. Should some people have more than ten "influentials" they can write more.

At this stage we prefer not to develop a discussion about the meaning of "influence" and "People who have influence." We let each person understand this as he or she wishes. When finished writing, each person retains his or her list for later use.

b. *Listing people you have ties with.* Each person has to bring to the meeting a list of people in his or her organization, arranged according to departments, teams, and committees. If we are dealing with managers in a large organization the list should be of people in departments or sections of the organization with whom the managers may have some on-going contact.

The participants now underline on their lists the names of every person with whom they have ties. We define "ties" as more than a nodding acquaintance; it is a relationship close enough so that those who share it can discuss things with one another and tell each other things about themselves.

When people have finished marking their lists we point out that now they have a picture of their ties with various departments, teams, and committees in the organization. They should check whether they have ties with the director of each such department, team, and committee. Having ties with the director and three other people of a seven-man team generally means more influence on that team than ties with one or two people of another similarly sized team not including the director.

If the organization has a number of important *informal* subgroups that have influence on what goes on; e.g., "old timers," "young specialists," a similar procedure should be gone through with them. First, each person must make a new list organized by informal subgroups. Then it is necessary to underline the names of people in that informal group with whom one has ties.

c. *Examining your influence on subsystems.* Each person now examines his or her list of "influentials" to see which teams, departments, and committees he or she can influence with their help, then writes the names of those "influentials" next to the name of the team, department, or committee on his list. A similar procedure is then carried out with important informal subgroups.

The group members now each have a list of formal and informal subsystems in the organization with the names of people with whom they have ties underlined, and the names of influentials marked next to them.

Taking these factors into account, each person then ranks each subsystem according to the amount of influence he or she has on it, using a reverse scale of from 1 to 5. Thus:

1 = I influence this subsystem very strongly.

5 = I have no influence on this subsystem.

Note that the most influence has the smallest number (1) and least influence has the highest number (5).

When each person has finished marking the subsystems (including the informal ones), he or she transfers the ranking to a newsprint in the form of concentric circles, as shown in Fig. 4.14. The inner circle represents the individual him- or herself. In circle number one the person puts the names of formal and informal subsystems which he or she influences very strongly, and so on until the last circle in which are listed the subsystems on which he or she has no influence. To make the illustration clearer, the informal groups can be listed on the right side of the circles.

Next the group members take turns in putting up the newsprint that shows their "Influence map" and next to it their list of goals. They have to explain to the group how they worked out the influence map and how it can help them achieve the goals they have listed for themselves. Others in the group listen to these explanations and clarify matters, question assumptions, enlarge possibilities, and point out factors and even eventualities that the person demonstrating did not think about. They often point out some critical part of the organization that was not covered in the influence map but that should be taken care of, or a "leverage point" which the person presenting the influence map did not mention.

4. *Examining what strengths are needed and which you have.* Each person in a subgroup writes down the "strengths" needed to perform their managerial function in the ideal way. "Strengths" would include qualities, behavioral style, experience, skills, knowledge, etc.

Each individual calls out his or her list and all individual lists are combined into one master list on newsprint. An attempt should be made to

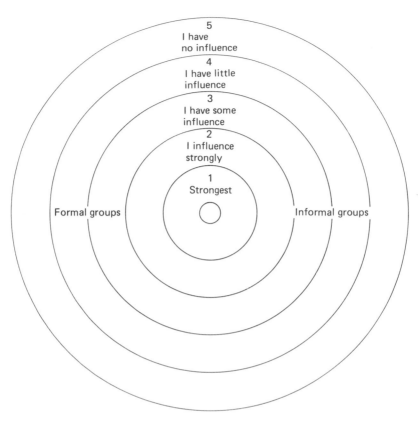

Formal groups

5
I have
no influence

4
I have little
influence

3
I have some
influence

2
I influence
strongly

1
Strongest

Informal groups

Fig. 4.14 Influence map

reach an agreement on this list. Items about which there are differences of opinion should be clarified and, if possible, consensus should be attained regarding all items on the list. If time is short, items with little support can be dropped.

Each person now copies the combined list in his or her notebook, giving each "strength" a rating on a scale of from 1 to 4.

1 = I am very weak in this "strength."

4 = I am very strong in this "strength."

When all have finished the rating each person in turn goes up to the newsprint and using different colors marks with a 1 the items in which he or she is very weak, and with a 4 the items in which he or she is very strong. All members explain why they give themselves the ratings, and the group members give their opinion on those ratings, give feedback, and discuss and clarify matters.

5. Self and systems: examining what others expect from you. Each person has to make a list of the subsystems: formal groups (teams, departments, committees) and informal groups (old timers, pressure groups, etc.). The names of the subsystems are to be written in a column on the left-hand side of the page in the individual's notebook.

Next to each subsystem, the person writes, in the form of a spoken request, the major expectation of that system from him or her. For instance, "Grant us a higher budget," "Leave us alone," "Get rid of team X," etc.

If a system is of low importance to the goals of the person concerned and if it has no expectations from him or her, it need not be included on the list.

Each person now transfers what he or she has written to a newsprint in the form of a small circle with spokes coming from it, as shown in Fig. 4.15. The circle is the self. The name of each subsystem is written close to the circle and its "spoken expectations" are written in its segment further on.

When all have finished preparing their newsprint, each person in turn does the following:

a. Puts up on the wall the first newsprint prepared with his or her goals, and next to it the newsprint with his or her Expectations Map.

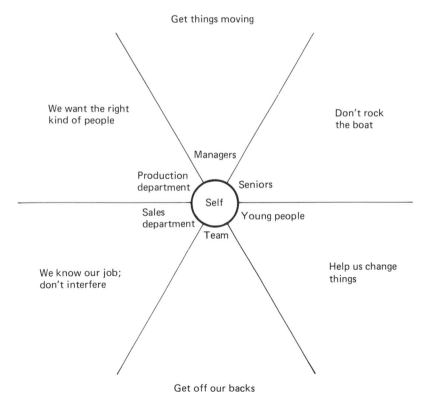

Fig. 4.15 Expectations map

b. Explains each expectation and states whether he or she is *interested in*, *wants* to, and is *able* to meet this expectation.

c. Examines whether there is any *connection* between his or her goals and the expectations of others. If not, why not? And what can be done about it?

When a person is explaining his or her map and answering these questions (they may be put on newsprint) other subgroup members may question him or her, clarify things, and voice their opinion about what he or she has told them.

Another approach requires that participants each explain their map and compare it with their goals list without any interruption. When they have finished, people give them feedback, voice opinions, etc. without them being allowed to answer back. All they can do is listen and write down the main points of what is said to them.

6. *Redefining goals and ranking them.* The participants are now requested to return to their original goal lists. Taking into account all they have been through:

a. They must consider whether they wish to keep the same list or make changes.

b. Do they wish to add goals; to remove goals; to redefine goals?

c. When they have decided these things they must rank their goals in order of *importance* and *feasibility*.

d. They should prepare on newsprint a new list of their goals written in order of importance and feasibility.

Everyone works alone on their goals list. Give as much time as possible.

7. *Planning action steps.* Each person has to continue working alone. Considering the first three goals, they lay out a *plan of action steps to implement each one separately.* They should use all the material they have prepared until now: the goals list, the influence map, the strengths rating, and the expectations map. With the help of these, each person writes down on paper an action plan for each of the first three goals selected.

When everyone is finished, pairs are formed and are given about one and one-half hours to discuss their plans.

When this is over, people are given time to make any changes and transfer their plans to newsprint.

Each person in turn displays his or her revised plans to the group. The group helps, gives suggestions, and adds ideas.

Creative problem-solving, decision-making, and implementation

5

CHAPTER OBJECTIVE

To offer a series of interventions that will help managers and teams handle problems more creatively and effectively, make decisions based on all relevant considerations, and ensure their implementation.

GUIDE TO APPLYING INTERVENTIONS

What is creative problem-solving?

- Problem-solving is a methodical way of treating problems in a step-by-step fashion.
- From defining the problem, one goes on to finding solutions; from this to evaluating solutions, and then to deciding which ones to adopt, and finally to ensuring their implementation.
- Creative problem-solving attempts to maximize the use of human ingenuity and creativity in the process of solving problems.
- A creative approach attempts to "open" the definitions of problems to form that will encourage a wide range of constructive solutions.
- Combining individual and team work, people are encouraged to let their imagination play and bring forth as many proposals as possible.

- People learn how to build on each other's ideas and create new alternatives by developing variations on other's thoughts.
- In order not to stifle creativity, the stage of raising proposals and solutions is clearly differentiated from the stage of evaluating them.
- People are helped to become more aware of the criteria by which they make evaluations.
- A practical, constructive way is sought to overcome the pitfalls of implementation.

About the interventions in this chapter. These interventions can be used in a number of ways:

1. *In a workshop:* They may serve as the main framework of a problem-solving and decision-making workshop for a management team, committee, or individual managers. In this case, it is worthwhile to follow the interventions in the consecutive order in which they are presented in this chapter.

2. *As an aid to team when working on other problems:* A facilitator can lead a team through one or a number of these processes. He or she might do this when the team is having difficulty handling a problem in the conventional way; e.g., a team has difficulty finding solutions to a problematic situation and the facilitator introduces brainstorming.

3. *As a learning input:* A facilitator can, at appropriate occasions, introduce an intervention as a learning experience. The purpose of doing this would be to teach the participants a method they can use in the future when need arises.

4. *As an aid to the individual manager:* A manager may practice using these processes independently with the purpose of improving his or her problem-solving and decision-making ability.

The interventions

1. *How to begin dealing with a problem.* This was developed after we had "problem-sensed with groups" in a number of organizations. We found that some management teams had difficulty dealing with the mountain of problems they had unearthed. We sought a methodical way of helping them. Building on ideas of N.R.F. Maier and others, we developed this process.

2. *Stages of dealing with a problem.* These took shape while we were working with management teams and committees. We were often surprised by the haphazard way decisions were made. Building on the ideas of Sidney Parnes, we developed these "stages of dealing with a

problem." In this process, participants get their first picture of the overall process of problem-solving.

3. *Defining a problem.* Here we examine and differentiate between different kinds of problems. Together with the participants we try out different ways of defining the problems. Here again, we are much indebted to Sidney Parnes.

4. *Creative solutions to problems.* This intervention was developed to help participants learn and practice brainstorming. We use brainstorming extensively in our work with teams. Therefore, we introduce this process very often when working with groups, not specifically within a problem-solving workshop.

5. *Weighing proposals.* We developed this intervention when we found that decision-makers were not often aware of the criteria which swayed them to prefer one proposal over another. This process was developed to aid decision-makers make their decisions in a more methodical way. We built on ideas of Y. Dror.

6. *Deciding between alternative solutions.* We developed this intervention from a process we learned from Jerry Berlin. Every time we use it we derive satisfaction from helping people begin to understand both sides of a question.

7. *Overcoming resistance to implementation.* This is a must at the end of any workshop and before the return home. The purpose is to implement what one has decided on or learned. Most facilitators know it under the name of "force field analysis"—first proposed by Kurt Lewin.

MATRIX OF INTERVENTIONS

Intervention	Use	Who can use	Time demand
How to begin dealing with the problems of an organization	Finding the suitable processes for dealing with different problems	Anyone with practice	6–14 hrs
Stages of dealing with a problem	Acquiring a systematic way of solving problems	Anyone with practice	2–4 hrs
Defining a problem	Learning a creative way of defining problems	Anyone with practice	2–4 hrs
Creative solutions to problems	Learning how to brainstorm	Anyone with practice	2–6 hrs
Weighing proposals	How to evaluate and decide between proposals	Anyone with practice	1–3 hrs

(Cont'd.)

Intervention	Use	Who can use	Time demand
Deciding between alternative solutions	How to choose between two solutions	Anyone with practice	1 hr
Overcoming resistance to implementation	Ensuring effective implementation	Anyone with practice	1 hr

Possible outcomes

1. More effective problem-solving.
2. Better decision-making.
3. More effective use of meeting time.
4. More involvement of team members in decision-making process.
5. More commitment of team members to team's decisions.
6. Better utilization of all available and relevant information and expertise.
7. Greater ability to see a wider range of solutions to problems.
8. More of a "win-win" attitude and less of a "win-lose" attitude.
9. Narrower gap between decisions and implementation.
10. Higher quality of decisions.
11. More use of different human resources in team.
12. More active listening.
13. Increasing receptiveness to others ideas.
14. More building on each others ideas.
15. Increased creativeness and innovativeness in the organization's life.

Recommended readings

1. Kepner, C. H., and B. B. Tregoe, *The Rational Manager: Systematic Approach to Problem-Solving and Decision-Making* (New York: McGraw-Hill, 1965).
2. Maier, N. R. F., *Problem-Solving and Creativity in Individuals and Groups* (Belmont, Calif.: Wadsworth, 1970).
3. Osborne, A. F., *Applied Imagination: Principles and Procedures of Creative Problem-solving*, 3d ed. (New York: Charles Scribner's Sons, 1963).
4. Parnes, S. J., *Creative Behavior Guidebook* (New York: Charles Scribner's Sons, 1967).
5. ————, *Creative Behavior Workbook* (New York: Charles Scribner's Sons, 1967).

Process to help management deal with its organizational problems; assisting team to decide procedures including people and decision groups for dealing with problems.

When to use

We generally use the process with a management team immediately after "Problem-sensing" with groups (see Chapter 2).

The management team has finished "sensing" the problems of the organization and may have fixed priorities for dealing with them. The task looks enormous, "How are we going to deal with and overcome all these major and often urgent problems?" The problems have been brought to the surface, but *how does one get down to tackling them?*

Often there is a tendency for the management team to immediately *start dealing with the issues;* people want to get their teeth into them. At this stage we find it most appropriate to introduce this process, the purpose of which is both *to help the team begin dealing with the problems* and, equally important, *to help the team avoid pitfalls* on its path and show how to minimize them.

In this intervention, as in others in the Handbook, we try *to maintain a healthy balance between ensuring that the team produces effective outputs and giving the team a learning experience* from which they will profit in the future. We often find that people want to deal with the *"task outputs"* of their team; *they want results* in the form of decisions and the changes they desire to bring about. The pressure is in the direction of "getting the job done" with a strong "task orientation."

When we lead the discussions and processes we are fully cognizant of the fact that through our efforts and support the team can indeed be more effective. However, there is often a significant lessening of effectiveness when the team has to work alone *without* our assistance. We, therefore, put much emphasis on the *"learning experience"* aspect of the processes. We try as much as possible to formulate the processes in such manner that when they are over, people will feel not only that they have accomplished something in team outputs, but that they have also had a learning experience from which the team and the individuals will profit *in the future.*

This intervention may be used at the appropriate time *during different kinds of management teams' workshop.* For instance, a workshop may be limited to a specific subject such as "organization structure." In the course of such a workshop many of the organization's structural problems may be unearthed. We might find it suitable to introduce this process to help the team begin dealing with those problems and at the same time learn how to do this in the future with other kinds of problems.

It is difficult, but possible, to go through the process with individual managers in a workshop comprised of people from different organizations. Usually it is possible to find a number of major organizational problems that are faced by most managers. These can serve as the raw material for the experience. In such case we would treat the process more *as a learning experience* and less as an intervention.

Sometimes, *toward the end of a workshop* with a team (not specifically a management team), a list of problems to be dealt with still remains which cannot be postponed to later meetings. In such a case we might use the process or parts of it. But then under these circumstances our specific purpose is to *help the team decide how to deal with the issues*. In this case, the learning experience aspect of the process would be secondary. The process, in the form as outlined here, is not to be used by a team in the first stage of dealing with its own problems. This should be clearly understood: the process is suitable for a decision-making body discussing problems of the organization or part of it. Its purpose is to learn how to handle such problems. If the team has interpersonal problems, effectiveness problems, internal conflicts, etc. there are other processes in this book to deal with them. In this case, we would use the processes detailed in this chapter only after first going through these other processes.

The question here is how does a management body begin dealing with its *organization's* problems.

Who can use: Anyone who has practiced this process even once with a noncritical, friendly team can try it later with other teams.

Purposes: 1. To help a decision-making body become aware of different ways of making decisions on problems
2. To help a management team decide by what processes to deal with various major organizational problems
3. To help individual managers in a workshop become aware of factors that influence effective processing of problems.

Participants: Preferably not more than 15 people if in a team. When used with managers in a workshop the number may be larger. The participants may be subgrouped by similarity of organizational problems which they face.

Materials: 1. Newsprint, felt pens, tape
2. Placard and handout with illustration of factors in "effective decision-making" (Fig. 5.1)

Time: 4 to 8 hours (depending on number and complexity of problems to be dealt with)

STEPS IN PROCESS

1. Introduction to process
2. Factors in effective decision-making on problems
3. Ways to process the problems
4. Processing the problems
5. Team makes decisions on processes

Note: We will detail the process in the form we would use after "Problem-Sensing with Groups" (see Chapter 2).

Detailed process*

1. *Introduction to process.* We begin by stating the purpose of the process. Three points are stressed:

a. Our major purpose is to process the problems by *deciding what to do with them* and how to deal with them.

b. We will try to learn what factors hinder or aid effective decision-making and implementation, and consider what to do about them.

c. Another important purpose is to become acquainted with a process which can be used in the future when the team may face similar circumstances.

If the team has not yet experienced or acquired an understanding of the differences between "process" and "content" we devote some time to clarifying these concepts.

We give examples from the problem list with which we will be dealing. In a few words we explain that "process" is the *way* we deal with a decision —how and with whom we make it—and that "content" is what the problem and decision *is about.*

We try to give some examples from experiences we have just had with the team. We now ask the team to give us examples of the possible process and content of two or three problems we are about to deal with.

Only when we are sure that all members of the team have grasped the difference between the two concepts do we go on to explain that this sitting will be devoted exclusively to the process by which we shall deal with the problems. As much as possible we shall try *not* to deal with the content of the problems, nor discuss or debate them. Our sole purpose is to decide by what process we can ensure a serious consideration of the problems and a successful implementation of the course adopted for their solution.

---

* In this intervention we have used many of the ideas of N. R. F. Maier.

We will consider:

- *what body* or bodies should discuss them
- *who* should participate in the discussion
- *what form* the discussion should take
- which problems are *ours;* which belong to *other bodies;* which belong both to other committees and to us *jointly*
- what problems need to be thrashed out *first* in one forum and then decided in a different or wider forum, etc. etc.

We now ask participants what factors, in their opinion, influence us in attaining an effective decision in a problem and its successful implementation. Participants voice their suggestions and we note them on newsprint.

To summarize this stage we write up the following decision formulae on newsprint and explain them.

Q = The *Quality* of the decision = having all the information expertise needed

I = The *Implementation* of the decision = being involved in making it

E = Effective decision-making

$E = Q \times I$ Effective decision-making = The quality of the decision × The implementation of the decision

We can have *low-quality decisions implemented,* i.e., decisions made when the necessary information or expertise was not available. We often have *high-quality decisions which are never implemented* because the people affected by them were not involved in the decision process.

Implementation without Quality gives bad results.

Quality without Implementation is being ineffective.

2. *Factors in Effective Decision-Making.* We now display the placard with the illustration of "Factors in Effective Decision-Making" (Fig. 5.1). We explain:

- The *horizontal* axis represents the two major factors in achieving a decision of quality: having all the pertinent *information* and all the *specific expertise* needed to make the decision.

- The left side of the horizontal axis represents *problems* on which we can make a quality decision *without need* for further information and/ or for expertise, knowledge, or experience. The right side of this axis refers to problems that *do need* relevant knowledge and/or expertise for making a quality decision.

- The *vertical* axis represents the *importance* of the decision *to the people it concerns.*

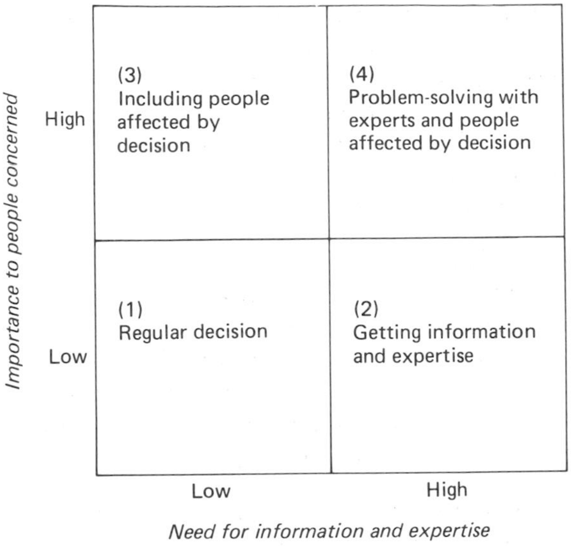

Fig. 5.1 Factors in effective decision-making

■ The bottom half of the vertical axis represents problems in which whatever decision is made will *not* concern the people involved; they have low concern for the outcome.

■ The top half of the vertical line represents problems which *are of great interest* to the people concerned. The outcome of the decision is highly important to the people involved in it.

We point out that combining the two axes creates four types of problems which should be treated differently in deciding by which decision-making process they be dealt with.

Type 1 *Low in need for expertise and information and of low importance to people concerned.* Problems of this kind can be decided by a regular decision, by whoever has to make them, *sometimes* even by the toss of a coin; e.g., should the supply of pencils be painted one color or many colors.

Type 2 *High in need for expertise and information but of low importance to the people concerned.* Problems of this kind demand that all relevant information be known to decision-makers, and all experts and experienced persons who can contribute *should participate* in the decision. These problems can sometimes be decided by the *experts alone;* e.g. what is the optimal freezing level to preserve all perishable supplies for making a product.

How to begin dealing with problems of an organization **133**

Type 3 *Low in need for expertise and information but of high importance to the people concerned.* At some stage of the decision-making process, problems of this kind demand *the inclusion of people who will be affected* by it. Those affected may prepare the discussion or participate in making it, or make the decision themselves; e.g., vacation periods for all members of a department.

Type 4 *High in need for both expertise and information and of great relevance to the people concerned.* These problems are the most complicated ones. They demand a problem-solving process to ensure consideration of all relevant information and expertise and the inclusion in the process of decision-making of the people affected by the decision; e.g., major changes in a production process.

We now request participants to give examples of problems, from their own experience, which fall under each of the four categories.

Enough examples are collected so that everyone understands this categorization of types of problems.

Here are four representative examples for the facilitator that may evoke some discussion:

Type 1 Which of two machines of equal price, quality, and performance—but of different manufacturers—does management decide to buy?

Type 2 Which of two machines to buy: They demand the same effort from the worker but are of different quality, price, and performance.

Type 3 Which of two machines to buy: All their details are known including price, quality, and output—but they demand different kinds of performance and effort from the men operating them.

Type 4 The factory must make a decision about changing its machine system. There are two alternatives. Neither of which is understood too well by the decision-makers from the technical, output, social, and economic aspects. It is obvious that whichever setup is chosen it will have major effects on the existing labor force, working conditions, hours, shifts, etc.

3. *Ways to Process the Problems.* The participants are now requested to list examples of different ways of processing problems confronting the team. All suggestions are written up on newsprint.

We usually begin with one or two suggestions to make our request understood, for example:

a. Discussion and decision in this management committee only.

b. Preparation by a subgroup with experts and decision by this committee.

c. Joint meeting with another body involved and decision together.

d. Creating a project team to deal with the issue, etc.

The suggestions are not connected to any specific problem. What we try to achieve is *a list of options in processing problems* in this particular organization.

4. *Processing the Problems.* We now begin work on the problems from the problem list. If a priority order has been fixed we begin with the problem given highest priority. Members of the team are requested to think some minutes about the most effective way *to process* this problem. They are to remember what we have learned about dealing with the four types of problems, and to jot down on paper a process to deal with this first problem. The process may have numerous steps, or a person can suggest just one step, after which *the decision process* itself may be decided on by others involved in it.

All suggestions are put up on newsprint, and the team discusses and decides on the process it prefers—always referring to the placard of "Factors in Effective Decision-Making," (Fig. 5.1).

When this has been done and we feel sure the participants know what is required of them, then we can begin processing the rest of the problems in *subgroups.*

The team is divided into subgroups of three people each. Each subgroup takes a number of problems from the list and is requested to prepare suggestions of processes to deal with the problems.

The subgroups are reminded that they can decide to recommend postponing dealing with a problem especially if it has low priority.

It is also worth remarking that if a process has a number of steps in which other people than those present must take part, it might be worth deciding about the process itself together with those other people.

Each subgroup is to prepare a newsprint with a Problem/Process Record Sheet in the manner shown in Fig. 5.2.

The newsprint should contain the process suggested by the subgroup for each of its problems. The subgroup should also suggest a person from among the participants who will be responsible for implementation and a date on which he or she is to report to the management committee which of the steps have been accomplished.

It should be clear that the person responsible on behalf of the committee is responsible *only to the committee itself* and has *not* of necessity to be the person who will be dealing with the problem in all stages of

The problem	Groups or people af-fected by problem	The process	Who is responsible for imple-mentation	Reporting date
1.				
2.				
3.				
etc.				

Fig. 5.2 Problem/process record sheet

problem-solving and implementation. A person may be nominated to be responsible only for the election of a project team that will take upon itself the complete responsibility for dealing with the problem.

We stress this point because we are aware of a tendency in management committees to load too much of the burden on their own members and at the same time leave excellent human resources throughout the organization unexploited.

Each subgroup gets down to its work in a different room or the corner of a large room. We move between the subgroups while they are working, giving advice, helping, and guiding in the process. If one subgroup finishes before the others we transfer to it problems not yet processed by a lagging subgroup.

5. *Team makes decisions on processes.* When all have finished, the total group is convened. Each subgroup in turn displays its newsprint and explains its recommendations. We prefer to follow the following system:

■ All recommendations *which were accepted without debate* are ratified as decisions.

The decision is written up on a fresh newsprint as the committee's decision. Care is taken not to omit the name of the person responsible for implementation and the date of reporting. It is the responsibility of the committee's chairman to see that the report is made on the specified date.

■ If a recommendation is *not* accepted without dissension we do not at this stage debate it. We pass on to the next recommendation, leaving all debatable recommendations for the end of this stage.

■ Each subgroup in turn follows the above procedure.

What is achieved is a sizable number of recommendations accepted by the team as decisions.

What remains to be done is to discuss and decide on the recommendations about which there are differences of opinion.

We follow the above procedure in order to ensure that the team accomplishes a good part of its work and *sees results*. If for reasons beyond our control time is short and not all problems can be processed, at least a large part has been accomplished.

If we are not short of time the team can discuss and decide on the remaining recommendations over which there has been disagreement.

If the team does not finish debating all processes, a date is fixed on which discussion will continue.

A handout with "Factors in effective decision-making" can be given to participants.

Note: The team has now finished deciding about *processes* relating to problems they face. The time has now arrived for it to begin dealing with problems on which it must make *its own decisions*. In short, the team should now pass on to the phase of discussing the *content* of the problems for which it is responsible for finding solution.

That process is described in the other interventions of this chapter.

Variation 1: Working on some immediate dilemma

We might use this variation when working with a team in which we are more interested in helping it overcome *its present dilemma,* and less interested in the intervention as a learning experience for future application and use.

In such case we would perhaps skip steps 1 and 3 and begin by explaining the placard, and then proceed directly to forming subgroups that prepare recommendations.

Variation 2: Helping team examine how it makes decisions

This variation is just a theoretical input which we might introduce to a team when we feel it is beginning to make decisions *without* involving people who would be affected by them.

Sometimes we might use it when a team begins to make a decision *without* the necessary information and expertise being available.

In cases like these we just draw the illustration of "Effective decision-making" and perhaps add one or two formulae. This input often leads the team to reexamine how it goes about making its decisions.

STAGES OF DEALING WITH A PROBLEM

Demonstrating to an individual or a group the steps in dealing effectively with a problem.

When to use

This process is used when the need is felt for improvement in problem-solving abilities.

A management team or a committee feel they are not making decisions in a methodical manner; people have difficulty in dealing with problems in systematic ways; people have difficulty in defining the problems they face; team members start debating solutions before deciding what the problems are; people weigh solutions before exhausting the possibility of finding alternative solutions; the team has difficulty deciding the angle from which to attack a complicated problem, etc.

This process is more effective *with a team that will continue to work together*. People can learn the process together and continue practicing it and improving their capabilities as they work together.

On the other hand, it also can be used with individual managers in a workshop. Although the managers may have some difficulty working with their team back home along the lines on which they were trained, it will, however, help them as individuals to do problem-solving systematically.

The process is suitable for a team of any kind that meets quite often and has to make democratic decisions. It is unsuited to a team in which the leader makes the decisions, and only asks the team members for opinions and advice. On the other hand, it is suitable for *anybody who wishes to train themselves alone* in this process in order to increase their problem-solving ability (see Variation 1).

This process is preferably used with the other processes in this chapter, but it is the initial opening process by which we get the team acquainted with the steps of decision-making.

It is undesirable to use this process without accompanying it with other interventions on the interpersonal and group level that may be hindering effective decision-making.

We often use this process toward the beginning of work with a team that shows resistance to working on the interpersonal level. The emotion-free, impersonal, and conceptual character of this process makes it acceptable to teams that are not yet ready to deal with their interpersonal problems.

Who can use: This process can be used by anybody after they have become acquainted with it. It is preferable to first try it out in a safe accepting team (possibly your own) and later with other teams.

Purpose: To help a team or individual manager become aware and familiar with a systematic method of dealing with problems.

Materials: 1. Newsprint, felt pens and tape, pen and paper
            2. A newsprint with "Dealing with a Problem" (Fig. 5.3)
            3. Handouts of "Dealing with a Problem"
            4. Problem list

Time: 2 to 4 hours

STEPS IN PROCESS

1. Problems displayed
2. Consultant explains purpose of process
3. Newsprint with "Dealing with a Problem" displayed
4. Consultant leads the group through the steps
5. Committee chairman or task force leader takes over

Note: You must be prepared to be very active and leading in this process. The trainer is more of a teacher here than in most of the other processes in this book.

Detailed process

1. *Problems displayed.* When working with a management team or a committee the consultant can request the leader of the team to prepare beforehand, on newsprint, a list of the problems on which the team will have to make decisions in its future meetings.

If this process comes soon after a problem-sensing session with a team, the items given priority by the team can be copied on newsprint and will serve the purpose. The data finally chosen after individual interviews and feedback can also serve.

If working with a group of managers from different teams, the managers should be requested to draw up a list of problems which each may have to tackle with his or her own team. Each manager then throws in a problem or two and these are listed on the newsprint.

Then participants are asked if they have any methodical way of dealing with problems and what, in their opinion, is the first step. The participants voice their opinions and the consultant lists them on newsprint.

2. *Consultant explains purpose of process.* The consultant explains that the purpose of this meeting is to become acquainted with the general outline of steps in dealing with a problem. People will not yet be proficient in using it at the end of the session, but they will be more aware of the different steps of a systematic way of dealing with problems.

The consultant can now make these points:

a. There is no best way of dealing with all kinds of problems.

b. Different kinds of problems require different ways of dealing with them.

c. Different problems require emphasis on different steps in the process.

d. In some cases the most important step is to define the problem itself; the rest comes fast and easy after that.

e. With other kinds of problems the important thing is to find many alternative ways of dealing with them. In such situations, the definition may be clear, but the group seems unable to find a creative solution.

f. For some problems the most important step is collecting all the relevant information. After this the solution may be self-evident.

g. In other kinds, the definition of the problem is clear, the alternative choices are known, and what remains to be done is to choose between alternative solutions.

h. Still another kind of problem is that even when the solution is known and decided on, the team is faced with the question of how to implement it successfully.

i. It is of great value to be able to see with what kind of problem we are dealing and what stages of the process are important in solving it. This is not easy and takes much practice. Sometimes, even after practice, when actually working on the problem, one discovers that the estimate was wrong.

People's comments can now be requested, and when finished, the consultant proceeds to the next step.

2. *Newsprint with "Dealing with a Problem" displayed.* The consultant now puts up the newsprint showing the steps in "Dealing with a Problem" and asks one of the participants to read it out aloud.

The version we use is shown in Fig. 5.3.*

---

1. Defining the problem
2. Collecting all relevant information
3. Finding alternative solutions
4. Weighing and choosing solutions
5. Ensuring successful implementation
6. Responsible individuals for implementation steps
7. Follow-up steps

Fig. 5.3 Dealing with a problem

---

*   This can be duplicated and used as a handout.

The consultant can make these remarks:

a. This is not the only version of ways to deal with a problem but is the one I use and find useful.

b. Each step has substeps that you will become acquainted with throughout the process. Meanwhile the purpose of this session is to get to know the general outline and to practice it.

c. It is important to recognize the steps and not jump to the later steps without being sure that the first ones have been adequately dealt with.

d. Mistakes often made are in not spending sufficient time on step 1, or step 2, or step 3, or step 4, or the "weighing" part of step 4. Quite often teams accept the definition of the problem as first stated and jump to choosing a solution and finish with that.

The participants are now asked if they understand in general terms what each step means. If some do not understand, others can be asked to clarify the meaning to them. If necessary, the consultant can add explanations, being careful not to go into details, but just being content to reach a general understanding of the steps.

4. *Consultant leads the group through the steps.* The purpose of this exercise is to get people used to the sequential steps in dealing with a problem. The consultant will take, one-by-one, the problems listed on the newsprint and, together with the participants, go through the four steps with each problem.

Here is how this is done:

▪ The consultant says: "Let's take the first problem. How would you define it; can you suggest other definitions?"

▪ People suggest definitions and the consultant writes them on the newsprint. He or she may remark: "You can see there are different definitions to a problem, and we shall go into this later."

▪ The consultant takes 2 or 3 definitions and, with the help of the team, lists the relevant information which might have to be collected before proceeding further.

▪ The consultant now chooses one definition which he or she believes opens the problem to a wide array of alternative solutions and says; "For the exercise we shall take this definition, and pass to step 3: 'Finding alternative solutions'." Everyone is asked to write on a piece of paper one or two solutions to the problem defined. When they have finished they are asked to read out their solution and the consultant puts them up on newsprint, remarking: "Well, that was Step 3, 'Finding alternative solutions'; let us now pass to Step 4, 'Weighing and choosing solutions.' Let us look at some of the solutions you have offered. By what criteria would you weigh their relative value in solving the problem? Will each of you think a moment or two and write down two or three criteria." After the participants have finished writing, the consultant lists their criteria on the newsprint.

The consultant explains that we have to find a way to evaluate which of the solutions best satisfies the most important criteria, and—at this stage —calls on the participants to volunteer an appraisal of which solutions best answer the criteria.

People give suggestions and the consultant writes them down on the newsprint.

The consultant now chooses one of the solutions, saying: "That was Step 4, 'Weighing and choosing solutions.' Now let's move to 5, 'Ensuring successful implementation.' The problem with many good decisions is that they never get implemented, or are ineffectively implemented. Some people have the feeling that by coming to a decision, they have made a change. But change only occurs when the decision has been effectively implemented in reality and not only on paper."

He asks the participants to give any suggestions or make any guesses as to what factors may obstruct the effective implementation of this solution.

People make suggestions and the consultant writes them down and asks: "Now, have you any ideas on how we could go about ensuring successful implementation?"

People make suggestions and the consultant writes them down. He then remarks: "In reality we would have to finish this process by deciding who is responsible for the implementation and by what date. We would also fix a date to reexamine what has been done and, if necessary, make changes in our plans."

5. *Committee chairman or task force leader takes over.* After the consultant has practiced this process two or three times with the team, he or she turns over the leadership to the person who regularly chairs the meetings, first requesting the team to help the chairman and then taking a seat among the participants.

The team's chairman then goes through the entire process with two or three other problems.

It should be emphasized that the goal is not to solve the problems but to *exercise the steps*. Therefore, the decision as to what definition or solution to choose rests with the chairman.

If there is another team member who sometimes chairs the meetings, he too can take his turn in leading.

If the process is being done with individual managers who are not a team, the consultant can give only one demonstration and then let each person in turn lead the group through the steps. Of course, if necessary, and if others do not do so, the consultant helps the person in leading.

At the end of the process each participant receives a handout of "Dealing with a Problem" (from paragraph 2 above).

Variation 1

For managers or people who have to make many decisions without the aid of a team:

Individuals wishing to learn the process can do so by themselves by taking a problem they are faced with and going through the steps, one-by-one. Wherever the text states that team members offer suggestions or solutions etc. the individual can make a list of suggestions or advance solutions of his or her own.

DEFINING A PROBLEM

Method used to get a better understanding of the problem being faced.

When to use

This process is a continuation of the problem-solving process previously described, and all the conditions there relate also to this process.

Who can use: Anyone who has tried this intervention with supportive team

Purposes: 1. To help a team or individual managers become aware of different aspects and ways of defining a problem
2. To exercise definition of problems

Materials: 1. Newsprint, felt pens, tape, pens and paper
2. Newsprint with "Defining a Problem" (Fig. 5.4)
3. Problem list
4. Handouts of "Defining a Problem"

Time: 2 to 4 hours

STEPS IN PROCESS

1. Simple, Complex, and Yes-or-No Problems
2. Simple problems: creative definitions and fixing level
3. Complex problems: listing different aspects
4. Further information and deciding what subproblem to deal with
5. Practice

Detailed process

1. *Simple, complex, and yes-or-no problems.* The consultant introduces the session with a few words as a continuation of the former process.

The purpose of the session is to learn to differentiate between different kinds of problems and to exercise the steps in defining them.

The consultant puts up the newsprint with "Defining a Problem" (Fig. 5.4).*

The consultant gives a working definition of simple and complex problems.

Simple problems have one major aspect and there is no great difficulty in defining them.

Complex problems have many different aspects of importance and there is difficulty in defining them.

Examples of simple problems are:

- Will we invest in this machine?
- Will we promote Mr. Bell to be Assistant Manager of sales?
- Should we extend the agreement with company X for another year?
- How much money will we grant to the Y fund?

We generally know how to approach simple problems. They have one major aspect and there is no great argument about what that aspect is.

Example of a complex problem: "Productivity has gone down considerably." Further questioning into this problem may lead some people to define the problem as "decreasing work morale in the factory"; others as "lack of supervision"; others as "how to catch up our lag in investment in modern equipment." One person may insist that the correct definition of this problem is: "How to make our management more effective."

---

1. Simple and complex problems
2. Simple:
   a. Giving a creative definition
   b. Deciding level of definition
3. Yes-or-No Problems: Moving to decision stage
4. Complex:
   a. Listing different aspects of the problem
   b. Combining similar aspects
   c. Further information, if necessary
   d. Deciding what subproblem to deal with
   e. Giving a creative definition

Fig. 5.4 Defining a problem

---

*   This can be duplicated and used as a handout.

In short, a complex problem is a "tangle" of different aspects, and there are different ways of approaching it.

The consultant takes one-by-one the problems listed on the Problem List, and asks the participants whether they see them as simple or complex. Whatever is decided is marked with an S or a C on the Problem List (which was prepared, you recall, by the team leader).

When there are differences of opinion the consultant gives this rule: "If for different people it is important that a problem be defined differently and in their way, the problem is called complex."

After completion of the list the consultant begins practicing defining simple problems.

2. *Simple problems: creative definitions and fixing level.* The consultant explains as follows:

We often tend to give "closed" definitions to problems that leave us few alternatives for solutions. A creative definition opens a problem to a variety of creative solutions.

How does one open a problem by creative definition? By changing the wording and placing, at the beginning of the sentence, the words "Ways to. . . ." For instance:

Ordinary Definition: "Productivity has gone down."
Creative Definition: "Ways to make productivity go up."

Ordinary Definition: "Decreasing work morale in the factory."
Creative Definition: "Ways to raise work morale in the factory."

Ordinary Definition: "Lack of supervision."
Creative Definition: "Ways to make supervision more effective."

The consultant may add that a problem is generally *the gap between an existing situation and the desired situation.* (The consultant may illustrate this visually on newsprint.)

The creative definition channels our thinking in the healthy direction of attaining the desired situation.

Not every problem, however, can be changed this way. The consultant requests participants to suggest creative definitions *where possible* to problems on the Problem List. The consultant writes these new definitions on newsprint.

The consultant now points out some problems that could not be changed by adding the words "Ways to. . . ." He or she suggests that a wider perspective of some of these problems can be attained by asking *"Why?"* or *"For what?"* Answering such questions leads to another definition of the problem, but at a higher level. For example:

Question: Will we invest in this machine?
Response: For what?
Answer: In order to increase productivity of machinery.
New definition: Ways to increase productivity of machinery.

This definition naturally raises further possibilities of increasing productivity of machinery other than "investment in this machine." Raising definitions to a higher level is like going to the top of a tower and viewing the landscape from a different and far wider perspective. Sometimes people ask: "You can go on raising a problem indefinitely. For each new definition you can go on asking 'For what?' Where does one stop?"

The answer is not to raise the problem to a level higher than that with which the team can cope within the framework of its responsibilities and resources (quite often, one level is enough).

Not every problem should be raised to a higher level, and sometimes this method is unsuitable. The best way is just to try and see if it helps in acquiring a wider perspective of the problem.

Yes-or-No Problems are those in which we are constrained to choose between two alternative solutions only.

Generally, yes-or-no problems can be left without change. Sometimes it helps to try a higher level but mostly we can only move on to making a decision. For example: "Do we or do we not grant Mr. Farmer's request for four months leave of absence from the firm to accompany his ailing daughter for treatment abroad?" There is no sense in asking here "for what?" We can proceed directly to the step of weighing the decision and making it.

The consultant requests participants to go over the Problem List and try out the method of "raising to a different level." When a participant feels that the method suits a particular problem, he or she calls it out, and the consultant writes down the new definition on newsprint.

3. *Complex problems: listing different aspects.* This step deals with finding ways to define complex problems. We demonstrate the process once or twice with explanations, and then let the participants do it on their own.

We take one of the complex problems from the Problem List and ask participants how they see the problem and how they would define it.

People make various suggestions which actually represent that aspect of the problem that seems important to them. The consultant lists all suggestions on newsprint.

When all suggestions are written, the consultant numbers them, and, with the aid of participants, groups similar items within a common category. (See Chapter 2, process entitled, "Problem-Sensing with Groups.")

As there are not too many definitions, the final categorization of definitions boils down to not more than four or five (often fewer) major aspects of the complex problem. We call these "subproblems."

4. *Further information and deciding what subproblem to deal with.* The consultant explains:

At this stage it is worth examining the different subproblems to see whether or not we have sufficient information to begin either dealing with them or deciding which ones are the main subproblems. If not, we will need

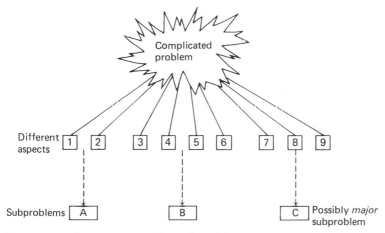

Fig. 5.5 Breaking up a complicated problem

further information. To help understanding, the consultant can draw an illustration similar to Fig. 5.5.

The complicated problem was broken up into its various aspects (1, 2, 3, etc.). These, in turn, were categorized into three major subproblems (A, B, and C).

At this stage we still do not know:

a. Which, if any, is the major subproblem that, if dealt with, will clear up the whole problem.

b. Whether we have sufficient information about each subproblem to find solutions for it.

Here we must make a decision: Do we wish to gather *further information* on these subproblems or not?

If we decide that we need further information, we should decide by whom and by when it must be collected.

If we decide we have all the information needed, or see no way of gathering further information, we can go ahead .

If we decide to go ahead, we can begin dealing with the subproblems.

If everyone is sure that one of the subproblems is *the* major one, we can give it a creative definition and go ahead with solutions.

If we are not sure which one is the major subproblem we can either deal with each subproblem, one by one; or divide our team into three subgroups, each subgroup beginning to work on solutions for its subproblem.

5. *Practice.* The consultant now practices the process described together with the team members. After one or two demonstrations the team chairman or someone else takes over and goes through the process of defining issues from the Problem List.

Summing up

The consultant remarks that people are sometimes confused by the definition stage and have difficulty grasping it.

It can actually be summed up quite simply:

1. If "yes or no," move on to decision stage.
2. If "simple," add "ways to" and/or raise to a higher level.
3. If "complex," define different aspects, seek information if necessary, and move on to solutions.

The consultant can end the process by giving each participant a hand-out of "Defining a Problem" (from paragraph 1 of this Detailed Process).

CREATIVE SOLUTIONS TO PROBLEMS

A method of determining a wide variety of creative solutions to a problem.

When to use

Unlike most of the other processes in this chapter the process described here—brainstorming—need not be part of training in effective problem-solving. Brainstorming is easy to learn and extremely useful, and it generally impresses participants very much.

It would not be worth working with a team on defining a problem without also going into the other stages of problem-solving. However, brainstorming is different; it can be taught on any suitable occasion, when working either with a team or with individuals. It is a powerful instrument and *worth introducing to most teams or individual workshops* or interventions.

Brainstorming is especially useful *with a committee that is set in its method of dealing with problems;* working without imagination or creativeness. This process opens the eyes to the unlimited vistas of human creativity, to the gratification in building on each others ideas, and to the realization that there are many different ways of solving a problem.

In short, this process can be learned on its own merits, whenever opportunity arises, or *it can be part of a creative problem-solving course,* or intervention, with a committee of any kind—managerial or otherwise. *An individual can also learn the steps* of the technique and do his or her own thinking in this way.

Who can use: Anyone who has tried it once or twice

Purpose: To acquire a creative method of seeking solutions to problems

Materials: 1. Newsprint, felt pens, tape, paper and pens
               2. Newsprint of "Brainstorming Rules" (shown later)
               3. Copies of "Brainstorming Handout" (shown later)

Time: 2 to 6 hours

STEPS IN PROCESS

1. Introduction by consultant
2. Brainstorming rules
3. Participants write solutions
4. Building on others
5. Participants practice brainstorming
6. Using the idea cube

Detailed process

1. *Introduction by consultant.* Consultant states that the purpose of the meeting is to acquire and exercise a creative method of seeking solutions to problems. This method is called "Brainstorming." The consultant can make the following points:

a. Generally, a problem is dealt with by explaining it to the group while presenting a previously prepared proposal of how to deal with the problem. Often the discussion revolves around the proposal brought forward or other counter proposals based on criticism of the first proposal.

The weakness of this method is that it may close the way of *many different solutions to the problem.* It hinders people from raising *creative ideas* and weighing them. This often causes people to entrench themselves behind their proposals without opening their eyes to the *advantages attached to the ideas of others.* They do not build on each others' ideas but criticize them.

For fear of criticism, people are afraid to raise far-fetched ideas that may be extremely effective. Some people are more restrained than others and seldom voice their proposals unless asked to do so—even though they may have much to contribute in finding a solution.

People may often censor an idea that comes to them because they have not thought it out thoroughly, even though this very idea could actually be the basis for a creative solution. This makes it less likely that the solution decided on is in fact based on all feasible possibilities and combines within itself the positive features of the different proposals.

Generally the decision taken is of a "win–lose" kind; i.e., one proposal "wins" the others are rejected. Often the decision is a compromise between various positions, and not really the best solution of the problem.

b. Brainstorming is used by some of the most creative managerial teams in highly successful and innovative organizations.

c. Brainstorming is a different way of finding solutions that attempts to eliminate or minimize the defects of the conventional way. It is based on two principles:

1) Most problems have *more than one solution.*

2) The step of *generating* solutions should be *separate* from the step of *evaluating* and deciding.

d. Most faults of the conventional way of discussing proposals lie in the intermixing of the two steps that should be kept separate—raising solutions, and weighing them.

c. By weighing solutions at the same time as we produce them, *we close the door to creativity,* stifle innovation, and intimidate many who could enrich the discussion.

Most problems have many solutions. You can arrive at the same goal by many different paths. Our engulfment in our own pet proposals closes our eyes to the rich variety of solutions and their combinations with one another which could serve us in reaching our goals.

2. *Brainstorming rules.* The consultant now puts up the newsprint with the following Brainstorming Rules (Fig. 5.6):

The consultant explains:

- At this stage we are after quantity and not quality. We want to get as many ideas as possible, as varied and different from each other as can be. So write down any idea you have.

A group of about 10 people can often generate about 40 to 80 ideas for dealing with a problem.

---

1. Bring forward as many solutions as possible.
2. No remarks or criticism or reactions are allowed when people are listing their solutions.
3. Do not censor yourself—express your ideas even if they seem farfetched and even if you doubt them.
4. Remember, separate the producing of ideas from the evaluation of them.

Fig. 5.6 Brainstorming rules

- If you criticize, snicker or joke about ideas which people bring forward—even if they are strange—you are stifling creativity. People will be afraid to bring forward unconventional ideas. Often the unconventional idea can trigger an associative track that leads to a good solution.

- Don't censor yourself. Censoring and evaluating will be done later. Let your mind play freely with ideas—whether strange, unusual, or seemingly impractical—and write them down.

- Sometimes the unusual and impractical solves the problem and can be made practical by changing some of its aspects.

3. *Participants write solutions.* The consultant should choose beforehand which problem on the problem list he or she wishes to use in demonstrating brainstorming.

For this first occasion it is worth choosing a complex problem worded in the form "Ways to. . . ." The problem should be of the kind that can encourage the participants to raise many partial solutions. For example:

- Ways to raise the morale of the organization's members.

- Ways to increase information flow from management to ranks and from ranks to management.

- Ways to increase productivity suggestions from the workers, etc., etc.

The consultant writes the problem on newsprint and sees that every participant has a pen and paper.

He or she now asks people to work alone and write down as many solutions, or partial solutions to the problem, as they can think of.

The consultant draws their attention again to the newsprint with Brainstorming Rules and rereads them out loud before they begin writing.

While they are writing, the consultant should try, as much as possible, to maintain quiet in the room and deter anyone from interfering with others who are still thinking and writing.

It does no harm, every now and then, to remark:

"Remember, we are after quantity"

"Don't censor yourself; we will evaluate the suggestion later"

"Even wild ideas are good; write them down anyhow, since they may be useful"

When some finish before the others, they are asked to continue thinking in case they have more ideas.

When all seem to have finished and exhausted their imagination, it is possible to begin listing the ideas on newsprint, giving each a serial number. We tend to be very strict in maintaining the rule of "no criticism and no remarks" while the ideas are being listed.

Often (especially toward the end of listing) people remark that many of their ideas have already been written on the newsprint as other people brought them up.

Our reply is, "If they are exactly the same as yours we shall mark the number of your idea with an asterisk (*). If it is slightly different, read it out and we'll list it separately.

When all have finished, participants enjoy seeing the long list of possibilities. Some even hurriedly copy them down for future use.

4. *Building on others.* The consultant explains: "We can increase the range of alternatives even further if we can get used to building on the ideas of others and using our imagination. For instance:

- Think of ideas you had, when we were listing the ideas, that were triggered off by someone else's suggestion. Put them in writing.

- Look through the list of suggestions and try to glean fresh ideas from the following manipulations:

a) Combine the two ideas and see if they can produce a new one.

b) Change magnitudes and media (someone suggested weekly meetings of the team—try, say, monthly meetings of the department; someone suggested publishing a weekly bulletin to employees; perhaps this could lead to the thought of mealtime broadcasts to employees).

The participants are given some minutes to write down any new ideas and then these are listed on the newsprint.

5. *Participants practice brainstorming.* After the first experience under the direction of the consultant, the participants can take turns in leading a brainstorming session. This can continue as long as time and patience allows.

6. *Using the idea cube.* If participants have shown interest and enthusiasm, one more element may be introduced during the exercise period.

The consultant explains another method of generating ideas: the Idea Cube (or Square). Here is an example:

The problem was: "Ways of improving two-way information flow between management and workers and between departments."

It is not difficult to see that there are a number of basic dimensions around which many solutions revolve:

a. Medium of transferring information: bulletins, broadcasts, notice boards, meetings, lectures, suggestion box, movies, symposia, etc.

b. Type of information: what is happening in production, in sales, workers' complaints, management's requests, social events, etc.

c. Time of interaction: before work, morning meal breaks, afternoon after work, daily, weekly, monthly, etc.

If each of these dimensions is put along one axis of a cube we get tens to hundreds of little boxes (See Figure 5.7)

Many of these boxes are meaningless, but quite a number of them can light up bright original ideas. Here is an example:

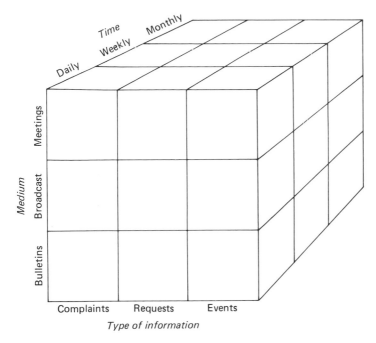

Fig. 5.7 The idea cube

Combining three boxes can give:

a. Monthly newsreel of what is happening in the factory shown during lunchtime break.

b. A broadcast during work hours every three months—Personnel manager interviewing workers on their complaints, etc., etc.

If using three dimensions seems too complicated, one can work with a square and play with two dimensions only.

The consultant chooses one of the problems from the problem list and asks for suggestions of various solutions. When these have been written up, the consultant asks participants to suggest three dimensions for the Idea Cube. When these have been agreed on, he or she draws a cube with the dimensions chosen on the axis.

He now requests participants to give various elements of these dimensions (i.e., the elements of "Time" may be: hourly, daily, monthly, yearly, etc.). When all elements have been written down, people are requested to suggest ideas that are brought to mind by any of the little boxes.

An *alternative* method of doing this is first to demonstrate the Idea Cube and then ask each person to choose a problem and try to generate solutions for it by means of the Cube.

If anyone has difficulty with three dimensions, he or she can work in two dimensions, with a square.

When the whole process is over each participant can receive the following handout:

Brainstorming Handout

Steps:

1. Each person write as many solutions as possible
2. List them on newsprint
3. Add solutions by building on others' ideas
4. Use the Idea Cube if necessary

Rules:

1. As many solutions as possible
2. No remarks or criticism
3. No self-censoring
4. Separate the producing of ideas from their evaluation

Variation 1

For those who prefer an experience with fewer "teaching" features, the process can be carried out in this manner:

Do not give introduction step 1, but begin directly from step 2.

In steps 2, 3, 4, and 5, just demonstrate the process with few explanations.

When finished, request participants to try and estimate what advantages this process has over the usual method of problem-solving.

Variation 2

If time is short—or the process is used not as a training experience, but in the midst of working with a team in consultation or otherwise—it is possible to do only steps 2 and 3.

Variation 3

Another, even shorter, version, often used in the midst of an intervention, is as follows:

The rules are not explained and participants do not write anything down. Participants are requested only to voice as many solutions as possible without justifying them and without others criticizing. These solutions are noted on newsprint.

A way to evaluate, decide between and improve proposed solutions to a problem.

When to use

We would use this process or part of it in either of two circumstances: (1) As part of problem-solving training of a management group, committee, or managers' workshop, or (2) As an input when working with any team.

1. *As part of problem-solving training.* This process is the continuation of the processes described previously and is the *fourth stage* in problem-solving steps after defining, collecting information, and brainstorming. If we are training a team or workshop in the whole problem-solving process, this is the next stage.

2. *As an input.* We often use various parts of this process as an input when working with a team. If we are consulting a team and it has brainstormed solutions to a problem we may choose to use parts of this intervention, i.e., steps 4, 5, or 6, or any combination of them, to help the team *process the proposals raised in the brainstorm.* The process is valuable for teams that are not effective enough in their decision-making and *jump from proposals to decisions without seriously evaluating the alternatives.*

It is also of value to teams that are *in a rut* in making decisions and process all decisions in the same manner; i.e., discuss proposals and vote thereon. The various experiences in this process open people's eyes to *the rich variety of ways* that can be used effectively to make a decision.

Who can use:
1. Anyone who has practiced using these processes
2. A manager can study various steps thoroughly and then try them out with his or her team when occasion arises

Purposes:
1. To become aware of various methods of processing a range of proposals to solve a problem
2. To gain experience in various methods of choosing different solutions

Participants:
A team of managers, a committee or a managers' training workshop, or any kind of team that often makes decisions together

Materials: 1. Newsprint, felt pens and tape
2. Newsprint and/or handouts of "Different ways of processing brainstormed proposals" (Fig. 5.8)

Time: 3 to 4 hours (Steps 4, 5, 6 require 1½ to 2 hours)

STEPS IN PROCESS

1. Forms of processing
2. Discussing the forms of processing
3. Differentiating between "multiple solution" and "alternative solution" problems
4. Choosing criteria
5. Weighing proposals by criteria
6. Choosing and improving proposals
7. Learning a variation

Detailed process

1. *Forms of processing.* When we have finished a brainstorming session we may be faced with a staggering array of from 40 to 60 proposals. The question inevitably arises: "How does one deal with this rich mine of ideas? *How does one decide* which to implement and which to discard?"

Often all value of brainstorming is lost in this stage because of the difficulties of processing and deciding between so many alternatives. The result is that after the first surge of enthusiasm on seeing the rich variety of proposals and the potential of brainstorming, people revert to the familiar methods of decision-making. Therefore, right at the beginning of this process we explain all this to the participants and then show them alternative ways of processing the proposals.

We do this either by writing the different ways on newsprint while explaining them, or by displaying a newsprint with the following points already noted on them, or by giving participants handouts containing these points (Fig. 5.8).

2. *Discussing the forms of processing.* After the facilitator has explained these different ways of processing the proposals, the team is asked to discuss the advantages and disadvantages of each way.

If it has not been mentioned in the discussion, the facilitator can draw attention to these considerations:

a. *Time* is a major factor in deciding which process to use. Dividing a committee into subgroups saves a great deal of time. The subgroups are simultaneously working on different proposals and the discussion

a. *Open Discussion*
The various proposals are discussed and examined by the participants with the purpose of choosing between the solutions and/or crystalizing combined solutions to the problem.

b. *Examining agreement and open discussion*
The open discussion can be shortened and improved by clarifying before the discussion *which proposals are accepted by all participants*. A fast run through the list of proposals is made. Proposals which are accepted by all are ratified as decisions. The open discussion following can then be focused on proposals over which there were differences of opinion.

c. *Shortening the list and open discussion*
An alternative to the previous method is to clarify before the open discussion *which proposals have no support* and to eliminate them from the list. This is also done by a quick run through the list and erasing proposals that no one wishes to discuss or accept. This is followed by *an open discussion of the remaining proposals.*

d. *Agreement, shortening, and open discussion*
Methods (b) and (c) can be combined. The Chairman runs through the list, eliminates unsupported proposals, and ratifies decisions on unanimous agreements. Following this, the team discusses the remaining proposals.

e. *Subgroups*
Team may be divided into subgroups, who then divide between themselves the list of proposals. The subgroups meet separately and *simultaneously* in different rooms or corners of a large room. Each subgroup processes its share of the proposals and *prepares its recommendations for the entire group*. When the subgroups have finished their work they reconvene as a team. Each subgroup explains its recommendations which are discussed and accepted as team decisions.
Subgroups are especially useful when the proposals can be naturally divided into areas that are not opposed to each other but *complement each other.*

f. *One subgroup*
One subgroup may be chosen *to process all the proposals* and bring its recommendations to the next meeting of the entire team. The subgroups can either *bring recommendations or* prepare the discussion for the team by *listing the pros and cons* of each proposal.

g. *Mixing the different ways*
It is possible to begin with an open discussion of the proposals and when the trend of opinion is discerned, pass the discussion on to subgroups. Various other combinations of the different methods of processing can be combined and used [for example (d) can be combined with (e) and so on].

Fig. 5.8 Different ways of processing brainstormed proposals

in a subgroup of three to four people takes less time than in a large committee.

b. *Trust* between team members allows a wider range of choices among ways to work on the proposals. When members of a team have not developed an adequate level of trust between themselves there will be *difficulties in accepting recommendations of subgroups.*

c. *Commitment* of team members to action on the proposals should be taken into account when deciding whether to use a subgroup or subgroups and whether they bring recommendations or prepare pros and cons. The more we wish all team members to have a reasonable measure of commitment to act on the decisions, the more they need to be involved in all stages of the decision-making process.

d. *Operationalism* (concrete statements). The problem of operationalism should be considered in deciding how to process proposals. Some proposals in a brainstorm are *wide recommendations* (e.g., "let's enrich people's work"). On the other hand, some proposals are *concrete suggestions* (e.g., "let's change shifts two hours earlier"). Wide recommendations need to be operationalized, that is, converted into concrete proposals. Discussing these two different kinds of proposals in the same manner may lead to absurdities. One should consider operationalizing wide recommendations by a subgroup or subgroups before discussing them in the forum of the entire team.

Note: A less structured way of going about steps 1 and 2 is to ask the team to suggest different ways of processing the brainstormed proposals. All suggestions are written on newsprint and if necessary the facilitator adds suggestions from the list.

The advantages and disadvantages can be handled in the same way. People are asked: what are the considerations, the advantages, the disadvantages of each way of processing. The replies are written on newsprint and the facilitator adds whatever he finds necessary.

3. *Differentiating between "multiple solution" and "alternative solution" problems.* The facilitator can begin by demonstrating the difference between multiple solution problems and problems in which a decision must be made between two alternatives.

This can be demonstrated graphically on newsprint by Fig. 5.9.

a. *Multiple solution problems* are generally broad problems that have a *large array of solutions*, each contributing in some measure to the total solution. Some solutions may be of major importance and some

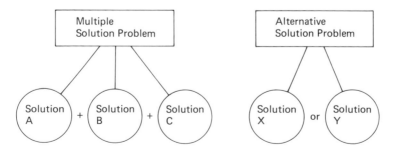

Fig. 5.9 Multiple and alternative solution problems

of lesser. The different solutions *may complement each other* in solving the problem.

(For example, "How to increase work satisfaction in the factory.")

b. *Alternative solution problems* are problems in which we have to decide *between two possible ways* of solving the problem.

(For example, "Will we appoint Mills or Bruner as Plant Manager?")

Note: It is important to stress that this classification of problems is a matter of convenience because most "Alternative Solution Problems" can be converted into "Multiple Solution Problems" by defining the problem differently. Nevertheless, everyday reality forces us quite often to choose between either one or two alternatives and we have to be practical and make decisions of this kind.

4. *Choosing criteria.* The facilitator displays the list of solutions engendered by the brainstorm. It is preferable to take a *shortened list;* i.e., one that has been processed by eliminating all proposals that are objected to by all team members and ratifying as decisions all accepted proposals. What remains is a list of proposals about which there are differences of opinion. If this has not already been done the facilitator may go through this process with the team.

The facilitator now asks the team members *by which criteria* they decide which proposals to accept and which to reject.

As people suggest criteria the facilitator notes them down in bold letters on the newsprint. Sometimes two criteria can be combined as one, and the facilitator draws attention to this.

If there is disagreement about the validity of a criterion, it is generally worthwhile to reach some agreement about it.

When people have finished putting forward suggestions the facilitator can draw attention to the list of criteria which is generally applicable to most problems (see Fig. 5.10).

Contribution: How much does the proposal contribute to solving the problem?

Money: Financial cost of implementing proposal.

Manpower: Difficulty in finding or allocating labor or specialists needed to implement this proposal.

Commitment: Difficulty in finding suitable people who will be committed to action on proposal.

Resistance: How much resistance to the proposal are we to expect from key people or others involved.

Problems: To what degree will implementing this proposal create other problems with which we may have to contend.

Fig. 5.10 Useful criteria

5. *Weighing proposals by criteria.* We now take a newsprint and prepare it in this manner: along the top we draw perpendicular lines in which we list the criteria. From top down on the left-hand side we list the proposals (see Fig. 5.11). We then begin, together with the team, *to evaluate each proposal by each criterion.*

We try to get a quick consensus on each point, and when we run into disagreement on a particular evaluation we try to reach a compromise. If this is difficult, we put a question mark in the appropriate space. The marks we generally use are as follows:

    + + Very good
      + Good
      0 Neutral or inapplicable
      − Not so good
    − − Bad

Another possibility is: 2, 1, 0, −1, −2.

We find the +, − marking easier to digest when later evaluating the proposals.

There are two possible ways of doing the evaluation:

1. Taking each *proposal* and evaluating it by each criterion; i.e., going *along the lines* one by one.
2. Taking each *criterion* and marking each proposal by that criterion; i.e., going *down the columns* one by one.

We generally do the evaluation by the first method; i.e., *along the lines,* as people seem to grasp it better that way. We are aware that going down the columns, although more difficult, may lead to less bias when evaluating.

	Contribution	Money	Manpower	Committment	Resistance	Etc.	
Proposal A							
Proposal B							
Proposal C							
Proposal D							
Proposal E							
Proposal F							
Etc.							

Fig. 5.11 Format for evaluating proposals

When all proposals have received their evaluation by all criteria, the picture becomes clearer. We are now almost ready to ask participants which of the proposals seem to be favorable by most criteria.

Note: Very often during the evaluation by criteria, people add other criteria they had not previously thought of. This is legitimate and worthwhile as it points to evaluative aspects of the proposals we could not preconceive but which do in effect sway our opinion.

6. *Choosing and improving proposals.* As stated, we are now almost ready to choose the suitable proposals. Nevertheless, we prefer to add two more considerations before making decisions.

We ask participants if they see all criteria as of equal values—and if not, which criterion, in their opinion, carries more weight.

People can generally agree about two or three criteria which should be accorded greater weight when evaluating proposals.

We generally mark at the head of the columns of these important criteria some sign, or alternatively emphasize their column lines with a different colored marker.

We can now ask participants which proposals *seem to have done best by most of the criteria* and *especially by the criteria which were given more weight.*

It is generally not difficult to achieve consensus on a number of proposals that get most of the plus signs (+ +) according to the different criteria. These proposals are marked on the newsprint with an asterisk * or any other sign.

We are now ready for the next step of *improving proposals.*

We ask participants if they can put forward suggestions on how *to eliminate or reduce the weak points* of some of the "good" proposals. For example: a proposal has achieved high marks on all criteria except "Resistance." Can we put forward suggestions to decrease potential resistance to the proposal? People generally give suggestions and these are noted down on the newsprint.

If we are working with a team on its real day-to-day problems we will, at this stage, examine whether the proposals can be ratified as decisions. Sometimes this can be done at once, because the weighing by criteria has eliminated most of the points that could cause argumentation.

Nevertheless, if the team is not yet ready for a decision on all recommended proposals, *the ones agreed upon can be ratified as decisions and disagreements left for further discussion* and clarification of the points of disagreement.

It is recommended not to let the discussion move away from the newsprint with the evaluations. Remarks made should refer to criteria and their evaluation. Maybe another criterion has to be added. A vague general debate at this point makes all the work pointless. Perhaps *further information* is needed to clarify an evaluation. The decision can then be postponed. However, with all the information and considerations posted clearly before their eyes, people can generally come to an agreement.

> *Note:* We have gone through this process with many teams. Inevitably we come to the same conclusion. *This is not a "one-shot affair"* that you show a team and from then on it begins using the process. If you practice this once with a team most people will admire the technique and some may have reservations and say it is cumbersome. But, in any case, you can be sure the team will revert to its regular way of making decisions.

This method, with its variations, only takes root if practiced again and again until it becomes second nature to make decisions in this manner and/or the team develops some variation of its own.

7. *Learning a variation.* This variation is *not* intended to be used in place of the preceding process. We suggest that the facilitator practice this variation with the team *after* it has become familiar with the more structured process.

In this variation no marks are given to proposals and all we do is just make the criteria explicit by writing them down. We take the list of proposals and ask people by what criteria they would evaluate them. People suggest criteria and these are written on newsprint.

At this point we are ready for a discussion on the proposals and people are requested to refer constantly to the listed criteria when making a point. Decisions can be made by consensus or majority vote.

We practice this variation with a team until the team is quite familiar with it. We suggest to the team that it use both methods as it sees fit. The less structured version is easier to adapt to and less complicated. The structured version is more difficult to use and to get used to but more thorough. The ideal achievement would be to be familiar with both methods and to use them alternately whenever suitable.

> *Note: Who decides what process to use* when discussing a problem in a team? *Who ensures* that these techniques are continually practiced? Learning these techniques without assuring their everyday implementation is, in our opinion, a waste of time. (See step 7 of the next section, Deciding Between Alternative Solutions.)

Variation 1

When working with a team, consulting, or training, we may use parts of this process just to help the team move ahead. In this case we would skip all theory and explanations. We might only go through steps 4 and 5 and the first part of step 6 (choosing the proposals).

Variation 2

Alternatively, under similar circumstances, we might choose to use *only* the variation described in step 7. A team may be faced with a list of proposals and may be having difficulty deciding how to make a decision. Our contribution would be to ask the team to make explicit the criteria which sway their decisions. These would be noted on newsprint and people would be requested to refer to them when discussing and evaluating proposals. (See step 7.)

Variation 3

When pressed for time and less interested in people gaining a thorough understanding of all aspects of this process, we might skip step 3. Sometimes we also skip step 2, step 1, and step 7. This helps the team at the cost of learning.

DECIDING BETWEEN ALTERNATIVE SOLUTIONS

A method to help a team to carefully evaluate alternative or different solutions to the same problem. It is particularly useful when team members frequently take sides against each other whatever the issue.

When to use

As in the former intervention this process can be used either as a part of the problem-solving training or as an input, on its own worth, when working with a team.

1. *As part of the problem-solving training* this process should follow the process described before (Weighing Proposals).
2. We have found this process to be *a valuable input on its own right* when introduced at the right moment to a management team, a committee, or any other decision-making body.

   When working with such a body the following might occur:

   We find it is faced with making a decision between two alternatives. We therefore might suggest to the team that they make the decision in a manner to which they are not accustomed. If the team agrees, we then proceed with the steps described in this process until the actual decision is made. At the end of the process, if the team has not experienced the process described in the previous intervention, we explain step 3 of that process. In other words, we explain the difference between "multiple solution" and "alternative solution" problems. We point out that the process they have just experienced is suitable *only for "alternative solution" problems.*

We have found this process of great value in *teams in which people entrench themselves* on one side and waste energy, breath, and the team's time in derogating the opposing view and extolling their own.

The process itself leads people to begin *evaluating opposing viewpoints* in a positive manner. The process is an eye-opener to the value of synergistic, win-win teamwork and decision-making.

Managers can also use this process *with their own teams*. They are advised to first read the instructions carefully, then try it out by themselves on some problem on which they are undecided how to choose between two alternatives. When they feel sure they know the steps, they can attempt the process with their own teams.

Who can use:	Almost anyone who has tried this out once can use it. A manager can try it privately and then proceed to introduce it to his or her own team
Purposes:	1. To experience and acquire a method of deciding between two alternatives
	2. Learning to value contending considerations and the opinions of others
Participants:	Any team or decision-making body. Preferably not more than twelve people
Materials:	Newsprint, felt pens and tape, paper and pen
Time:	1 to 2 hours, when practiced as a learning experience; 30 to 60 minutes when used as a decision-making process

---

STEPS IN PROCESS*

1. Differentiating between "multiple solution" and "alternative solution" problems
2. Writing criteria
3. Choosing important criteria
4. Deciding between the alternatives
5. Improving the chosen solution
6. Discussing the experience
7. Deciding on process responsibility and continued use of process

---

* Those steps are those which we would follow when teaching the process as part of problem-solving training.

Detailed process

1. *Differentiating between "multiple solution" problems and "alternative solution" problems.* This is Step 3 in "Weighing Proposals." If we have already gone through this step with the team while training in the former process, we will only remind the members of the main points. We explain that now we will practice a method of dealing with the second type of problems: "alternative solution" problems. If we are working with a team which is training in problem-solving but has not yet done the former process we will go into all the details of this step.

If we are introducing the process as an input when working with a team, we skip this step at this point and return to it only after making the decision.

2. *Writing criteria.* Together with the team we choose a problem with which they are faced which has two alternative solutions. We begin by drawing a line horizontally across the middle of a newsprint. Near the top right corner we write one alternative solution. Near the bottom right corner we write the second alternative.

We now ask the participants to give their reasons for supporting either of the criteria. They are requested:

a. Not to explain their reasons and criteria but just give them in a few words.

b. Not to react to one another's criteria, reasons, or considerations as we only wish to write them down without yet evaluating them.

Whenever a person gives a reason, consideration, or a criterion supporting one of the two options, we write it in one or two words on the side of the alternative it supports. We encircle it and draw a line from the circle to the line dividing the middle of the paper, as shown in Fig. 5.12.

When people voice considerations, we are careful:

a. Not to allow sarcasm or remarks that will intimidate suggestions.

b. To convert negative considerations against one alternative into affirmative considerations for the other (e.g., "alternative A will demand a large investment" is converted into: "small investment" in support of alternative B).

c. Not to allow debate or discussion of the validity or weight of any suggestion at this point.

3. *Choosing important criteria.* When the preceding step has been terminated, the time has come to decide which reasons or criteria supporting both alternatives really carry weight in the eye of the participants. Time is now allocated for an open discussion of the criteria. Often half an hour is sufficient time for this.

Following the discussion each participant is requested to allocate 10 points among the considerations supporting *each* alternative. Make this

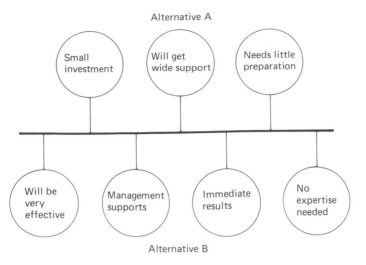

Alternative A

Small investment

Will get wide support

Needs little preparation

Will be very effective

Management supports

Immediate results

No expertise needed

Alternative B

Fig. 5.12 Form of writing down reasons supporting alternatives

clear: 10 points *for each alternative*. The points are awarded to each factor according to the amount of support it gives to the alternative. When all have finished allocating the points, each person should then read out in turn his or her allocation and the numbers are noted near the appropriate criteria.

In our opinion, this part of the process is the most important. Its value is that it actually brings people to think about the *weight of considerations even for a viewpoint to which they may be opposed.*

When all have finished reading their allocation, the points for each criterion are summed up and written on the newsprint.

It immediately becomes apparent that some considerations received no points at all, and that two or three on each side got most of the points. It is convenient to take a clean sheet of newsprint and draw a similar figure with the alternative solutions but including only the two or three considerations or criteria on each side which scored the highest.

4. *Deciding between the alternatives.* The participants are now requested to divide 10 points between the remaining criteria *supporting both alternatives*. They may divide the points in any way they wish; either on both sides or on one side only.

They are requested to try to give value to considerations supporting the alternative which they do not accept. From our experience most people give from about two-thirds to three-quarters of their points to considerations supporting their viewpoint and the remainder to specific considerations supporting the opposing view.

When people have finished writing down or considering how they will allocate their 10 points, each participant in turn states his or her allocation. The points are marked on the newsprint next to the appropriate criteria.

When all have finished we sum up the points allocated to the criteria of each alternative. It now becomes clear which alternative has been given the most points. (See Fig. 5.13 for an illustration of what the newsprint looks like when summing up.)

5. *Improving the Chosen Solution.* We will point out to the participants that the alternative with the higher number of points has disadvantages and the alternative with fewer points has advantages. These can be clearly seen on the newsprint. Our task is *to reduce the disadvantages and increase the advantages of the alternative with the higher number of points.*

People are asked to suggest ideas about how to do this. This is not a discussion or debate but a *suggestion collection* that should be of help to the people who will later have the responsibility of implementing the decision.

All suggestions are noted on newsprint which will later be handed to the person or body responsible for implementation.

6. *Discussing the Experience.* If the process is *part of the problem-solving training* we will now suggest to the participants that they discuss the experience.

We leave the discussion completely open. People generally voice their appreciation of being able to weigh the contending views. Quite often, someone describes how at the beginning he or she supported one alternative, but after evaluating the criteria, changed his or her mind. Some people are critical of the structuredness of the process and sometimes there are remarks about the validity of the mathematical summing up as a decision-

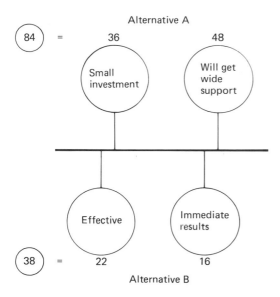

Fig. 5.13 Summing up the decision

making tool. More often, however, its value has been greatly appreciated, and the desire has been expressed to continue using it in the future.

When the process was *not* part of problem-solving training, discussion about the experience is optional. Generally we do allocate some time to this discussion and people's reaction to the process. In any case we have to explain to the participants that this process is only suitable for "alternative solution" problems, and at this point we go through step 1 of this process (see Intervention, "Weighing Proposals, Detailed Step 3").

7. *Deciding on process responsibility and continued use of process.* The more we have to experience in training people in this process, as well as the other processes in this chapter, the more we come to realize that the problem to overcome is that of *continuity* of implementation. Generally this process, like others in this chapter, is received enthusiastically. People enjoy it and express a wish to continue using it. But from wish to practice—the path is long. In many cases, especially when we began this kind of training, the process left its mark in the form of using newsprint when making decisions, acceptance of the stages in decision-making, some use of brainstorming, and an awareness of the importance of making criteria explicit. But this still falls short of being regular use of the process.

We therefore place much importance on doing as much as possible to ensure regular use of the processes. One way to do this, is to spend sufficient time in *training, retraining,* and *practicing* the processes until they become second nature.

A second approach, complementing the first, is for the team to *choose a member* whose responsibility it will be to ensure that the group uses the processes. It will be that member's duty to remind the acting chairmen when to use a specific process. And should the team forget its training and revert to previous accustomed ways, he or she will have the responsibility of insisting on a decision about the use or nonuse of the processes. It will be that member's duty to discuss with the chairman, before a meeting, what processes will be suitable for each specific item on the agenda. He or she may even have to make sure that all materials needed (e.g., newsprint, felt pens, tape, etc.) are available.

A third aid to continued use is a *group decision.* We prefer not to leave things vague, but to get the team to make a formal decision, if possible, that in future it will use the processes it has been trained in as the regular way for its decision-making. A decision of this kind is not so easy to back out of.

Variation 1

Instead of the structured, regulated format of step 2, it is possible to hold a discussion of the pros and cons of each alternative. While people are speaking, the facilitator notes down on the newsprint (which retains the same setup previously described), the criteria which they mention and notes them in place on the side of the alternative they support. The discussion can have a time limit or not, according to circumstances.

Doing it this way, of course, makes discussion of suggestions (proposed in step 3) unnecessary. The rest of the steps on the process can remain unchanged.

Variation 2

If time is very short, the discussion can be skipped entirely, with only the other steps in the process being dwelt on. However, the time-saving is at the expense of going through a formal structured process, leaving no place for free expression.

Variation 3

The open discussion can be postponed until after step 3. This focuses the discussion only on the criteria which team members feel to be important. This might be more effective, but on the other hand its disadvantage is the delay in letting people speak out freely what is on their minds.

OVERCOMING RESISTANCE TO IMPLEMENTATION

Using a problem-solving method to help decrease resistance to change or program.

When to use

This may be regarded as the next step in the problem-solving sequence. We will use this intervention after a decision has been made and what remains is *to implement it*. The question is: "Will the decision be implemented and what can we do to assure implementation?"

This process is especially valuable when the team has accepted a resolution on *making some major change in the organization*. People are aware that there will be resistance, opposition and many difficulties in the way of turning the decision into reality. People opposed to the decision may "sabotage" it by doing things to ensure its failure. People in doubt may not give a hand. There may be financial, technical, and formal difficulties on the way. The problem is: "How to go ahead with all these potential difficulties facing you?"

This process can be introduced to a team *not only within the context of problem-solving training*. Whenever we are working with a team that has made an important decision, which we feel may go aground in the implementation stage, we might introduce this intervention.

The process may be used as formerly described as an intervention with a team facing the problems of reality. It can also be imparted, *as a learning experience,* to a group of managers from different organizations in a workshop. This is especially important *toward the end of the workshop,* when people have begun thinking about how they will implement changes in their organization back home.

Who can use: Anyone who reads this description can try it out either for his or her own use, or together with a group of people

Purposes: 1. To become aware of the problems of implementing a decision
2. To find ways to decrease resistance and opposition and increase support

Participants: A team, or strangers in a workshop, or an individual by himself or herself

Materials: Newsprint, felt pens, and tape

Time: ½ to 1 hour

STEPS IN PROCESS

1. Drawing the force field
2. Examining possibilities
3. Deciding on action steps

Note: The steps described here are those we would use when actually working with a team faced by a problem of implementation.

Detailed process

1. *Drawing the force field.* Our situation is that we are working with a team that is now facing the problem of how to go about implementing an important decision and that is going to meet resistance. We say to the team that we would like to help them overcome their problems with the help of "force-field analysis."

We draw a line across the middle of a newsprint lengthwise. We now ask the team members to enumerate all the major forces in the way of effective implementation. These may be individuals or groups or populations. They may be potential resisters—opposers—who may come out openly to annul the decision, or latent resisters, who may work "below the surface" to ensure failure.

We ask the team not to debate suggestions or try to prove them, but just to call them out, so that we may put them down on newsprint.

We note the names of the "resisting forces" on the top half of the newsprint, some distance from the midline, and one next to the other. From each "resisting force" we draw a line, ending in an arrowhead, down toward the midline.

We now ask the team to enumerate forces in the system which will help, support, and strengthen the proposed change. The same procedure is carried out with the "supporting forces" as was carried out with the obstructing forces. They are written on the newsprint, on its bottom half, below the line. From each "supporting force" an arrow is drawn to the midline (see Fig. 5.13).

2. *Examining possibilities.* We now point out the possibilities open before us to ensure implementation success or at least decrease the chances of failure.

We may *exert more pressure on the resisting forces* with all the means within our control. We can push up the line. We demonstrate by drawing the midline higher up and thickening the arrows below the line. "We are increasing the pressure put by us on the resisting forces."

What is the result of our doing this? We ask the team, "What does the opposition do when we exert more force on it?" "It resists even more, opposes with more energy and pushes our line back to the equilibrium position it held before." *Using pressure tactics on resistance generally increases the resistance.*

We have another alternative and that is to work on decreasing the resistance. We can do this by alleviating anxieties as to the outcomes of the proposed changes, by finding contacts with people who may resist and gaining their support and trust.

We now ask the team members to brainstorm suggestions aimed at decreasing resistance and opposition, and increasing acceptance and support of the proposal.

All suggestions are noted down on newsprint.

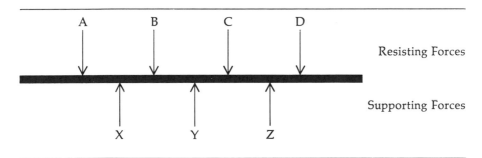

Fig. 5.13 Force-field analysis

3. *Deciding on action steps.* The brainstorm suggestions are now processed in one of the ways described in "Weighing Proposals."

This process should not be terminated without a newsprint list of: Who?—does what?—until which date? This, of course, will include steps of creating ties with resisters in order to discuss the proposals with them and alleviate anxiety.

Variation 1

Force-field analysis can be used not only as an aid to decrease resistance and strengthen support.

Sometimes the difficulties facing implementation are not resistance by people. Difficulties may stem from obstacles such as cost, inexperience, time factors, etc.

In this case we can use the force field to analyze what these obstacles are and what are the advantages and supporting factors. We can then brainstorm in order to find ways to minimize the obstacles and to maximize the advantages and supporting factors.

Variation 2

We often use force-field analysis as a learning experience within the framework of a workshop with managers from different organizations. In this case we will make every effort not to just illustrate the technique, but to use it while working on a genuine problem. This means we will choose a problem facing the workshop members in the context of the workshop. In other words, we will endeavour to work on a genuine problem and not a simulation.

Variation 3

Toward the end of most workshops people begin to think about back-home implementation of what they have learned. In this case, we ask each person (or group of people from the same organization) to prepare a newsprint with a force-field analysis implementing the changes they wish to make back home. The analysis should include how they intend to decrease resistance and obstacles and ways to develop support and increase advantages.

When the people have finished, they break up into subgroups. Each person (or group from the same organization) displays, in turn, the newsprint with his or her analysis and listens to the suggestions, criticism, comments, and ideas of the others in the subgroup.

If the workshop consists of teams from different organizations, each team jointly prepares its analysis. Later the teams convene. Each team displays its work and receives suggestions, ideas, and criticism from the other teams.

Team development

CHAPTER OBJECTIVE

To offer a series of approaches for increasing trust, openness, better communication, mutual acceptance and open confrontation of conflicts in a team.

GUIDE TO APPLYING INTERVENTIONS

What is team development?

- The underlying aim of team development is to increase trust among team members.
- People work better together when there is *open* and *honest* sharing about the problems and difficulties that they have with one another.
- A team functions more effectively when members build on one another's strengths, skills, and resources.
- People work better with each other when they learn to accept others—their weaknesses included.
- A team's efficiency is lowered and tension increases when feedback is avoided. Lack of clarity about the meaning of a statement becomes the rule rather than the exception.

- Considerable practice is required to achieve appropriate and well-timed feedback.
- Learning to listen actively makes messages clearer and shows respect for the sender of the message.
- Learning to differentiate process from content will allow for better problem-solving and reduce abstract arguments during meetings.
- Personal conflicts can be dealt with through a process of personal contracts.
- In a personal contract, all parties are clear about the elements of the conflict, the series of steps necessary to reduce the conflict, and the fact that all parties gain from the reduction of the conflict.
- There are some specific skills that can be used to increase the effectiveness of interaction, such as clarifying and innovating, and others that interfere with interactions, such as overtalking and blocking.

About the interventions in this chapter

We are convinced that before applying any of these interventions, a thorough analysis of the situation in the department or the organization is required. The basic question is: If an intervention is required, what is the most appropriate intervention at that particular time?

Further, there should be the awareness that once an intervention has been applied within a team, there will often be some impact on other parts of the organization. Team development activities often result in participants trying what they have learned in meetings with co-workers from other departments.

In applying these interventions, we have found that teams and situations require variations in what we include and the sequence of the different components of the intervention. We recommend to a facilitator that he or she modify the intervention to fit his or her style and the situation in which the intervention is being applied.

The interventions

1. *Basic steps in team development.* This was developed after reviewing many possible first steps in team development. We were looking for the essential skills and knowledge that we thought would make the change from just a group of people working together to an open and effective team of individuals who can use one another's resources.

2. *Improving interpersonal relations.* This approach requires team members to look at differences among members of the team and determine how those differences might be interfering with the effectiveness of the team. It requires as a prerequisite the increased degree of trust and openness that often is achieved after some basic work on team building.

It is in part built on our knowledge of learning theory and specifically learning styles (Kolb et al.).

MATRIX OF INTERVENTIONS

Intervention	Use	Who can use	Time demand
Basic steps in team development	Building trust; developing basic skills in working together	Manager with OD experience; outside consultant	about 11 hrs
Improving interpersonal relations	Focusing on differences in perception and communicating styles	Manager with OD experience; outside consultant	8–9 hrs

Possible outcomes

1. More recognition and acceptance of differences among team members.
2. More effective use of each other as resources.
3. Problem-solving and decision-making handled more efficiently with wider involvement of all team members.
4. More assumption of responsibility for day-to-day operations by team members.
5. More clarity in definition of responsibility and authority within team.
6. More willingness to go beyond own job in assisting another member of the team.
7. More personal satisfaction in carrying out own work as part of a team.
8. More creative use of departmental or team resources for organization-wide activities.
9. Greater support for each other in the carrying out of team functions.

Recommended readings

1. Bates, M. M., and C. D. Johnson, *Group Leadership* (Denver: Love Publishing Co., 1972).
2. Johnson, D. W., *Reaching Out* (Englewood Cliffs, N. J.: Prentice-Hall, 1972).
3. Pfeiffer, J. W., and J. E. Jones (eds.), *A Handbook of Structured Experience for Human Relations Training*, Vols. I, II, III, IV, V (LaJolla, Calif.: University Associates Press, 1971, 1972, 1973, 1974, 1975).
4. ————, (eds.), *Annual Handbook for Group Facilitators* (LaJolla, Calif.: University Associates Press, 1972, 1973, 1974, 1975).
5. Johnson, D. W., and F. P. Johnson, *Joining Together Group Theory and Group Skills* (Englewood Cliffs, N. J.: Prentice-Hall, 1975).

BASIC STEPS IN TEAM DEVELOPMENT

Recognizing and accepting differences among team members as key ways of building trust and effective ways of working together.

When to use

We have found that basic team development is often sought during times of crisis, periods of growth, or when some new procedure or process is being instituted within the organization.

Basic team development seems to work whether it is introduced by corporate headquarters as a total organizational activity or as the limited action of a department head.

We have used it with large organizations, starting from work with the personnel department. In this case, the management team of the personnel department goes through the basics of team development. Then on a low-key basis, the experience is made available to any departments interested in trying it out. As the personnel people begin to develop further skills in team development, the offer for such team development is made more visibly. This might increase the awareness of the more sensitive managers—the ones who are somewhat more willing to experiment. The awareness raising results in some units deciding to ask for such assistance.

We have also started with the top management team. Usually, this begins with the top executive. He or she might have experienced some basics of team-building at a conference or attended a workshop for presidents.

The series of steps we will take in team-building in the organization is usually worked out with a planning group. One such program involved first the executive committee, then each vice president and his next level managers, then those managers and their group leaders, and so on, including all supervisory personnel. Where there were special highly technical groups, then all employees in these departments were included in the team-building as separate units.

Smaller organizations, such as partnerships or professional groups, have also found team-building very useful. In most instances, all partners or members of the group were involved at the same time. We have found that with such groups the process is a longer effort. Usually team-building comes after there has been considerable history and experience together. In this case, there tend to be more unresolved conflicts than we usually find in organizations where the turnover is greater.

Who can use:
1. A manager who has participated in team development and has co-led team sessions with a consultant. Such a manager can work best in a different department than his or her own
2. Consultant to organization

Purposes: 1. To recognize and accept differences among members of a team
2. To build *trust* between members so that the work of the team can be handled more smoothly and effectively
3. To learn to use other members of the team as resources

Participants: 1. All members of a team; however, if the number exceeds 9 or 10, natural subgrouping should be arranged, for example, by function or by where people work in the organization
2. In a workshop, in groups of 6 to 9

Materials: 1. Newsprint paper, felt pens, tape, pencil and paper
2. Optical illusion material, for example, old woman/young woman (Fig. 6.1)
3. Journal or notebook

Time: About 11 hours

STEPS IN PROCESS

1. Brief problem-sensing
2. Examining effect of differences in perception
3. Listening and clarifying
4. Giving and receiving feedback
5. Looking at process and content
6. Developing interactive skills
7. Personal contracting with team members
8. Follow-up procedures

Detailed process

1. *Brief problem-sensing.* Elsewhere in the Handbook (see Chapter 2 "Problem-sensing with groups") there is a detailed explanation about problem-sensing. We suggest that you consider Steps 1, 2, 3, and 4 of the problem-sensing intervention as the initial phase of any basic team-building. If we are working with a team that we know has many *serious problems* we will not begin team-building without personal interviews of the team members. We would be very reluctant to begin working with a problematical team without first collecting all the information we need before beginning the team-building. The process we would use is described in the intervention: "Individual interviews and feedback," in Chapter 2.

The same considerations would influence us when working with the *first team* at the start of work within an organization. Here again we would tend to begin with personal interviews and not problem-sensing with groups. We would want to be sure that the team-building process is what that team really needs.

Again, we tend to use individual interviews when we are approached by an organization to work with *one* particular team that has problems. If we are approached in this way, we would be careful to interview the team members before beginning the team-building.

The problems identified in the individual interviews and displayed as feedback to the team would be the focus of our team-building activities and other processes we would go through with the team. If we did not interview the team members and are beginning the work with the team directly from Step 1, we might consider another alternative to begin with. The alternative we might use is the Schein questionnaire and the process we would go through is described in the intervention: "What is hindering effectiveness?" in Chapter 9. We have found that by going through this process first we achieve a number of advantages:

1. The team itself defines which aspects of team-building it wishes to work on.
2. This step often gains legitimacy to the subsequent team-building process.
3. We can give more time to particular aspects of team-building—guided by the team's diagnosis.
4. The questionnaire gives the group a commonly accepted set of concepts and terms by which people can understand the elements of effective team functioning.
5. The consensus-seeking part of the process necessitates that each person become thoroughly aware and understand clearly the basic concepts of team development.

We recognize the need for a warm-up into team-building. Each member of the team wants to bring out his or her feelings about the issues or problems facing the team. During the problem-sensing, participants will often include their worries or expectations about the team-building process. Such feelings and thoughts must be considered as important as any other problem that is raised.

It has been our experience that issues caused by differences between team members on work procedures or who is responsible for what, usually surface. The problem of "communication" will always be raised. Confusion about who has agreed with whom about what never failed to surface. When people raise the specific problems that are troubling them, the experience usually becomes more personal and meaningful for them.

We have found that the following steps have usually covered most of the items suggested by team members, particularly in the beginnings of active team-building. Of course, we keep the specific issues in the forefront while going through the other steps. We are always looking for ways of intertwining the particular ideas of participants with the general learning that comes from the steps in this intervention. If people raise other problems than those covered by this process, they must be dealt with. This should be done concurrently with the team-building process and intertwined with it. Other processes described in this book can be used to deal with various problems that will be raised.

2. *Examining effect of differences in perception.* First of all, we suggest a very brief statement highlighting the following points:

a. We have a few ground rules in working together. Our first step has tried to demonstrate the basic one of respecting and listening to each others' ideas (referring back to problem-sensing).

b. Sometimes these games or exercises that we try may seem silly or not to the point. Please bear with us. Try them, and then later give your feedback—your thoughts on what was useful or not useful.

c. Try to put yourself as much into these activities as you can—but of course it is entirely up to you about how much you can get into each one.

We have used a variety of perception (tricks or optical illusions) to get the group involved. We have found the old woman/young woman face (Fig. 6.1) to be very attractive and involving. As time goes on, more people have seen "her" so that "her" usefulness is decreasing. However, any photograph or diagram that can be seen in two ways might serve the same purpose. Sometimes we use a few examples of optical illusions.

With the old woman/young woman, we would show the picture to the team by holding it in front of the group. We let each person take a good look at it. On the newsprint in front of each group, we have some questions like:

a. How old do you think she is?

b. What kind of work do you think she does?

c. Would you want to live with her/marry her/have her a member of your team? (Or some question like that.)

We then ask the group to split into subgroups based on whether they have answered the last question yes or no—those who said "yes" in one group; those who said "no" in the other. (Before we begin the process we say that we are going to show a picture that some people have seen. If people have seen it they are requested to raise their hand and not say anything.) We ask participants who have seen it before to act as observers or join one group or the other to play the game. The facilitator moves from one group to the other to help keep the discussion going.

Fig. 6.1 Old woman/young woman

After 10 minutes or less, the groups should be asked to select the strongest spokesman for each position to sit together in front of the whole team and continue the discussion on "why or why not the woman should be included."

The process works best when each debater has chosen a different face in the picture. Most of the time that is exactly what has happened. In any case, the different perceptions are vigorously exposed. The follow-up discussion is crucial.

The whole team is brought together and people bring out their thoughts on the exercise: what they felt; what they learned about how people see things differently; how easily they got into the heat that is raised over such a question. The facilitator should then bring the discussion to *application in work*. Every exercise must be brought back to application within the team.

We may pose a question like: Give examples of how your perception was different from that of someone else on the team in the work situation—and what happened? Some important things usually come out. The participants should be asked to write down what they have learned. They should also be asked to keep track of any issues they might want to work on either with the entire team or with one or two other members. Such issues can be used later in the workshop or be part of the action steps identified at close of workshop.

3. *Listening and clarifying—demonstrating and practicing.* After the previous step, there will be plenty of examples of good and poor, or active and inactive listening. We have found it useful to introduce listening as an activity with a short statement, including:

a. Some studies have shown that, during lectures and other large group presentations, less than 20% of what is spoken is heard by the listeners.

b. Many things distract the listeners from hearing what the speaker (whether in group or one-to-one) has to say. Such things may be physical discomfort, outside noises, fantasies—or day-dreaming, tiredness, disagreement with speaker's position, the way speaker appears, etc.

c. Active listening requires *working* at listening and understanding what the other person has to say.

First, we find it very useful to demonstrate active listening. Someone is asked to volunteer from the team to tell something about himself or herself. The facilitator listens to the story and works at bringing out and clarifying both the content of the story and the process (the way the person is feeling about what she or he is saying). This activity on the part of the facilitator is what we call active listening—*understanding without judging* either positively or negatively. The facilitator might ask such questions as:

a. How did you feel in the situation?

b. What happened after you completed the conversation?

c. What did you have in mind when you said that?

In addition to questions the facilitator might make the following kinds of statements.

a. It sounded like you were really excited and interested in what was going on.

b. You really do get involved when you are talking with someone.

c. As I understood it, you were hoping that the situation would change.

d. What you said made me feel as though I was right there with you.

After the demonstration, we suggest that the team divide into groups of three. The purpose of the subgrouping is to practice active listening and clarifying. One person tells the story, another person is the active listener and the third person functions as an observer. We call the third person a *process observer*, since he or she will be observing the interaction between the two others. Particular attention is placed on the active listener, since this is the skill we are attempting to develop in all members of the team. Each member of the subgroup takes a turn at each role.

Prior to inviting the subgroups to locate themselves in different parts of the room or in different rooms, a copy of the Active Listening Checklist (Fig. 6.2) is given to each person on the team. The team is asked to read over the items and ask any clarifying questions. After this discussion, we usually suggest that the observer record his or her comments in the notebook and journal so that detailed feedback can be given to each active listener. A final suggestion is that each pair *look at each other* while carrying on the conversation.

While the interviews are going on, we usually visit the subgroups and listen into the exchanges for short periods of time. Such availability of the facilitator keeps the level of seriousness higher, allows for suggestions right on the spot and permits the participants to ask any questions that arise. The disadvantage of feeling ill at ease generally is easily overcome particularly, since the very presence of the process observer has already brought some level of discomfort which probably has been worked through. This part of the process takes about 45 minutes.

The team reconvenes and there is a group discussion of what has been learned about active listening. Usually we find participants will begin to comment on their own level of listening as well as the type of listening shown by others in the subgroup. Most often these comments come out

---

What is active listening? Focusing your attention on what the other person has to say in words, actions and feelings. It is more than listening to just the content of the message; it is also trying to understand what is behind the content.

Check yourself on the following *blocks* to good listening:
1. Feeling that you *must* answer or come to a decision about what is being presented to you.
2. *Evaluating* what is being presented to you.
3. *Being hurried* and listening on the run.
4. *Hearing what you want to hear*—selecting what stands out for you.
5. *You have something to say*–and you want to take time away from the presenter.
6. *Other things on your mind*—those things fill all available space so there is no room for what presenter has to say.
7. *Disagreeing* with the other person's point of view.
8. Seeing the person as *different* from yourself, that is, from another group, another culture, another race.
9. *Looking away* from the presenter or *staring* at the presenter.

Fig. 6.2 Active listening checklist*

---

*   Modification of a checklist developed by John T. Shoup.

in the form of jokes or sarcastic humor. After the discussion we ask each participant to record what he or she has learned about active listening, about him- or herself and about other members of the team.

4. *Giving and receiving feedback.* The process of feedback has already occurred during the previous steps in this intervention. We intentionally want the feedback process to take place with as much spontaneity as possible prior to reaching this point in the team development procedure. By this time, the word feedback has probably been introduced. Also, we usually find that some people are becoming a little tense about the use of open and hopefully honest evaluation of such "simple" acts as perceiving things, talking, and listening to each other.

Without any more preparation than: "Now, we have come to the third step of the team development process—giving and receiving feedback," we ask the team to discuss their experiences with feedback since the workshop began or on other occasions. Either at the top of a chalk board or on two sheets of newsprint, we place the words "Giving Feedback" (on one side of the board or on one sheet of paper) and "Receiving Feedback" (on the other side of the board or other piece of paper).

Then, we pose the question: "What does giving feedback mean to you?" We record all the main points that are made by the team. They often cover how they give feedback, feelings about giving feedback, comparisons between giving and receiving feedback, experiences before and during the workshop when feedback was being given. With little more than a lead-in comment, we then ask the team to think about receiving feedback by asking: "What does receiving feedback mean to you?" Again the thoughts are recorded on the newsprint or board.

Usually, the discussion of receiving feedback has a higher level of feeling associated with it. Often, a member of a team will report on some painful experience he or she has had during an evaluation session at work. Sometimes there will be a report of such an uncomfortable feeling during step 3 of this process. The discussion is continued until all members of the team have commented. If time permits, we may explain the Johari window and give some examples. (See Appendix II, Basic and Standard Exercises.) At this time, the handout on Giving and Receiving Feedback is distributed (Fig. 6.3).

The team is given a chance to review the handout and make whatever spontaneous comments they wish to make. Also, clarifying questions are solicited. Then, we ask the team to think of the different members of the team—one by one. If it seems right, we ask them to actually look at each person so that they can jog their memories.

Write down in your notebook the names of each person on your team. After each name write down at least one piece of positive feedback and one piece of negative feedback. Be sure you are following the rules of giving feedback as you write down these statements.

What is giving feedback? Presenting to another person some observation, some view, some feeling that you have about that person based on the *readiness* of the person to receive the comment.

What is receiving feedback? Receiving what is presented to you with an open mind and a readiness to listen and understand what is being presented.

Consider the following factors in helping you give and receive feedback?

1. It is more *descriptive* than evaluative. As such the receiver is more likely to stay open to the feedback.

2. It is *specific* rather than general. Refer to a specific experience that both of you have had.

3. It takes into account the *needs* of *both* the *receiver* and the giver. You must think through what both of you will gain from the feedback.

4. It takes into account the *readiness* of the receiver to make use of the feedback. If the person is into many other things, the result can be negative. So check first.

5. It is directed toward *behavior* the receiver can do *something about*. If the receiver has no control over the behavior or even feels that way, the outcome is negative.

6. It is *solicited* by the *receiver*. The readiness is the highest when the receiver asks for help in a certain area.

7. It is *well-timed*. Shortly after the event is usually the best time to give feedback if the receiver is not so troubled by what has happened that he or she is just not ready.

8. It is *checked* with the receiver after you have given it. The receiver must be sure that he or she has heard you correctly. Sometimes it helps to have the person repeat.

9. It is useful to give in a *group* or with a third person. The observers can check the accuracy of the feedback.

Fig. 6.3 Giving and receiving feedback*

After the team has completed the lists, we suggest that each person find someone in the team to whom he or she wishes to give some positive feedback. After a partner has been found, each person should go off to some other part of the room and give the feedback. If the two people can exchange positive feedback, then the exchange should be made. If not, the partners should split and find some other people.

After one exchange, the group should reconvene and discuss the experience of giving and receiving positive feedback. We have found at times that people have much trouble carrying out this part of the process. We give the group a good chance to discuss the experience and relate other times when such feedback was given or received.

---

* Modification of various lists of the rules on feedback, including the ideas of John Anderson.

At this point there is a moment of decision. With some groups, we find that many pairs go into negative feedback, that is, after giving the positive feedback, someone asks for the negative feedback as well.

If we sense that many pairs have started to exchange negative feedback, then we suggest to the team that each member select a person to whom they have not given negative feedback or continue discussing the feedback with a team member if they were interrupted by our reconvening of the whole team. We usually limit this discussion to about a half hour.

If we sense that negative feedback has been avoided by the pairs, we then set up a demonstration of giving and receiving negative feedback. We ask for a volunteer pair. Usually, one person will turn to another team member who has been a friend as well as co-worker and suggest or tease the other person into doing it.

If there is agreement, we suggest that the "giver" take the "receiver" off to the side of the room and check the "receiver's" readiness to receive feedback on the subject. If there is agreement, the two return to the front of the group and the feedback is given.

The facilitator helps the process along by checking that the rules of feedback are followed including the active listening.

Usually, we do not continue with more work on negative feedback. See Variation 1 for reasons to continue.

5. *Looking at process and content.* We find it useful to focus on the differences between process and content. During this intervention, we want the team to become aware of the difference between process and content particularly when the team functions as a whole. Thus, we engage the team in a discussion about some team issue that has been raised, for example, a problem that has been attributed to differences in perceiving why a new procedure was established for reporting sick leave and vacation time.

We allow the discussion to go on until there is sufficient involvement. When it is apparent that, let's say, some people saw the change as based on people not reporting their days off and others saw it as based on the new computer system that was introduced to the company—at this moment, we would write *"Content"* on one sheet of newsprint and *"Process"* on another sheet. Then, we say to the group, "OK, now what is process and what is content?" Usually, it takes a while to get out of the content discussion, but soon people start looking at their behavior and offer suggestions. The ideas are appropriately recorded on the two sheets.

Usually, the process list includes: feelings about the issue, the way people talk about the issue, the staying with the topic or going off on tangents, who was talking a lot, who was talking very little, who was trying to resolve the differences, etc.

The content list includes: what was the topic, some details about the topic, etc.

We have the team consider the value of stopping a team discussion and looking at the process. Usually, someone comes out with, "We waste so much time going off on small points or someone just takes over and talks all of the time." On the other side, we sometimes get comments that looking at the process just wastes more time or, "We won't have a facilitator around at work."

We try to work on both sides of this by looking at the positives and negatives of process observation. For example, the problem of: "Who will do it?" We explain that anyone in the team can be assigned to or volunteer for the job. After the team has been trained in practice process observations, the assignments can also be rotated. We assist the team members in thinking through the usefulness of such a process and help them arrive at a consensus about whether or not they wish to use a process observer at team meetings. If there is agreement to try it, arrangements are made to have the facilitator meet with the team at a subsequent regular or special team meeting. (See Step 8, "Follow-up procedure.")

6. *Developing interactive skills.* We would now devote a period of time to developing awareness of individual behavior during team meetings. First of all, we try to build lists of constructive and negative behavior with the help of the team. We would ask them: "Which individual behaviors in a team meeting interfere with the progress of the team meetings (constructive) and which help the meeting process (negative)?" We would note people's suggestions on newsprints. We then would display our placard with constructive and negative behavior in team meetings. See Fig. 6.4 for some suggested constructive and negative behaviors.

We prepare a tally sheet with people's names along the top of the sheet and the list of constructive and negative behavior in the left column of the page.

We will mark in the suitable place on the sheet each time a person displays one of the behaviors identified on the page.

A. *Constructive*
1. *Building:* developing and expanding the ideas of others
2. *Bringing in:* harmonizing, encouraging others to participate
3. *Clarifying:* restating, ensuring understanding, seeking relevant information
4. *Innovating:* bringing in new relevant ideas, information, feelings, etc.

B. *Negative*
1. *Overtalk:* interrupting, talking together with speaker
2. *Attacking:* deriding, belittling, criticizing person
3. *Negating:* cooling, cynicism, undermining morale

Fig. 6.4 Constructive and negative behaviors

The team then begins a discussion of one of the controversial subjects on its agenda. We stress that this topic should be a real item with which the team must deal. We do not participate in the debate, but only tally the behaviors.

After an hour or more the discussion is terminated and we read out the results of our observations. We put the results on a prepared newsprint for the entire team to review.

Then we may work out percentages with the help of team members. For instance: What percentage did each member have of the total number of "building" behaviors, or what percentage did each member have of the "overtalk" behaviors in the meeting? Another way of looking at the results is: What percentage of the total percentage of each member's behavior falls into each category? For example: Dave had 20% "building," 15% "overtalk," etc., until we reach 100% of Dave's recorded behavior.

Team members discuss the feedback and people take upon themselves assignments to increase specific constructive behaviors and decrease specific negative behaviors. If there is time, the team can resume discussion with a new topic and the whole process is repeated. This can be done a number of times and adopted as a procedure in the team's meetings.*

> *Note:* Effectively recording behavior by the method described here needs practice and skill. Another way of doing this, probably less effective, is to do without the observer's recordings. The list of behaviors is developed with the team. This is followed by a discussion. When the discussion is over each person roughly estimates which behaviors he or she used a little or a great deal and then takes it upon himself or herself to change assignments.

7. *Personal contracting with team members.* The procedure for personal contracting is described in detail in the intervention entitled, "Resolving one-to-one conflicts" (see Chapter 7).

We suggest that such a process is useful in basic team development. However, when time does not allow this step, it can be handled as a totally separated activity.

8. *Follow-up procedures.* The total team is convened to review what has been learned and to identify what the next steps should be. As a way of getting started, we like to ask for feedback about the way the workshop has been carried out:

a. Look at us as facilitators and indicate how well or poorly we have practiced accepting differences, listening and clarifying, feedback, etc.— all the skills we have asked you to work on.

---

* An excellent book devoted to this process is Rackham, N., P. Honey, and C. Colbert, *Developing Interactive Skills* (Guidsborough, Northampton, England: Wellers Publishing, 1971).

b. What were the steps that were the most and least helpful to you?

c. Did you find practical applications to your work?

First, we ask the participants to record their reactions in their notebooks. Then we have a general discussion.

We will end up with identifying the next steps. We ask the team to think of what action steps they wish to take individually and as a group. The team is asked to report all of the team action steps it intends to take and we list them on newsprint. We include such items as: the form of facilitating a team meeting, any problems that may have come up during different parts of the workshop, etc. After each action step, the team should identify the responsible parties and the dates related to implementing the items. See Chapter 10 for dealing with such follow-up procedures.

Variation 1

During step 4, it may be advisable to continue the pairing on negative feedback. After the demonstration and discussion have concluded, we suggest that each member of the team select a partner to give negative feedback. The process is identical to that of giving positive feedback.

We have found that some teams just want to get into these negative feelings. Members might comment, "It's so easy to say nice things, we must go beyond that." If team members have had previous experience in working openly with each other, we suggest going on into this phase of feedback. If we have completed the basic team development, we probably would have the group work on negative feedback at a subsequent session or workshop.

IMPROVING INTERPERSONAL RELATIONS

Reducing the confusions and tensions building up in the team through a greater awareness of the problems resulting from differing perceptions and communicating styles.

When to use

Interpersonal issues and problems often grow from minor differences to major gaps and finally to splits within the team.

When we start working with a recently organized team, we find it worthwhile to have members look at their differences. Through such awareness, confusion and misinterpretation can be avoided, and, on the positive side, resources can be identified.

With established teams, a common history will often produce unsolved problems, and issues may be brought out in an attacking way to make a point or win an argument.

We find that this intervention is requested and/or appropriate when there is:

- Pressure from top management to become more efficient
- A relatively new manager who has come up from the ranks of a department
- A manager who has been around for 6 or 8 months and has tried everything he knows and still does not have the department working well
- A complex assignment given to a work team particularly when the new assignment requires more contact with other resources or departments in the company

We also find that this process is useful in a three- to five-day workshop after a team has gone through sensing problems, basic team development, skill training, and confronting learning and communicating styles.

Who can use: 1. A manager who has participated in team development experiences and has co-led team sessions with a consultant. Such a manager can work best in a department other than his or her own
2. Consultant to organizations

Purposes: 1. To become aware of the kinds of problems that interfere with good problem-solving and communications
2. To build a higher level of trust among members of the team
3. To reduce confusions and tensions among members of the team

Participants: 1. All members of a team; however, if the number exceeds 9 or 10, natural subgroupings should be arranged—for example, by function or by where people work in the organization
2. In a managers' workshop, in groups of 6 to 9

Materials: 1. Newsprint, felt pens, tape, pencil and paper
2. Folders for notebook or journal
3. Materials needed for "Problem-sensing with groups" (see Chapter 2)
4. Materials needed for "Confronting your learning style" (see Chapter 3)
5. Materials needed for "Resolving one-to-one conflicts" (see Chapter 7).

Time: 8 to 9 hours

Detailed process

1. *Preparing team for working on interpersonal relations.* We find that bringing up the topic of *interpersonal relations* seems to raise the anxiety of many team members. We therefore begin this intervention with a discussion of what we *will be doing* and what we *will not be doing.*

On a newsprint we develop two lists, namely, activities *included* under interpersonal relations work and activities *not included* under interpersonal relations work.

Firstly, we indicate that this process is not sensitivity training and write that on the "not included" list. We explain that sensitivity training is used to work on deep feelings with the goal of personal growth.

We indicate that this process is task-oriented and works on issues interfering with getting the job done at work, and we write those items on the "included" list.

Then we narrow the focus down to working specifically on the differences in the way the team members learn and communicate and how such differences cause tension and lowered efficiency within the department or team. A summary of those ideas is written on the "included" list.

We now open up the discussion to the team. We request that people suggest what they think will be included or will not be included. By the end of this brief discussion, we have a good list of specific items for each list.

Through this step, we make sure that the real purpose of this intervention is understood by everyone. The two charts are taped on the wall and kept in sight throughout the workshop.

2. *Problem-sensing with team.* In a way, we have begun the sensing process in Step 1. To refine this, see the intervention in Chapter 2 entitled "Problem-sensing with groups," which can be used in its entirety modified to focus on issues concerning interpersonal relations.

We have found that the warmup to this intervention (step 1) helps the group in limiting the problems to interpersonal issues. When other problems are mentioned, we ask the team member to make note of the problem and be sure to bring it up at a future team meeting or ask if she or he can restate the problem in terms of interpersonal relations.

At the completion of step 8 in "Problem-sensing," we indicate to the team that we would like to start with problems that are generally referred to as communication issues—both the sending and receiving of information within the team and from the team to other departments. We have found that the tensions in teams are more readily reduced if we start with such issues.

After sharing this limitation with the team, we suggest they carry out step 9 of the "Problem-sensing," and develop the priorities agreed on by the team. (Note: We keep newsprint with identified problems clearly posted on the wall throughout the intervention.)

3. *Confronting learning styles.* After a break we ask the team to step back from the problem-sensing so that the members can gain a clearer idea about how each person on the team takes in (learns) and sends information. We see these as the basis of building good communication patterns.

We now suggest that the team go through steps 1, 2, and 3 of the intervention entitled "Confronting your learning style."

At the end of step 3, the team again reviews from the newsprint the identified problems listed during step 2. With the additional sensitivity gained about their learning styles, the problem which was given the most points is discussed by the group as a whole. There tends to be a deeper understanding of the problem. There is also a greater level of involvement in the direct work on the issue. Frequently referred to problems are: "Work does not progress smoothly because things get piled up on some person's desk"; or "We get quickly mumbled orders while he is on the run"; or "Never clear about who is responsible for a given piece of work."

4. *Working on one issue—a demonstration.* We write the problem on a separate sheet of newsprint.

We then ask each team member to write on a piece of paper some recent experiences he or she has had with this problem, including the name or names of the team members involved.

We list the names of all the team members on newsprint and then ask the group to call off the names they have listed on their own paper, including their own if they have been involved. The final tabulation will show how often certain team members have been a part of the problem.

Usually, people are quite aware of their part in the problem. It is also common that the name of the manager of the department is mentioned many times.

The group usually needs some time to reflect on the results. Often, someone tries to restate the problem. Always there are more specific examples presented. The facilitator should record the better statements or the more specific examples on the same newsprint on which the problem was originally written.

The members of the team whose names are mentioned most are asked whether they would like to work on the problem in front of the team. In our experience, there has never been a refusal.

The first step in working on the problem is to have the two or three participants state the problem as each person sees it. We try to get each of the volunteers to state the problem using "I" terms; that is, accepting the problem as much as possible as his or her own. For example, "I am in the office after everyone else, but I still can't get through all of those reports. It's just too much for me." Or "I have so many things to do that I can't spend more time giving instructions."

As the problem is talked about in these personal terms, we record each person's comments and place his or her initials next to the statement.

After some discussion by these participants, the rest of the team members are asked to restate the problem as specifically related to the people in front of the group. This process of restatement goes on until the subgroup reaches agreement on the definition of the problem.

We find that the tension, which usually is strong at the start of the demonstration, gradually becomes less. There is a growing atmosphere of helping each other within the subgroup as well as among other team members.

Of course, at times angry feelings are expressed and comments are misinterpreted. We must deal with those feelings and comments by keeping the attention of all the participants directed toward defining the problem for the subgroup.

When a definition of the problem has been accepted by the subgroup, a personal contracting process can begin. (For a description and application of personal contracting, see step 3 of "Resolving one-to-one conflicts," Chapter 7.) We then work with the subgroup through the elements of personal contracting so that the two or three people have a workable agreement.

5. *Clarifying what are the problems among team members.* Each person on the team takes one piece of newsprint paper, places his or her name on the top, and then lists all of the previously listed problems that he or she contributes to.

Next to each of the problems, the team member puts the names of other team members who are also involved. All participants tape their newsprints on the wall. (See Fig. 6.5 for an example.)

Team members go around reading the different lists and add their name with a different color if they also feel they are involved in or part of the listed problems with the person whose name is at the top of the newsprint paper.

Name of participant: Joe Smith		
Problems	Names of team members	Names added by other team members
1. Things get piled up on someone's desk	Tom, Ron, Jane	(Rose)
2. Get mumbled messages	Tom	
3. Never clear about who is responsible	Tom, Jane	(Ron)

Fig. 6.5 Personal listing of team problems (an example)

6. *Personal contracting among team members.* We suggest to the team that each member establish as many contracts with other team members as he or she can. As the pairs or groups of three or four work through their contracts, we keep ourselves available to assist in any steps of the contracting.

7. *Follow-up procedure.* At the conclusion of the contracting, we will ask the team to reconvene to discuss the necessary follow-up process. We indicate that very often the excitement and glow of the workshop becomes dim when the day-to-day pressures return. Thus, we feel some type of total team review process should be established.

We suggest that at least two three-hour sessions should be convened, the first one about one month after the workshop and another about four months after the first follow-up meeting. The purpose of the follow-up sessions is to reinforce some of the learning gained during the workshop.

In preparation for the follow-up sessions, we ask the entire team to identify what seems to be different about the team at this moment. "Look around the room. Get a sense of what seems to be happening between yourself and the others. Then write down in your notebook a description of what you see and feel." After giving the participants a chance to record their thoughts, we ask them to report these thoughts out loud while a list of them is made on the newsprint.

From this list we select the main themes and use the themes as an indication of how far the group has come. The following kinds of themes have been suggested: increased feeling of trust; understand Tom and Joe in a different way now; more people are talking; people are listening better to each other, etc. A list of the themes is typed and distributed to the team members as early as possible.

During the follow-up sessions the themes are again brought out and used as a guide for looking at what has happened to the interpersonal relations within the team after the workshop. Also, built into the follow-up sessions is a review of personal contracts. It is expected that the individuals involved in the contract will have set up their own review procedure.

Variation 1

When this process is used in a workshop of managers from different organizations, steps 2, 5, 6 and 7 are not included. During step 4, common issues from the different organizations are identified. Usually we will use role-playing to work on some of the common interpersonal problems that stem from sending and receiving information.

Resolving conflicts

CHAPTER OBJECTIVE

To assist managers and consultants work on the resolving of conflicts within a team that result from either conflict over who does what and how (the role) or personal matters that interfere with getting the job done.

GUIDE TO APPLYING INTERVENTIONS

What is meant by "resolving conflcts"?

- It means to examine what is causing trouble between two people and interfering with getting the job done.

- It means bringing two or more people together to look at the conflict.

- It means helping people to be clear about their expectations of each other.

- It means breaking down the elements of the conflict so that the parties can deal with them one at a time.

- It means learning how to use constructive feedback so that issues do not pile up and end in underlying, difficult-to-get-at conflicts.

- It means learning how to use help from a third party—*when necessary.*

About the interventions in this chapter

We have found that people have trouble in just sitting down and working on conflicts. The tendency is to avoid confronting the problem and to try to avoid the person who is causing trouble.

In many organizations, a difficult person is either fired or segregated from the people he or she is not getting along with. Minor irritations are usually allowed to build until they become barriers to getting problems identified and solved. People often feel that bringing out problems will hurt feelings and then things will be worse than if you just let the situation alone.

It is our view that by working on conflicts by means of orderly and organized approaches, the benefits far outweigh the temporary tensions that may arise in facing the conflict.

The interventions

1. *Resolving role conflicts.* Developed out of Roger Harrison's "Role Negotiations" to help team members who have different expectations and viewpoints about each other's job, this intervention is useful with team members who have worked with each other for a time.

2. *Resolving one-to-one conflicts.* This intervention should be used with a team when working on smaller or larger conflicts. It is a method for getting many underlying problems out into an open problem-solving confrontation. It offers a series of steps to try to handle the conflicts.

MATRIX OF INTERVENTIONS

Intervention	Use	Who can use	Time demand
Resolving role conflicts	Working on role conflicts in long term teams	Outside consultant	6–10 hrs
Resolving one-to-one conflicts	With personal tensions between two people; with style differences between two people	Manager with practice; consultant	6–12 hrs

Possible outcomes

1. Clarity on the definition of jobs within team.
2. Better understanding of what to expect from different team members.
3. Smoother working relations among team members.
4. More enjoyment of work relations.
5. Quicker identification of problems.

6. More willingness to work on problems rather than going off into long discussions or arguments.

7. More willingness of team members to help each other.

8. More freedom in asking for help from others on team.

9. Less collecting of unexpressed resentments.

10. More open airing of difficulties people are having with each other's way of doing things.

Recommended readings

1. Bennis, W. G., K. D. Benne, and R. Chin, *The Planning of Change* (New York: Holt, Rinehart, & Winston, 1961).

2. Harrison, R., "Role Negotiations," in *Readings in Organizational Psychology,* 2d ed., edited by Kolb, D. A., I. M. Rubin, and J. M. McIntyre (Englewood Cliffs, N. J.: Prentice-Hall, 1974).

3. Sherwood, J. S., and J. E. Glidewell, "Planned Renegotiation and Norm Setting," *Annual Handbook for Group Facilitators in 1973*, edited by Pfeiffer, J. W., and J. E. Jones (Iowa City: University Associates, 1973).

4. Walton, R. E., *Interpersonal Peacemaking: Confrontations and Third-Party Consultation* (Reading, Mass.: Addison-Wesley, 1969).

RESOLVING ROLE CONFLICTS

Assisting team members to examine their roles and reduce the conflict based on the unclarity of their roles.

When to use

From our experience most teams need this intervention; each team to different degrees. People working together are not in the habit of sitting down and trying to deal with the everyday tensions between them. These conflicts are generally caused by role conflicts based on different expectations between members. People expect things of each other as role bearers. If people work together as a team, each person is dependent on the others. *What* one person does affects the others. *How* a member of a team performs what is expected of him or her has great significance for the other members.

As this process generally pays rich dividends, the question more correctly put might be: when *not* to use this intervention? Here is a list of circumstances under which we would choose *not* to use this process:

- A relatively new team: We would not use this intervention with a team in which the members have not yet worked together for at least a number of months. When people have not yet crystallized what they will be doing and how they will do it; when members have not yet developed mutual role expectations and experienced one another's way of performing their roles, it is not advisable to use this intervention.

- A group that is not a team: We would not use this intervention in a group of people who are not interdependent with a division of work and responsibility; i.e., this is unsuitable for a strangers' workshop of managers who do not work together.

- A committee that does not meet weekly: The intervention will not work with a committee that does not meet regularly (at least every week) and so has little interaction between its members.

- A large group: In the form detailed here, the intervention is unsuitable for a group of over 15 people. Going through the entire process with a large group is difficult and impractical.

- Important replacements expected: We have found that using the intervention with a team that is expecting replacement of some important members is a wasted effort.

- Central people with personality disturbances: We are wary of trying to resolve role conflicts when it seems to us that the problems stem from personality disturbances. If key members of the team are extremely difficult, very aggressive, authoritarian, and critical, settling the role conflicts is not going to help for long.

The intervention must be repeated regularly. Settling role conflicts is not a one-shot affair. It is a process that a team must go through regularly and periodically.

Conditions always change. New people join; others leave. Tasks are altered; interfaces change; technology develops. Everything changes all of the time. Change necessitates reexamining, revising, and coming to mutual agreement about the division of work, responsibility, and authority. Change demands a regular harmonizing of role expectations and thus a reduction in role conflicts.

Who can use: This is one of the interventions in this Handbook that is recommended *only to consultants.* Many potential flareups can exist in the process, and if not handled by someone with experience can do more harm than good

Purposes:
1. To bring out into the open confrontation of conflicting role perceptions
2. To help the team members decrease role conflict by agreeing to change their role content or performance

Participants: A team of any kind—managers, a work group, etc., who have at least weekly meetings or contacts. Preferably not more than 15 people

Materials: 1. Newsprint, felt pens, and tape
2. Half sheets of newsprint
3. Paper and pen for each participant
4. A placard or newsprint illustration of "A model for planned renegotiation" (Fig. 7.1)

Time: 6 to 10 hours

STEPS IN PROCESS

1. Consultant's introduction to the process and explanation of model
2. Participants prepare lists of role content
3. Participants request changes in role content
4. Consultant explains conditions of feedback
5. Participants request changes in role performance
6. Unconditional acceptances
7. Clarified acceptances
8. Conditioned acceptances and conflicts
9. Summing up
10. Feedback on whole process

Notes:

1. The complete process is divided into two major parts.
The first part is aimed at bringing out the differences in role expectations, the second part is spent on dealing with the differences.
We have found it worthwhile to have a meal break between the two parts. This allows the information received to "sink in" and makes for a more balanced resolution of differences.

2. We differentiate between role content and role performance. The first is "what we do"; the second is "how we do it."
"What we do" is the content and responsibilities of our role or job—such as, say: lathing; being responsible for dispatching the merchandise, keeping accounts, loading materials, superintending work, etc.
"How we do it" is the particular manner in which we perform these activities such as: coming late to work, not submitting requested reports, putting pressure on subordinates, shifting unpleasant tasks to others, etc.
We shall consider role conflicts of both types, pertaining to role content and to role performance, and in the first stage will also deal with each separately.

Detailed process

1. *Consultant's Introduction to Process and Explanation of Model.*

    a. Consultant describes the goal of the meeting, elaborating on the points given in "Purposes" above.

    b. Consultant displays the placard showing "A Model for Planned Renegotiation" (Fig. 7.1) and explains the model, beginning from the top and making the following points:

    1) People who work together, in interdependence, with division of labor, need to share information and role expectations. If this is ensured there will be role clarity, and, other things being equal, people will be committed to the team and its purposes. This, of course, will contribute to the stability and productivity of the team. However, change is inevitable and must be anticipated. So we must expect that the "pinch" (something disruptive) soon will happen.

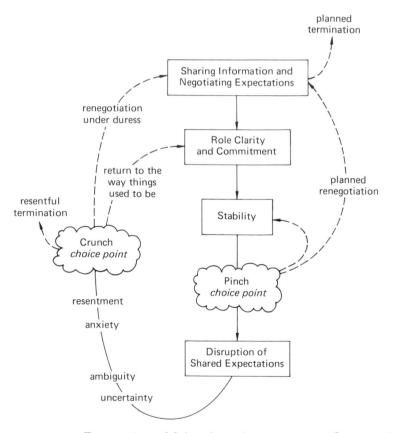

Fig. 7.1 A model for planned renegotiation (© 1971 John L. Sherwood. Used by permission.)

2) Change is inevitable, and in present times rate of change is generally increasing. Our "turbulent environment" constantly forces new situations and new problems upon us. New people join, others leave; new activities are needed. All this necessitates redefining role expectations and sharing the information. When these steps are not taken in time the result is disruption of shared expectations. ("I expect something from you and you act differently.")

3) If the problems and potential conflicts are brought to awareness by the "pinch" of something being wrong, the parties affected can openly confront the new situation, plan renegotiations, redefine role expectations, and achieve a common settlement of the problems. This leads to a further period of shared expectations—commitment, stability, and productivity. Sometimes, of course, the planned renegotiation may lead to planned termination of the relationship.

4) If the new situation is not dealt with in this way, the result is uncertainty about how to behave and how the others will behave. This leads to anxiety and resentment in relationships, disrupting the functioning of the team. A choice point is reached; this is no pinch but a crunch. One direction may lead to resentful termination of the relationship. And trying to return to the way things were before the new factor appeared does not work because the change demands that new role definitions be commonly accepted.

Settlement of the differences and redefinition of roles is essential at this point. This is more difficult after anxiety and resentment have already loaded the problem with emotional entanglements. This is renegotiation under duress and is difficult. The best policy is to openly confront and settle role conflicts as soon as they become apparent.

2. Participants Prepare Lists of Role Content. The consultant explains that in the first stage we will deal with role content—"what we do," and later with role performance—"how we do things." He or she asks each participant to write down in point form *all* the various activities and responsibilities included in that participant's role, as actually performed by him or her.

The list should be detailed enough to give a picture of the person's activities but not so detailed as to make understanding difficult. From 10 to 16 items is about right.

Each participant copies his or her list on the top two-thirds of half a newsprint and attaches it to the wall next to those of other participants.

Under the last item listed, a line is drawn across the paper to separate this list from whatever is added later.

Note: We have met with some difficulty when working with a committee consisting of some persons who are regular members of the group and other participants who have been on periodic yet continuous contact with the group. In such a case we ask the latter participants to put down on the newsprint their activities connected with the committee and then to join one of the office holders and help list his or her items.

It should be apparent that settling role conflicts is suitable if participants fill roles which are interdependent and in some ways complementary.

3. *Participants Request Changes in Role Content.*

a. Participants are now requested to walk around and read all the lists. If they find on any person's list: (i) any activity or responsibility which they do not think should be there, or (ii) if they feel that any person's list has left out an activity or responsibility that should have been included, then they briefly state this information on the appropriate newsprint below the horizontal line, and sign their names.

b. Participants finding such a remark on any newsprint can add their own signatures next to it if they agree with the remark.

c. When participants have finished writing all requests and remarks, they are asked to study the remarks on their own sheets. At this stage the consultant is advised not to allow any remarks or requests for clarification; he or she can promise the team that this will come later.

4. *Consultant Explains Conditions of Feedback.* As the following activity may create problems in a team that has not experienced previous human relations training, we explain at this point that the next activity will demand more risk-taking and openness to feedback. The team members are told that they will be asked to prepare short notes to each other containing "things I would like to request you to do differently from the way you do them now" (it is advisable to put this on newsprint). Members are requested to sign their names on the notes and fold them so that only the name of the receiver is on the outside.

However, before they begin writing their notes we find it essential to list the conditions of giving feedback on bold newsprint and explain them to the team. We stress that:

- The request must be within the ability of the person to perform (e.g., he or she must have the abilities, resources, and legitimacy to do what is requested).

- The request must be worded concretely and not generally (e.g., "Please do not check my performance," rather than "Don't be distrustful").

- The request should be motivated not to hurt the other person but to help him or her.

- The request must be not to change character but to change a behavior or activity.

Note: We have also found it sometimes useful to precede the explanation of "conditions of giving feedback" with an illustrated explanation of the Johari Window.*

5. *Participants Suggest Changes in Role Performance.* Participants are requested to write the notes and hold on to them until everyone is finished writing. Then the notes are passed around and each participant reads the notes addressed to him or her. We may mention that in most teams the team leader gets most of the notes.

We prefer to have a meal break at this point, and we request that participants not discuss the requests they received during the break.

6. *Unconditional Acceptances.* The following process was developed after we found, by trial and error, that it is much easier to develop a positive atmosphere and get agreements if we first deal with suggestions for role changes or additions that are relatively easy to accept.

The consultant asks the team members: "Who has received a request or requests *either on the newsprint or in a note* that he or she is willing to accept *unconditionally* and *without clarification?*"

When a person states such a request, accepted by him or her, this is written up on his or her newsprint list (above the line). All accepted requests are written down, and when that person has finished the others follow suit. On the many occasions we have gone through this process we have never found difficulty in getting the first volunteer or others to follow. This first stage often clears up about half the suggestions. We still find it advisable to curb requests for clarification and "conditional acceptances" (i.e., "If what you mean is . . . then I might think of . . .).

7. *Clarified Acceptances.* When the above stage is completed the consultant asks the team members "are there any suggestions you have received that you think you can or will accept if you have some clarification?" This stage also inevitably leads to some acceptances that are noted on the newsprint.

The consultant will probably have to intervene here to make sure the suggestion is understood by the receiver. The intervention to "Repeat to the other person what he has said to you and receive his confirmation that you understood him correctly," comes in very useful here.

8. *Conditioned Acceptances and Conflicts.* The problematic role conflicts and interpersonal problems find expression at this stage. However, the preceding two stages have helped to prepare the conditions of working through confrontations and settlement. The atmosphere of acceptance and willingness to concede to others and accept feedback generally helps to make this last stage fruitful.

---

* For an explanation of the Johari Window see Appendix II.

The consultant first asks for "conditioned acceptance"; i.e., "Suggestions you have received that you may be willing to accept under certain conditions." When these have been dealt with, team members are asked to speak about suggestions received that they tend *not* to accept. This is the most difficult stage of all for the consultant, who must now use all his or her skill of intervention at the right point. The consultant will be using the intervention of asking a person to repeat what has been said to him or her to the satisfaction of the person who said it; may have to help bring into the open long nurtured resentments that are disturbing healthy role relationships; and may have to ferret out "hidden agenda" that are interfering with agreement.

Sometimes a consultant helps two people negotiate a "working agreement" in which each agrees to accept a part of the other's requests. In short, at this stage, the consultant needs to use all of his or her Third Party intervention skills.

As in former stages, all acceptances and agreements are put up in writing.

It is difficult to fix time estimate for this stage as it depends mainly on the specific problems of each team. If the whole process has an objective time limit determined by other circumstances, the discussions may have to be stopped without attaining resolution of all conflicts. Even then, however, the team as a whole is generally very satisfied with the agreements that have been reached.

9. *Summing Up.*

a. We tend to read out aloud all acceptances and agreements that have been reached.

b. A date is fixed to reexamine what has worked out and what has not. If necessary, unfinished business can be dealt with at that date.

c. The placard of "A model of planned renegotiation" is once more displayed and explained in the light of what has taken place. Participants are asked for comments and conclusions on how to deal with role conflicts in the future.

10. *Feedback on the Whole Process.* (See notes on feedback, Chapter 2).

RESOLVING ONE-TO-ONE CONFLICTS

Reducing conflict between two people through a process of personal contracting.

When to use

Many problems in an organization start with a conflict between two people. While it is true that external forces can increase the level of conflict within

the organization, the kinds and intensity of the conflict are often determined by the individual pairs that make up the organization.

We think that finding ways to reduce one-to-one conflict can be one of
the most profitable skills a manager can develop. Obviously, there are many
ways to approach such a problem. We are suggesting this process since it
seems to have worked well in many situations, such as:

1. Two managers competing for the same position and not being able to
   to bring the conflict out into the open.
2. A manager and his or her assistant who were gossiping about each
   other as a way of reducing personal tension between them.
3. A production manager and supervisor who were avoiding each other
   because of a "bad" evaluation.
4. Two managers who teased each other in front of the president because
   of some conflicts between members of their families.
5. Two vice presidents who would almost always take opposite sides at
   executive committee meetings whenever a problem would be considered.

This process is more successful under these conditions:

1. The two parties voluntarily come to a skilled *third party* to assist in
   resolving their conflict.
2. The problem has existed for a relatively *short* period of time.
3. The problem has a rather narrow definition—either it involves just the
   two parties or it is easily defined by both parties.
4. The definition of the problem is readily agreed to by both parties.
5. Both parties can gain through a successful resolution of the problem.

Who can use:
1. A manager who has participated in team development
   and has co-led team sessions with a consultant. Such a
   manager can work best in a department other than his
   or her own
2. Consultant to organizations

Purposes:
1. To develop a problem-solving orientation within a team
2. To reduce tension and the level of conflict among members of a team
3. To deal with the tension between a manager and the
   members of his or her group or department

Participants:
1. All members of a team unless the team numbers more
   than 15; then subgrouping is required
2. In a workshop, in groups of 6 to 9

Materials:
1. Newsprint, felt pens, tape, pencil and paper
2. Folders for notebook or journal

3. Materials needed for steps 1, 2, 3, and 4 of "Basic steps in team development" (see Chapter 6)
4. Materials needed for steps 5 and 6 of "Improving interpersonal relations" (see Chapter 6)

Time: 6 to 12 hours (includes 6 hours for follow-up sessions)

STEPS IN PROCESS

1. Reducing one-to-one conflicts—a lecturette

2. Some basics in team building

3. What is a personal contract?—a lecturette

4. Personal contracting without the help of a third party

5. Working on personal contract requiring third party

6. Follow-up workshop

Detailed process

1. *Reducing one-to-one conflicts—a lecturette.* We like to make the following points in the lecturette and discussion that precedes working on the conflicts:

a. All teams have conflicts or tensions among their members.

b. The longer the team has been working together the greater the chance of having lingering conflicts, that is, unresolved problems that have been shelved.

c. Most often conflicts arise from people not relating to each other in an open and honest manner, and not revealing what the other person does that is bothering them.

d. Most conflicts of short duration can be handled by the two people involved *if* both have been trained in using some system of conflict resolution.

e. Conflicts of a longer duration may need a third party to help the two parties actively listen to each other and work through some misconceptions that probably have accumulated over time.

After these main points have been presented, we suggest a discussion of the meaning of each idea. When there is time, the facilitator might try to elicit examples or experiences from the participants. We might also display Fig. 11.2 and explain as detailed in step 2 of "Dealing with tension between teams" in Chapter 11.

2. *Some basics in team building.* We feel that a team must go through steps 1, 2, 3, and 4 in "Basic steps in team development" (see Chapter 6)

prior to working on personal contracting. These team development steps might help the team members build a greater readiness to understand each other.

3. *What is a personal contract?—a lecturette.* Usually, conflict is based on unclarity between two or more people. The unclarity is most often associated with certain differences in the style or makeup of the two people coupled with external pressures or unclear definitions of responsibility and authority. Further, it is often obscured by other matters until it is hard to even identify the issues that are causing the problem or conflict.

We have concluded that the legal sounding term "contract" has a positive and clarifying effect. That is, legal contracts have an objectivity about them. The words of the legal profession are sometimes very confusing, but the awe with which some people approach contracts seems to have a stronger overall impact than the negative effect of the confusing words.

The elements of the personal contract include the following (we suggest listing the elements on newsprint):

a. *Problem clarification.* There must be a clear statement of the problem to which both parties agree.

b. *Gains by both parties.* In order for a personal contract to be initiated, all parties must benefit. The more ways all parties benefit by the resolution of the problem, the more likely the problem will be worked on.

c. *Agreed-upon action steps.* All steps taken by both parties must be identified and agreed upon by the parties involved. When possible, all action steps should have a date associated with them. Minimally, each party has an identified first step and a date associated with it.

d. *Sanctions, if appropriate.* Some people require some form of punishment or inducement to ensure the ongoing work on the contract. Some sanctions might be specified in the contract if agreed to by both parties.

e. *Review and evaluation of results.* Specific ways of measuring the desired changes (reduction in problem) must be included in the contract. In addition, the dates and time for such reviews must be specified.

f. *Renegotiation of contract.* After each review period, there can be a renegotiation of the contract. The procedure for renegotiation must be specified.

We find that much discussion follows the presentation of these elements. Here are some of the types of questions we are asked, with our usual answers:

a. *Do you mean all these things have to be written down, and why?* Yes, it is essential that all the parts are written down and both parties sign the agreement. We find that when a contract is written and all parties have copies, the specific language can be referred to at some later date and this helps all parties to more accurately recall the original discussion about the contract.

b. *How can we figure the details about when to work on such a contract? So many things happen to interfere.* We know about the interferences and pressures at work. Conflicts stay conflicts because we almost always look for ways of avoiding them, rather than actually handling them. We think that you must take time now to look over your work days and figure the best time to work on the conflict. Mark it on your calendars and have very good reasons to change those agreed-upon dates. In fact, we suggest that the parties to the contract agree that the only way to change those dates is by mutual consent after a full explanation for the change has been given.

c. *What is an example of a sanction?* Remember, not everybody needs sanctions—but be sure you don't if you decided not to include them. People have used payment of money either to the other party or to a previously identified charity. Others have used setting up a point system, with points being deducted for any failure to comply with the contract. Sometimes, with the point system, a chart showing the "score" is visibly displayed on the departmental bulletin board or in the office of the parties involved.

d. *How do you measure the reduction of a conflict?* It isn't easy. We recommend that you make the means of measurement as specific as possible. For example, if the problem has to do with one person not showing enough respect for the ideas of another person, then the measure is the number of ideas that have been carefully listened to and discussed to the satisfaction of the offended party. A record of these discussions is kept. Usually, the implementation of the agreed-upon ideas are felt as benefits that both parties gain in such a contract. If the problem is that the manager is not clearly and frequently evaluating the performance of each department member, then the measure might be keeping of a written record of the evaluations. During the review period the parties discuss the issues of clarity and frequency. To repeat, we find it necessary to use very concrete behavior as measures.

e. *Should the contract be written in a certain form?* We feel that the parties should decide on the form as long as *all elements* are covered. If there is some trouble about the form, someone else in the team might be helpful in assisting the parties.

4. *Personal contracting without the help of a third party.* We suggest using steps 5, 6, and 7 of "Improving interpersonal relations," Chapter 6. That procedure allows team members to define how they are related to conflicts that have been identified to the whole team as general team prob-

lems. In addition, we suggest that time be allowed for team members to make private agreements.

For example, if two team members recognize their part in an identified conflict, the pair might decide to develop a contract with each other. In some instances the pair will choose to be open about the contracts, in other instances they will handle it in private. The facilitator should make it known that either approach is acceptable.

Usually, we find that as team matters are discussed and contracts are written, some previously undisclosed issues may be recalled by a team member. The facilitator should suggest that such issues should be noted in the journal and, when time and circumstances permit, a contract be written.

The public or open contracts should be written on newsprint and displayed on the wall for review and comment by all team members. Clarifying questions usually help strengthen the contracts. Any suggestions agreed to by all participants in the contract should be written into all copies of the contract. The contracts are worked on after the team returns to the work place. The contracts written on newsprint should be saved for the follow-up workshop. (*Note:* we are trying to build in a system of conflict resolution that can be achieved *without* the assistance of a professional facilitator. Thus, our *primary* goal is to assist participants to identify the conflicts and write the contracts.)

5. *Working on a personal contract requiring a third party.* We ask the team members to think about the different contracts which the team members established during the previous step. We might say: "Think about the nature of the conflict that you are having with the other party involved in each of your contracts. Do you see a lot of problems in working on the conflict? Do you imagine that the other party is not going to do his or her part? Do you feel *you* will have trouble really taking steps toward a resolution of the conflict?"

We then suggest that each participant select one of his or her contracts which he or she thinks will be a difficult one to resolve without some outside help. Each participant should go to the other person involved in the contract (if available) and see whether he or she is willing to work on the conflict in front of the group. The facilitator chooses from the group of pairs willing to work on their conflicts.

The facilitator and the two team members form a small fishbowl within the larger circle of the team members. The two team members face each other and begin by reading the problem. The facilitator helps them with any unclarities there might be in the statement of the problem. If there is difficulty in defining the problem, the facilitator attempts to identify the underlying issue and asks the two team members if such an issue does indeed cause them trouble. If they agree that it does, the facilitator may have to help them redefine the problem, and an attempt is made to reach an agreed-upon contract. Such an attempt may have to be repeated a few times.

Much of the time we find that the intensity of the conflict is directly related to the number of issues that are hidden under the one issue that has been initially brought to the surface. At other times, we find that there are glaring differences in learning, communication styles, or other basic differences in how the people operate.

At times we must conclude the attempt of working in front of the group if agreement cannot be reached. The involved parties might need some private sessions with the facilitator or another person who is more skilled in resolving more involved conflicts among team members.

6. *Follow-up workshop.* A follow-up four-hour workshop is scheduled from four to six weeks after the initial work on contracting. The primary objectives of the workshop are:

    a. To review the accomplishments of team members in working on contracts and reducing the conflicts.

    b. To learn from each other what methods are effective and not effective in the real work situation.

The whole team, including all subgroups, should meet in the same room. All public contracts should be displayed on the newsprint and taped on the walls of the room.

The facilitator asks participants to discuss the following questions:

    a. What helped you work on your contract?

    b. What interfered with your working on your contract?

The helps and interferences are recorded on separate sheets of newsprint. At the end of the discussion, all participants are asked to write in their journals what was learned and how they can apply the learning to working on their own contracts.

The second part of the workshop focuses on successes. The facilitator asks for examples of positive changes resulting from the work on the contracts.

Finally, the team considers the need for any further follow-up sessions. Usually we find merit in scheduling another follow-up in six months.

Variation 1

The intervention can be completed without step 5. If the team has been working together for a long time and there are many more involved conflicts, the use of step 5 may just cause too much stress in the group. We find that it is useful just to get the personal contract process in use for awhile at the work place. After it has been successfully employed on less deep conflicts, we can then try to get team members to work on more difficult conflicts at some later workshop.

Enriching work life

CHAPTER OBJECTIVE

To offer a number of interventions meant to increase work motivation and raise the quality of work life.

GUIDE TO APPLYING INTERVENTIONS

What is job enrichment?

- Job enrichment is a way to increase motivation, production, and satisfaction of people at work.

- Job enrichment is based on the idea that basic human needs for variety, autonomy, task identity, task significance, etc., have to be satisfied if work is to become meaningful and motivating.

- Motivation to work comes from the satisfaction of people's needs, though these needs may vary in intensity from person to person, and people are not always aware of their needs.

- Such factors as wages, work conditions, fringe benefits, etc. (extrinsic factors) strongly affect work satisfaction. A change to the worse in these factors causes dissatisfaction.

- These extrinsic factors are not work motivators. Work motivation stems from factors connected to the work itself and its content.
- Changes can be made in the work itself, with the purpose of increasing work motivation.
- Changing work content basically includes three elements: extension of the work cycle, integration of production and services to production, and decentralization of authority and responsibility.
- Individual job enrichment, as practiced by Herzberg and others, attempts to *enrich individual jobs* by enlarging them to include tasks they did not previously encompass.
- The *autonomous work group* approach, as practiced in Scandinavia, differs from Herzberg's approach in that the target unit is the work group and not the individual.
- The factors stressed in the group approach are: increasing the group's autonomy, adding meaningful elements to the group's task, increasing individual satisfaction and growth through training in more than one skill, and developing overlapping competencies in workers.
- The *interprofessional team* approach attempts at one and the same time to improve the quality of work life and raise work effectivity.
- This approach stresses the combination of *social*, *structural*, and *technical* changes in the workplace—with the purpose of improving work life and work effectiveness.

About the interventions in this chapter

Three of these interventions are intended to bring about concrete change in the work life of a team or a department. These are neither short inputs to help a team with a particular problem, nor learning experiences from which the team may later gain an insight. These are interventions with the purpose of change.

The interventions

1. *Motivating team members.* This intervention was developed by us out of the ideas of Henry Murray, David McClelland, and Kolb, Rubin, and McIntyre. We are keenly aware of the interest in finding ways to increase motivation at all levels of work. More awareness of the needs that motivate may increase a manager's options in assisting team members in doing a more consistent and effective job.

2. *Enriching jobs of team members.* This is based on an analysis of the critical factors to be considered before committing ourselves to a job enrichment program. When working on this we developed a comprehensive list of elements which can be focused on in enriching jobs. This list is included in the intervention.

3. *Initial job enrichment.* We designed this for a team's first plunge into job enrichment, and we were quite satisfied with our creation until we came across Merrelyn Emery's *Participative Design Seminars—A Description.* We tried including elements from that design and ideas about team structure from Fred Emery and P. G. Herbst. The various approaches fell into place and strengthened the intervention.

4. *Developing an interprofessional team.* Here is a detailed description of all the stages and considerations in the process of developing an interpersonal team in the organization. The description covers all details from planning to developing such a team, through the various phases of its work until its final disbandment.

MATRIX OF INTERVENTIONS

Intervention	Use	Who can use	Time demand
Motivating team members	Finding ways to motivate team members	OD experienced manager; OD consultant	4 hrs
Enriching jobs of team members	What to do and consider before embarking on job enrichment	Only OD consultant	Undefined
Initial job enrichment	The first intervention with the work team	OD consultant; experienced facilitator	8–12 hrs
Developing an interprofessional team	How to develop an interprofessional team in an organization	Only OD consultant	16 hrs; until pilot project

Possible outcomes

1. More personal satisfaction in carrying out own work as part of team.
2. More satisfaction from the work itself.
3. More involvement and commitment to work.
4. Less absenteeism and worker turnover.
5. More productivity and effectivity of work team.
6. Creative use of departmental, or team, resources for organization wide activities.
7. More support for each other in the carrying out of team functions.
8. Increased flexibility of work group and department to accommodate itself to changing conditions.
9. More willingness to go beyond one's own job in assisting another member of the team.

10. More creativity at work.

11. More awareness of the needs that motivate in the work situation.

Recommended readings

1. Ford, R. N., *Motivation Through the Work Itself* (New York: A.M.A., 1969).

2. Herbst, P. G., *Autonomous Group Functioning* (London: Tavistock, 1962).

3. Herzberg, F., "One More Time: How Do You Motivate Employees?" *Harvard Business Review*, **46** (1968), pp. 53–62.

4. Herzberg, F., *Work and The Nature of Man* (Cleveland: World Publishing, 1966).

5. Maher, J. R. (Ed.) *New Perspectives in Job Enrichment* (New York: Van Nostrand-Rheinhold, 1971).

6. McClelland, D. C., *The Achieving Society* (Princeton, N. J.: D. Van Nostrand, 1961).

7. Myers, S. M., *Every Employee A Manager* (New York: McGraw-Hill, 1970).

8. Emery, F., *Democracy at Work* (Leiden: Martinus Nijhoff, 1975).

MOTIVATING TEAM MEMBERS

Becoming more aware of the relationship between needs and work; taking steps to increase the motivation of members of a work team.

When to use

There is much talk about increasing the motivation of workers. Like the word communication, it is more spoken about than acted upon. We are aware of a number of situations that might call for work on motivation, such as:

- People in a department keep their eyes on the clock; take breaks for long periods of time; just cannot wait for the work day to end.

- In a discussion with a number of workers in a department, the general feeling is "down"; the work is boring; everyone else seems to be getting the promotions and raises; it just isn't worth making the effort.

- In another department, there are a lot of people out sick; lateness has become a regular event; turnover is high.

- The manager of an engineering department says that the department members are always griping; they rarely give help to a co-worker who may have been slowed up for some personal reason; he feels there is no clearly defined purpose for the department.

- In one company there was a lot of talk and "flashy" programs to keep motivation high; the methods applied were having a positive effect on some employees, but really missing a lot of others.

We have found that when situations like these are experienced for extended periods of time, some special effort should be made to look or relook at the issue of motivation. Of course, it is important to analyze the situation to see whether there are other interventions that might be more useful.

In an organization that has established a management and team development program, motivation can be an excellent area to work on after some basic work has been completed. It helps to refine the thinking and action within the team, that is, the members focus more actively on what they are gaining from the work experience. It allows each person to ask: What in my work life is important to me? How is my work life satisfying me as a person?

Who can use:
1. A manager who has participated in team development and has co-led team sessions with a consultant. Such a manager can work best in a department other than his or her own
2. A consultant to organizations

Purposes:
1. To increase the work satisfaction of each member of a team
2. To become clearer on what motivates each member of a team
3. To increase the benefits of all kinds of motivating factors and lessen the negative impact of conflicting needs

Participants:
1. All members of a team; however, if the number exceeds 9 or 10, natural subgrouping should be arranged, for example, by function or by the physical location in the organization
2. In a workshop, in groups of 6 to 9

Materials:
1. Newsprint, felt pens, tape, pencils, and paper
2. Folders for notebooks or journal
3. Magazines with many photographs of people, alone and in groups, and/or Kolb, D. A., I. M. Rubin, and J. M. McIntyre, *Organizational Psychology: An Experiential Approach* (Englewood Cliffs, N. J.: Prentice-Hall, 1974). See photographs on their pp. 55–66.

Time: About 4 hours

1. Some thoughts about motivation and work
2. Personal need satisfaction and motivation—a way of measuring needs
3. Discussing needs with team members
4. Heightening awareness about strongest needs
5. Applying the understanding about needs and motivation to the work itself

Detailed process

1. *Some thoughts about motivation and work.* At the beginning of the workshop, we like to share some thoughts with the team or workshop participants about needs, motivation, and action. These thoughts include the following:

a. A need is a sense of incompletion or dissatisfaction within a person.

b. Motivation comes from trying to satisfy a need or needs.

c. In order to reduce a need, a person must take some action.

d. There are essentially two types of needs, safety needs and growth needs. *Safety needs* are related to food, protection from harm, security, a reasonably predictable environment, physical health. *Growth needs* are related to independence, development of interests, pursuit of knowledge, creativity, etc.

e. Something that starts out as a need—let's say, to be protected from harm–may be expressed as another need—for example, seeking closeness to others (affiliation). One need may cover or conceal another need. Further, the more visible (conscious) need, in this case affiliation, can itself become a motivator. Thus a person can be motivated by both needs—the underlying need (concern about being harmed) and the more surface need (affiliation).

Needs are funny that way, they can start as a deep concern and even when the need at the deeper level is cared for, we may continue the behavior that was started by the original need. We have developed a habit and it becomes a part of our daily life.

f. Many authors have written about needs and their relationship to motivation, including Abraham Maslow, Henry Murray, David McClelland, and Fred Herzberg. It is a very complicated subject. We are interested in giving enough about the subject so that the understanding will help in being more effective in the work situation—not that a thorough understanding of the subject will be achieved. For further understanding, read: McClelland, *The Achieving Society*, and Herzberg, *Work and the Nature of Man.* (See Recommended Readings.)

g. Fred Herzberg has concentrated on applying an understanding of motivation to the work situation. Robert N. Ford, one of Herzberg's students and colleagues, makes the strong point of connecting satisfaction with the work itself.

Ford's studies with employees of American Telephone and Telegraph Company (AT&T), reported in *Motivation through Work Itself* (American Management Association, 1969), indicate that motivation comes out of increasing the satisfaction with the work or task itself. He concludes, "The surroundings of the task can produce dissatisfaction, but not long run satisfaction. Good policies, good administration, good wages and benefits, good supervision—all these merely set the stage..." The tasks in many AT&T departments were reordered so that the workers "were provided greater chance for achievement, for recognition, for responsibility, for advancement, and for psychological challenge and growth." (p. 39)

h. We are suggesting that as needs and motives become clearer to members of a team, tasks can be better organized to satisfy these needs. Of course, there are other initial steps which can be taken to increase satisfaction including job enrichment, the interprofessional approach. (See appropriate interventions in the Handbook.)

2. *Personal need satisfaction and motivation—a way of measuring needs.*

   a. We have found that certain needs are particularly useful to consider with regard to the work situation. These include:

   1) *Need for security*—the sense of protection and safety that comes with being in the same physical surroundings, the same environment; having things happen the same way day after day, etc.

   2) *Need for affiliation*—wanting to be close to people; relating to others in any way possible.

   3) *Need for competence*—the desire to master the task or skill at hand.

   4) *Need for achievement*—the desire to accomplish the task or reach the goal.

   5) *Need for power*—the desire to have control over or influence others.

   b. We have found that it is important for participants to discover how these needs are expressed within them. Many people can take a good guess about the level or intensity of each of these needs and get fair agreement from close friends or colleagues. However, we have been convinced that going through the following exercise helps to increase awareness of these needs and sets the stage for increasing motivation within the team.

Henry Murray developed the Thematic Apperception Test to look at the needs of people as a way of understanding their personality dynamics. This same approach has been applied to industry and personnel work. Simply, the participant is asked to make up a story or answer some questions about a picture.

c. There are two ways that we approach the measuring of these needs.

1) If the workbook by Kolb, et al., is available, pages 53 through 73 can be used to work on three of the needs, namely: affiliation, power, and achievement. The outlined procedure in that workbook is quite similar to the one we use.

At the completion of the workbook task, step 3 of this intervention which is the "Discussing needs with team members," is the next best step.

2) Another possibility is to go through the following steps:

a) Team members should be given a pile of magazines in which there are pictures of people either alone or in groups. They have 15 minutes to go through the magazines selecting and tearing out pictures which show:

(1) Someone who is sitting or standing who looks like he or she is dreaming.

(2) One person who is giving directions to another person.

(3) Someone who looks as though he or she is achieving or in the process of achieving a goal.

(4) A group of people doing something together.

The team is asked to pile the pictures in the four groups indicated above.

b) After the team members have completed separating the pictures, the team is asked to select the picture from each of the four piles that best represents the atmosphere in their work situation. We find that going through the pictures and personalizing the choices increases the involvement and work relevance in making up the stories at the later stage of this exercise.

Each of the selected four pictures should be mounted on separate pieces of newsprint.

c) The team members are then requested to take out their notebooks, and, while looking at the pictures one at a time, write a story about each picture. The story should answer the following questions:

(1) What do you see happening in this picture? What are the doing or saying? How are they feeling?

(2) What do you think happened before this situation? What might have led up to this scene?

(3) What do you think will happen after this scene is over? What will the people do or say later?

d) We distribute the handout entitled, Work-Needs Scoring Criteria (Fig. 8.1). We then ask the participants to read the examples and ask clarifying questions.

e) Then we suggest that each of the participants score their own stories with the five needs in mind. We ask the participants to refer to their criteria and scoring sheets. (See Figs. 8.1 and 8.2.)

f) Our instructions are: Read through each of your stories, keeping the Examples of Story References in mind. On your Work-Needs Scoring Sheet, rate the level of each need present in your first story by circling one of the choices—high, medium, low, or ab-

The Needs	Examples of Story References
1. Security	"Place feels so good." "Never want to change things." "Why can't people leave things where they find them?" "I walked into the room and everything is just the way I left it."
2. Affiliation	"Being around people feels so good." "Why don't we have more people around?" "This is a very lonely spot." "I dream of my family all huddled together." "I feel so close to him."
3. Competence	"I learned that well." "It takes a while but I can really handle myself." "She can type very well." "As she walked into the room, there he was going through his exercises preparing for the big race." "She is really a scholar—a master at carefully reviewing all sources of information before acting."
4. Achievement	"I like to win." "She did everything possible to get the job done. Time just didn't matter." "When I came in the people were just wasting time and not getting down to work." "It was so good to see the fine piece of work, done well and efficiently."
5. Power	"The boss always has the right answer." "I like to get my point across and see how it changes things." "Running the business has its hard part, but if I were there I could make it hum." "My father knew how to get what he wanted." "People need a lot of direction to get things done."

Fig. 8.1 Work-needs scoring criteria

Need	Picture 1	Picture 2	Picture 3	Picture 4	General Tendency
1. Security	High Medium Low Absent	High Medium Low Absent	High Medium Low Absent	High Medium Low Absent	High Medium Low Absent
2. Affiliation	High Medium Low Absent	High Medium Low Absent	High Medium Low Absent	High Medium Low Absent	High Medium Low Absent
3. Competence	High Medium Low Absent	High Medium Low Absent	High Medium Low Absent	High Medium Low Absent	High Medium Low Absent
4. Achievement	High Medium Low Absent	High Medium Low Absent	High Medium Low Absent	High Medium Low Absent	High Medium Low Absent
5. Power	High Medium Low Absent	High Medium Low Absent	High Medium Low Absent	High Medium Low Absent	High Medium Low Absent

Fig. 8.2 Work-needs scoring sheet

sent—in the "Picture 1" column. Complete all five needs for that story before going on to rate your second story in the "Picture 2" column, and so on. After you have completed all the stories, review the rating for the four stories and circle one of the choices for each need in the column entitled "General Tendency."

g) Reviewing the "General Tendency" column will help to determine the rank of each need. Try to select one or at most two outstanding needs.

3. *Discussing needs with team members.*

a. We suggest that the team divide itself into groups of three to discuss the information gained through the measuring of the personal needs.

b. Participants usually have a lot to say after going through the story writing and the scoring. Sometimes there are surprises.

During one session, a very quiet man discovered that he had a high need for power. In the subgroup, the discussion started at a low level and became increasingly loud. The two other members were confirming his need for power. The surprised person became increasingly defensive. With the help of the consultant, it was possible to clarify with the team member that power was *not* all bad. Teams need people to influence the behavior of others. Often suggestions motivated by power or influence will result in breakthroughs. The issue becomes—*how is the power used?*

c. We ask the participants to think through the ranking they determined to see whether or not their performance in the work situation is consistent with that ranking. They are encouraged to get the opinion of other team members.

If there is *disagreement* based on the additional observations and feelings of the team member, we suggest that the General Tendency rating be changed. People should include any general and relevant comments on the scoring sheet.

d. We ask each participant to spend a little time privately thinking about which of the five needs is his or her most prominent one, so far as work is concerned. After thinking about it, we suggest that each person record those thoughts in a notebook or journal.

e. After the private time, we reconvene the team and have an open discussion of what was learned regarding needs, including how different team members view the manner in which their coworkers' needs are seen in the work situation. Again, participants are asked to record any new insights.

4. *Heightening awareness about strongest needs.*

a. We suggest that the team divide itself into subgroups based on their strongest needs. That is, all people who are high in Affiliation should group together, all with high ratings in Power, etc. If any one person is left with no partner, we suggest that he or she join the group that is based on his or her second-highest need.

b. The participants in each subgroup are instructed to discuss the meaning of their need and how it motivates them to act. Then they are asked to find ways they often behave that might possibly be an expression of the underlying presence of that need. For example: if we are considering the Achievement need, the following kinds of feelings may be identified: discomfort when people just go on and on talking; feelings of excessive energy that must be expended by just doing or making something; or the feelings of satisfaction when some work is completed.

c. After the subgroups have some time to discuss the behavioral expressions of their dominant need, they may write these statements on newsprint. The subgroup must determine some way of expressing or acting out some key behaviors associated with the need. Some subgroups have acted out a work situation reflecting the need, but the method of expression can take any form—such as role-play, a dialogue, or doing something artistic.

d. Each subgroup presents its "creation." Following this presentation, there is a discussion of what has been learned by the team about the central needs of team members.

5. *Applying the understanding about needs and motivation to work itself.*

a. Each participant is now asked to take some time to think specifically how his or her highest ranking need is expressed in the work situation. The participant should consider both the positive and the negative ways the need shows itself. He or she should record these ideas in a notebook.

b. Then each person is asked to take a piece of newsprint and record the ways that the need motivates him or her at work. All the newsprints are taped on the walls so that all team members can read and review them. They are told to look for common themes that may lead to some back home projects on increasing motivation in the team. Team members should record these common themes in their notebooks.

c. The team reconvenes and begins to discuss the common themes. These themes are listed on separate pieces of newsprint. One list is made for negative ways that the needs affect team members and another list is made for the positive effects.

At times, we have seen how the need for Power on the part of the manager has brought out anger in many team members. The anger has resulted in the team members being willing to do only what was required and no more.

On another occasion, the high Affiliation need resulted in lowered efficiency. On a third occasion, the high Affiliation need brought frequent comments from other departments that everyone in such-and-such a department seemed to enjoy coming to work.

Frequently we find that the team reaches agreement on one or two of the most important negative and positive ways in which the needs seem to motivate action.

d. At this time we suggest that the group break into subgroups to work on the themes. Each subgroup should consider ways of implementing the changes at work that might either increase the positive ways in which the needs show themselves or reduce the negative ways. Each group must come to some clearly stated objective on how to achieve the change. Some interventions in Chapter 5 might be helpful both in reaching a clearly stated and agreed upon objective and in helping to implement that objective. (See particularly the section on Overcoming Resistance to Implementation, in Chapter 5.)

e. The following are some examples of common projects:

1) The manager of a team or department recognized a high need for Power. It was understood by almost all team members that such a need is appropriate, particularly for someone in their position. However, team members were feeling cut off from decisions and connections with other parts of the organization. The project involved setting up regular review meetings for a half hour each morning and one hourly meeting at the end of the week.

2) Another team was faced with many people with a high need for Affiliation which was interfering with getting the work done. The more Achievement-oriented members had the burden of either doing a larger share of the work or feeling great discomfort at not getting the job done. The team set up a "To do" board, which was displayed where everyone could see it. The board showed all the tasks for the week; when they had to be completed; and who was responsible for each. When larger jobs involving many members of the team were completed, the group treated themselves to some "fun" activity.

3) One team member had a strong need to have his space respected. There were two others who felt free to go into anyone's office and either borrow something or use the office for a while. The member with the high Security need was becoming less and less motivated. Once his need was recognized by the team, contracts were made between him and the other team members that they would be sure to clear with him before using his office or materials.

Variation 1

When this intervention is used in a workshop with managers from a number of companies, step 5 is changed. The managers are asked to think about their own work situations and consider the positive and negative ways in which their needs are expressed. After these are recorded in the journal or notebook, each participant thinks of ways to apply these learnings to the back-home work situation. We assist each participant in arriving at a plan.

ENRICHING JOBS OF TEAM MEMBERS

The first stages, their elements, the considerations and possibilities before deciding to help a work team create more satisfying growthful jobs for its members.

Explanatory note

This process differs from others in this book in that it describes *steps and considerations* before actually beginning the interventions.

Therefore, the steps in the process will not describe the steps of a particular intervention but will attempt to detail the different stages before beginning to work with a team on job enrichment. An example of the first interventions will be described in this chapter. It is called "The Initial Job Enrichment Intervention."

When to use

The idea to begin job enrichment with a specific team may have been initiated by:

a. An organization's management

b. The team's or department's head

c. The personnel manager

d. Suggested by a consultant

1. The management of an organization may be interested in job enrichment in the organization. After an analysis of the situation, there is a joint decision to begin the project with one particular team or department. Generally, this will be a trial project which, if successful, we hope will be initiated in other departments in the organization.

2. A team or department head approaches us—on his or her own initiative and with management's accord—seeking our help to initiate a job enrichment program with his or her team or department. Usually, the team head has received the agreement of the team members for this venture. In both these cases (request of the top management or department manager) the reasons for deciding to approach us are probably a combination of two factors:

a. *Problems and dissatisfaction.* There are problems of manpower turnover; people are leaving their jobs; people are expressing dissatisfaction with their work; there is a high rate of absenteeism; people are complaining of boredom, lack of challenge, lack of motivation; work outputs are low and ineffectiveness is rampant.

b. *Individual initiative.* Management or the team's head have heard about job enrichment and have been impressed with its potentials. They wish to give it a trial and see what benefits may be derived.

3. *Suggested by consultant.* We have been working with a work team, department, or factory for some time in training, consultation, and interventions. We came to the conclusion that it would gain much from a job enrichment program and suggested this to the team and management, and they accepted our proposal.

4. *Some initial considerations.* The initial consideration on whether to begin working with a particular team cannot be settled without some pre-

liminary interviews and observations for more data. Nevertheless, even before beginning to collect further information, we generally give thought to the following considerations:

a. Wanted by the team

b. Kind of technology

c. Measure of team autonomy (henceforth we will use the word "team" for either a department or a team)

d. Team, manager, and management support

e. Willingness to invest resources

f. Should this be the first team in the organization?

We will need to get further information on these considerations by collecting information, and only then can we make a decision. Sometimes the first interview with the team's head, or management, is sufficient for us to decide that we will not go further with this venture. In any case, we can only make a positive decision to go ahead with the project after we have finished collecting information on these questions:

a. *Wanted by team.* Does the team need job enrichment now? Or are there other basic things it must do first, such as team-building, team-effectiveness training, etc.?

b. *Kind of technology.* Is the technology the team uses in its production of the nature that allows jobs to be enriched? Maybe the technology itself needs to be changed, and this might necessitate a socio-technical intervention. If this is the case then we are facing a different problem that might require changes and resources for which the organization is not ready.

c. *Measure of team autonomy.* What leeway has the team got in deciding how it will work? How will it divide the labor? What will be the flow of its production? How does it divide authority? What control method shall be used?

If the team has little autonomy and these things are decided by higher echelons in the organization, there is little we can do.

Note: We are aware of the fact that a number of these considerations would not be accepted by some consultants. These are considerations we found suitable for the organizations with which *we* worked. We have, however, received information that in Norway, for example, job enrichment or socio-technical changes are successfully implemented from the top down. That is: a group of people from an organization (probably including the team's/department's manager, some engineers, supervisors and workers) participate in an offsite workshop. They plan the steps they will take back home in the workshop itself and then return to the factory and implement them. The workers in the team or department are not involved in planning the changes. These are prepared by the group that participated in the workshop. The changes that will take place and their rationale are explained to the people involved, and of course if they (or the union) seriously oppose them, there may be difficulties. A serious attempt is therefore made to convince the workers of the advantages. Nevertheless the concept is one of planning the changes from *outside* the team and not involving the team in planning the changes.

The process as described by us herein is one that involves the team planning the changes itself, and is suited to the type of organizations with which we have worked. We are aware that other organizations may introduce job enrichment in a way similar to the Norwegian approach.

d. *Team, manager, and management support.* Do the majority of the team members, the team's manager, and the management support this attempt to work on job enrichment? If the team's manager does not support this move, or if management is not cooperative, or a sizable number of the team's members are against it, then it is very doubtful if we should do this intervention.

e. *Willingness to invest resources.* Everybody in management and the team may be supporting the venture, but when it comes down to the practical realities of spending money or allowing the team time off for a week's workshop, difficulties arise. Are all the people involved willing to invest the resources of work, time, and money needed for this type of project?

f. *Should this be the first team in the organization?* Is this the team we should begin with? Is this the kind of team in which job enrichment will give observable results? Is this the team we would choose to begin with in that organization if we had a free choice? Is this a team that other teams in the organization would wish to follow if it shows effective changes?

5. Before beginning the second stage of collecting information, we may be of the opinion that the team does not meet the criteria given above. In such case we might suggest another intervention or training and not begin with job enrichment. We would not, however, give a definite answer before collecting all information. Should the information already in hand show us that job enrichment is *not* for that team, we would let it be known and save the organization the further expense of having us collect more information. In any case, we make no final commitment before going through the second stage of collecting information.

Who can use: Only a trained consultant.

Purposes:
1. To examine the feasibility of enriching the jobs of members of a work team/department
2. (Sometimes) to decide whether this can serve as a trial run in order to investigate job enrichment throughout the organization.

Participants: A work team, a department.

Materials and time: Vary with circumstances.

STEPS IN PROCESS

1. Collecting information
2. Deciding on general lines of action

Detailed process

1. *Collecting information*

   a. The major goals of this stage of collecting information are to:

   1) Have sufficient information to enable us to decide whether or not we shall commit ourselves to this project.

   2) Gain direct personal experience of the team at work, the work process, the work climate, the division of labor, authority, etc.

   3) Have sufficient information to enable us to roughly estimate what aspects of the team's functioning we shall focus on.

   4) Have sufficient information to enable us to roughly outline how to work with the team.

   5) Create personal contacts with the team members and gain their trust.

   b. The sources of information and methods of collecting it will vary with circumstances, from team to team. The following methods and sources will probably be included in one form or another:

   1) Personal interviews with the team members;

   2) Personal interviews with the head of the team, his or her superiors, and possibly interviews with some people from top management;

   3) Personal interviews with people from other teams and with individuals who interact a great deal with the team itself;

   4) Personal talks with specialists in the area in which the team works;

   5) Observation of the team at work.

c. The information we collect will probably include the following:

1) *The work process itself.* What materials come in? What is the transformation process, the stages in this process, and the product (outputs).

2) *The division of labor.* Who does what? Who is responsible for what? What rotation is there of responsibilities; subteams, etc.?

3) *The division of authority.* Who has authority? In what areas? To whom is he or she accountable? Who has power? Who has less power than he or she wants? Who plans? Who gets things done?

4) *The control system.* Who checks what? How do individuals get feedback on how they are doing? On what do they receive feedback? In what way? Does the team receive feedback on its output? How?

5) *Work satisfaction.* How satisfied are people with their work? Do they want to remain in their jobs or not?

6) *Factors affecting work satisfaction.* How much autonomy do people have in their jobs? How much control? How much challenge? Is there variety? Is the job monotonous or physically difficult, etc.?

7) *Managerial and supervisory style.* Is it autocratic, democratic, problem confronting, supportive, collaborative, etc.?

8) *Ways of making major decisions.* Are they team decisions, clique decisions, managerial decisions, etc. How often the whole team meets? On what?

9) *Interpersonal relations.* What is the climate of relationship in the team: conflicts and antagonisms, collaboration, trust, mutual aid, openness, cliques, difficult individuals, etc.?

10) *Information systems.* What information do team members get? How? How often?

11) *Careers.* What possibilities, advancements, career planning, studies, courses, etc. are there?

12) *Openness to change.* Is there willingness to try new ways of working together, openness to innovations, etc.

13) *Hard data.* What about the team's outputs throughout the years; labor turnover, absenteeism, etc.

14) *Expert opinion.* What is known about possible ways of reorganizing the work process; alternative work arrangements and division of work as found in similar teams, etc.?

15) *Answer to questions we put at the beginning.* Is this what the team wants? Kind of technology? Measure of team autonomy; team, manager and management support; willingness to invest resources. Should this be the first team in the organization?

2. *Deciding on general lines of action* (after collecting the information).

a. The items we may wish or have to decide on are: (1) Whether or not to commit ourselves to the project; (2) Team-building; (3) Working on interfaces (the points of connection between departments, etc.); (4) Other areas of work; (5) Using an outside expert; (6) Creating an "internal change agent" team.

1) *Whether or not to commit ourselves to the project.* Are we going to commit ourselves to this project of job enrichment with this team or are we not willing to do so? If not, does the team need other activities that we are willing to commit ourselves to? If not with this team, are we going to suggest we work on job enrichment with another team in the organization?

2) *Team-building.* Is team-building *prior* to job enrichment a condition to our agreeing to go ahead? Is it unnecessary in this particular team? Or can and should we plan a process of work with the team which will involve both elements?

3) *Working on interfaces.* Do the circumstances demand focusing attention and working on troubled interfaces; i.e., problematic points of interaction and contact between the team and other teams or individuals? Can we do this at a later stage or must we plan this before going ahead with the job enrichment interventions?

4) *Other areas of work.* Are there other areas of team functioning to which we will have to devote time? Will we need to deal with managerial style, team decision-making processes, defining the team's areas of responsibility, dividing responsibilities, establishing objectives, etc.? Will we have to do this before, while, or after dealing with job enrichment?

5) *Using an outside expert.* Should we consult with an expert on the area of work of this team? With whom can we consult and on what do we want information and advice? On different possibilities of work flow? Different divisions of work responsibilities, innovations, etc.?

6) *Creating an "internal change agent" team.* Should we begin examining the possibilities of creating a small group within the team that will be a "linking pin" or coordinating unit between us and the entire team? Its functions may need to be defined: Liaison? Coordinating our meetings with the team? Planning general strategy with us? Planning detailed interventions with us? Leading interventions? Giving us feedback, etc.?

b. The general outlines of what we intend to do as worked out by us, may include the following questions: (1) Which elements of job enrichment should we focus on? (2) What processes and interventions should we use for this? (3) What processes should we use for other purposes?

(4) What should be the sequence of interventions? (5) What should be the broad framework of our work? (6) What demands will this make on the work team and its organization? (7) What feedback system should we create?

1) *Which elements of job enrichment should we focus on?* There are different ways to enrich jobs. Not all will be suitable for this team. Which ways should we bring to the attention of the team? For instance, jobs may be enriched by: (a) Increasing autonomy and achievement in each individual's work; (b) Increasing the interest, challenge, and satisfaction in each individual's work; (c) Rotation and double jobs; (d) Promoting individual development and growth; (e) Increasing autonomy and achievement in the team's work; (f) Widening the variety and span of the team's activities; (g) Improving work conditions.

a) Increasing autonomy and achievement in each individual's work. Individuals:

  (1) Plan, do, and control their own work;
  (2) Decide on their own how they will do their job;
  (3) Decide for themselves the priority of their activities;
  (4) Fix their own work speed;
  (5) Set their own work objectives;
  (6) Check their own output;
  (7) Have full authority in their work area;
  (8) Have a longer time span of personal decision.

b) Increasing the interest, challenge, and satisfaction in each individual's work:

  (1) Each person's job allows him or her to finish something meaningful (if not the whole product).
  (2) Each job is made to include more challenging elements, more complex activities.
  (3) Each job is made to demand more skills.
  (4) The job is organized to cover a greater variety of different activities.
  (5) The day is broken up to allow the person to do different kinds of things.
  (6) The person changes his or her physical location during the day.
  (7) The person changes his or her tools and machines during the day.

c) Rotation and double jobs:

  (1) Jobs in the work cycle are rotated among team members.
  (2) The team is broken into autonomous subgroups with internal rotation.

(3) People have part-time interesting jobs outside the team.

(4) People have two professions which they alternate periodically.

(5) The person works some days each week in a different job.

d) Promoting individual development and growth:

(1) Plan the individual's work career and advancement.

(2) Promote people's participation in courses that deepen and widen their knowledge and capabilities in their work.

(3) Encourage people to learn and acquire various other skills and professional abilities not directly needed in their present work.

(4) Encourage people to learn all the different jobs in their work team.

e) Increasing autonomy and achievement in the team's work. Have work teams:

(1) Plan and control their own work.

(2) Decide on their own internal division of labor.

(3) Establish their objectives by themselves.

(4) Check their own output.

(5) Make all their own major decisions.

(6) Exercise authority in their areas of responsibility.

(7) Hold regular team meetings on all matters of importance to the team.

f) Widening the variety and span of the team's activities:

(1) The team finishes a product;

(2) The team extends its activities to include those which were formerly performed by others (activities performed *before* the team's work; e.g., market research, buying materials;)

(3) The team extends its activities to include those which were formerly performed by others (activities performed *after* the team's work; e.g., packing and selling products).

(4) The team broadens its scope to include servicing activities formerly performed by outsiders (e.g., repairing machinery);

(5) The team enriches its activities by including jobs formerly performed by experts from outside the team;

(6) The team's work includes all skills needed to finish a complete cycle (or product, if possible).

g) Improving work conditions:

(1) Improve comfort, lighting, noise level, temperature, background music, etc.

(2) Replace physically difficult or monotonous jobs with mechanization.

(3) Create work conditions that allow people to speak and interact with each other.

(4) Train supervisors to be supportive and servicing.

2) *What processes and interventions will we use for this?* By what
processes will we introduce the aspects of job enrichment on which
we will focus? Different types of job enrichment may require different processes.

We may already have developed processes for introducing some
types and we may have experience in them. For other types we
might have to develop new processes.

3) *What processes will we use for other purposes?* We shall probably
have to do some team-building and may need to introduce the team
to interpersonal competence and decision-making skills. How will
we go about doing this? Which types of process and intervention
will we use?

4) *What will be the sequence of our interventions?* Now we have a
rough idea of what we want to do and how we are going to do it.
We need to have a tentative plan of the order in which we will go
about doing things. What needs to be done first; what has priority;
what actions and interventions have to precede others; what can
wait for later? In short, we need to draw in rough sequence a list
of things we intend to do. (See Chapter 13: "Formats in using the
interventions.")

5) *What will be the broad framework of our work?* We will need to
draw in broad outlines the first estimate of what we are committing
ourselves to.

How will we work with the team? Will we begin with a workshop?
If so, then roughly for how many days?

Will we meet regularly with the work team? If yes, how often and
for how long?

Can we begin to give a rough estimate of how long the whole project will take? How many consultants from our team will be involved? How much of their time will this take? What other resources will this undertaking demand of us? Do we have them?
What's their cost?

6) *What demands will this make of the work team and its organization?* How much "work time" will the team have to spend with
us in the workshop and at meetings? What other demands does this
project make on the team and the organization? What will be the
rough cost of all this? Even if our contract is based on payment for
hours of consultation and training, the team's organization will
want a rough estimate of what it is committing itself to.

7) *What feedback mechanisms will we create?* What feedback mechanisms will we have to install:

- to follow up what changes are taking place in the team,
- to determine how effective the interventions are,
- to detect how people are feeling about what is happening,
- to sense what new problems have arisen as a result of the change,
- to determine how other teams and individuals are reacting to what is happening.

(See Chapter 12: "Feedback on Interventions.")

INITIAL JOB ENRICHMENT

The first intervention we might use to introduce job enrichment to a work-team.

When to use

We would use this intervention as the major element in a three-day offsite workshop with the entire team, including the manager.

The workshop would probably consist of three major elements:

1. The initial intervention to introduce job enrichment;
2. Team-building interventions and simulations;
3. Team effectiveness interventions and simulations.

The team-building and effectiveness elements are introduced in order to create a healthy supportive group climate and an effective orientation in the team. These two factors will enrich and fertilize the soil in the team so that the seeds of job enrichment will be planted under the right conditions and will develop a healthy, sturdy growth. Team-building and team-effectiveness training encourage and enhance job enrichment; and job enrichment, in turn, restrengthens them.

If during the interviews we discover significantly deep interpersonal conflicts, we may choose to deal with them by working for a day or so with the persons involved *before* the workshop. Team-building in the workshop will be oriented to the whole team and not to a specific interpersonal conflict.

What we learn from our interviews with the team members will determine what interventions and simulations of team-building and team effectiveness training we use.

For considerations on mixing and sequencing interventions, see Chapter 13.

Who can use: A consultant or experienced facilitator

Purposes: 1. To bring to awareness the need for job enrichment
2. To analyze the team's structure and division of jobs
3. To examine other possible structures and job divisions
4. To decide what steps to take to implement job enrichment

Participants: A work team, including supervisor

Materials: 1. Newsprint, felt pens, tape, paper and pens
2. One copy per person: "Job satisfaction and democratization," by F. Emery (optional)
3. A list of all team skills
4. Placard "Psychological job requirements" (Fig. 8.3)
5. Handout (optional) "Psychological job requirements explained"
6. Placard per person: "Estimating jobs by psychological criteria" (Fig. 8.4)
7. Placard: "Forms of team structure and task allocation" (Fig. 8.5)
8. Placard and handout per person: "Multiskilling table" (Fig. 8.6)
9. Placard and handouts: "Different ways to enrich jobs"

Time: 8 to 16 hours

STEPS IN PROCESS

1. Preparing a list of all team skills and prereading
2. Explaining placard of psychological job requirements
3. Examining if team members' jobs satisfy psychological requirements
4. Lecturette and discussion on different forms of team structure and task allocation
5. Examining team members' skill competences
6. "Different ways to enrich jobs" displayed and explained
7. Subgroups discuss ways of enriching jobs in the team
8. Team hears recommendations and makes implementation decisions

---

1. *Decision-making:* The need for some minimal area of decision-making that the individual can call his or her own.
2. *Learning:* The need for being able to learn on the job and go on learning.
3. *Optimal variety:* The need for the content of a job to be reasonably demanding in terms other than sheer endurance while providing a minimum of variety (not necessarily novelty).
4. *Mutual support and respect:* The need for some minimal degree of social support and recognition in the workplace.
5. *Meaningfulness:* The need to be able to relate what you do and what you produce to your social life.
6. *Desirable future:* The need to feel that the job leads to some sort of desirable future (not necessarily promotion).

Fig. 8.3 Psychological job requirements (Adapted from Trist, Eric, "A Socio-Technical Critique of Scientific Management," Department of Organization Behavior and Ecology, University of Pennsylvania. Unpublished paper, 1970.)

Detailed Process*

1. *Preparing a list of all team skills and prereading.*

   a. Prior to the workshop we meet the team supervisor and one or more experienced team members. We draw up with the supervisor a list of all the skills involved in doing the team's work, including those of the supervisor. We check this list with one or two more experienced members of the team and add items, change items, delete items, and rearrange the list in an organized fashion, grouping similar items.

   b. If possible, participants should read, before the workshop, the article "Job satisfaction and democratization," in Emery's *Democracy at Work* (see recommended readings).

2. *Explaining placard of psychological job requirements.* We display the placard of psychological needs that determine job satisfaction (Fig. 8.3). We explain that these were found to be major factors affecting job satisfaction in different work cultures.

---

* We had for some years been using a job enrichment process similar to the one described here. We came across the ideas of Fred Emery and Merrelyn Emery and found that their approach was similar to ours. We incorporated in our process parts of their process that we found valuable, and are therefore deeply indebted to them. The "Psychological job requirements" explanations and some of the "Forms of team structure" are taken from Fred Emery; the "Multi-skilling table" and method of examining whether jobs satisfy "Psychological job requirements" are taken from Merrelyn Emery. We are indebted to P. G. Herbst for ideas on structure and some of the "Forms of team structure." The "Psychological job requirements" are from Eric Trist.

We may add the following six items which we adapted from Fred Emery. They may be distributed to the participants as a handout, if that is desired.

Psychological job requirements explained:

1. *Decision-making:* Adequate elbow room. You should be able to have a sense that you are your own boss and that you do not have a superior breathing down your neck unless the circumstances are exceptional. But not so much elbow room that you just don't know what to do.

2. *Learning:* Chances of learning on the job and going on learning. We accept that such learning is possible only when people are able to set goals that are reasonable challenges for them and get a feedback of results in time for them to correct their behavior.

3. *Optimal variety:* An optimal level of variety. You should be able to vary the work to avoid boredom and fatigue and to develop a satisfying rhythm of work.

4. *Mutual support and respect:* Conditions in which you can and do get help and respect from your co-workers. Avoid conditions in which it is to no person's interest to lift a finger to help another; in which people are pitted against each other so that "one's gain is another's loss; or in which the group interest denies the individual's abilities or inabilities.

5. *Meaningfulness:* A sense that one's own work meaningfully contributes to social welfare. You should not have to feel that your job could as well be done by a trained monkey or an industrial robot machine; or that it is something that society would probably be better served by not having done at all, or at least by not having it done so shoddily.

6. *Desirable future:* Quite simply, not a dead-end job; hopefully one that will continue to allow personal growth.

Team members now discuss the psychological job requirements and their attitude and feelings about them.

3. *Examining whether team members' job satisfy psychological job requirements.* The team now gets down to a concrete examination of how the various jobs of the team members satisfy the psychological requirements.

In a team in which the jobs can be clearly broken up into a number of classes or skill groupings, the group can work on these together. The classes of jobs or skill groupings are listed lengthwise along the top row of a placard and the psychological job requirements are listed in a column on the left (see Fig. 8.4).

The team's objective is to estimate each class of job by every one of the criteria. This is done on a scale of 1 to 10 (10 is most ample; 1 is most insufficient) or on a scale of $-0+$ to indicate "insufficient, adequate, ample."

Psychological Criteria	Class of Job or Skill Grouping			
	Typist	Filing clerk	Receptionist	Accountant
Decision-making	2	1	7	9
Variety optimal	4	2	5	6
Learning	3	1	6	8
Mutual support and respect	3	3	0	0
Meaningfulness	3	1	5	7
Desirable future	4	2	2	9

Fig. 8.4 Estimating jobs by psychological criteria [From Merrelyn Emery, "Participative Design Seminars: A Description," in Emery, Fred, *Democracy at Work* (see recommended readings).]

If the team has a complicated and intricate division of work that cannot be broken up into conventional skill groupings or classes of jobs, an alternative way of estimating jobs by psychological criteria is to list the names of team members instead of classes of jobs, and to estimate how each person is satisfied in his or her present job by each of the criteria (using the same 1 to 10 or $-0+$ scale).

If we are dealing with a team of over eight people, this scoring may be done by subgroups on suitably prepared sheets of paper and later transferred to newsprint for all to see.

When the scoring is done, team members comment on the results and discuss their implications.

Note: Figure 8.4 has been completed to show how it should be done. Of course, the placard or handouts you use should have no entries on the right-hand side, for those are to be provided by the team members.

4. *Lecturette and discussion of different forms of team structure and task allocation.* We now put up the placard illustrating different forms of team structure and task allocation (Fig. 8.5). We explain:

a. *Bureaucratic-Hierarchical:* Control and coordination are done by the supervisor.

1) The supervisor specifies what each individual (A, B, C, etc.) will do vis-à-vis the task allotted to him or her (X, Y, Z, etc.).

2) The team's achievements are attributed to the supervisor's ability to control and coordinate.

3) The tasks of team members are specified by norms and rules.

4) Each man's competence is one specialized task.

5) The assumption is that the environment is stable.

1. *Bureaucratic — Hierarchical*

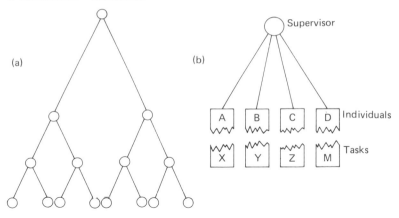

2. *Autonomous Work Team*

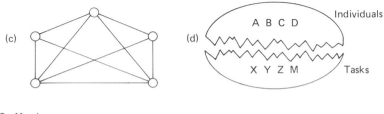

3. *Matrix*

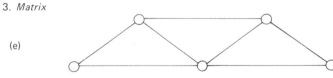

Fig. 8.5 Forms of team structure and task allocation [Parts (a), (c), and (e) are from Herbst, Philip G., "Non-Hierarchical Forms of Organization," *Acta Sociologica* **19**, 1 (1976); parts (b) and (d) are from Emery, Fred, *Democracy at Work* (see recommended readings).]

6) The structure is rigid and difficult to change.

7) Job-related communication is through the supervisor.

b. *Autonomous Work Team:* Control and coordination are shared by team members.

1) Members A, B, C, etc., share and allocate amongst themselves the requirements for control and coordination of their task-related activities, X, Y, Z. They are also responsible for task interdependencies.

2) Each person in the team can perform all tasks. They may be rotated as needed. When people are absent others can replace

them. When there are work loads the team can be organized accordingly.

3) The assumption is that the environment is in constant change.

4) The structure is flexible and can be adapted as needed to task requirements.

5) Communication is direct, person to person.

c. *Matrix:*

1) Control and coordination are shared by group members.

2) Members share and allocate among themselves the requirements for control and coordination.

3) Each man in the team has a specialized task, together with overlapping competence with other members.

4) The assumption is that the environment is in constant change.

5) A basic structure is given by the pattern of overlapping competencies, but within this a variety of structures may be adopted.

6) Communication is direct, person to person.

We now ask the team members which team structure would most suit a task allocation to give maximum satisfaction to team members of their psychological needs. The team discusses this subject and clarifies the differences between the three forms of team structure and between each form and the team's present structure.

5. *Examining team members' skill competencies.* If the team wishes to progress in the direction of a more flexible structure, either as an autonomous work group or a matrix structure, it will need *multiskilling* and *overlapping competences* of team members.

We will now examine the present position of overlapping competencies and multiskilling in the team for two purposes:

- To see what freedom this allows the team in replanning jobs.
- To see what training needs exist which will enable the team to create greater freedom and choice in planning jobs in the future.

We now hand out to each team member the page of team skills prepared by us with the supervisor and others before the team meeting (Fig. 8.6). The skills are written on the left column and members' names are listed along the top row. If people wish to add skills that were omitted, these are now added to the list.

The team now breaks up into subgroups, and each subgroup has to consider a certain number of skills and mark which members have them. The combined marking of all the groups is then transferred to a prepared placard (Fig. 8.4).

Skills \ Names	David	Joe	Ed	Ron	Mel	Sam
a	√	√		+	+	+
b	√	+	√	√	√	√
c		√	√	√	√	√
d	+	√	√			+
e	√	+				
f	√			√	+	+
g	+	√	√	+	√	+
h	√	√		+	+	

Fig. 8.6 Multi-skilling table (an example)

Note: It is possible to arrive at a skills list working together in the workshop instead of organizing it beforehand. This takes time, of course, but has its payoff as a combined team effort.

We give a simple working definition to the word "skill": A skill is a specific work activity that in order to be done effectively needs the relevant *experience* and *know-how*. People often say they have the know-how without sufficient experience in performing a particular skill. It is possible in such cases to agree on a particular symbol to signify this. We use a plus (+) sign to signify "Know-how *without* experience," and a (√) sign to signify "has the skill" that is, know-how and experience.

An alternative way of doing the marking is for each of the participants to do the marking on their own, and later to transfer it themselves to the prepared placard. This, of course, means that each person decides what his or her own skills are without hearing the opinion of others.

A third way to do this is to have each person mark his or her own skills and then have the team break up into small subgroups that examine each person's markings and suggest changes and corrections.

People are given time to absorb the list and discuss its implications: Who needs training in more skills? Which team members need training in what specific skills? Which skills are known to only one or two people, which others must acquire? Who has few skills and needs to widen his or her range of skills? In general, has the team sufficient multi-skilling and overlapping competency to allow it to be flexible in dividing up work, rotating jobs, and changing internal structure?

6. Different ways to enrich jobs displayed and explained. We now put up a placard which we prepared beforehand showing different ways of enriching jobs.

This list is one we prepared by taking from the long list titled: *Which elements of job enrichment should we focus on?* (See page 230.) We chose only elements that are *suitable* for the particular team we are working with. The list we display might contain all suggestions from the complete, detailed list, or, generally, only some of them that might be applicable to this team.

Members are also given handouts of this list. We explain the items briefly one by one. Questions are answered and items which are not clear are clarified.

7. *Subgroups discuss ways of enriching jobs in the team.* The team is now broken up into subgroups. Each subgroup takes a number of suggestions from the job enrichment list and examines them to see whether any can and should be made applicable to their team. When doing this, the subgroup should bear in mind the estimation of jobs by psychological criteria (Fig. 8.4) and the Multi-skilling table (Fig. 8.6).

Each suggestion for change should be examined in terms of:

a. Its contribution to job satisfaction of team members,

b. Its effects on productivity,

c. Its feasibility in terms of multi-skilling;

d. The skill training it will involve,

e. Job allocation changes it will lead to,

f. Changes in team structure it will involve,

g. Changes it will lead to in the way team members work together,

h. Resources (costs, investments, time) it will demand.

Each subgroup prepares recommendations of changes suggested in connection with the items from the job enrichment list it is considering. These are prepared on newsprint.

8. *Team hears recommendations and makes implementation decisions.* The entire team reconvenes. Each subgroup refers to its newsprint and explains its recommendations.

a. Items that are agreed upon by the entire team are ratified as decisions or as *conditional trial* decisions.

b. Items that need further information and thinking out are transferred to a "job enrichment subteam" chosen for the purpose.

c. Items over which there are differences of opinion are also transferred to this subteam if they cannot be easily settled by the entire team.

d. The job enrichment team is also to begin to organize the active implementation of decisions.

e. Dates are fixed for reporting on implementation, progress, and discussion of the job enrichment team's proposals.

DEVELOPING AN INTERPROFESSIONAL TEAM

Selecting and training a cross-section of people from the organization to deal with complicated problems that have social, technical, and structural implications.

When to use

There is a growing interest in using the thinking and skills of varied professionals working on the same organizational problem. We have developed some different and less elaborate uses growing out of the thinking and action referred to as socio-technical approach. We have used the approach in working on problems and planning changes in a plant locker room, reorganizing a production system, and revising the operations of a whole company. Work in Norway has gone as far as reorganizing total industries. We will use social-technical to differentiate from the more narrowly used phrase, socio-technical. We have found that the interpersonal team can only be introduced after considerable basic work in team and organizational development. We are aware of the fact that in Scandinavia the experts would differ with us on that issue. Some of the factors that must be looked at to determine whether or not to develop such a team would include:

1. The social and technical parts of the unit or department where the intervention might be made must be clearly differentiated from the rest of the organization.

2. What goes into and comes out of the operation of this unit must be easily defined and measurable.

3. The initial application should have a high chance of success.

4. There should be chances of a high degree of "ripple" effect; that is, effect on other parts of the organization.

5. There should be a sufficiently high degree of interest in experimentation among the employees who are involved.

6. There should be sufficient complexity in the situation in which the interprofessional team will operate, or the use of such a wide range of talent will be questioned.

Such an interprofessional team has usefulness either working on previously identified problems or as a "think tank" which can review the organization and detect problems that are interdepartmental and demand both social and technical changes. These may be problems with government regulatory agencies, municipal organizations, interest groups, etc.

We have found that the way such a group thinks can break through barriers. It may, for example, come up with ways of looking at a supply problem that is *different* from approaches suggested by purchasing people.

In one organization, we set up a series of interprofessional subgroups to work with all departments in the organization in detecting the inter-departmental problems. While many of the problems were similar to ones that the departments detected without such a team, there were a number of very significant problems that were found as a result of the special kind of thinking such a team brings to a unit.

There are much broader applications of the interprofessional approach. Those readers interested in the more complex applications are referred to the efforts of the Work Research Institute in Norway or the writings of Eric Trist.* We are suggesting a use that is in the grasp of an informed manager with the aid of consultants to organizations.

Who can use: Only consultants to organizations

Purposes: 1. To detect interdepartmental problems that may not be recognized by regular department members
2. To identify and think through unique problem solutions that are creative, technically sound, and efficient
3. To make the organization aware of issues that go beyond its boundaries and into the community that surrounds the organization

Participants: Selected managers and other employees from within the organization who represent different departments and different professional backgrounds

Materials: 1. Newsprint, felt pens, tape, pencil and paper
2. Materials needed for steps 2, 3, 4, and 5 of "Basic steps in team development," in Chapter 6.
3. Materials needed for steps 1, 2, and 3 of "Confronting your learning style," in Chapter 3.
4. Interprofessional Team Matrix (Fig. 8.7)

Time: 16 hours to point of working on pilot project; beyond that point, time very variable

---

*   See Trist, E. L., "On Socio-Technical Systems," in *The Planning of Change,* edited by Bennis, W. G., K. D. Benne, and R. Chin (New York: Holt, Rinehart & Winston, 1969).

Detailed process

1. *Organizing a small temporary planning team.* The idea of an interprofessional team may come from anyone in the organization; however, in order for it to be accepted and encouraged, we have found that a top executive must be behind it. In our experience, a combined social and technical intervention can gain acceptance only after basic work in team and organizational development has been introduced to the organization. Other specialists in the field have been successful without such preparation.

The planning team may be comprised of the top executive and members of the personnel department or it can be the members of the executive group or committee.

An explanation of the interprofessional concept used to work on social and technical operations should be presented. The essential ideas that we include are as follows:

a. Firstly, what is a social-technical system? It is the joint operation of two major aspects of work life: the social part is made up of people who do the work, and the technical part includes the tools, techniques, and the structural division of work; that is, the way the work is divided among the employees involved.

b. The social-technical system does not operate in a vacuum, but continually influences and is influenced by the environment or situation in which the work system operates.

c. Looking at the work system as having two main parts which interact can provide a useful way of analyzing and designing work as well as of detecting some of the central problems that may arise in and around the work.

d. In thinking about work units as social and technical systems, we recognize that there are different ways of thinking associated with different kinds of work and professions. The engineer thinks and problem-solves with a step-by-step logic; he or she sets a plan and goes to work. The marketing or sales specialist is thinking of the reactions of people to each idea; he or she will change an approach quickly to meet the immediate demands. The personnel type will get lost in the personal needs of a worker and forget that the work has to be done.

While these generalizations do not exactly fit all the engineers, sales people, and personnel specialists, we have found that there is a sufficient similarity to warrant such statements. *The interprofessional team must have the thinking of different types of people who make decisions in the organization.*

e. When working by social and technical principles, the organization must allow *experimenting* (trying things out) under rather protected conditions. Management should be prepared to allow some ideas to be tested so that they can be studied; as useful and effective methods emerge they can be applied more extensively in the organization. Not enough time for experimenting and/or too early application to the rest of the organization can kill the approach.

f. The organization requires a certain degree of openness. As indicated earlier, we prefer not to introduce the approach described here until there has been extensive prework in the basics of team and organizational development.

g. It is vital that the people who will be involved in the changes will be part of developing the change. We recognize that not everyone can be involved at all points. However, everyone must be thought of and approaches developed to include all appropriate people in the organization during the suitable stages.

After presenting this explanation, we now ask the planning group to think through two considerations:

- What should be the purposes of such an interprofessional team?
- According to the purposes, what essential subgroups (departments) and functions must be represented in this team?

The group members go through a brainstorming of possible ways interprofessional teams could operate: as a think-tank, a problem-solver, a generator of new ideas; as a training experience for developing generalists for the organization; to bring about social and technical change in a department in the organization; etc.

After the brainstorming, the planning group tries to narrow down the choices through consensus decision-making. During this process, many issues and needs of the organization may surface. The facilitator must help the planning group stay with the objective of defining the purposes of the interprofessional team. Quite often, the planning group identifies a broad purpose or purposes with the idea that the interprofessional team itself should have a chance to become more specific.

2. *Selection of the members of the interprofessional team.* The membership question is always a sticky one. This kind of team or special group (particularly if it is a first of its kind) gets a lot of attention within the organization. We suggest that initially, very little attention and status should be given to this team. We also suggest no publicity.

There are certain categories of members that we suggest, and then we ask the planning group to add more. The categories we suggest include:

- Representatives of all major functions, such as production, finance, engineering, marketing, personnel.
- A mixture of women and men.
- Specialists in communication.
- People with formal power in organization.
- People with informal power in the organization.

We have found that there should be a core of from six to nine people, and the inclusion of other interested employees could bring the group up to as many as 20 people. The other interested employees are involved as needed for special inputs or projects. Ideally, all people who have any involvement in the process should have had a workshop on basic steps in team development.

An "Interprofessional team matrix" (Fig. 8.7) is constructed on the basis of the information generated with the planning group. The matrix is drawn on newsprint paper. The functions or characteristics are listed on the column on the extreme left, and the names of people in the organization who fit the description are listed in the columns to the right.

Each member of the planning group is asked to list the names of the people he or she thinks would have the best qualifications for membership in such a team. The planners should privately list those names. Then, each planner reads his or her list and the names are recorded on the matrix. The group discusses the names and decides which nine people will be invited to the first organizational meeting of the interprofessional team. The planners must choose the nine people who can bring the widest range of characteristics to the team. Thus, if one person is a woman, a specialist in communication, and in personnel, she covers three categories.

The invitations should be made informally by the top executive or his or her designate. The potential member should fully realize that this is a voluntary position, that if the team does not gel there may have to be some replacements, that the first meeting is just an organizing meeting, and that all invitees have the right to withdraw if they are not interested.

3. *The first interprofessional team meeting.* The major purpose of this first meeting is to acquaint the potential members with the interprofessional approach to social and technical operations and the process that the planning group has completed. Thus, we organize the meeting in the following manner:

Functions and Characteristics	Suggestions by Members of Planning Group				
	Planner 1	Planner 2	Planner 3	Planner 4	Final Choices
1. Production					
2. Finance					
3. Engineering					
4. Marketing					
5. Personnel					
6. Women					
7. Communication specialist					
8. Formal power people					
9. Informal power people					
10. Troubleshooter type					
11.					
12.					

Fig. 8.7 Interprofessional team matrix

a. Explanation and discussion of the interprofessional concept. See step 1 of this process.

b. Displaying the Interprofessional Team Matrix with all of the suggested names and the names of the people who were finally chosen.

c. Discussion of the kinds of people included in the team.

d. Finally, the results of the planning groups' view of the need for such a team are presented and discussed.

After this experience, the invitees are asked to think over the whole idea and decide whether or not they would like to continue. They should recognize that such work is above and beyond their usual work assignment. Working with this group might require some extra time for special development sessions. The benefits of personal and professional growth to each person should be identified. The value to the company should also be indicated.

Usually, we find that there is acceptance by the people who have been initially invited. If not, then the planning group should consider replacements, getting help from interprofessional team members. Most people who were suggested and did *not* become team members are additional resource people and are called on as needed.

4. *Workshop in team development with interprofessional team.* We find that steps 2, 3, 4, and 5 of the "Basic steps in team development" (see Chapter 6) are important beginning points. It may well be that members of the team will have experienced such training. The work should be modified to fit the experience of the team members.

Two other experiences should be included: (a) Developing the purposes and goals of the interprofessional team; and (b) "Confronting your learning style" (see Chapter 3).

    a. *Development of purposes and goals of the interprofessional team*

    1) Each team member is asked to write down what she or he thinks could be accomplished by the team.

    2) Team members should pair and discuss the ideas, trying to reach some agreement on the best two or three possibilities.

    3) The team comes together and discusses all the suggestions. Some effort is made to find at least one idea that everyone agrees with.

    4) Before the end of the workshop, a subgroup should be selected to consider all of the suggestions for a report at a future meeting.

    5) Some issues that emerge in this session often include: How will team leadership be handled? What will be the group's approach to problem-solving and decision-making? etc.

    b. *"Confronting your learning style"*

    1) Before the end of the workshop, we like the members of the team to become more aware of the differences in their styles. In an interprofessional team the differences are even more visible.

    2) Steps 1, 2, and 3 of "Confronting your learning styles" (see Chapter 3) can be followed as written.

    3) At the completion of step 3, we suggest a discussion on how the different styles will help and interfere with the functioning of the Team. The positives and negatives should be recorded on newsprint. After the session, the lists should be copied and distributed to team members.

5. *Identifying the initial pilot project(s).* At the meeting following the workshop, the report of the subgroup on purposes and goals is considered. After listening to the report, the team brainstorms various types of projects that might fit its purposes. A list of criteria for selecting the best projects is made. Frequently used criteria include: realistic, accomplishable within a relatively short period of time, low budget, visible to other employees, etc. We suggest that the purpose statement remain in force for no more

than six months, and that, at the end of that time, the purposes, actions, and membership be reviewed.

In the beginning effort, we sometimes find it useful to agree that the Team will be dissolved and reconstituted so that members can easily drop out or be dropped out if things have not worked well.

One team decided to set up a series of projects. The thinking went: "We want everyone involved. We should find a series of small projects in the organization to test our methods." After identifying the projects the group divided itself among the projects and found other co-workers who could give the additional social or technical input. Each subgroup designed and carried out its project. Such an approach mainly tests the effectiveness and usefulness of people who think differently.

A more orderly way of handling the approach is to select one project that the total team is involved in. Certain members are in the action team, that is, the direct implementers of the project, and others are providing special assistance and advice.

6. *Working on the pilot project(s).* Once the team has identified the project(s), the necessary agreements must be gained. The project must be considered by the top decision-making body as an appropriate task, as well as one that will fit into the operation of the organization. After that level of agreement, the specific section or work unit which will be the target of change must be presented with the idea.

a. The process must be explained to the decision-makers of the unit.

b. Appropriate members of that department must be involved in all steps of the project.

c. We have found it essential to do some team-building between the interprofessional team and the members of the target department or work area.

d. With each phase of the project, a report back to the team is scheduled. In this way, the process can be followed and the advice and direct help of some team members can be readily obtained.

e. At times, we have found that external consultants are necessary for certain phases of design or evaluation. The team meeting is a place for the discussion and selection of such consultants.

7. *Working on the "ripple" effect throughout the organization.* As suggested earlier, we feel that the team should have an established life of about six months. Thus, the choice of projects must be limited to a period somewhat less than six months.

There are certain steps which might be taken to achieve a ripple effect during the implementation period. These steps may include meetings with top executives, meetings and work with relevant departments concerning the project, and use of other resource people.

We suggest a review of the project with the top executives. At this time, the results are carefully looked at to determine whether or not there were any practical benefits and whether these might prove useful in other parts of the organization.

In one organization, the benefits suggested and supported the idea of establishing an operating committee which would deal with the day-to-day problems of the organization. When it was established, it seemed to free the top executives from feeling they had to run the business. It allowed them to become more active in long-term planning.

If the project seems to have more general use, the team may be reconstituted with the same or somewhat changed membership. After appropriate team building, it can begin to look for other projects.

Often many projects are identified while working on the first project. People from other departments have either helped with some part of the project or have heard about it. They may have voiced an interest to some member of the team.

The newly constituted team must then review all of the possible projects and choose the one which is the next best step toward building a more interprofessional orientation into the organization.

Once this process has been instituted effectively, it has a good chance of fanning out into the organization as a whole. When this occurs, special resources must be provided by the personnel or human resources development group. But generally, most of the manpower comes directly from the regular work forces.

Team
effectiveness

To present a number of interventions aimed at increasing effectiveness by having a team examine how it is functioning and seeking ways to function more effectively.

GUIDE TO APPLYING INTERVENTIONS

What is team effectiveness?

- The basic idea behind team effectiveness interventions is that a team can learn how to function more effectively in the future if it takes a good look at *how* it is functioning in the present.
- "How it is functioning" means: the ways it does things, how it makes decisions, how it performs its responsibilities, how it conducts its meetings.
- The assumptions underlying this approach are that a team is capable of becoming more aware of the way it functions and can understand the basic dimensions of effective and ineffective ways of functioning.
- When a team becomes aware of these ways of functioning, it can take practical steps to function more effectively and avoid ineffective ways of doing things.

- The principle guiding this approach is that of a system monitoring itself by getting feedback on how it is doing. This is the same approach used by many therapeutic schools: To increase a person's awareness of how he or she is functioning gives that person greater freedom of choice about how to function in the future.

- Help a team become aware of how it is functioning. Provide the team with a set of relevant concepts with which to understand and evaluate the way it is functioning, and the team will find ways to improve its effectiveness.

- The basic ideas guiding this approach were developed by Edgar S. Schein of M.I.T., and are known as "process consultation."

- A commonly accepted way of doing process consultation is for an outside observer to give the team feedback on its functioning processes. In the interventions described in this chapter the team itself is its own "process observer." On the basis of its own observations and evaluations, the team decides what changes it wishes to make in its way of functioning.

About the interventions in this chapter

The interventions described in this chapter are all built on the same principle, which is described above. The team is provided with a method, a technique, concepts and evaluative procedures to observe its way of functioning. After understanding and working with these tools the team decides what action to take to increase its effectiveness.

We generally use these interventions when working with teams in workshops, but they can also be used as part of a series of short regular meetings with a team.

These interventions are especially suitable for management teams. With suitable variations they can be used with other teams, such as work teams and committees.

The interventions

1. *What is hindering effectiveness?* We use this intervention probably more than any other in this book. It is versatile and can be applied to many purposes: diagnosis, the learning of essential concepts, developing awareness of the team's way of functioning, monitoring improvements in functioning, guiding the facilitator in choosing what to focus on, etc. It can be used with all sorts of groups, teams, or departments. It can be used at the beginning, middle, or end of a workshop. It raises hardly any resistance. The process was developed around the Rating Group Effectiveness Questionnaire, proposed by Edgar Schein in his book on Process Consultation (see Recommended Readings).

2. *Are we doing what we should be doing?* This was developed specifically for top management teams, after we discovered that some of them were not doing what they should. The ideas guiding us in creating this intervention were drawn from Peter Drucker's concepts of the functions of management and the idea of "the turbulent environment" drawn from Terrebery's, *Causal Texture of Organizational Environments.*

3. *Improving practical aspects of team functioning.* We developed this in answer to the requests of many teams we worked with. People asked us to help improve the practical aspects of their team meetings. They asked for our assistance in changing outdated procedures and introducing more creative, involving, effective, and practical ways of running their meetings.

MATRIX OF INTERVENTIONS

Intervention	Use	Who can use	Time demand
What is hindering effectiveness?	Diagnosing what factors of a team's functioning require attention	Anyone	2–6 hrs
"Are we doing what we should be doing?"	Deciding what management should change in what it is doing	Consultant or facilitator; manager not with his or her own team	Excluding prework, 2–6 hrs
Improving practical aspects of team functioning	Making team meetings more effective	Facilitator; manager	2–4 hrs

Possible outcomes

1. Achieving a common set of concepts by which to evaluate team functioning.
2. Understanding what needs to be worked on to increase effectiveness.
3. Increased overall effectiveness of team functioning.
4. Better teamwork.
5. Introduction of a permanent form of monitoring team functioning.
6. More effective decision-making.
7. Management doing what it should be doing.
8. Management focusing on essentials.
9. More pre-thought and more planning.
10. Greater survival capability in a changing environment.
11. More initiatives from management.

12. More pro-action and less reaction.
13. Matters more under control, fewer surprises and unexpected crises.
14. More effective meetings.
15. More time in meetings for basic organizational problems.
16. More involvement and commitment in meetings.
17. More implemented decisions.
18. Higher satisfaction with meetings.

Recommended readings

1. Schein, E. H., *Process Consultation: Its Role in OD* (Reading, Mass.. Addison-Wesley, 1969).
2. Drucker, P. F., *The Effective Executive* (New York: Harper & Row, 1966).

WHAT IS HINDERING EFFECTIVENESS?

Helping a team become aware of the major factors which determine a team's effectiveness. Pinpointing which of these factors is hindering the team's effectiveness and need to be worked on.

When to use

This one of the interventions we use most widely. We have seldom found teams that did not benefit from it. The value of the process is that it gives us *a set of accepted terms* in common with the team members, as well as a list of *goals* the team wishes to achieve in order to increase it effectiveness.

At the end of the process, team members achieve a relatively acceptable understanding of some of the most essential concepts of group process. More than that, they come to accept the need for improving the performance of their team according to the standards set by these concepts.

We therefore generally go through this process in the first or second day of working with a team. We find that the process guides us in deciding which *aspects* of the team's functioning we will focus on in *future* training. Going through the process also gives *legitimacy* to other training activities which we shall be doing later with the team.

At the end of managers' workshops, participants give a high rating to this process as a way of helping the team increase its effectiveness.

We find the process valuable in helping work teams of different kinds to attain the same goals set for management teams. We achieve a common language of concepts, an accepted set of goals and standards which the team wishes to attain, a guideline for working with the team, and legitimacy and support for working in such areas of team functioning as need improvement.

As will be later explained in detail, we use a questionnaire to suit the type of team we are working with. Thus, a committee will not be working on the same set of concepts that we would give, say, to a work group.

This process can also be used in an individual manager's workshop, but only toward the end of the workshop. If the participants have worked in subgroups, it is preferable they go through the process in the subgroup and evaluate the subgroup as their team. In this context the purpose of the process will be to help the participants become familiar with the major factors influencing their team's effectiveness back home. In this sense, it will be more of a learning experience than a team intervention.

Who can use:
1. Anybody who follows the instructions
2. Teams without a facilitator who just follow the written instructions but are led by a team member other than the manager

Purposes:
1. To help a team understand and agree on major factors that influence a team's effectiveness
2. To bring out into open confrontation differences between team members regarding areas of team functioning that hinder effectiveness
3. To pinpoint and agree on which of these factors need working on to improve the team's effectiveness

Participants: A team of any kind; especially useful for management teams and committees; can be suited to individual stranger managers in a workshop; in teams of preferably not more than 14 people

Materials:
1. Newsprint, felt pens, tape, pens
2. "Team Effectiveness" questionnaire for each participant
3. Newsprint for "Team Effectiveness" rating

Time: 2 to 6 hours (depending on which method will be used)

STEPS IN PROCESS

1. Introduction and explaining questionnaire

2. Filling out questionnaires and recording results

3. Discussion of results

4. Deciding which items to work on

Detailed process

1. *Introduction and explaining questionnaire.* The facilitator can introduce this process by elaborating on the points under the heading of "purposes." He or she can also connect the experience with requests probably received to help the team function more effectively, explaining that in order to function more effectively the team needs first to become aware of the factors that contribute to, or hinder, a team's functioning. More than that, the team should agree which factors in particular need to be worked on in their own team.

We generally point out that the list we will soon be presenting is the distillation of much research and scientific effort in the field of group dynamics over recent years.

A: Goals

Poor	1	2	3	4	5	6	7	8	9	10	Good

Confused; diverse; conflicting; indifferent; little interest.

Clear to all; shared by all; all care about the goals, feel involved.

B: Participation

Poor	1	2	3	4	5	6	7	8	9	10	Good

Few dominate; some passive; some not listened to; several talk at once or interrupt.

All get in; all are really listened to.

C: Feelings

Poor	1	2	3	4	5	6	7	8	9	10	Good

Unexpected; ignored or criticized.

Freely expressed; empathic responses.

D: Diagnosis of group problems

Poor	1	2	3	4	5	6	7	8	9	10	Good

Jump directly to remedial proposals; treat symptoms rather than basic causes.

When problems arise the situation is carefully diagnosed before action is proposed; remedies attack basic causes.

Fig. 9.1 Team effectiveness questionnaire [From Schein, Edgar H., *Process Consultation: Its Role in Organizational Development* (Reading, Mass.: Addison-Wesley, 1969), pp. 42–43. Used by permission.]

E: Leadership

Poor	1	2	3	4	5	6	7	8	9	10	Good

Group needs for leadership not met; group depends too much on single person or on a few persons.	As needs for leadership arise various members meet them ("distributed leadership"); anyone feels free to volunteer as he sees a group need.

F: Decisions

Poor	1	2	3	4	5	6	7	8	9	10	Good

Needed decisions don't get made; decisions made by part of group; others uncommitted.	Consensus sought and tested; deviates appreciated and used to improve decision; decisions when made are fully supported.

G: Trust

Poor	1	2	3	4	5	6	7	8	9	10	Good

Members distrust one another; are polite, careful, closed, guarded; they listen superficially but inwardly reject what others say; are afraid to criticize or to be criticized.	Members trust one another; they reveal to group what they would be reluctant to expose to others; they respect and use the responses they get; they can freely express negative reactions without fearing reprisal.

H: Creativity and growth

Poor	1	2	3	4	5	6	7	8	9	10	Good

Members and group in a rut; operate routinely; persons stereotyped and rigid in their roles; no progress.	Group flexible, seeks new and better ways; individuals changing and growing; creative; individually supported.

Fig. 9.1 (cont.)

We hand out the "Team effectiveness" questionnaires to the team members and ask each member to read them on his or her own (Fig. 9.1). When the team members have read the questionnaires, they often raise questions about the meanings of concepts or sentences which we answer to the best of our ability. We value this questioning, as it clarifies essential concepts and goals of group functioning.

2. *Filling out questionnaires and recording results.* When everyone has finished reading, we explain that each person will now be requested to mark on the questionnaire how he or she sees this team functioning according to each criterion on the questionnaire. We add that we know it is difficult to give numbered scores. If a person thinks the team requires no change on a particular criterion, then he or she can give it the maximum number of points; if it's very bad, minimum points; if medium, toward the middle of the range, and so on.

Filling the questionnaire can be done in either of two ways: each person at his or her own pace, or each question in turn by all team members at the same time. We tend to do it the second way. In the first way we found that when a person asked questions on a certain point while others were concentrating on something else, this seemed to be disruptive and distracting.

The way we now do it is to ask a person with a clear voice to read out both sides of the first line, whereupon everyone marks down the score on his or her questionnaire. If there are problems of meaning, they can be clarified before moving on to the next question. When all the team members have scored themselves, the second question is read out, and so on. We have found this procedure allows better concentration, greater clarification, and less distraction than the first way.

We explicitly request participants not to discuss or debate scores until we have finished filling in the questionnaire. We explain that at this stage we would like to receive each individual estimation uninfluenced by others.

Almost every time we have worked with a team on the questionnaire we have run into the problems of statements with two variables. Let us explain: Some statements contain two or three sentences. A team member often says that by the criteria of one sentence he or she would give the team a high mark, but by the other sentence, a low mark. What should one do? For example, someone might remark that the goals (the first item) appear to be "clear to all," but that only two or three people really feel "involved." How, then, should this question be scored? We are aware that this problem applies to a number of statements in the questionnaire. We usually answer that people should take into account all the sentences in one statement and score accordingly.

While the team members are filling in the questionnaire, we put up on a wall or easel a newsprint of a "Team effectiveness" rating. This newsprint contains the same text as in the questionnaire.

When all have finished filling in the questionnaire, we begin marking on the newsprint the scores given to each heading. We call out the name of the first heading, "Goals," and each person in turn calls out the rating he or she gave that heading. We mark each person's score on the newsprint by a small × next to which we write his or her first name. We carry out this procedure with all headings until we have every person's score for each question marked up on the newsprint.

A. Goals

```
                        × Phil
          × Sam    × Lee    × Joy
          × Dave   × Ron    × John
          ─────────────────────────
          1    2    3    4    5    6
```

Confused; diverse;
conflicting; indifferent;
little interest.

Clear to all; shared by
all; all care about the
goals, feel involved.

B. Participation

```
                    × Joy
          × Ron    × Dave
  × Leo            × Sam    × Phil   × John
  ───────────────────────────────────────────
  1       2        3        4        5        6
```

Few dominate; some
passive; some not
listened to; several
talk at once or
interrupt.

All get in; all are
really listened to.

Fig. 9.2 Team effectiveness rating: Some examples of scoring

We explicitly ask people not to be influenced by the ratings of others and to give the original score they wrote down. In order to decrease the possibility of some people influencing others, we often change the order of calling out scores and begin with different people.

When completed, the newsprint should look like Fig. 9.2.

3. *Discussion of results.* With the newsprint marked with scores in front of everyone, we can now begin discussion of the results. We conduct this discussion in two different ways:

First way: We take each heading in turn and ask people who gave either higher or lower scores than most to explain why they did so. The team then discusses their reasons and threshes out the differences of opinion. On the newsprint we mark the average score given to each item.

Second way: We ask the team to try and reach a consensus on the score for each item. This should be accomplished within a specific time period. We tend to give from two to three hours for this task. The time depends on a number of factors: the extent of differences of opinion among team members as expressed in the range of their scores; the amount of time we can allocate to this experience; and our evaluation of its importance to the team members.

People often do not know what we mean by "consensus." We tell them that consensus means simply group agreement on one of the scores. They must arrive at this score by convincing each other and clarifying the reasons for their differences of opinion. They may not vote and should not use group pressure to bring dissenters into line. They should try to agree through a consensus on one score to all headings within the time limit we allocate.

Until the end of the time allocated, we try not to intervene in the proceedings. We say nothing about chairing the discussion and do not nominate anyone to be responsible. We leave the team to its own resources. Our only intervention may be to mention how much time remains to finish the discussion.

In practice we started with the first way, but now we almost always do it in the second way. We used to do it with the Schein questionnaire on a 10-point scale (see Fig. 9.1). The 10-point scale in Schein's questionnaire accentuates differences of opinion, and is suitable for the first way where we want to widen the differences. For the second way we prefer a six-point scale (see Fig. 9.2) in order to make achievement of consensus easier to attain.

We have found the consensus method to be an excellent way of bringing team members to a relatively thorough understanding of the concepts of effectiveness, and it provides a painstaking scrutiny of the way the team works together.

As mentioned previously, we began doing the process with management teams using the Schein questionnaire. As we gained experience we began using different questionnaires with different types of teams. We would delete or add categories according to what we found suitable for the particular kind of team. For example: when we are training a work team we tend to decrease the number of headings that deal with team discussions and decisions. We may add categories more suitable to a work situation, such as equity in carrying the burden of the less attractive tasks. Figure 9.3 shows an example of the categories we used when working with a team of women who were in charge of a kindergarten.

Here is another example—when we used the questionnaire with top management teams at the beginning of their training, we ran into difficulty with item 3, "Feelings." Management teams that had not previously gone through any human relations training had difficulty at this stage in digesting the ideas embodied in this item. We therefore preferred to delete this item from their questionnaire, and would introduce it only with a team that had gone through some experimental training in examining feelings. Instead of the "Feelings" item, we introduced one dealing with the division of responsibility and authority in the managerial team. To sum up: We see the original questionnaire as an excellent crystalization of items dealing with team effectiveness. But we use them with discretion, deleting and adding items specifically suitable to the kind of team we are working with.

4. *Deciding which items to work on.* By this time the stage is set for the last step in the process. The team can actually see for itself which aspects of its functioning require to be worked on and improved. This, of course,

A. Work Goals

1	2	3	4	5	6

Confused; diverse; disagreement

Clear to all; shared by all; all care about the goals.

B. Involvement and Commitment

1	2	3	4	5	6

Indifference or lack of commitment; some try to pass the buck to others.

Everyone cares about getting the work done well; each tries to do her best.

C. Division of Duties and Responsibility

1	2	3	4	5	6

There is no accepted division of duties, responsibility, and work—or people do not perform according to it, or adhere to it rigidly.

There is an accepted division of duties, responsibility and work; all perform with flexibility as need arises.

D. Trust

1	2	3	4	5	6

Members distrust one another—are careful, closed, guarded; afraid to criticize or be criticized.

Members trust one another, are not afraid to say what they feel, can freely express negative reactions without fearing reprisal.

E. Problem Solving

1	2	3	4	5	6

Problems are not acknowledged and faced; problems are ignored or coverd up.

When a problem arises it is acknowledged and discussed in a sincere attempt to solve it.

F. Discussing Problems

1	2	3	4	5	6

Members try to "win"; do not value others' opinions; dissenters are overruled or ignored.

When discussing problems people try to understand one another's viewpoints; dissenters and differences are appreciated and used to improve decision.

Fig. 9.3 Team effectiveness in a work team (an example)

depends on the team having reached consensus on all the items. We have worked with teams which did not succeed in reaching consensus on all items. In such cases, we either lengthened the period of discussion, if possible, or terminated the discussion without achieving overall consensus. In any case, even if consensus on all items is not achieved, the picture is already clear to team members. It is not difficult to pinpoint two, three, or four of the items that most members of the team agree need to be worked on and improved. We ask the team which of the items they think we should focus on and mark these on the newsprint.

Our next step depends on which items were chosen by the team. Most of the items on the original questionnaire are of the kind that need to be worked on through a period of training. In fact we can use the team diagnosis to plan the following stages of the team's training. For example: if the team thought it should put effort into improving its performance on item D ("Diagnosis of group problems") we might suggest we go through a period of training in group problem-solving. If the team is inclined to accept this suggestion, we will work with the team on the types of processes and interventions described in Chapter 5 of this book. If the team has marked for improvement item G ("Trust"), we will probably plan a series of experiences as described in Chapter 6.

For most items in the questionnaire there are suitable processes and interventions in this book. Some of the items, like C ("Feelings"), might need to be dealt with by simulations and experiences of the kind used in most human relations training programs. Some of these are described in Appendix II, "Some Basic and Standard Methods."

We end this process with the team making a formal decision to devote time and training in the following days, or near future, to the improvement of performance in those items in which improvement is needed.

Variation 1

With a workshop of managers who are strangers to each other, this process should be used within subgroups and only after the managers have worked for some time together in the workshop. In this case the purpose of the experience is not to improve the subgroup's functioning but to increase the participants' awareness of some of the essential aspects of—and detriments to—effective team functioning.

Variation 2

With some teams we may not use this process at the beginning of training. If we are short of time and have already diagnosed the major aspects of team functioning that need attention, we may ask the team to reach consensus only on these. Let this be clear: the members mark *all items* on the questionnaire and *all scores* are listed on the newsprint. But we may choose, because of time considerations, to ask the team to achieve consensus on only three of the items. The rest of the items can be summed up by working out the average and marking it up on the newsprint.

Variation 3

This variation is intended for use without a facilitator. We would use it in a managers' workshop with the subgroups. Its advantage is that a single facilitator can run a number of subgroups at the same time. Each subgroup is given the materials needed for this experience (as listed). Each subgroup is given an instruction sheet with directions (Fig. 9.4).

Variation 4

If we are working with a team for which we have not managed to prepare suitable questionnaires beforehand, we may go through the process *without* individual questionnaires.

We prepare a newsprint with categories suitable to this particular team; e.g., the Schein questionnaire or a work-team questionnaire. The newsprint should contain the full text of each item. With the newsprint before them, on the wall or easel, the participants mark their scores on paper. Let us repeat, there is only a newsprint and people write their scores on a paper or notebook. One person reads out the full text of "Goals." Each then writes "Goals" on his or her paper and the score he or she wishes to allot to the team on this item.

The team continues in this way until it has completed all items on the newsprint.

---

1. The team should nominate a person who will read out these instructions, check time, and see the procedure is carried out. *Do this now.*
2. The one selected now gives each person a Team Effectiveness questionnaire.
3. Each person individually reads his or her questionnaire and marks down on it the ratings he or she wishes to give this subgroup's performance by the criteria listed in the questionnaire.
4. Put up the Team Effectiveness placard. Each person, in sitting order, calls out the score he or she gave to "Goals." Mark these on the placard with an ×, and the person's name. Continue similarly with rest of the items.
5. Within a period of two hours the team should reach consensus on the score it wishes to give each item. Consensus means: clarification of differences by giving reasons and examples and reaching agreement on a score, without group pressure and voting.
6. For 20 minutes, discuss the experience and the possibilities of using this procedure with a team you work with back home.

Fig. 9.4 Instruction sheet for team effectiveness

"ARE WE DOING WHAT WE SHOULD BE DOING?"

Examining whether a top management team is doing the things it really should be doing; deciding what needs to be changed and how.

When to use

This intervention was developed specifically for management teams, and especially for *top management teams*. Experience has shown us that many of the top management teams we worked with were neglecting some of the most essential functions of management. They were dealing mainly with everyday routine affairs and not giving thought to what lay ahead.

Some teams seemed to be reacting mainly to problems brought to them, and were not devoting time to initiatives of their own. We found teams overburdened with everyday routine problems, spending most of their time putting out fires that should have been taken care of by others, and with little energy left to face basic issues confronting their organization.

Many of the teams gave no thought to planning ahead. All around them conditions were changing, and changes were also taking place within the team. But they were unaware of these changes and were not planning how to meet the demands of the changing environment and of their internal disequilibrium.

When we work with the top management team of an organization, and we observe that it has one or more of the weaknesses described above, we use this process. We can reach this conclusion through a number of ways; i.e., after an interview with the *top manager*, prior to a workshop with his or her team; after interviewing *individual managers* from the team before a training period; or from *observation* alone after working some time with a management team.

We found this intervention pertinent and timely in almost all top management teams of the organizations with whom we have worked. Nevertheless, it would be rash to generalize and apply this to all other top management teams.

This process can also be used with other than top management teams. When to use it can only be decided after knowing what the functions and responsibilities of that management team are. The reader is advised to read through the process and understand its purpose before deciding to use it with any management team other than top level.

Who can use: 1. A trainer or facilitator with the top management team
  2. With a middle management team, if found suitable, it can also be handled by a manager on the same or a higher level

Purposes: 1. To become aware of and understand some of the essential functions of management
2. To examine how the team is filling these functions
3. To decide what needs to be changed and improved
4. To find ways of doing this

Participants: A management team, especially a top management team

Materials: 1. Felt pens, newsprint, pens, and paper
2. On newsprint "What do we do?"
3. A categorized list of the items on the agenda of the last 10 meetings
4. "What do we do?" questionnaires (Fig. 9.7)

Time: About 3 to 4 hours
1. Prework, by one person from team (with secretarial aid)
2. The process itself can take from two to six hours, depending on the number of areas covered and the amount of effort put into finding ways to change the existing situation. The last stage may be the focus of a week-long workshop

---

STEPS IN PROCESS

1. Prework—preparing list of items on meeting agenda

2. Introductory lecturette

3. Examining the team's agenda

4. Scoring the questionnaire

5. Scoring how the team wishes to function

6. Discussing results and deciding what to deal with

7. Deciding what changes to implement

Detailed process

1. *Prework: preparing list of items on meeting agenda.* Some time before meeting the entire team to go through this process (generally, at least one month, preferably a few months), we meet the top manager. We ask him or her to arrange that when we hold the meeting we have a categorized list of the items on the agenda for the last ten meetings held by the management team.

We ask the top manager to have the list prepared in the following manner:

a. Before we meet the team, a list should be made of all the items that were discussed during the last ten meetings.

b. With the aid of the minutes of the meetings, the secretary (with the help of other members of the team) tries to remember how much time was devoted to each item, and writes this down on the list. If we meet the top manager a few months before the training, we request him or her to arrange to have the secretary note down in the minutes of the meetings how long each item took. If the meetings were taped, as is the custom with some management teams, there will be no difficulty in calculating the time spent on each item.

c. The items should be roughly grouped under the following categories:

1) Everyday routine practical decisions,

2) Items that could possibly have been handled by other bodies,

3) Routine reports,

4) New initiatives,

5) Dealing with basic organizational issues,

6) Examining trends and planning ahead.

If an item could fall under two categories, put it under either one, marking the other category next to it in brackets. For example: If an item suits both category (a) and category (b), put it in category (b) and mark next to it an (a). Should an item not fit any of the categories, add your own category to suit it.

d. Rewrite the items on a new list, under their new categories, writing next to each item the time spent on it.

e. Sum up the time spent on each category of items.

f. Copy this on newsprint in the form shown in Fig. 9.5.

g. Calculate what percentage of the total meeting time was spent on each category of items, and prepare this on newsprint as shown in Fig. 9.6.

Routine decisions		Could be handled by others	
Item a	20 minutes	Item f	50 minutes
Item b	40 minutes	Item g	45 minutes
Item c	25 minutes	Item h	25 minutes
Item d	90 minutes	Total	120 minutes
Item e	15 minutes		
Total	190 minutes		

Fig. 9.5 Items on agenda of last 10 meetings

Items	Time (%)
1. Everyday routine practical decisions	40%
2. Items that could possibly be handled by others	30%
3. Routine reports	15%
4. New initiatives	5%
5. Basic organizational issues	5%
6. Examining trends, planning ahead	5%
	100%

Fig. 9.6 Percentage of time spent on different items

h. Bring the newsprint with you to the team meetings (or workshop or training).

2. *Introductory lecturette.* We begin this intervention with a short lecture, the purpose of which is to clarify some of the essential functions of top management in a changing world.

We often accompany the lecture by noting the major points on a blackboard or newsprint. Some of these points are as follows:

a. *The pace of change has increased immeasurably.* Organizations today must survive in a turbulent environment. In this environment there is change in the quality of change itself. No organization can relax, content with past achievements. The rapid rate of change affecting all aspects of the environment continuously bombards the organization with new problems that reverberate within the organization itself and call for innovative, creative solutions.

b. *The aspects of the environment are increasingly interrelated.* Changes in one area instigate changes in other areas, more than ever before. Social changes cause political changes; political changes cause economic changes and vice versa. Geographically we live in an "infectious" world where changes in one country cause changes in another.

c. *The changing environment infiltrates into organizations and constantly creates problems within them.* Social, racial and economic unrest penetrate the walls of the organization and create problems within. No organization is immune to the turbulent changes around, and not only must it find answers to the problems of a speedily changing environment, but it must also find creative solutions to continually changing internal situations and problems.

d. *The constant changes create pressure on the top decision-makers in various ways.* They have to allocate their time to the essentials—looking at causes, planning and implementing long range change. It is no longer sufficient to do well what they did before; i.e., handling the day-to-day problems; their choices must be right on target or the organization will go down.

e. *They cannot afford only to react—they must initiate in order to survive.* Dealing only with everyday problems may lead to a situation in which undercurrents of tense situations will burst out, without management being prepared to handle them. Problems need to be detected and faced in their first stages of development, and before they become uncontrollable.

f. *Top management must keep its feelers on developing situations* in the environment and in the organization, and plan accordingly. Management cannot afford not to plan ahead in the light of developing trends.

g. *A management that overburdens itself with everyday matters may not find time to deal with basic problems facing the organization.* The everyday routine decisions, reports, and small emergencies may flood the meeting's agenda and leave no time for confronting fundamental issues that, in the long run, may shape the organization's future.

h. *Management must do what only it can do.* Shortage of time, the number of new problems that have to be confronted, the need to deal with basic problems, the necessity to have full information on developing problems and trends, the need to plan ahead, the time needed to make quality decisions on fundamental issues—all these lead to the conclusion that top management has no time to deal with problems that could be handled by others. Management has to examine whether it is doing what it really should be doing. Management has to find ways of transferring to other bodies such problems and issues as the latter can deal with and for which it has the responsibility.

Team members are encouraged to discuss all these points made in the lecturette. Issues can be elaborated on, and clarified.

3. *Examining the team's agenda.* The two newsprints that were prepared in the prework are now displayed before the team. The person who prepared them explains what he or she did and how the items were categorized, then begins explanation on the newsprint with the detailed list of items, and ends with the summary in percentages.

Team members are given sufficient time to read and digest the material. People may wish to make comments and ask questions, and so time is allotted for this. There may be differences of opinion regarding the categorization of some items. If needed, some categorizations of items can be altered. It is not worth spending too much time debating whether a certain item should be in one category or another.

Note: Although the prework instructions seem clear, we sometimes find the prework on the newsprint papers something quite different from what we asked for. It is therefore advisable, before the meeting begins, to check the prework. If there has been a misunderstanding, and if time allows, the necessary changes can still be made.

4. *Scoring the questionnaire.* We now hand out the questionnaires titled "What do we do?" (Fig. 9.7) and ask participants to read them. When all

---

What do we do in our meetings?

1. Basic Problems

1	2	3	4	5	6	7	8	9	10

Deal with everday emergencies and routine problems.

Deal with basic organizational problems and issues.

2. Initiating

1	2	3	4	5	6	7	8	9	10

React to problems others bring to us.

Initiate by ourselves problems and subjects that we will deal with.

3. Problem-Sensing

1	2	3	4	5	6	7	8	9	10

Deal with problems when they reach a critical stage.

Sense problems when they are developing and then deal with them.

4. Planning Ahead

1	2	3	4	5	6	7	8	9	10

Deal with the practical problems of today.

Plan ahead to keep abreast of changing trends.

5. Delegation of Authority

1	2	3	4	5	6	7	8	9	10

Deal with subjects that are, or could be, the responsibility of others.

Deal only with what we should. Delegate authority and resources to others to handle their responsibility.

Fig. 9.7 What do we do?*

---

* We wish again to remark that these are the items we found suitable for the organizations with which we worked. Sometimes we ourselves changed them to suit a particular organization. You are advised to change wording, delete or add items suitable to the organization you are working with.

have finished reading, we explain that this is not a questionnaire to evaluate the team as "bad" or "good." Every management group also has to do things described on the left side of the questionnaire. Management cannot ignore everyday emergencies and must make routine decisions. It must react efficiently to problems placed before it by others; it cannot think only in terms of tomorrow and plan ahead without controlling what is going on today; it must react to critical problems, and sometimes deal with problems which others have neglected.

The question is not whether one does either this or that. The issue is one of *balance*. Are we doing *too little* of this and *too much* of that? Are we neglecting one way of functioning because we are overburdening ourselves with other kinds of activities?

We then request the team members to once more study the summaries on the newsprint dealing with items on the agenda of the last ten meetings. After doing so they should score the questionnaire by marking a number for each item (from 1 to 10) which, in their opinion, expresses how the team has been functioning.

They are asked whether they have any questions about how to fill in the questionnaire, or about the meaning of its contents. After all questions are clarified, participants score their questionnaires individually.

When scoring is completed, the results can be recorded. While the participants have been busy scoring, the facilitator puts on newsprint "What Do We Do?" This is worded exactly the same as the questionnaire, only on a large sheet of newsprint.

The participants, in seating order, call out the score they gave to "Basic problems" and the facilitator notes the scores on a clean sheet of newsprint. He or she then works out the team's average score and writes it on the newsprint. The same procedure is carried out with the rest of the items on the questionnaire.

Now it is advisable to devote some time to examining the range of scores. If in a certain item there was a difference of five points or more between individual scores, this should be clarified. Differences in estimation of three or four points can be expected and need not be dealt with. A greater difference in score deserves discussion, clarification, and some form of consensual scoring. If after clarification a new score is decided on, this should be accepted as the team's score.

All team scores (average and corrected) are now marked on the newsprint "What Do We Do?"

5. *Scoring "how the team wishes to function."* The first scoring gave the team a picture of how it was functioning to date. The next step is to attain agreement on how the team wishes to function in the future.

This is explained to the participants and they are requested to score the questionnaire according to how they would wish to see the team working from now on. They should put a different mark on their questionnaire.

If previously they underlined a number, they should now put a circle round a number.

We stress the following points:

a. A person who is satisfied with the way a team is functioning on a certain item should not give a different score than he or she gave before.

b. It is not to be taken for granted that the aim is always to attain number 10 on the scale. A certain proportion of the team's time has of necessity to be given to the items in the left side of the questionnaire.

c. On the other hand, an attitude of "things can't be changed" will not help the team to control its way of functioning.

When all have finished scoring, the scores are written down, averaged, discussed if necessary, and marked on the "What do we do?" newsprint. This should be done the same way as the first set of scores. The team's scores on "how it wishes to function" should be marked on the newsprint in a different color or with a different form of marking.

6. *Discussing results and deciding what to deal with.* With the newsprint before it, the team is invited to comment on the results, to discuss them and to suggest what items should be given priority in an attempt to change the way the team functions. The discussion can be open and unstructured, preferably chaired by a member of the team.

It should be stressed that at this stage the discussion should preferably *not* be about *how* to bring about changes. The discussion's purpose is to react to the results and to decide on *action priorities* in respect to the items.

It often happens that discussion widens into debates about why the team functions as it does, and what factors cause difficulty and hinder change or improvement. We would prefer such discussion at a later stage, but nevertheless, if now it arises, we do not intervene.

The team should finish this stage with a formal decision about which items it wants to work on, and, if possible, the order of their priority.

7. *Deciding what changes to implement.* How this stage evolves depends on how many, and which, items the team wishes to deal with, and more particularly, how much time and training it is able and willing to devote to doing so.

If we have only a few hours at our disposal for this process, we tend to lead the team through a series of problem-solving sessions in the manner described in Chapter 5. We will probably minimize and even eliminate the learning and training aspects of this process, using them only to reach a series of decisions on steps the team wishes to implement in order to change its mode of functioning.

We will probably take each item in turn in the priority order previously decided on, beginning by listing the different aspects and causes of the present situation. We will brainstorm a list of proposals to deal with these aspects and causes. The team will choose from these and decide which it intends to implement and who will be responsible for implementation. The procedure used will probably be to pass as decisions all proposals accepted by everyone without debate; delete all proposals that receive no support; elect a subgroup to prepare, clarify, and gather information and recommendations on proposals over which there are differences of opinion, or which are very abstract and need to be made more concrete and operational.

A date is fixed when the subgroup will report, and this meeting may take place without the participation of the consultants.

All these problem-solving processes are described in Chapter 5, and readers who wish to refresh their memory can turn back and look through them. Once again we stress that because of lack of time we probably will only lead the processes, and skip all theoretical learning and training aspects as described in Chapter 5.

The weakness in completing the process in that way (at least in many teams we worked with) is that they have not learned and integrated the process. They need further expertise, inputs, training, and interventions in order to achieve effective lasting changes in their way of functioning. In other words, we have found that it is far better if the team decides it can allocate time and training to work on changing its way of functioning.

If the team decides to do this, there are various combinations of the processes described in this book that can be of practical value in helping them overcome problems that hinder them from functioning in the desired way.

Here is a list of processes that can be used:

a. Training in the processes of Chapter 5 "Creative Problem-Solving, Decision-Making, and Implementation" can help a team that has trouble dealing effectively with complex basic problems. This can also increase the effectiveness of other decisions and make time for the basic problems, planning, etc.

b. In Chapter 2, the section on "Problem-Sensing with Groups" and the questionnaire method described in the section on "Questionnaires and Feedback" can help the team define the basic problems it needs to deal with.

c. In this chapter, "What is Hindering Effectiveness?" can help the team find ways to function more effectively.

d. "Determining the Team's Responsibilities" in Chapter 10, can help the team think about developing trends in the environment and in the organization, and plan ahead.

e. In Chapter 4, "With Whom Should You Make Decisions?" can help the top manager to filter out of the meetings' agenda those items that can be settled elsewhere.

f. "Improving Practical Aspects of Team Meetings," the next section of this chapter, can help with the technical and procedural aspects of the meeting that are making it difficult for the team to do what it really should.

g. Whichever way we work on this stage, whether in a few hours or with a series of interventions, there is one team decision that is inevitably made. This decision is that the top team will meet regularly once a month for half a day or a full day (in a place where they cannot be reached by telephone) to deal with basic organizational problems, problem-sensing, analyzing environmental trends, planning ahead and taking new initiatives, etc.

Generally, someone from the team itself raises this suggestion and the team makes a decision affirming it. If no one brings up the idea, we do so ourselves and suggest that the team discuss it and decide on it. Needless to say, a decision of this kind has little chance of being implemented unless the team also decides on:

a. A fixed day of the month and time of day;

b. The place where the meeting will take place—away from any interference;

c. The date, hour, and place of the first meeting of this kind;

d. A person responsible for implementing this decision who might also help the chairman prepare the agenda.

IMPROVING PRACTICAL ASPECTS OF TEAM MEETINGS

Taking a new look at procedural, structural, technical, and other aspects of the team's meetings. Changing what needs to be changed and deciding on innovations.

When to use:

This intervention is useful with committees, with management teams, and with other teams that have frequent team meetings. The process can be helpful to most committees or task forces. It is especially suitable after observations or interviews have shown that the technical and procedural aspects of team functioning are lacking.

Sometimes, in a workshop, a committee specifically requests us to help it become more effective in this aspect of its meetings.

Who can use: 1. A facilitator
                    2. A manager with his own, or another team

Purposes:
1. To become aware of outdated ineffective procedural, technical and structural aspects of team meetings
2. To think out ways to change these and decide how
3. To become aware of innovative practices in this area
4. To decide to try some innovative practices

Participants: A committee, a management team or any other team that has frequent meetings

Materials:
1. Newsprint, felt markers, tape, pens and paper
2. Handout: "Items to be examined" (Fig. 9.8)
3. Handout: "Idea list" (Fig. 9.9)

Time: 2 to 4 hours

STEPS IN PROCESS

1. Individuals work on handout, "Items to be examined"
2. Adding proposals from the "Idea list"
3. Processing the proposals

Detailed process

1. *Individuals work on Handout, "Items to be examined."* The team meets. The facilitator says a few words linking the process with the issue(s) which indicated the need to request consultation. The purposes of the process can be explained as they are listed in "Purposes" above.

Participants are now given the handout, "Items to be examined" (Fig. 9.8).

When team members have finished writing their proposals these are listed on newsprint as in brainstorming (see Chapter 5).

2. *Adding proposals from the "Idea list."* There are innovations used in team meetings that would never enter the minds of a group that has for years maintained the same regular formal procedure. It is possible to confront people with new ideas by at least letting them hear about them. Anxiety as to what will happen if they are adopted can be diminished by conditional decisions. The team can decide to adopt a procedure for a number of months and reconsider it after trying it out. The facilitator gives each participant the handout—"Idea list" (Fig. 9.9). Each person reads the list and marks ideas he or she would like to try out for some time in the team's meetings.

Participants are asked which items they have marked for "trial implementation" and these items are added to the list on the newsprint paper.

Working some time together, teams often adopt procedures that either were not given serious thought or have now become obsolete. Often, the technical and structural aspects of team meetings are not as effective as they could be.

Here is a list of such items that might be worth examining. Mark items you think might need change and make a list of what changes you suggest.

1. How often the team meets
2. The weekday on which the team meets
3. The hours of the day at which the meeting is held
4. How long the meeting lasts
5. The physical meeting place: chairs, seclusion, noise, ventilation, temperature, etc.
6. Interfering telephone calls to and from people in the meeting
7. People interrupting the meeting to see participants
8. Refreshment arrangements
9. Visual aids
10. The size of the team from the aspect of decision effectiveness
11. The composition of the team: what office holders belong
12. The composition of the team: what members of the organization are represented
13. The meeting agenda: Who suggests? Who prepares? Who reviews and rejects items? Who fixes priorities?
14. How are agenda items prepared? Is there written information given before the meeting?
15. Who is invited to participate in working on the items?
16. Accepted meeting procedures: appeals, changing priority, order of items, etc.
17. How are decisions made? Vote? Consensus?
18. Who chairs the meeting? Is chairing rotated?
19. How are decisions recorded?
20. How are decisions brought to the attention of those concerned?
21. How does the team decide who will implement decisions?
22. The procedure for checking decision implementation
23. The subjects that are brought for decision
24. The subjects on which the team gets information and reports
25. The percentage of team time devoted to items 23 and 24

Fig. 9.8 Items to be examined

3. *Processing the proposals.* The facilitator can use any one of the different ways of processing brainstorm proposals suggested in Chapter 5's section on "Weighing Proposals." We do it this way:

    a. Quick run through the entire list.

    b. Items agreed on without discussion are ratified as decisions.

Here is a list of innovative ideas collected from various teams. Each one of the ideas has been used and found useful by some team. Of course that does not necessarily mean that it will suit your team.

Mark items that you would like to try out for a trial period in your team:

1. Asking team members at beginning of meeting if they have items they wish to add to the meeting agenda.

2. In some meetings, organizing the priority order of the items at beginning of the meeting

3. When this is done, making a timetable allocating time to be given to each item

4. Putting up the agenda and time allocation on newsprint

5. Organizing the agenda so that quick "easy" items are at the beginning and finished off first

6. Rotating chairmanship of meetings

7. Taking turns in chairmanship in long meetings

8. Writing the main points of what people say on newsprint

9. Writing team decisions on separate newsprint

10. Sending typed copies of meeting decisions to all members

11. Sometimes breaking into subgroups during meetings to discuss different aspects of a problem

12. Sometimes going round the room to check opinions.

13. Using brainstorming when suitable

14. Sometimes making decisions to try something out for a certain period of time (conditional decisions)

15. Using a subgroup to prepare work on a complicated problem for the entire team

16. Using task groups to deal with team projects

17. Making use of subcommittees

18. When important item is very controversial, trying to reach consensus and not vote

19. Checking before discussing an item if people meaningfully affected by it are present

20. Writing next to each decision who is responsible for implementation

21. Fixing a date to check implementation of difficult decisions

22. Using a process observer (a team member) who follows the way the team operates and at the end of the meeting reports his or her observations

23. Sometimes devoting time at the end of a meeting to discuss the process of meeting and draw conclusions

24. Allocating a regular monthly (or bimonthly) meeting for discussing basic problems for which the team never seems to find time

Fig. 9.9 Idea list

c. Items agreed on without discussion as conditional decisions are ratified, with a date for their reexamination.

d. Items no one supports are eliminated.

If time allows, the remaining items are divided among subgroups. The subgroups prepare recommendations.

The team reconvenes and ratifies or rejects the recommendations.

If time is short, controversial items are delegated to a subgroup for preparation. The meeting date for the report is established. The name of the person responsible for implementation is put down next to each item decided on.

After the meeting, each team member receives a typed copy of the decisions.

Variation 1

Adding proposals from the "Idea list" (step 2) may be skipped if time is short.

Management through objective-setting

10

CHAPTER OBJECTIVE

To present a series of interventions that are basic building blocks in introducing management through objective-setting to an organization.

GUIDE TO APPLYING INTERVENTIONS

What is management through objective-setting?

- It is an effective method of management, a motivation system one can
  introduce to an organization, a democratic way of functioning that
  enables people to plan and control their own work goals, an effective
  control system, a way of thinking and planning ahead, a method by
  which to clarify and define managers' functions and responsibilities, a
  method of dividing authority and responsibility, etc.

- Management through objective-setting has been developing, in the last
  few years, as a form of management which is both complementary and
  suitable to an organization that uses organizational development.

- An increasing number of consultants support the idea that an optimal
  strategy of working with organizations should be a two-headed effort,
  using OD with and between teams and MBO (management by objectives) as the management system for controlling and running the
  organization.

- It may begin with managers and teams defining their areas of responsibility; that is, what they are responsible for.

- Management teams will have to clarify the division of responsibility and authority between the managers who compose the team.

- Managers and teams will need to begin thinking in terms of a changing environment; that is, what changes are taking place outside the organization and within it that may impinge on what the managers are doing and should be doing.

- Following clarification of areas of responsibility, objectives will have to be established for each area. Managers will have to define the objectives they will try to attain and teams will have to do the same.

- The emphasis in a manager's work is transferred from "doing things" to "getting results."

- Objective-setting will be done by the persons who will be responsible for attaining those objectives; it should not be imposed from above by superiors.

- These objectives will be coordinated with the objectives of peers, superiors, and subordinates, and linked with the overall objectives of the organization.

- An attempt will be made to establish objectives that are specific, time-bounded, and measurable.

- Some method of checking and reviewing the attainment of objectives will also be ensured.

- Following the establishing of objectives, managers will have to draw up plans and schedule activities in order to attain the objectives at predetermined dates.

- The basic ideas of MBO were developed by Peter Drucker, George Odiorne and Peter Humble. We have found *Effective MBO*, as developed by W. J. Reddin, practical and suitable for our needs. (See Recommended Readings.)

About the interventions in this chapter

We have included in this chapter six interventions that are basic building blocks in the management-through-objective-setting implementation.

The first three interventions deal with defining a team's responsibilities and dividing the responsibility and authority between the team's members. The fourth intervention serves a manager in defining what his or her responsibilities are; the fifth intervention teaches how to establish objectives, and the last intervention deals with planning how to attain them.

The interventions

1. *Determining the team's responsibilities.* This intervention was developed under the influence of Alvin Toffler's *Future Shock*. We try to introduce a team to thinking in terms of a changing environment entailing "future shocks," and planning ahead to meet these changes.

2. *Dividing responsibilities in a team.* Developed for a management team whose members did little sharing of responsibility, this intervention guides the team through the process of assigning responsibilities among its members. This is just the hard, inescapable job of deciding who will be responsible for what.

3. *Clarifying responsibility and authority in a team.* An alternative to the intervention just described, this intervention should be used with a team which already has a division of responsibility. The team will take a new look at its responsibility and authority assignments, clarify matters, make changes, and cover areas of responsibility that are not adequately taken care of.

4. *Defining and improving managers' jobs.* This was developed to help managers define their areas of responsibility. In the process of doing so the managers reexamine what needs to be added, dropped, or changed. This process can help managers take a new look at what they are doing and may lead to many changes in their way of functioning.

5. *Establishing objectives.* This intervention trains managers and teams to establish objectives in their areas of responsibility. People work on establishing objectives for their actual work responsibilities.

6. *Planning how to attain an objective.* This is a training session in using a simplified form of PERT. The team members apply it to their actual work objectives. They go through the steps of planning activities and scheduling them so as to attain their objectives on time.

MATRIX OF INTERVENTIONS

Intervention	Use	Who can use	Time demand
Determining the team's responsibilities	Fixing areas of team functioning in a changing environment	Facilitator; manager who has observed the process	4 hrs
Dividing responsibilities in a team	Deciding who does what in a team	Facilitator; manager	3–5 hrs
Clarifying responsibilities and authority in a team	Reexamining the division of responsibility and authority	Facilitator; manager	3–4 hrs

Intervention	Use	Who can use	Time demand
Defining and improving managers' jobs	Helping managers redefine what their responsibilities should be	Facilitator; manager	5–7 hrs
Establishing objectives	Learning how to define actual objectives	Facilitator; manager	4–6 hrs
Planning how to attain an objective	Learning to plan and schedule events	Anyone	2–3 hrs

Possible outcomes

1. Organization better prepared for changing circumstances.
2. Organization better prepared for changes developing within it.
3. Management oriented for better thinking and planning.
4. More initiatives to confront developing trends by management.
5. Fewer areas of responsibility having no one clearly responsible.
6. Easing the load of the top manager.
7. Wider use of task groups.
8. More initiative to start new projects.
9. Less conflict stemming from ambiguity in division of responsibility and authority.
10. More motivated managers and teams.
11. More effective managers and teams.
12. More people knowing what is expected of them.
13. More people checking their own performance.
14. More internal control by people themselves.
15. Less external control by rewards and punishments.
16. More focus on essentials by managers.
17. Decreased need for personality appraisals.
18. Higher profits.

Recommended readings

1. Beck, A. C., and E. D. Hillmar, *A Practical Approach to OD Through MBO* (Reading, Mass.: Addison-Wesley, 1972).
2. Drucker, P. F., *Management for Results* (New York: Harper & Row, 1964).
3. Reddin, W. J., *Effective Management by Objectives* (New York: McGraw-Hill, 1971).
4. Toffler, A., *Future Shock* (New York: Bantam, 1971).

DETERMINING THE TEAM'S RESPONSIBILITIES

Clarifying and deciding what are the areas of team responsibility. Taking into account current trends and changes, deciding on new initiatives.

When to use

This process should be done *every year* by many kinds of organization teams. In the form described here it is suitable for most committees and management teams.

We use this process with committees and *management teams* with whom we begin work. We try to help the teams build into the organizational structures and procedures the mechanisms that will ensure the regular yearly performance of this process. We believe it is essential in any *newly formed* group.

We try to encourage every organization that we work with to assign the responsibility of ensuring and facilitating the implementation of this process to some particular body. In other words, *some person or some group should consider itself responsible for the yearly implementation* and facilitation of this process in the management teams and committees of the organization. Who will be responsible depends on the particular organization. It may be Personnel, it may be an OD unit (if the organization has one), it may be an MBO (Management by objectives) team nominated for this and for other activities, or it may be an extra function added to the responsibility of an existing committee.

When done with a management team as a "one-shot" affair, this process is effective and pays dividends. Nevertheless, the goal should be that it becomes a regular yearly procedure of all management teams and committees in the organization.

When, as often happens, we do this first with the top management team, we then have a leverage point to encourage the use of the process with other teams of the organization. We encourage the top team to make a decision on this, and to nominate the person or body responsible for implementation and facilitation throughout the organization. Experience has shown that although the process is not very difficult, most teams do not do it without outside guidance and facilitation. We have come to the conclusion that to ensure implementation, someone from outside the team must see this as his or her particular responsibility.

The process, as described here, is *not* suitable for a work team that has not much control over what it does. If the work team is on a lower level of a hierarchical organization, and others decide what it does and how, there is no purpose in it using the process described here. (In Chapter 7—the section on "Resolving role conflicts"—and in this chapter we describe interventions that would be suitable for a work team that has some control and discretion in deciding what it should be doing.)

We often go through this process after the Chapter 9 section "Are we [the team] doing what we should be doing?" This is especially suitable if the team has signified that it wants to deal with its weaknesses in "not following trends and changes in the environment and in the organization," and is only "reacting and not initiating."

We sometimes lead the process ourselves in a number of committees, accompanied by the person or persons from within the organization who will facilitate their implementation in the future. After observing us go through the process with two or three committees, the future facilitator takes over responsibility for implementation. We accompany him or her as observers, and sometimes give aid for as long as necessary.

Who can use:
1. As a regular practice: A facilitator or consultant from outside the team or anyone who has had some experience (as described above) as observer
2. As a one-time act: By following the instructions, a manager can try it out with his or her own team; this is preferable to not doing it at all if no facilitator can be found

Purposes:
1. To decide on the areas of team responsibility
2. To begin thinking in terms of current trends and changes and their effect on the team's responsibilities
3. To initiate new projects and activities

Participants:
1. Any team that has some discretion over what it does
2. Suitable for most organization groups, especially effective for top team

Materials:
1. Newsprint, felt pen, tape, pens and paper for participants
2. Team Responsibilities questionnaires (Fig. 10.1)
3. Summary of questionnaires on newsprint

Time: Answering the questionnaire—1 hour prework; the meeting itself—4½ to 5 hours (preferably less)

STEPS IN PROCESS

1. Individual prework—answering the questionnaire
2. Preparing the feedback for the team
3. Deciding on areas of team responsibility
4. Deciding on new projects and initiatives

---

1. *Individual prework—answering the questionnaire.* At least a month before meeting the entire team, we have a meeting with the team's chairperson or boss. In this meeting we explain to him or her the purpose of the intervention and, in general terms, the procedure we will follow.

We make it clear that the boss will have to take over in leading the meeting during part of the procedure. We explain which parts these will be, and how we would like him or her to do it. (This will be detailed later to the reader.)

We give the boss the questionnaires (Fig. 10.1)—one for each participant—and go over them until we are sure that he or she thoroughly understands the meaning and purpose of each question, for it will be the boss' responsibility to explain them to the team members and answer any questions they raise. We ask the boss to do the following within the next week:

a. Meet the team and give them the questionnaires.

b. Read the questionnaire together with the team members, and make sure that all of them understand the meaning of the questions and what they are requested to do.

c. Have the team members answer the questions individually (it takes about one hour) either during the team meeting or at home, and return the questionnaires to the boss. (The handout should allow more space for answers than we have shown in Fig. 10.1.)

d. Collect all the questionnaires after they have been answered and send them to us so that we receive them at least a week before we meet the team.

Alternatively: If we are holding a workshop of at least a few days with a team, we may ourselves hand out the questionnaires to the team members and explain their contents. Members will be requested to fill them in individually in their spare time and return to us the next day. This we will probably do on the first day of our meeting with the team.

The disadvantage of this is that it uses valuable training time for an activity that could be done without us. A second weakness is that it is difficult to find time during an intensive workshop to prepare the questionnaire for feedback to the team.

2. *Preparing the feedback for the team.* When we receive the filled-in questionnaires, we prepare them for feedback to the team.

a. The answers of all team members to each specific question are typed as one list. Each answer is numbered. Lists of answers to different questions are typed on separate pages.

b. We now go over the answers to each question separately. Similar items are marked; one of them is chosen to represent the others, and the others are erased.

Your name

Your team's name

Name of organization

Please answer the following questions to the best of your ability and give thought to each one separately. Try to think things out. The answers to the questionnaires will serve the team in deciding what its responsibilities are, what changes should be made in its functions, and what new projects and initiatives it should undertake.

Before answering, please read all four questions and be sure you understand their intent, and the differences between them.

1. What at present, are the routine areas of team responsibility?

   What are the team's regular functions?

   Please answer in short phrases (not over 5–6 words each sentence).

   Try to write down not less than 8, and not more than 14 regular functions and responsibilities of the team.

1	8
2	9
3	10
4	11
5	12
6	13
7	14

2. What should be added?

   What should the team do regularly that it does not do today?

   What new routine functions and regular responsibilities should the team take upon itself?

   Please answer in short phrases.

3. What changes are taking place in the organization and outside the organization that might affect matters the team is responsible for?

   What new trends are discernible that might effect the team's areas of responsibility?

   a) Changes and trends *within* the organization:
      (For example—workers increasing demand for job satisfaction; rising educational level of employees, etc.)*

   b) Changes *outside* the organization:
      (For example—tightening markets, rise in price of fuel and raw materials; specific competitor innovations, etc.)*

4. What demands do these trends and changes make on the team?

   Please write down your ideas of new projects and initiatives that the team should undertake in order to handle and confront these changing conditions.

   You may also add new projects and initiatives that you suggest the team should undertake, not specifically connected with these changes.

   Please write in short phrases and short sentences.

   Mark with an asterisk the two projects you see as most important and urgent.

Fig. 10.1 Team responsibilities questionnaire

---

*   We have given examples suited to the top team of some industrial organizations. The consultant should insert here examples suitable to the particular team and organization he or she is working with.

c. Listed items that appear to stem from a complete misunderstanding of the question are deleted.

d. Items worded unclearly are made understandable.

e. Long answers are condensed to a few words.

f. After this treatment, the final list of answers is put up on newsprint. A short version of the question is written on top of the newsprint (e.g. "Responsibility areas," "New Responsibilities," "Changes in Organization," etc.). The answers to each question are listed on a separate sheet of newsprint.

g. In question 4, "New Projects and Initiatives," items are marked with asterisks if so marked in the questionnaire. If the same or similar item has been marked by two or three people, two or three asterisks are marked against the item.

h. In questions for which one answer was chosen to represent other similar answers, the one chosen should be marked on the newsprint with some sign (say, plus marks: + + +) to signify the number of people who suggested this same or a similar item.

i. In the answers to question 2, we sometimes find items that are not new areas of responsibility to be included in the team's routine duties. People sometimes write here suggestions which should go under question 4; i.e., "New Projects and New Initiatives." If we find such items we transfer them to the correct place under question 4.

j. One problem we generally meet when preparing the feedback is that people answer on different levels of generality. An example will make this clear. In reply to the first question, one person may write that the team is "responsible for maximizing the profitability of the enterprise." A second person may list as separate items the different components of "profitability."

It is not easy to decide what to do in this situation. We have tried to avoid this in the first question, to a certain extent, by requesting people to list between 8 and 14 items. While this helps, it does not solve the problem. We are, therefore, sometimes forced to decide for ourselves what level of generality is preferable, and to choose the best representative answer. On the newsprint, we can add next to it, in brackets, a word or two relating to other answers which are encompassed by it. This problem is not of great importance to questions 3 and 4, but can create difficulties when deciding on the team's areas of responsibility and functions (questions 1 and 2).

3. *Deciding on areas of team responsibility.* We begin the team meeting with a short introduction to its purposes (as outlined in "Purposes" above). We explain that the team cannot take for granted the areas of responsibility and functions which were decided on in the past.

If the team has already participated in the process "Are we doing what we should be doing?" (see Chapter 9), there is no need to repeat the lecturette and we need only add that an unpredictable environment and changing organizations demand regular reappraisal of the functions of the organization, and of the subunits within it. Rigid structure and functions cannot be retained in the face of such change.

If the team has *not* been through "Are we doing what we should be doing?" then we may present the major points of the lecturette which we gave in that process.

The sheets of newsprint with the team's replies to the first two questions are now put up on an easel or wall for all to read.

Team members are given time to peruse the newsprint. When all have finished, any team member's questions or general comments about the way in which the material was prepared and displayed may be answered.

We tell the team that its objective now is to decide on its areas of responsibility and functions. We suggest that the team follow this procedure:

a. First, from the items listed for question 1, take those that were mentioned by a sizable number of team members (marked by a number of + signs) and see if they can be ratified by a supporting decision.

b. Next, take items suggested by two or three people and try to reach a quick consensus on them.

c. Finally, take, in writing order, all remaining items on the first list and determine whether or not the team supports them. If they can be decided after a short discussion, have the team members do so. If they cannot be quickly decided but are of importance, mark them for discussion at a later date.

d. Follow the same procedure with the list of answers to the second question.

e. If time allows, begin discussing and making decisions on items of importance over which there were differences of opinion.

f. All areas of team responsibility agreed and decided on should be written up on fresh newsprint. This can be done by one of the team members during the discussions.

We hand over responsibility for leading this discussion to the team's regular chairman.

In step 1—"Individual prework—answering the questionnaire"—we mentioned that we discussed this stage of the process with the team's chairperson or boss when we explained in detail what he or she would be doing. Now we repeat it for the whole team.

The team has two hours at its disposal to accomplish this aim. Whatever has not been settled by that time will have to be postponed for a later meeting of the team—without us. If the chairman and team adhere to the procedure we suggested, most teams succeeded in processing many of the items within two hours.

If we see the team sinking into a lengthy debate over one item, before finishing off other items that can be agreed upon easily, we do not hesitate to intervene and help the team return to course.

When we first began using this process, we used to lead the discussion ourselves. Experience has taught us that it was far more effective to leave it to the team's regular chairperson.

When the time period is up, the discussion ends. The team has prepared the major part of its list of areas of responsibility and functions. It may also have a short list of items to be discussed and decided on at a later date.

4. *Deciding on new projects and initiatives.*

   a. We introduce the following ideas: What with the change in the quality of change itself, the changing conditions demanding more interdependence between people, and the growing influence that factors external to organization have on the inner developments within the organization, the necessity to take initiatives (pro-active) and not just be "reactive" becomes critical for survival and viability. By "proactive" we mean initiating, acting, doing things out of your own impetus, planning new projects and implementing them, thinking ahead and creating accordingly, sensing trends and confronting them, and discerning problems and solving them before they reach a critical stage. One can live reactively in a slowly changing society, but organizational existence today depends on being proactive.

   b. We now put up the newsprints: 3a, "Changes in the Organization," and 3b, "Changes outside of the Organization." (See Fig. 10.1.)

   People read them at their own pace, and when they are finished, time is devoted to clarification, comments, and discussion of the ideas on the newsprint. There is no necessity to reach agreement on trends and developments in and outside the organization. It is sufficient that people begin to think in these terms and so can influence one another to begin considering how they affect the team's functioning.

   c. The team now moves on to its last goal: that of deciding which new projects and initiatives it will take upon itself.

   The last newsprint—number 4,—"New Projects and Initiatives"—is put up for all to read. (See Item 4, Fig. 10.1.)

   If items are not clear, the people who proposed them are requested to explain. Alternatively, a few minutes are devoted to each item and the person who suggested the item explains his or her reasons for doing so.

   The team's regular chairperson takes over and leads a discussion on which projects and initiatives the team wishes to take upon itself.

Before this discussion begins we are careful to remind the team of the restraints in deciding on new projects should they entail heavy investment of funds, high budgets, or other demands from the organization's resources.

Choosing which projects to adopt can be done by the regular method by which the team makes its decisions.

It is preferable to commence the discussion on projects which were accorded a number of asterisks (*); i.e., those that a number of people thought important and urgent.

It may possibly suffice to decide on a number of these projects which were regarded as important and urgent, and to assign the remaining suggestions to a subgroup for clarification and recommendation prior to discussion by the entire team at a later date. We give the team an hour to make decisions on projects. Those projects decided on are listed separately on a newsprint.

Projects to be postponed and prepared by a subgroup are written on a separate list. The team nominates members to the subgroup that will have to bring recommendations, and fixes a date for their discussion.

If some of the projects decided on are dependent for implementation on resources not within the authority of the team, the subgroup has also to clarify the possibility of obtaining such resources. Their report should be submitted to the team when it meets again to settle the final list of projects.

Note:

1. It will be noticed that we limit the time for discussion on responsibilities and projects, and end discussions on time, even if the team has not completed its mission. There are three major reasons for doing this: (a) the process is heavy work, and stretching debates without end often leaves the participants exhausted; (b) decisions can be made without our participation, and it is therefore a pity to waste training time; and (c) some items always need further information, expertise, and clarification. After preparation in a subgroup they can be decided on more effectively with a fresh outlook in another meeting.

2. Most committees and management teams do have some internal division of responsibility for implementing areas of team responsibility. It is therefore generally necessary to follow the process just described with the process following, see Dividing Responsibilities in a Team, Chapter 10.

Variation 1

The discussions on items in questions 2 and 4 can be shortened even more by use of the matrix form of dividing 100 points, described in Chapter 2, the section on "Problem-sensing with groups." After using the matrix, the discussions can focus only on those items receiving a sizable number of points.

Variation 2

Some consultants in our team prefer to do it slightly different. They request that before the meeting, the team's top manager, prepare (either alone or with advice and assistance) the answers to question 1, putting it all on newsprint for the team. Then the team's first discussion focuses on the list the top manager has made. Members suggest changes and corrections and these are discussed and decided on.

The questionnaire in this case, contains only questions 2, 3a, 3b, and 4, and these are answered by all team members. The rest of the process remains unchanged.

Variation 3

Some prefer doing it this way: Newsprints 3a, 3b, and 4 are displayed at the same time. Members read them together. There is no separate discussion of newsprints 3a and 3b. The discussion and decisions on the projects and initiatives (no. 4) are made with people having the option of pointing out the connection between them and the changes referred to on newsprints 3a and 3b.

Variation 4

This is a combination of variations 2 and 3 (and, if so desired, 1). This is the shortest way to do the process.

Variation 5

A less structured, easier, but less thorough way of going through this process is without the questionnaire and prework.

Each question is dealt with separately at the meeting without the use of questionnaire. The facilitator asks the team what its present areas of responsibility are and lists all suggestions. The team discusses and decides on them. He or she asks for suggestions on new functions that should be regularly performed, and these are written down and discussed. The same procedure is carried out with the other questions. This can, of course, be combined with variation 1.

DIVIDING THE TEAM'S RESPONSIBILITIES

Deciding who will take care of each area of the team's responsibilities, and who will be responsible for team projects in a group that has not developed a satisfactory division of responsibility.

When to use

We generally use this process immediately after the one previously described ("Determining the team's responsibilities"). In that process the team decided what it should be doing, and in this process it decides who will be the doers.

This process is suitable for teams in which there is *some measure of division of responsibility* among team members.* It is *not* suitable for:

1. A group whose only function is to make decisions on matters put before it by the chairperson or some other person. Such groups exist and fulfill a specific function of decision-making, and the members have no responsibilities or functions as members other than to come to meetings and participate in discussions and decisions. For such a team, the process preceding this one is more suitable.

2. A management team whose members are selected because of the specific functions they fill outside the team. There are many management teams of this type, composed of top managers of various sections, such as sales, production, etc., and among the responsibilities of such teams is often included the coordination and guidance of each individual manager; i.e., the team supervises, directs, counsels, or guides its members in the performance of their duties outside the team. In cases of this kind we prefer to use an intervention presented later in this chapter, entitled "Defining and improving managers' jobs."

3. Teams of people who work together in a workplace of any kind. Under conditions of high interdependence, as in a workplace, more appropriate processes would be either the next one in this chapter—"Clarifying responsibility and authority in a team"—or the one on "Resolving Role Conflicts," in Chapter 7.

To repeat: This process is suitable only for a group that has some division of responsibility among its members and that meets regularly. It deals with the division of duties and responsibilities *that accrue from team membership* and that legitimately belong to that team. We have found the process helpful when a team is ineffective because *the responsibilities of its members are not clearly defined,* and everyone expects someone else to attend to things. That is, the team may make decisions, but no one sees it as his or her particular responsibility to implement them.

Another common problem of teams is that *the top person is overburdened.* The team expects the boss to take care of everything. He or she is neck deep in work and cannot fulfill all his or her obligations; consequently

---

* For teams that already have complete division of responsibilities, task groups, subcommittees, etc., see the next process—"Clarifying responsibility and authority in a team."

decisions are not implemented and necessary actions are not taken. In such cases it is of great value to *spread* responsibility among team members and ease the burden on the top person.

Assuming responsibility is, moreover, a healthy antidote to *lack of commitment* on the part of the rank-and-file members of a group. Members who bear responsibility for particular functions of the team are more inclined to feel involved in the team's business and committed to raising the standard of its effectiveness. The process described herein helps such a team in this direction.

We have found this process of value to teams that think only in terms of individual responsibility, and that do not utilize the potential that could be unleashed by the use of *project teams* and *task groups* (these terms will be explained later).

Who can use:
1. An outside facilitator should prepare the team's chairperson in the method of leading this process
2. A person or body in the organization should see it as their responsibility to help all teams go through this process once a year
3. With no available consultant following the instructions, a manager can lead the process in his or her own team.

Purposes:
1. To divide responsibility among team members and subgroups for the team's areas of responsibility and projects
2. To ensure that someone is responsible for each function and project
3. To increase effectiveness by easing the load of the top manager
4. To increase commitment by diffusing responsibility and strengthening involvement
5. To encourage the use of "task groups"

Participants: A team in which there is some division of responsibility

Materials:
1. Newsprint, felt pens, tape, pens and paper
2. Division of team's responsibilities and projects (Fig. 10.2)
3. The list of the team's areas of responsibility and projects

Time: 3 to 5 hours with a team that has not done "Determining the Team's Responsibility"

2 to 3 hours otherwise

Detailed process

1. *Preparing the meeting with head of the team.* Prior to meeting the entire team we have a meeting with the team's head, boss, or chairperson (in this example let's say this person is male) in order to:

   a. Explain to him what is to be done in the team's meeting;

   b. Arrange with him what his part will be in that meeting;

   c. Decide with him how he will do what he has to do;

   d. Prepare him for the prework he will have to do before the meeting.

The meeting may take place under either one of two circumstances:

   a. The team has already decided on its areas of responsibilities and projects; i.e., it has already gone through the process entitled "Determining the team's responsibilities."

   b. The team has not yet defined its areas of responsibility and projects.

In each case, we detail below how we proceed with the chairman:

   a. *Where the team has done the process entitled* "Determining the team's responsibilities," described earlier in this chapter:

   1) We detail the steps of the process we intend going through with the team and note the chairman's comments.
   2) We tell him that he will take over chairing the meeting during part of the process when the team decides "who is responsible for what."
   3) We discuss with him and decide together the best way to do this in his team (more about this later).
   4) We ask him to prepare prework, namely:

      a) Copy the list of the team's areas of responsibility and projects as previously determined and record on newsprints in the form given in Fig. 10.2.
      b) Add to each responsibility and function the name of the person presently responsible for it. If there is no one, leave a blank space (as in Fig. 10.2). Write the names of those responsible in the column headed "Person responsible." If necessary, use a separate newsprint for projects. The newsprints are to be shown at the team's meeting.

Dividing the team's responsibilities   **293**

Responsibilities	Suggestions	Person Responsible
1. School services		Jerry
2. Teacher employment		Jerry
3. Teacher supervision and guidance		
4. Curriculum		
5. Student problems		Sonia
6. Relations with parents		
7. School budget		Lakin
8. School facilities		Jack
etc., etc.		

Projects	Suggestions	Person Responsible
1. Establishing a student-staff committee		
2. Starting a new auditorium fund		
3. Revising school's bookkeeping system		
etc.		

Fig. 10.2 Division of team's responsibilities and projects

b. Where the team has *not* done the process entitled "Dividing the team's responsibilities," we follow steps 1), 2), and 3, immediately preceding, with the chairman. Then we:

4) Explain to the chairman what we mean by the "Team's area of responsibility and functions" and ask him to prepare a list of these. We do this together with him, helping and advising. We transfer the list onto newsprint.

5) Ask the chairman to suggest new areas of routine responsibility and regular functions, and we put these suggestions on a separate newsprint.

6) Ask for suggestions of new projects and initiatives, and these also are put on a separate newsprint.

2. *Deciding on team's responsibilities and projects (if not yet done).* If the team has not yet decided on its areas of responsibility and projects, we generally go through this process in the shortest possible way. We lead this process ourselves, thus:

a. We explain its purpose.

b. We put up the newsprints which we had prepared with the chairman and explain them.

c. We ask participants to add new items to all lists and suggest changes in the first list, if any are required. All suggestions are noted on the newsprints.

d. We try to reach a quick consensus on the first two lists: (1) Team's Areas of Responsibility; and (2) New Routine Areas of Responsibility. If there are major differences of opinion on an item of importance, we may decide to postpone decisions on this item to a later meeting.

e. If needed, we use a matrix to decide on priority of projects, see "Problem-sensing with groups," in Chapter 2.

f. At the side of each area and function we add, with the aid of team members, the name of the person presently responsible for it.

g. We transfer the results of the team's work to fresh newsprints in the form shown in Fig. 10.2.

The team has now reached the same stage as a team which has already done the process, "Dividing the team's responsibilities."

3. *Assigning the responsibilities.* If we are working with a committee in which *the chairman is overburdened with responsibilities,* and other committee members have few responsibilities, we may remark about this.

We show the team how this affects team effectiveness and both the involvement and commitment of team members. We might suggest that the team make an effort not to give the chairman any new responsibilities or projects. In fact, we may sometimes suggest that the chairman be relieved of one or two current responsibilities, if he wishes this.

The second point we make, and which we found important for the teams we work with, is *the value of using subgroups as "task groups."* Most of the teams we work with think in terms of either team responsibility or individual responsibility. In other words, the entire team holds itself responsible for some things, while for others it nominates or chooses individual team members. Formal subgroupings of team members for specific functions are not common.

Teams also think habitually in terms of *permanent* functions and responsibilities. In this framework it is hard to envisage *changing* functions and *temporary* responsibilities.

Combining these two ideas leads to the use of "task groups," which are temporary subgroups chosen to carry through specific time-bound projects.

In this context we mean by "projects" something that is devised or planned, a new plan or scheme.

When one fulfills functions of routine everyday work, there is little time to think about starting something new, making changes, planning something not in the usual run. Task groups can perform this function. Utilizing the team's human resources effectively entails creating various task groups that will take upon themselves the implementation of projects and other initiatives of the team.

Team members are asked for their reactions and opinions on these ideas and, if necessary, we clarify them further.

The chairperson now takes over from us and leads the team through the stage of assigning responsibilities and functions. In our earlier separate meeting with the chairman we discussed and decided with him how this should be done, and he now follows the procedure decided on.

It is difficult to suggest one procedure that would be suitable for all committees. The way in which people are assigned responsibility can differ greatly, even in organizations of the same culture. A basic difference is whether people are *nominated* to their responsibility within the group by the head of the group or are decided on by the group itself.

We give the following suggestions for different procedures suitable in a team where the team members (and not the head) make the decision on responsibility assignments:

Possibility 1: People study the list and, taking in turn each unmanned area of responsibility, offer suggestions which are noted on the newsprint. The team then discusses the suggestions and decides by consensus or vote.

Possibility 2: People study the list and suggest in which particular area they themselves are willing to assume responsibility. The suggestions are put on the newsprint. This is discussed and decided on by vote or consensus. Areas for which there are no volunteers are assigned by the method described in Possibility 1.

Possibility 3: Possibilities 1 and 2 are combined. People can either volunteer themselves or suggest others. All names are written on newsprint for the team to discuss and decide on.

Possibility 4: Each person studies the list, then suggests, in writing, who should be assigned to unmanned areas of responsibility. He or she may volunteer for any assignment. When all have finished writing, they read out (in seating order) their suggestions, which are put up on the newsprint. Where a person has volunteered, the suggestion is marked differently (the name may be circled). The team then discusses and decides by consensus or vote.

It should be clear that the example shown in Fig. 10.2 is used for the assignments. Names of people suggested are put in the "Suggestions" column. Names of those elected for responsibility are put in the column headed "Person responsible."

4. *Assigning projects.* When the team has finished assigning responsibility for its functions and responsibilities, the same process is gone through with the projects. The difference in assignments between the projects and

areas of responsibility is that for projects the committee will probably nominate not an individual but a subgroup (or, as we call it, a "project team" or "task group").

Of course, it may happen that the team has also elected subgroups for some responsibility area. Some teams do work with permanent groups, and if this is needed, deciding on these subgroups and their membership should be done when decisions are made about responsibility areas.

These groups should be differentiated from "task groups" responsible for projects that are more of a one-time, preplanned, and time-bounded character. Generally, groups are chosen for areas in which the person responsible for implementation is in need of some kind of small advisory group in order to make decisions.

The committee assigns a number of people to each project, and one person in each "task group" of this kind is nominated to head it. (His or her name should be underlined on the newsprint.)

Note: It may be noticed that in the actual assignment of responsibilities in the team meeting, we, the facilitators, hardly intervene at all. It is therefore quite feasible that we do not participate in the meeting if the chairman has done his prework thoroughly.

If the team has not decided on team responsibilities and projects, we generally lead this part of the meeting, using the variation described here. Again, this may be led by the chairman if he is thoroughly familiar with the process.

CLARIFYING RESPONSIBILITY AND AUTHORITY IN A TEAM

Clarifying and settling differences in perception concerning responsibility and authority in a team, with complex division of responsibility and authority among members.

When to use

This intervention should be used with a team that *already has a complex division of responsibilities and authority* among its members, and wishes to clarify issues and misconceptions, and to ensure that every area of its activities has someone responsible for it.

Areas of responsibility and projects are already defined; team members have responsibilities for different areas; the team has task groups and subgroups. The team has worked for some time in this way and the need has arisen to clarify misconceptions, to settle differences of opinion as to who is responsible or has the authority in a specific area, and also to make sure that each area is covered.

This intervention is generally suitable for a team of *professionals* or a team of experts who have wide control over what they do; who decide for themselves how and with whom to do things.

It is also suitable for a team of *managers* working together in close interdependence, who have developed a complex division of responsibility and authority in areas of team responsibility.

It is *not* suitable for a management team in which the division of responsibility relates only to responsibilities *outside* the team. That is, it is unsuitable for the kind of committee to which each person has been elected because of his or her specific function outside, and when the committee (team) coordinates and guides each manager in fulfilling his or her duties. See the next section in this chapter: "Defining and improving managers' jobs."

The process is also unsuitable for a work team that has *little control* over what it does and who does what.

Who can use:
1. A manager in his or her own team
2. The intervention can be facilitated by someone outside the team, following the instructions given here

Purposes:
1. To clarify and settle differences in people's perception of who is responsible for what
2. To clarify and settle differences in people's perception of who has authority for what
3. To ensure that all areas of team responsibility and all projects are taken care of by someone

Participants: A team of managers, professionals, or experts who have a complex division of responsibility and authority for the team's responsibilities

Materials:
1. Newsprint, felt pens, tape, pens and paper
2. Newsprint with "Clarifying Responsibility and Authority" (Fig. 10.3)

Time: 3 to 4 hours

STEPS IN PROCESS

1. Preparation
2. Introduction in team meeting
3. Team members list their responsibility and authority
4. Transferring individual lists to the newsprint
5. Clarifying and settling differences

	David	John	Sam	Jerry	Alex
1. Area a					
2. Area b	R	R	R		
3. Area c	A	[R]			
4. Area d			A		A
5. Area e					A
6. Area f	. `			R	
7. Area g	A				
8. Area h	A				
9. Area i		[R] R	[R] R	A	
10. Area j		A			
11. Project A			A	[R] A	
12. Project B				A	[R] R

Fig. 10.3 Clarifying responsibility and authority

Detailed process

1. *Preparation.* The preparation for this intervention does not require much time. If the team has already defined its areas of responsibility and its projects, the chairperson prepares a newsprint in the form shown in Fig. 10.3.

The names of areas of team responsibility and projects are listed in the left column of the newsprint. Some space should be left at the bottom of the column for other areas that may be added during the team meeting. Names of the team members are listed along the top row of the newsprints. (The letters entered in those columns will be explained shortly.) If the team has not devoted a recent meeting to defining its areas of responsibility and projects, the chairperson prepares two sheets of newsprint: one similar to Fig. 10.3, but with no areas of responsibility and projects listed; and another with a list of the team's areas of responsibility and projects as the chairperson conceives them. We may help him or her prepare this list if we are being consulted.

2. *Introduction in team meeting.* The introduction is short. The chairperson introduces the process by explaining its purposes and how it will be done.

Purposes may be stated as:

a. To clarify who is responsible for each area and project of the team.

b. To clarify who has the authority in each of these areas and projects.

c. To settle differences in viewpoints of team members.

d. To be sure each area has someone in charge of it.

This is done as follows:

a. Each person writes down what is his or her own responsibility and authority.

b. Members' statements are compared.

c. Differences are settled.

If the team has not decided on its areas of responsibility and projects, such decisions must be finalized. The chairperson will display the second newsprint with the list of areas and projects as he or she sees them. Team members will discuss these and make changes, additions, or deletions.

The final list will then be rewritten in the first column of the first newsprint (see Fig. 10.3).

3. *Team members list their responsibilities and authority.* The chairperson now instructs the team members how to list their responsibilities and authority, which each does individually, on a sheet of paper. The instructions are given more or less in these words:

a. First, read the newsprint column listing the areas of team responsibilities and projects.

b. Going down the column, if you find an item that you alone are responsible for and have authority in, write on your paper the name of that area with the letter A (for authority) next to it.

c. If you find an area for which you are in charge of a subgroup or a task group, write that area or project on your paper with an A next to it. But also add the names of the subgroup or task group members, or your assistants in that particular item.

d. If you find an item on the list for which you are partly responsible —either as a member of a subgroup or task group or as an assistant— write the name of the area or project on your sheet and put an R (for responsibility) next to it.

e. Should you find that an area of team responsibility or a project for which you have authority or responsibility is not listed, write that down.

So that the instructions should be clear to all members, they can be printed up on newsprint in brief:

1) Write A if you have authority in an area.

2) If you write A, add names of people with you in that area (unless you are alone).

3) Write R if you are partly responsible.

Individual work is now commenced.

Inevitably during the individual work, someone raises questions concerning the difference between responsibility and authority. We clarify this in the following manner:

a. A number of people may have joint responsibility for an area or project where they work together.

b. In our opinion, *only one* person can have the final authority for that area, at any given time or for any given task—although such authority can be shared and rotated. The task team or subgroup may be super-democratic, with all members participating in decisions; or it may have a clear division of responsibilities. But either way, only one person can be the authority, the one who has the final responsibility for this particular area to the entire team. This person may divide his or her responsibilities among others, but he or she must carry the final responsibility for the functioning of the subteam, and must bear the responsibility for whether or not the subteam functions effectively—unless by agreement such authority is assumed by another member.

c. Two or more people may alternate having the authority during different periods. But only one person can be in authority (A) at any given time.

d. We define as responsibility (R) any form of joint responsibility with the person in authority (A) in that area. The responsibility may be as a member of a task group or subgroup; in the form of regular consultation or assistance. All these forms of aid in varying degrees of responsibility, we call responsibility (R).* When all have finished writing we proceed to the next step.

4. *Transferring individual lists to the newsprint.* The individual work is now transferred to the newsprint prepared for it. (See Fig. 10.3.) The chairperson does this in the following manner:

a. Each person, in turn, reads out his or her individual work and this is noted on the newsprint.

b. If a person says he or she is R in a certain area, this is marked in the box under his or her name in the row for that particular area. (Note, for example, that Jerry is responsible for Area f.)

c. If a person says he or she is A in a certain area, this too is marked in the box under his or her name in the row of that area.

---

* We have tried this intervention with more categories than A and R, using, for instance, categories such as: "Expects to be consulted in this area"; "Expects to get information about this area"; "Expects to be notified about decisions," etc. However, we found this too complicated and cumbersome in the teams we worked with, and finally settled on the two category system only.

d. A person who is A in a particular area should also give the names of the other people he or she considers R in that area. This is done by marking the appropriate box with the letter R in brackets, thus: [R].

e. If the person who is A in an area is *solely* responsible, he or she should state this, and then nothing will be marked under boxes of other people.

The chairperson tries as much as reasonably possible to postpone discussion and remarks, for it is better to hold such discussion, to seek clarifications, and decide differences in an orderly manner only after all have finished reading out their individual viewpoints.

5. *Clarifying and settling differences.* The time has now come to clarify differences in viewpoint and to ensure that each area is adequately covered by someone responsible for it.

a. Starting from the top of the newsprint, each area (row) in turn is examined to see if there are any problems stemming from different viewpoints as to who has authority (A) and who is responsible (R).

b. Each area is taken separately. If there are no problems, a check mark ($\checkmark$) is made next to it on the newsprint, and the team moves on to consider the next area.

c. If there are problems connected with a specific area, these are clarified, discussed, and settled by agreement or by a decision and the newsprint row appropriately marked.

d. After each row has been examined, the chairperson asks the team if there are any remarks. A row may formally be in order without any apparent conflicting views, yet it may need discussion. For example, one person may write only A for a particular area while nobody else writes anything. Team members may wish to make changes for that area, such as either replacing the person who sees him- or herself as A, or giving him or her assistance of some kind (by adding R's).

The problems that usually need to be dealt with are as follows:

a. Nobody sees themselves responsible for or having authority in one of the areas. (See row 1 in Fig. 10.3.)

b. In a subgroup or task group, nobody saw themselves in charge (A). (See row 2.)

c. A person in charge of an area erroneously thought that he or she had assistance of some kind. (See row 3.)

d. Two people both thought that they alone were responsible and had authority in an area. (See row 4.)

All decisions made by the team are written on the newsprint, and appropriate marks (preferably with different colored markers) are made in the boxes of the people who have new authority or responsibility assigned to them.

When the meeting is concluded, the team's secretary types a copy of the final layout of the newsprint for each member of the team.

DEFINING AND IMPROVING MANAGERS' JOBS

A team of managers working together to help each individual manager improve the way he or she functions in a managerial capacity outside the team.

When to use:

This process should be used with a team of managers, each of whom fulfills *a managerial capacity outside the team.*

This process should be of aid to most managers and we therefore use it with many of the top teams of managers with whom we work.

It is especially important in cases where observation or reports show that individual managers are *not doing their job as effectively* as they could. During our interview of managers or subordinates we may hear remarks and criticisms of how individuals are performing in their managerial capacity. Consequently we may decide to go through this process with that team.

In our opinion it is of value to go through this process regularly—once a year, or every two years—with a team of executives.

Individual managers in a workshop can also profit from the experience, although the feedback they receive in the team part of the process may be of less relevance in their case than if they were with their co-workers. Managers can do the first part on their own and gain insight by so doing, even without aid.

This intervention is *not* suitable for use with people who do not fulfill a managerial capacity; also, it is *not* intended to improve either team functioning or coordination between managers.

Who can use:
1. A facilitator with a management team
2. A facilitator with individual managers in a workshop
3. A manager with his or her own team
4. A manager on his or her own

Purposes:
1. To help managers clarify what they are in effect doing in their managerial capacity
2. To help them clarify what needs to be changed
3. To help them define what changes to make

Participants:
1. A team of managers
2. Individual managers in a workshop

Materials: 1. Pens, tape and paper
                  2. Instruction sheets (Figs. 10.4 and 10.5)
                  3. Five newsprints and two felt markers of different color for each participant

Time: 5 to 7 hours

STEPS IN PROCESS

1. Individuals work on the first instruction sheet
2. Subgroups give feedback to individuals
3. Summing up

---

1. *Individuals work on the first instruction sheet.* The purpose of the experience is explained as in "Purposes" above. The team is told that there will be two major stages in the process. In the first stage they will work on their own according to written instructions; in the second stage they will help one another in subgroups.

Each participant receives:

1. One instruction sheet: improving your managerial job
2. Two or three pieces of newsprint
3. Two differently colored felt markers

The participants have about two hours to do the individual work called for in the instruction sheet handout (Fig. 10.4), after which the group reconvenes in the meeting room. If practicable, the group members should be in separate, adjoining rooms while doing this assignment— or at least in separate parts of the meeting room—while the facilitator remains on hand to be consulted if needed.

Participants are told that if there is anything they do not understand in the instruction sheet, they can come to the facilitator for help, they will probably come to the facilitator for aid in defining their areas of responsibility. Aid should be given without relieving the individuals themselves from giving serious thought to the subject.

People may have problems in alloting the percentage of the time they devote to each area. In doing this they may discover that a sizable percentage of their work time is frittered away on trivialities. They should put this down on the newsprint as "wasted time." When listing their action steps they should give thought to this item.

2. *Subgroups give feedback to individuals.* At the appointed time the team reconvenes in the meeting room. Participants are divided into subgroups of three or four people. The subgrouping should be thought out by the facilitator while the people are doing their individual work, and should

1. Make a list of the areas of your responsibility as a manager. List not less than 8 and not more than 16 things for which you are responsible.

   The complete list should cover 100% of your work time.

   Write in short phrases; i.e., less than 8 words for each area of responsibility.

   Be careful not to include areas for which other people are responsible.

2. Next to each area of your responsibility write an estimate of what percentage of your work time you spend on doing it. The sum total of all areas should be 100%. If, when doing this, you find other areas that occupy your time, add them to the list.

3. Copy the list onto a newsprint in the following manner:

   Leaving a wide margin on the left, write down the areas one under the other, numbering each one.

   On the right of each, write the percentages of work time.

4. *Now study the list on the newsprint.* In which two areas should you show more initiative? Mark these with a "V" in a different color in the left margin. (Note: Use the same color for marking the other letters.)

5. In which two areas are you weakest? Mark with a "W" in the left margin.

6. In which two areas are you strongest? Mark them with an "S" in the left margin.

7. Which two areas are of greatest importance to you? Mark them with an "I" in the left margin.

8. In which two areas should you stop doing anything, or spend less time? Mark them with an "L" in the left margin.

9. In which two areas should you do more, or spend more time? Mark them with an "M" in the left margin.

10. Do you take regular weekly "chunks of time" to think things out, to plan ahead and decide what to initiate? If not, try to decide now on a regular weekly day and hour when you can do this, and an undisturbed place to do it. Write these at the bottom of the newsprint.

11. Study again what you have written. Now make a list of all the action steps you intend to take in order to improve the way you function as a manager. Copy this list on a separate newsprint.

Fig. 10.4 Instruction sheet: Improving your managerial job

be based on a roughly equal spread of clarity of thought, constructiveness, understanding, and cooperativeness.

Each person is now given a newsprint and an "Instruction sheet for subgroups" (Fig. 10.5). Each subgroup is also given some masking tape, and is allotted from three to four hours for its work. The subgroups convene in different rooms and follow the procedure detailed on their Instruction sheets. At an appointed hour they reconvene in the meeting room. During their work in the different rooms the facilitator visits them and sees how they are progressing.

Choose one person to read these instructions aloud to the subgroup. He or she will also be responsible for seeing that instructions are followed and that the team keeps to the timetable.

A. Now a person is chosen, or volunteers, to do the following five steps, taking *not more than 40 minutes* altogether.

    1. Display the newsprint he or she prepared about his or her responsibilities.

    2. Answer team members' questions to clarify what he or she wrote.

    3. Explain, item by item, why he or she gave the marks "V, W, S," etc. to particular areas of responsibility.

    4. State his or her decision about alloting a "chunk of time" to planning, etc. (Instruction 10.)

    5. Display the second newsprint prepared by him or her and explain which action steps he or she plans to implement.

B. Next, each subgroup member, in turn, gives feedback to the above which may be:

    ■ Intended to clarify matters to the receiver of the feedback.

    ■ Remarks intended to help.

    ■ Suggestions and ideas.

    ■ Intended to open the receiver's eyes to contradictions, etc.

The person receiving the feedback is instructed not to answer back or speak during this part of the process, but to write on newsprint the essential points of what is being said to him or her.

This feedback should take not more than 20 minutes. Thus, for one person to go through parts A and B should take not more than one hour—and may take less.

C. When the first person has finished, the same process is followed for the next person, and so on until all people in the subgroup have displayed their individual newsprints and received feedbacks.

Fig. 10.5 Instruction sheet for subgroups

3. *Summing up.* The entire team meets after the subgroups have completed their meetings; and people are:

    a. Invited to comment on the experience.

    b. Advised to plan in detail and, at the earliest possible opportunity, give the action steps they intend taking to implement the changes they have decided on.

Variation 1

The first part of the process can be done by the facilitator reading out the instructions and having people following them. This allows more clarification to be given.

Variation 2

"Summing up" can be skipped if time is short.

Variation 3

The instruction sheet "Improving your managerial job" can be prepared in the form of a questionnaire, leaving space after each instruction for people to write in.

People may copy what they have written on the newsprint after they finish filling the questionnaire.

ESTABLISHING OBJECTIVES

Learning how to establish objectives with each manager setting objectives in his or her areas of responsibility.

When to use

Fixing objectives is an effective way of working, and is of value to most managers and other people who have control over what they do at work. It is therefore worth going through this process in management courses and workshops of all kinds, whether the managers work together or not. The intervention can also be used effectively with most management teams that have control over what they do, and have an internal division of responsibility. It is especially useful for top management teams composed of managers who are each in charge of something outside the team. We generally use this intervention in sequence after working with a management team on defining the areas of responsibility of its individual members. After deciding what a person is responsible for, the next stage is for him or her to fix goals that he or she will try to attain in each area. Defining objectives and striving to attain them is an eye-opener for a team or a manager that is all the time busy and hurried but whose effort shows poor results. The stress which "defining objectives" lays on outputs, results, and goals and objectives, can help to change a person's way of functioning.

Who can use:
1. An internal consultant who ensures that managers define and establish objectives on a regular basis
2. A facilitator handling workshops of strangers
3. A manager leading his or her own team in the process
4. A manager reading this and working on his or her own objectives

Purposes:
1. To help people become aware of the importance and value of establishing objectives for their responsibilities

2. To assist people in learning how to define objectives
3. To help people define the objectives of their areas of responsibility

Materials:
1. Newsprint, felt marker, tape, pens and paper
2. A placard—"How to define objectives" (Fig. 10.6)
3. Forms for listing the objectives of an area of responsibility
4. Handouts (for each person) "How to define objectives"
5. Instructions for subgroups

Time: 4 to 6 hours, depending on variation used

STEPS IN PROCESS

1. Lecturette on the value of establishing objectives
2. Each person defines an objective which team discusses
3. Each person defines the objectives of his or her areas of responsibility
4. Improving objectives in subgroups
5. Summing up and decisions

---

1. *Lecturette on the value of establishing objectives.* We generally accompany this lecturette by noting its main points on newsprint during our talk. The points we stress are as follows:

a. There is a world of difference between being busy doing things, on the one hand, and *getting results,* on the other. Some managers seem to be overburdened with work; they may be energetic and extremely active doing all sorts of things, but the question is: Do they show results? Are they contributing to the solution of problems? Are they suggesting and implementing new ideas?

b. Establishing objectives is a powerful *motivative force.* A clear definition of what we are trying to attain will itself push and pull us to try to reach the goals we have set.

c. Establishing objectives helps us *to clarify to ourselves and to others what our goals are.* Defining the objectives makes us think things out and forces us to get down to the root of the matter. We have no way to circumvent the basic question of what our goals really are.

d. The very act of fixing objectives defines *the level of our performance.* Will we be trying to attain last year's results? Are we trying to maintain the status quo; or have we put our sights on higher standards of performance?

e. Establishing objectives allows us *to check how we are performing*. By giving both a quantitative and a time aspect to objectives we have in our hands a means by which we may receive feedback on how we are doing.

f. Fixing objectives is not done just once for all time. This is a procedure we should go through *at regular intervals*—every year or season, or whatever interval we decide on.

Comments and questions are called for, and people are encouraged to discuss the remarks if they wish.

2. *Each person defines an objective which the team discusses.* Each person is now requested to write down one objective in any area of responsibility he or she chooses. In defining his or her objective, a person must try to follow the instructions on the placard which we now display: "How to define objectives" (Fig. 10.6).

We explain:

a. Many people define as objectives what we would call "activities"; e.g., "Give three courses in Management by Objectives (MBO) by the end of this year." This is an activity. In terms of results, the *objective* of this activity might be: "To have three work teams using MBO by the end of this year."

b. Fixing the level of an objective to what we know we can easily attain may be playing safe, but it won't move things forward. Fixing a level beyond our ability is impractical. Can we raise our sights a little?

c. It is difficult to measure all objectives. Many qualitative objectives cannot be quantified. Nevertheless, we should make an effort to express the objective in measurable quantitative terms; e.g., not "Increase production," *but* "Increase production by 10 percent." Such measures are ways of checking the results.

d. Dates by which objectives should be attained are obligatory. Without them the objectives are meaningless. Dates should be written explicitly; e.g., "until the end of 1977," "by the end of March 1978," and so on.

The OBJECTIVE should:
1. Be defined in terms of results, and not as an activity (doing something).
2. Be at a higher level than usual, yet attainable.
3. Contain measurable quantity, if possible.
4. Have a date of attainment.

Fig. 10.6 How to define objectives

Team members are now requested to define an objective they wish to set. This should not be an imaginary one, but a real objective. The guidelines on the placard should be adhered to.

When all have finished writing, the team examines what each person wrote. Each in turn reads out his or her objective, and this is put on the newsprint. The team examines it checking to see whether it follows the instructions on the placard. This is the time when people learn how to write objectives.

The remarks, questions, and discussions that now take place clarify many difficulties people have in defining objectives. People suggest alternative phrases to those a person wrote. Measures are suggested for an objective which a person thought was immeasurable. Activities are transformed into outputs, etc.

3. *Each person defines the objectives of his or her areas of responsibility.* (*Note:* This step in the process can be given to the team members as homework which they must finish by a certain hour.) Each person in the team receives about 20 forms for listing objectives. (See Fig. 10.7) and a copy of "How to define objectives" (Fig. 10.6).

Team's Name _____

Your Name _____

Responsibility Area _____

No.	Objective	Completion Date	Way of Checking
1			
2			
3			
4			
5			
6			
7			
8			
9			
10			

Fig. 10.7 Form for listing objectives

We give the following instructions:

a. Each form is for one area of responsibility.

b. For one area of responsibility we may have a number of objectives. List these on the form associated with that area.

c. Do not write the objectives of different areas of your responsibility on the same form.

d. Be sure to fill in "Completion date" and "Way of checking"; that is, ways of measuring when that objective has been reached .

e. Take the list of your areas of responsibility. Write the name of each area on a separate form, and then begin establishing objectives for each area.

f. Put down your name, the name of the team, and the name of responsibility area, on each form.

g. Check to see whether you are doing things correctly by referring to the handout "How to define objectives" (Fig. 10.6).

If the above is being done on the spot (not as homework), people do the work individually in different parts of the room or in adjoining rooms. We are available in the main room for help, clarification, etc. We allot about two hours for this activity.

4. *Improving objectives in subgroups.* After the individual work the team reconvenes. We then divide the team into subgroups of three people and give each subgroup the written instructions shown in Fig. 10.8.

People now break up into subgroups to fill their assignment. Before they break up we notify them at what hour the team will reconvene.

The purpose of this activity is to help each person improve his or her objectives. Follow this procedure:

1. The first person reads objectives from one form to the other two members of subgroup.

2. The other two people comment on this list, suggest changes, improvements, and corrections where needed. (Use the handout "How to define objectives," Fig. 10.6.)

3. The first person is not to argue back but only to make notes and give clarification if asked for.

4. When this is done, the second and third persons, each in turn, follow the same procedure.

5. The first person now displays his or her second form, and so on.

6. You have two hours at your disposal. Try to work as effectively as possible.

Fig. 10.8 Instructions for subgroups

5. *Summing up and decisions.* When the team reconvenes, we may have a summing up of the experience. People comment about their reactions, difficulties, and discuss the value of defining objectives.

a. A date must be fixed when the team will meet again to appraise objectives' lists submitted by all subcommittees and task groups. These subgroups should, of course, meet and prepare the lists before that date.

b. A date must be fixed when people will submit their final corrected forms for typing. People may have to make changes in lists which the subgroup commented on. They may also wish to reappraise forms, which is a step the subgroup did not find time to deal with.

c. The team may need to decide who will receive typed copies of the list of objectives of each team member. Should it be the top manager alone, or all team members?

d. The team may wish to make decisions about the adoption of procedures for defining objectives regularly, the time periods when this will be done, the person responsible for implementation, and the next date when this will be done.

Variation 1

The process as a whole remains unchanged; however, in addition, the team's head receives all lists of objectives and makes written remarks on them, and returns them for reappraisal and final submission.

Variation 2

The process as a whole remains unchanged, but in addition, each person has a meeting with the team's head to go over and discuss the person's list of objectives.

Variation 3

Step 3 may be lengthened by having each person prepare two objectives. Step 4 is skipped, and each person discusses his or her individual lists with the team's head, as in Variation 2.

Variation 4

This variation was mentioned in step 3. The preparation of individual lists of objectives may be done as homework between two team meetings.

PLANNING HOW TO ATTAIN AN OBJECTIVE *

Learning how to plan a series of actions and events in order to meet an objective on time.

When to use

Most people, especially managers, will find this useful. The process can be learned by strangers or in a team; it can be done in a managers' training workshop or as part of the regular training of a management team.

Preferably, one should go through this process after learning more about establishing objectives. Establishing objectives is determining the goals we wish to attain. In this process we learn how to get down practically to the implementation. We examine what steps have to be taken; in what order and by what dates, in order to reach our goal on time.

Who can use: 1. Any manager for him- or herself
2. Manager with his or her own team

Purposes: 1. To become familiar with a methodical way of planning events and activities to meet an objective
2. Learning how to schedule events in order to attain the objective on time

Participants: 1. Anyone
2. Managers of different organizations
3. A team of managers, etc.

Materials: 1. Newsprint, felt marker, tape, pens and paper
2. Placard—"Kinds of networks" (Figure 10.11)

Time: 2 to 3 hours

---

* This process is just a simplified form of PERT (program evaluation and review technique). Experience has shown us that the managers we work with are not in need of the sophisticated version. We therefore settle for this simple and easier form, which demands less practice and has more chance of being used.

STEPS IN PROCESS

1. Introduction
2. Listing events
3. Arranging events into concurrent series
4. Scheduling events
5. Planning with networks

Detailed Process

1. *Introduction.* The purpose of the activity is explained as in "Purposes," above. These points may be added.

a. Having objectives without planning how to attain them is the same as not having any objectives at all. In order to reach a goal we have to think out *how we go about attaining it.* Most goals can be reached only *by a series of steps.* If we avoid taking them, no elevator is going to lift us to the top. There is no substitute for the plain hard work of analyzing what has to be done, in what order and by what time. *Planning* is the tool that moves us from our present situation to a desired situation in the future. (This may be illustrated on newsprint.)

b. Planning can save much wasted effort and disappointments. We will have *fewer unexpected crisis periods* if we think things out thoroughly and plan ahead. Scheduling events ahead of time allows us *more time to prepare them well.* Scheduling saves us from unpleasant surprises—such as suddenly realizing that something important which we had relied on to take place has not materialized. Planning and scheduling relieves us from that common ailment of most organizations—"What! They're not finished *yet?*"

2. *Listing events.* We give a working definition of "activities" and "events":

- An *activity* is doing something. An activity takes time.
- An *event* is a point in time. An event (in this context) does not take time, it has no duration.
- Eating breakfast is an activity.
- Having finished eating breakfast is an event.
- Having a meeting is an activity; having had a meeting is an event.

Events are often *sequential*—that is, one event cannot take place before the other event is over.

```
1   2   3   4
0—0—0—0
```

Fig. 10.8 Events and activities

0 = Events; $-$ = Activities

In building a two-storied house the events may be:

1. foundations laid
2. first floor construction finished
3. second floor construction finished
4. roof finished

We write the above example on newsprint and illustrate it on newsprint as in Fig. 10.8.

People are then requested to choose one objective which they have established from any of their areas of responsibility.

They are to list in a column the rough order of events that must come about to attain the objective. Attainment of the objective is the last event at the bottom of the list.

We point out the example of the two-story building and request that people list the events in a form similar to this. At this point they should not worry about the order in which they write those events that can take place at the same time. We will deal with that later.

When people have finished, one or two examples are listed on newsprint and discussed. We sum up this stage by explaining that this is the most usual and simple way of planning and sometimes it is all we have to do.

3. *Arranging events into concurrent series.* We give an example and illustrate it on newsprint.

If we plan to hold a meeting of our team we need not finish each activity before beginning the next one. We can deal with a number of matters together *during the same period of time.*

We may decide what the agenda will be and then prepare written information for the participants concerning items that will be discussed. During the same period of time we are doing this, we (or our secretary) may be verifying the date and hour most convenient for holding the meeting and making arrangements for a meeting place.

We illustrate this procedure on newsprint as in Fig. 10.9. We are careful to convert the activities into events, and we point this out to the participants.

| 1. Agenda decided | 3. Date and hour of meeting decided |
| 2. Written information prepared | 4. Meeting place arranged |

Fig. 10.9 Arranging a meeting

We then request the participants to study the list of events they prepared beforehand. Each person is to try to divide his or her list into a number of lists of events that can take place simultaneously. This should be done in writing in a form similar to the example we have just illustrated.

When the participants have finished, two or three examples are copied on newsprint and discussed.

We sum up this part by pointing out that if there are no time constraints and no need for a tight schedule, sometimes this is all we have to do in order to plan how to attain our objectives.

4. *Scheduling events.* We explain: Objectives have *time constraints* and often we have to know by what date we will finish something. Sometimes we have *datelines* and we need to know whether we will be able to attain our objective on time. We can do this by scheduling events. *Scheduling events* means affixing dates by giving estimates of the time that will elapse between one event and the next. Scheduling is done by estimating the time it takes to perform the activity between each two events. We use our former example to illustrate the scheduling, as in Fig. 10.10:

a. Today is Monday; we can finish preparing the agenda today. That means it will be finished in one day. We mark a *1* with a different colored marker to the left of the first item on the newsprint.

b. Preparing and typing the written information will take, say, another three days. We mark a *3* with the marker to the left of the second item.

c. It will take our secretary two days to coordinate a convenient date and hour. We mark a *2* to the left of item 3.

d. It will take our secretary another day to arrange a suitable meeting place out in the country. We mark a *1* to the left of item 4.

e. For the notices to be typed and mailed and delivered by the post-office will take four days. We mark a *4* to the left of item 5.

f. We cannot normally expect that participants will be able to attend a meeting the same day they receive notice of it. So we allow a day for them to arrange to attend—and we mark a *1* to the left of item 6.

Now we ask the participants what is the earliest possible date for which we can set the meeting. The answer is: nine days from now. In our example, that would be Wednesday of the following week.

1	1. Agenda decided	*2*	3. Date and hour of meeting decided
3	2. Written information prepared	*1*	4. Meeting place arranged
	4 5. Notification of meeting received by participants		
	1 6. Participants arrange to attend meeting		

Fig. 10.10 Scheduling events

You can see how we reach this total in Fig. 10.10. We add up the days listed in the left-hand column (items 1 and 2) and then we add up the days listed in the right-hand column (items 3 and 4). We take the larger total, which is four days (the left-hand column), and to it we add the days required for item 5 (four days) and item 6 (1 day). This makes our total of nine days.

Participants are requested to schedule events on their lists and work out the earliest date they can achieve their objective. If they have difficulty estimating the time needed for one of the activities, we suggest this equation:

$$\frac{\text{Estimated maximum time} + \text{Estimated minimum time}}{2} = \frac{\text{Average time}}{\text{needed}}$$

When the group members have finished, two or three schedules are displayed on newsprint and discussed.

5. *Planning with networks.* We explain that when there are more than about 12 items in a plan and they are not sequential, it becomes difficult to schedule events and estimate when we will attain our objective.

We illustrate this with a placard showing different kinds of networks (see Fig. 10.11). We explain that:

a. Each circle represents an event.

b. The number in the circle indicates what event it is on our list.

c. The lines represent activities.

d. The number above the line indicates the number of days the activity takes.

e. The first net is a sequential one like our first example of building the house.

f. The second net represents a series of events somewhat similar to the example of arranging the meeting.

g. The third net represents a common situation in which we decide on something (1). We or others have to do a number of things concurrently (2, 3, 4). When they are all ready we can move on to achieve

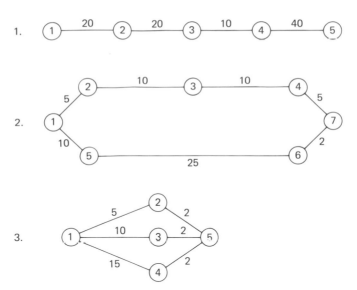

Fig. 10.11 Kinds of networks

our objective (5). (We decide to have supper; you cook; he sets the table and she prepares the salad; and when we are all ready we can wash our hands, sit down, and have supper).

To help understanding we ask each person to work out the shortest time it will take to reach each one of the three objectives in the networks. The answers are: (1) 90 days, (2) 37 days, (3) 17 days.

Participants are then requested to:

a. Choose another objective from their areas of responsibility.

b. Draw a network for this objective, with time estimates.

c. Calculate the minimum time needed to attain the objective.

When people have finished this assignment the group is broken up into subgroups of three people each. In the subgroup, each person in turn displays the network he or she has drawn and the others comment and give help if it is needed.

When the subgroups have finished, the group reconvenes and discusses the learning experience. People may ask questions and make comments. It is worth discussing the possibility and practicality of using this method of planning.

Variation 1

All the illustrations in the different figures may be prepared beforehand on newsprint. This may be less spontaneous, but it saves time.

Increasing effectiveness between teams

11

CHAPTER OBJECTIVE

To assist managers and consultants in building closer working relationships between teams through reaching out to each other, thus gaining a better understanding, achieving more effective listening and reducing interfering tensions.

GUIDE TO APPLYING INTERVENTIONS

What is increasing effectiveness between teams?

- It is finding ways to bring two teams together to work on common problems.

- It is recognizing differences between teams and not allowing those differences to keep the teams apart.

- It is getting people to listen more actively to each other even though they may have different starting points or different styles.

- It is assisting two groups which might merge into one team to prepare for a smoother transition.

- It is anticipating problems before they arise between two teams that work together.

- It is helping people become more aware of factors that may be maintaining an unrealized barrier.

What does increased effectiveness between teams do?

- It affords an opportunity to learn about different communicating styles.
- It helps bring out feelings about power and influence and allows team members to handle such issues better and place them in a proper perspective.
- It helps people become clearer about their different ways of dealing with conflict.

About the interventions in this chapter

These interventions are designed to help two groups or two teams from the same organization to work together more effectively. They are particularly useful when the two teams have frequent contacts, work on mutual projects, and are brought together to think through new directions for the organization. Our word is *interface*; that is, they have many overlapping duties or programs.

In our experience, the most effective application of these interventions requires both teams to meet *without interruption*. Thus, we strongly recommend leaving the site of usual business and spending at least a night and a day together. If this is impossible, some of the interventions can be accomplished during an evening session.

We are also careful to try to provide methods of applying what has been learned in the work environment. Very often, inter-team workshops can end in a "good time," but with little ongoing payoff. The interventions are structured as much as possible to avoid such an outcome.

The interventions

1. *Reaching out to other teams.* This was specifically designed to help two teams examine their differences and out of these differences discover creative ways of working together more effectively. There are many characteristics that can keep people (and teams) apart, such as: physical location, professional background, educational differences, racial differences, etc. These very characteristics can also be directed toward more creative problem-solving, but the differences must be understood and bridged.

2. *Listening to each other.* A special form of "reaching out," this intervention focuses on a most important tool in interpersonal relations: listening. There are many ways of presenting information—some methods fit one kind of person and other methods do the best job for other kinds. This intervention assists the two teams in learning about and practicing different ways of presenting and using information.

3. *Increasing understanding between teams.* This intervention is particularly useful in bringing two groups or teams together that must find better methods of joint operation, particularly if they will merge in the future or if they must work together and have different ways of operating. We often find that members of the different teams have many unspoken concerns about a future merger. It is important to confront such issues before the merger or some unnecessary problems will be experienced.

4. *Dealing with tension between teams.* This is useful as a method of catching a major problem in the bud. If tension and feelings are very strong, this intervention must be preceded by some calming-down procedures. There is a strong effort to help create a "win-win" problem-solving attitude between the two teams; that is, helping them to find ways in which *both* can win in a given situation.

MATRIX OF INTERVENTIONS

Intervention	Use	Who can use	Time demand
Reaching out to other teams	Overcoming differences between teams; increasing use of creative solutions to problems	Experienced manager not with his or her own team	5–7 hrs
Listening to each other	Poor information flow between departments; errors in communication between teams; limited benefit from joint meetings	Experienced manager not with his or her own team	4–6 hrs
Increasing understanding between teams	Before two teams will merge; two teams wanting to work more closely	Consultant to organizations	2½–4 hrs
Dealing with tension between teams	Help teams, groups realize how they are hurting each other; create positive atmosphere between teams	Consultant to organizations	3–6 hrs

Possible outcomes

1. Understanding and more acceptance of differences in people.
2. Discovering more creative ways to solve problems.
3. Increased links between participating departments.
4. Increased quality of teamwork within and between departments.
5. More effective ways of exchanging information.
6. Better use of active listening.

7. Better understanding of how other people feel about interteam problems.

8. Reduced anxieties about future changes and mergers.

9. More ease in speaking out about underlying issues.

10. More positive understanding between teams.

11. Finding more ways to have both teams benefit from joint actions.

Recommended readings

1. Fordyce, J. K., and R. Weil, *Managing with People* (Reading, Mass.: Addison-Wesley, 1971).

2. Lawrence, P. R., and J. W. Lorsch, *Developing Organizations: Diagnosis and Action* (Reading, Mass.: Addison-Wesley, 1969).

3. Pfeiffer, J. W., and J. E. Jones, *A Handbook of Structured Experiences for Human Relations Training*, Vols. I, II, III, IV, V (La Jolla, Calif.: University Associates Press, 1971, 1972, 1973, 1974, 1975).

REACHING OUT TO OTHER TEAMS

Attempting to increase creativity on the basis of differences between two departments or groups that work or are planning to work together in the organization.

When to use

Within an organization each department tends to develop a way of life of its own. Lawrence and Lorsch (see Recommended Readings) stress how differences in the environment that each group faces (stability and certainty versus instability and uncertainty, etc.) affect each group's style of functioning, time frame, managerial style, and orientation to goals. These in turn create communication and linkage problems between groups. Some circumstances that we have found contributing to keeping groups apart include: physical location; nature of the work; professional background of team members; seniority; age; educational, social, and racial differences between groups; totally female or male work force; and orientation of the manager.

These differences can sometimes be overcome. In the normal work experience, pressures to get an interdepartmental job done will often break established barriers. We have noticed that even if these barriers are removed temporarily, as soon as the job is over most of the people return to their own area and regular task. Occasionally there will be a continuing connection between two people from different departments. These natural links can be used to build better working relations between departments. However, a forward-thinking manager should not leave interdepartmental connections just to chance or special personalities.

We find that the following situations might necessitate using a "reach-out" program:

1. Company plans indicate that two departments will be working closely together on a series of projects.

2. The company is looking for creative solutions to equipment redesign or new product development, and it is clear that the thinking of two or more departments will be essential for optimum results.

3. One department seems to be operating very successfully and it seems advantageous to try to spread the effectiveness to other departments.

4. There is a merger between two companies or organizations and two similar departments must be integrated into one larger department or must coordinate their efforts.

5. There is a government inspection team based at the plant and there is also a quality control department. The functions of the two teams somewhat overlap, and should be coordinated.

6. There are two departments that have (or should have) frequent contact with each other; e.g., Marketing and Research and Development, or Purchasing and Production. There is interest in achieving a better working relationship.

Such a "reach-out" effort is *not* suggested when there are particular tensions between departments. (See "Dealing with tensions between teams," later in this chapter.) The "reach-out" approach is an attempt to start a process and see what can be gained from the increased creativity that might be generated by it.

Who can use: 1. A manager who has participated in team development and has co-led team sessions with a consultant. Such a manager can work best with departments other than his or her own

2. A consultant to organizations

Purposes: 1. To develop stronger links between two teams or departments

2. To identify and support natural ties among members of two teams or departments

3. To stimulate more creative solutions to organization-wide projects or problems

4. To spread the effectiveness of departments that seem to have a high quality of team work

Participants: All members of both teams or departments. When necessary, the teams may have to be divided into subgroups

Materials:
1. Newsprint, felt pens, tape, pencils and paper
2. Folders for notebooks or journals
3. Materials needed for Steps 2, 3, and 4 of "Basic steps in team development," in Chapter 6.
4. Materials for creative presentations, including magazines, paints, scissors, paste

Time: 5 to 7 hours

STEPS IN PROCESS

1. Warm-up and basics in team development
2. Identifying differences among team members within each team
3. Sharing differences within total group
4. Interteam joining on identified differences
5. Creative presentations of themes associated with differences
6. Planning some joint company project(s)

Detailed process:

1. *Warmup and basics in team development.*

a. We suggest that some introduction exercise be used at the beginning of the session. See Appendix 2, "Some Basic and Standard Methods" for suggestions about a warmup.

b. The use of steps 2, 3, and 4 of "Basic steps in team development" must be tailored to the experience and receptiveness of both groups. At times we have faced one experienced team and one that has not had any team development. While such a situation is quite challenging, we find that the experienced group *is quite willing* to repeat some exercises. After taking the whole group through an exercise, we usually invite the more experienced participants to comment on how they have applied what they have learned. It is also interesting to have them remark about the differences between their previous experience and this one.

c. By the completion of steps 2 and 3 of "Basic steps in team development" there often is a good feeling built up in the group. They have shared the discoveries of perceptual differences and they are more aware of the difficulties in good active listening. We usually hold the feedback exercise to just giving and receiving *positive* feedback. We want the participants to learn the lesson well and prefer to keep the tensions down.

2. *Identifying differences among team members within each team.*

a. At this time we invite the two teams to separate and go to different parts of the room or to different rooms. If the teams have more than nine people per team, we suggest that the teams subdivide into two smaller units per team. However, it is best to keep the team together whenever possible.

b. After they have separated, we explain that we would like them to discover as many differences within their group as they can find. For example, if there are men *and* women; if there is an older group *and* a younger group; if there are some members who have more seniority *and* others with less seniority; if there are some people who are left-handed *and* others who are right-handed, etc.

c. Usually, the team can reach the differences through total group discussion. However, if there seems to be difficulty, we suggest that the group have a series of interviews in a "fishbowl" form. One team member interviews another on the differences he or she brings to the group. All the differences should be listed on newsprint paper and the names of the team members who are identified with each side of the difference should be listed next to the appropriate side.

d. When the teams have completed their task, they should take down the newsprint and come together. Both sheets should be taped to the wall side by side.

3. *Sharing differences within total group.*

a. Going down the list of differences can bring both laughter and, at times, a little tension. We have found that when racial or religious differences are brought forward, some people have become a little uneasy, and sometimes tension has developed around sex or age differences. Most of the time the group listens and discusses each of the differences with growing amazement about how many differences can be found within a group of eight or nine people.

b. We now ask the group to notice whether there are any common differences between teams. As these differences are identified, we circle the items on both sheets in another color. At the same time, we mention the names of the people who are identified with each side of the difference.

c. We look for enough differences so that all members of both teams have been identified with at least one difference. It is usually quite easy to achieve this end. In the rare occasion that one person was not included, it was possible to include him or her by raising or lowering the age range for the older/younger age split or some other slight revision in another category. While the differences are being identified we write down on the newsprints the names of the people identified with each difference (next to that item). This helps us with the next step.

4. *Interteam joining on identified differences.*

a. In going over the differences we try to select those that will allow for "difference subgroups" of at least three people and preferably four or more. Sometimes it is necessary to do some juggling to form balanced groups.

b. We ask the members of one team to join with the members of the other team who line up on the same side of a given difference. For example, we ask the women of both teams to join together and likewise the men of both groups to join together.

After separating the groups into subgroups of all men and all women, we then require further splits. Each group might then divide by age, into older and younger members. The older and younger members of the men's group would then join the appropriate women's subgroup.

Now we would have four possible subgroups: all women; all men; one group of younger men and women; and one group of older men and women. As we look over the subgroups, we want to make sure that there is a good mix of both teams. After all, that is the main purpose of this step.

c. Once the subgroups have been set, they go to different rooms or parts of the large room and begin to examine what the difference really means to the members of the subgroup. One time there was a discussion among the "tall ones" that led the participants to become aware of how it feels for a tall person to enter a room or fit into spaces that are generally made for the average-sized person. Sometimes the left-handed participants become enraged at how frequently they are at a disadvantage in this right-handed world.

d. The second stage of the discussion involves how the differences are noticed within the work situation. In some instances, the subgroup can find no special way that being a young man will make a difference. But we have been surprised about some observations.

One time a young, fair-skinned man revealed to his subgroup's surprise that he thought he was employed by a company with predominantly middle-European employees because of his light complexion and seemingly different ethnic background. Sometimes the discussion might emphasize the unfairness of the company to women employees or to the minority groups.

e. Finally, we ask the subgroup to review their discussion and then think of some way to express the special sense of their subgroup to the total group. The creative expression can take the form of a skit, a collage made up of clippings cut out of magazines and displayed on some newsprint, a poem or song, etc. *We encourage each subgroup to include something about the company when possible.*

5. *Creative presentations of theme associated with differences.*

a. Each subgroup is given a chance to present its creative work with as much freedom of expression as possible. After each presentation, the total group has a chance to discuss the meaning of the presentation. We suggest that each person record in his or her notebook what has been learned from the presentation, particularly as it might relate to company matters.

b. At the end of the presentations, the group is asked to list the ideas that came to them during the series of offerings. We list these ideas on newsprint. Usually, the group finds two or three items particularly interesting, and lets the discussion go off into these directions. We are attempting to help the group identify some interests that cut across team lines. This is usually very easy to accomplish.

6. *Planning some joint company projects.*

a. The groups now choose a joint project to work on together. When two teams are going through this process because they will be working together in the future, they will probably choose a project related to that future work. For example, two teams who were identified as the ones responsible for new products moved very quickly to brainstorming new product ideas. (See the section on "Creative solutions to problems," in Chapter 5, on how to apply brainstorming in such a situation.)

b. Teams that are brought together to learn from each other (or for one team to learn from the other about better ways to organize or handle departmental business) have identified processes of working together on some change in the operation of the department. It has been interesting to see that the so-called "better functioning" department has often left the session with methods it has learned from the other department.

In one case, two departments had a series of joint meetings back at the plant. There was a different departmental procedure presented at each meeting. The procedure was critiqued with both departments benefitting from the careful and respectful analysis of the procedures.

c. After a project has been identified, the total group identifies the necessary steps to implement it. This includes setting objectives, taking action steps, nominating the responsible team members, and agreeing on some review procedure to evaluate attaining objectives. We refer you to Chapter 5 for assistance with any part of the decision-making process and Chapter 10 for setting objectives.

Usually we have interteam subgroups formed to handle at least some of the action steps. In one such session, the issue chosen was "Better utilization of the talents of women." The idea came from the women's subgroup presentation. The action steps involved reviewing the use of women managers throughout the company.

d. After the project or projects have been worked on, the total group discusses their learnings, focusing on the questions:

1) What have I learned about the other team that I didn't know before this workshop?
2) What am I likely to do differently when I return to work tomorrow?

Finally, we ask the participants to record what they have learned in their notebooks or journals.

Variation 1

This intervention can be used in a workshop for managers from different companies to increase awareness of differences and how they influence behavior at work. Steps 1, 3, 4, and 5 can remain essentially the same.

Step 2 will have to be modified. We suggest that the workshop participants form into two groups with equal distribution of men and women. The two subgroups operate as though they are teams from the same company.

Step 6 can be eliminated or modified so that each participant thinks of a project that emerges from the differences he or she can carry out on returning to his or her organization.

LISTENING TO EACH OTHER

Attempting to increase effective listening between two departments or teams that work or are planning to work together.

When to use

The "Listening" intervention is a special form of reaching out. See "When to use," in the preceding section: "Reaching out to other teams."

Some additional circumstances for using "Listening" are when:

1. Two teams have started to work together and after joint meetings there is much unclarity about what has been discussed.

2. The managers of two teams with coordinated functions meet regularly, but the joint efforts of the teams have not been very fruitful.

Who can use: 1. A manager who has participated in team development and has co-led team sessions with a consultant. Such a manager can work best with departments other than his or her own
2. Consultant to organizations

Purposes: 1. See "Purposes," in the section on "Reaching out to other teams"
2. To increase awareness of different forms of presenting information between teams
3. To practice some different forms of presenting information

Participants: All members of both teams or departments. When necessary, the teams may have to be divided into subgroups

Materials: 1. Newsprint, felt pens, tape, pencils and paper
2. Folders for notebooks or journals
3. Materials needed for steps 2, 3, and 4 of "Basic steps in team development," in Chapter 6.
4. Materials for step 4 including magazines, paints, scissors, and paste
5. A large meeting room
6. Typewriters and carbon paper

Time: 4 to 6 hours

STEPS IN PROCESS

1. Warmup and basics in team development
2. "Parallel chairs" listening exercise
3. Blocks to information flow and understanding—a lecturette
4. Practicing different ways of communicating information
5. Staging a joint meeting on a current issue

Detailed process

1. *Warmup and basics in team development.* See step 1 of "Reaching out to other teams" (the preceding section).

2. *"Parallel chairs" listening exercise.*

a. We indicate that active listening is difficult even under quiet circumstances. We are usually faced with all kinds of pressures and influences while trying to listen in group situations. The "Parallel chairs" exercise is an exaggerated form of this pressure type of situation.

b. The participants are asked to set up their chairs in two rows, facing each other. The rows should not be longer than six pairs of chairs. Thus, if the teams are 10 to 12 each, then there would be two rows of either five or six pairs of chairs. If two sets of rows are necessary, the sets should be placed as far from each other as possible to lessen interference. With teams of unequal size, the larger team should "loan" members to the smaller team for this exercise.

c. We ask the participants to sit in the chairs facing each other. We would say: "I am going to ask you to discuss a topic with your partner for three minutes. After three minutes, I will give the signal, and each person in the row on my right will change seats with the person on his or her right and the last person in the row will take the first seat. The people in the row on my left will just remain seated throughout the exercise. Each discussion will last three minutes. By the end of the exercise everyone will have had a chance to talk to everyone else. Now, I'll write the topic on this paper."

d. We usually use very timely topics that are likely to evoke strong opinions and lively conversation. Such topics as the following have been used: "What is blocking cooperation between our teams?" or "What is the most serious problem we are now facing in our organization?" or "How can our company become more efficient?"

e. Once the topic is written on newsprint, the signal is given for the first conversation. At the end of three minutes the facilitator gives a loud signal and helps people move to the next seat as quickly as possible. Pressure mounts as the conversations become more lively.

f. At the completion of the conversations both teams are brought together for a discussion about what was learned about listening. We find that there are some surprises, such as: "I didn't think I could hear my partner with everyone else talking so loud," or "I began hearing some of my arguments coming back at me almost in the same words." There is a heightened awareness of how information is misinterpreted; how misinformation is passed along; how strong people seem to get their influence felt; etc.

3. *Blocks to information flow and understanding—a lecturette.*

a. We usually start the lecturette with the questions: "What do you think interfered with getting your thoughts across to someone else in a group meeting? What are the factors in yourself or the other people?" Most often, the group will identify all the factors in bits and pieces. All of the thoughts are written on newsprint.

b. The lecturette is formed around the ideas of the participants. The main issues are:

1) *Different communicating styles.* Some people are just very talkative and others are very quiet; some people give a powerful message in a few words and others use many words and say very little. Some people can communicate better in writing; others are far better on their feet—and so on.

2) *Interest in the subject.* People differ in their interest in a specific subject; the same person may have different levels of interest in the same subject at different times.

3) *Pressure in the situation.* The job must be done quickly and there is little time to share thoughts or information; everyone is enthusiastic or angry about the job to be done; an outside person is attending the meeting, a visitor from the parent organization.

4) *Language or dialect differences.* The confusion can result from different ways of pronouncing the same words or from special expressions associated with different sections of the country. When people have different mother languages, there is more difficulty in getting ideas across.

5) *Unspoken disagreements and other feelings.* Unclear messages are also the result of underlying feelings which have not been shared openly. The anger or frustration behind the words comes through to the other person. Such feelings also influence our word choices so that more inflammatory words may be used when anger is felt.

c. After the lecturette, we ask for further comments and press for connections between the "Parallel Chairs" exercise and the blocks to information flow and understanding.

4. *Practicing different ways of communicating information.*

a. We want to increase awareness of different ways of communicating. Through greater awareness and practice, we have seen teams become better at sharing information and thus function better together.

b. We ask all the participants to think of specific examples of subjects exchanged between the teams at meetings, in memos or conversations. The participants should write these examples down. Then we ask everyone to report what they have written and a list is made on newsprint.

c. We select a number of items from this list and write each one on a separate piece of note paper. We choose items that: arouse the interest of the participants; are neither too simple nor too complex; and that contain implications for both teams.

d. The group is divided into groups of four—two from each team. The participants have freedom to choose their groups. Each subgroup receives one item written on note paper. On the outside of the note paper on which the item has been written we indicate the way each subgroup must present its item. The following five ways can be used and each one is alloted to a different subgroup:

1. Written as a memo
2. Oral, as a report at a meeting
3. Presented as a dialogue
4. Demonstrated to group
5. Drawn or made from clippings as a pictorial presentation

e. The subgroups of four take the sheet and review the contents. They must organize a communication which will be presented to the total group. They must have a product which will be available in the form dictated by the directions on the outside fold. They have about one-half hour to complete the task.

f. The total group is reconvened and each subgroup has a chance to present its message. After each message is presented, there is a critiquing of its clarity. Is there agreement in the total group about what was being communicated? Clarifications are made by the subgroup members.

We try to have the group consider whether the form of delivery was the best way of communicating the message. In that way, we have the participants really examine options that can be used.

We help them begin to examine how these different forms of communicating can increase clarity during their regular work encounters— either at large meetings, exchange of written communications, or meetings of two or three at a time.

g. We ask the participants to write down in their journals what they have learned about communicating as it might be applied at work and especially between the two teams.

5. *Staging a joint meeting on a current issue.*

a. We suggest reviewing with the group "How to run a participative meeting," from Appendix II. We ask everyone to take notes on the meeting since all members will have a chance to report the content of the meeting.

b. While we are setting the agenda, we ask for issues that have concerned members of either team and require attention. The items are written on newsprint in the order presented.

c. We help the group see connections (if there are any) between items and set priorities. Finally the group selects one item which we will work on.

d. The group now begins to discuss the item it chose. During the discussion, if we see people who indicate (whether by their comments or their nonverbal expressions) that they are having trouble understanding, we stop the meeting to get at clarity.

e. At the end of the discussion, we ask the group to think about which of the five forms tried earlier would be the best way to convey the ideas brought out during the meeting to anyone who might not have attended. We allow some discussion of the options.

f. We end the meeting with the suggestion that everyone choose one of the previously suggested five forms of reporting a meeting and (as back-home work) organize a report of the content of this meeting at a follow-up session. Examples of the different forms of reporting should be used. At the follow-up session, the examples of different methods of reporting should be presented by any team member who *volunteers*. After each presentation, the group should comment on how well the message got across.

g. We find that a follow-up meeting has much merit. It allows the participants a place to review what they have learned. They can test which forms of communicating are realistic in the work setting. They can reexperience some of the benefits of different reporting methods and ways of listening that were achieved during the workshop—only now in the real-life work setting.

Variation 1

This intervention can be used in a workshop with managers from different companies. Steps 1, 2, and 3 can be used without modification. In step 4, we ask participants to think of subjects that they have difficulty understanding either during or after a meeting. We usually eliminate step 5.

Variation 2

When time is limited, we eliminate step 5 and suggest such an activity as part of a regular meeting at work.

INCREASING UNDERSTANDING BETWEEN TEAMS

Helping two teams understand each other better, become closer, and deal with common problems, or lay the basis for merging.

When to use

We would use this intervention for either of two different purposes:

1. To lay the groundwork for two groups that were separate and are either intending to merge or to work closer together in the future.
2. To bring closer together two groups that interact with each other but do not understand one another's problems, viewpoints, and feelings.

1. *Laying the groundwork for two groups intending to merge.* Merging two separate groups may create many problems: Each group may have its own way of doing things. In each group there may be people who are worried about changes that will take place when the groups merge. People may feel uncertain about what will happen to them in the new setup.

The purpose of this intervention will be to allow free expression to people's anxiety in order that the problems may be openly confronted and dealt with.

2. *To bring closer two groups that have difficulty understanding each other.* This situation is often found in organizations and communities.

In organizations the problems may be between two departments; e.g., Sales and Production.

In communities we may find misunderstandings between different generations, between people from different economic or racial backgrounds, or between two groups that interact on one specific level (such as teachers and parents). In this case, the purpose of the intervention will be to lower the barriers between the groups, to decrease misunderstanding and stereotyping, and to help both groups to better understand and accept one another's feelings and problems.

We would *not* use this intervention to deal with severe tensions between two groups. When tension between groups is high, we prefer to use the next intervention in this chapter: "Dealing with tensions between teams." We also would *not* use the intervention unless *both* groups have expressed their willingness to find some way of becoming closer to each other. It is difficult to get people to cooperate in going through this process if they have not first explicitly decided they want to do something about their relationship with another group. It is therefore not sufficient that *one* group wants to become closer to another. Members of each group may have different degrees of enthusiasm and support for doing this. But if the key people and the majority of *each* group want to do something about their relations with the other group, this will be sufficient for us to go ahead.

Who can use: A consultant or experienced facilitator, preferably with the aid of a co-facilitator

Purposes: 1. To help members of two different groups listen to one another's problems and better understand one another's feelings
2. To bring the two groups closer to each other
3. To help the groups deal with common problems
4. To alleviate people's anxiety before a merger and confront problems they see in the merger

Participants: Two groups—not more than 15 people and not less than four people in each group

Materials: Newsprint, felt pens, and tape

Time: 2½ to 4 hours

STEPS IN PROCESS

1. Introducing the experience
2. "Fishbowl" with group A inside
3. "Fishbowl" with group B inside
4. Defining problems and dividing into mixed subgroups
5. Recommendations and reactions in total forum

Detailed process

1. *Introducing the experience.* The process begins with the two groups sitting together in as small a circle as possible. Large open space created by from 20 to 30 people sitting in a circle is often a cause of discomfort and embarrassment.

We begin in either of two ways:

a. We relate what circumstances have led to convening this meeting; *or,* better still, one person from each team (prearranged with us) relates briefly (in not more than five minutes) what led him or her to initiate holding this combined meeting.

b. Following this opening, whichever of the two ways was used, we say a few words and present an illustration showing problems of interface in general. (This actually is the same opening used by us in the intervention "Dealing with tensions between teams.") We draw on a newsprint two interlocking circles (see Fig. 11.1) and mark the area of

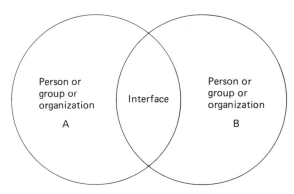

Fig. 11.1 Point of interface

overlapping. We explain that this is the "interface" of two systems. Each circle represents a system which can be an individual, a group, or an organization. The area of interaction—the interface—is where problems, misunderstandings, and misconceptions develop. To deal with these we must become aware of them, know what they are, and then confront them openly together in a problem-solving way.

A second point may be made about *stereotyping*. We explain the need people have to organize information in a consistent form. Thus, if we know someone is young, we might associate this with a number of other characteristics such as "unsettled," "rebellious," etc. We tend to organize our perception of groups of people in such stereotypes, and this leads to misconceptions and misunderstanding.

c. If we are dealing with two groups that intend to merge, we will probably mention the point about stereotyping and add a few words about people's *anxiety*. We will point out that a group of people who work or interact together for some time develop a set of agreed norms and role expectations. People in a group develop accepted ways of doing things and in time come to agree about what is done and what is not done. They also build up a set of expectations from each other, how each will behave in his or her specific role within the group.

When two groups merge, both the norms and the role expectations may change. People are anxious. The stability they achieved is endangered; their way of doing things and their expectations from others may change. This uncertainty can breed anxiety. People are not sure of their place and role in the future setup. They are afraid that the familiar and accepted ways of doing things will be disrupted. It is therefore important that these anxieties be brought to awareness and openly confronted. If this is not done, the problems will simmer under the surface and will affect the level of openness and trust in the new combined group.

2. *"Fishbowl" with group A inside.*

a. The place where the two groups meet should be large enough to allow organization of the participants into two circles, an inner one and an outer one. The seating arrangements should not be sofas or armchairs, but light movable chairs.

b. We now ask the members of one group (henceforth group A) to arrange themselves on chairs in a closed circle in the middle of the room. The members of the second group (henceforth group B) arrange themselves in an outer circle surrounding group A. Both groups face inward.

If we are dealing with two groups of unequal power and influence, we tend to put the *weaker* of the two groups inside the fishbowl (group A).

The same with two merging groups; the one with the *highest level of anxiety* should be group A.

We now request the members of group A to begin discussing among themselves problems—the difficulties, misconceptions, and anxieties— that may have a bearing on their relationship with members of group B. This needs further clarification. The subject of discussion will depend on who the two groups are, and the problems between them which are to be dealt with. If we are dealing with two groups that are going to *merge*, the subjects might be, for instance:

1) How do I feel about the merger?
2) What am I anxious about regarding the merger?
3) What would I like to ensure and/or achieve with the merger?
4) How will the merger affect me individually?
5) What hopes have I of the merger?

If we are dealing with two groups that do not know each other sufficiently and have *difficulty understanding and getting closer to each other*, the subjects might be.

1) What are our problems, as I see them, that group B members may not be aware of?
2) What is of importance to me and/or us that may not be felt by members of group B?
3) What do I find to be difficult for group B members to understand in our way of seeing and doing things?
4) What, to my mind, interferes with the two groups becoming more understanding and closer to each other?

If there are some *difficulties* between the groups we might add the following questions:

1) How do I feel when I come into contact with members of group B?
2) What difficulties do I have in my relationships with members of group B?

c. We sometimes run into the problem of *silence and embarrassment* in the inner group. People may find it difficult to speak freely with another group of people sitting around them listening and watching. If we see signs of this problem we request one participant who generally speaks easily in public to begin, and then continue with each person speaking in turn in seating order.

The questions suggested above may be written on newsprint, and people can refer to them when they speak. We would prefer a less structured form of discussion—more of a give-and-take kind—and if this develops we encourage it.

d. While group A members are speaking we are careful to ensure that group B members are listening, but we stop any oral comments. This can be more easily achieved by dispersing group B members completely around the A circle at roughly equal distances, for if group B members cluster together in pairs or groups at some point in the circle, they tend to exchange remarks and reactions among themselves regarding what is being said and going on. We might have to remind them that they will have their say in turn, and that their objective at this point is to try to listen as much as possible, and to understand what group A members are trying to express.

3. *"Fishbowl" with group B inside.* After a certain time the two groups change places. Group B sits in the inner circle and group A sits in the outer circle.

When to make this changeover depends both on the total time at our disposal for the entire process and upon the flow of talk in group A. When group A members begin to repeat comments, we call such repetition to their attention. Frequent repetition of items suggests changing to group B. We must take into account that group B must also have its say. It seems better to make the changeover when both groups are still interested, than to do it when they have begun to lose interest. Group B now begins to talk along the same lines and answer the same questions that group A dealt with.

The difference, of course, is that group B has heard group A, and therefore it is to be expected that people will refer to things and react to things that were said by group A. Nevertheless, we are most interested in having group B members speak of their problems, difficulties, anxieties, etc. We may point this out, and while we do not discourage reactions to what was said before, we do encourage people to speak about what is troubling them.

4. *Defining problems and dividing into mixed subgroups.*

a. If we are very short of time, and if we are dealing with two groups that wished to understand each other and become closer, we might eliminate step 4 and proceed directly to some form of summing up and practical conclusions if needed. We would convene the two groups and suggest that they offer suggestions that would help bring the groups closer in the future. Quite often the groups elect a liaison committee to ensure ways of meeting together in the future.

When we are dealing with two groups that will merge or have misunderstandings, we always go through Step 4 and try not to omit it.

b. While both groups are in the fishbowl, we keep notes of the major problems raised. We do this privately in a notebook, not on newsprint. Writing the problems on a newsprint would divert people's attention. Toward the end of group B's session in the fishbowl, we transfer the major problems raised by both teams onto a newsprint. If we are working with a co-facilitator, we prefer that one of us prepare this newsprint outside the meeting room.

Generally, it is worthwhile to lead the intervention with two facilitators. During the fishbowl one facilitator takes care of the process and the other concentrates on keeping notes on the problems and later prepares the newsprint. When group B has finished its turn in the inner circle, we display the newsprint to the groups. We do this without moving the groups from their two-circle seating arrangement. Then we ask if anyone wants to add suggestions or if we have missed any major problem.

c. The two groups are now divided into subgroups made up of people from both teams. Their purpose is to deal with the problems raised. During the fishbowl, the second facilitator can prepare a plan to divide the groups into mixed sub-groups. Alternatively, if preferred, the groups can be broken up arbitrarily by dividing them into subgroups of from three to five people, combining segments from the two circles. That is, two or three people from the inner circle join together with two or three people who are sitting behind them in the outer circle.

Each subgroup is notified which problem or problems it will discuss. The subgroups are asked to discuss the problem, clarify it in a *constructive, problem-solving way* and, if needed, prepare *suggestions or recommendations concerning it*. We specify a time limit of from 30 to 60 minutes for the subgroup discussions. We ask the subgroups to keep notes on their discussions and to put their recommendations, if any, on newsprint. The facilitators move between subgroups to help with the problem-solving process.

People now begin discussing the issues they have to deal with in their respective subgroups. If one group finishes its assignment before the others, we may transfer to it a problem from one of the other groups that is lagging in its discussion. Alternatively, they may join another subgroup and follow its discussion passively or join in actively. If preferred, a subgroup that has finished can just sit together and wait for the others to finish.

5. *Recommendations and reactions in total forum.* When time is up, the groups convene in one circle. A member from each subgroup relates briefly what the discussion was about in his or her group and presents the various viewpoints. If there are conclusions or recommendations, these are displayed on newsprint. If possible, they are ratified by both teams. If there are difficulties in doing this, a mixed liaison committee is formed. At this stage the committee will have before it two functions:—

a. To discuss and bring *recommendations on unsettled issues.*

b. To be responsible for *implementing accepted recommendations.*

If it is decided to form such a committee, one of the members is requested to follow the discussions and (1) write on newsprint the accepted recommendations for implementation, and (2) list separately the issues that the committee will have to deal with.

When the discussion is over, people are requested to give their feelings and reactions to what has happened to them throughout the entire process. This final expression of feelings can sometimes be the most emotional, heartwarming experience of the entire process, and often does much to bring the two groups closer together.

Variation 1

During the fishbowl, an empty chair can be left in the inner circle. Any one member of the group in the outer circle can occupy this chair for a time by just getting up and going to sit on it. The person who does this can ask a question to clarify something or express an opinion on what has been said in the inner circle. Using the empty-chair technique might make the discussion livelier and help clarify an issue. On the other hand, the method might give the fishbowl a more controversial debating quality than was intended.

Variation 2

This was mentioned in step 3. If we are dealing with two groups who wish to become closer, and if time is very short, we may omit step 4—dividing into subgroups. Nevertheless, this choice should not be made lightly. Even if time is short it might be preferable to shorten the sessions in the fishbowl and still have mixed subgroup meetings. We are often forced to face such a dilemma because we are frequently limited to only two and a half to three hours for the total process.

DEALING WITH TENSION BETWEEN TEAMS

Helping two conflicting groups settle their differences constructively.

When to use

This intervention is used with two teams who must work together in an organization and who have problems at their interface. That is, they do have to interact with each other and there are problems and tensions that arise at the points of interaction. These may be two work teams; a service group and a production group; a number of supervisors and a work team, or some other combination.

We find this intervention suitable also for two groups that cannot be defined as teams in an organization. For example: teachers and the parents of the children they teach. The parents are not a "team" but they may have similar interests and tension may develop between them and the teachers.

There are a number of circumstances under which we would not make this intervention. We would *not* use this process:

1. If we were sure that the tension had reached an explosive stage of extremely intense conflict and great emotional involvement. In such a case we would need a series of interventions and experiences to begin clearing the air.
2. If we were not sure that the people in the two groups really wished to work out their differences and try to settle them.
3. If we diagnosed the situation to be caused mainly by one or more extremely difficult people. In such case we would suggest giving these people help before we made an attempt to deal with the tension between the groups.
4. If there was extreme conflict within the teams themselves, we might have to deal with this first before beginning on the outside interface.

Who can use: A consultant or an experienced facilitator. Both would be advised to work with a co-facilitator throughout the process.

Purposes:
1. To help each group realize what it is doing that hurts the other group
2. To create a positive understanding atmosphere between the groups
3. To help them deal with differences between them in a constructive, problem-solving way

Participants: Two teams or two groups of not more than 12 people in each group. This needs further clarification: We have sometimes been requested to deal with tensions between a very small group (say three people) and a relatively large group (20 people or more). The groups may consist of supervisors and workers, or teachers and parents, etc. The discrepancy in size creates problems. As detailed here, the process is suitable for two groups that are not disproportionately different in size. When the groups are disproportionate, we examine the feasibility of holding more than one meeting and breaking up the larger group into smaller groups. Each meeting will be between the small group and a part of the large group. This, of course, is not easy either for the small group or the facilitator, since they must go through a similar experience a number of times.

Another solution we have tried—but are not too happy about—is to go through the whole process with the smaller group and a representative team from the larger group. The remaining members of the larger group sit and watch the process without taking an active part in it.

Materials:
1. Newsprint, felt markers, tape, pens and paper
2. Placard "Ways of dealing with problems" (Fig. 11.2)
3. Handouts: "Ways of dealing with problems" (optional)

Time: 3 to 6 hours (not including initial interviews)

STEPS IN PROCESS

1. Pre-meeting individual interviews
2. Introducing the experience
3. The groups prepare their lists
4. Lists compared: some problems settled, others defined
5. Mixed subgroups problem-solve the remaining issues
6. Summing up

Detailed process

1. *Pre-meeing individual interviews.* We have gone through this process without interviewing individuals from both groups. However, we feel more prepared if we do speak to a number of people from each group before going through the intervention. Oftentimes a team we have been working with may make its own decision about going through this process. It may decide to deal with one of its problematic interfaces with another group. In this case we are already aware of the problems as seen by the team we have been working with, and therefore all we need to do is to speak to a number of people from the other group.

In any case, we should perhaps not call what we do an "interview." The short talk which we have with people is not the same as the long and thorough interview which we hold in, for instance, the intervention entitled "Individual interviews and group feedback" (in Chapter 2).

All we try to do in the talks we have with a number of people is to get a rough estimate of the answers to a number of questions:

a. Is the tension between the groups such that we will be able to deal with it through this intervention, or *has the tension reached such an emotional intensity* that it will have to be dealt with through a series of interventions?

b. Are the people willing to sit down and deal with their differences in a constructive way, or are the people in the groups (or perhaps members of one group) indifferent to what is happening and *not ready to invest energy in changing the situation?* If this is the case, we may decide not to do the intervention.

c. Do the sources of the tension, and the events that trigger them, lie mainly in the areas of faulty communication, different ways of seeing and doing things, and different orders of priorities? Or do the problems stem mainly from *one or more extremely difficult and maladjusted people?* If the latter, then those people may need personal help before we attempt to deal with the groups.

d. Is each group relatively cohesive? Or is one (or both of them) *torn from within by extreme internal cleavages and conflicts?* If the latter, we should consider whether we will be able to work with the two groups without first dealing with the internal disruptions.

e. Are both groups roughly equal in their power and dependence on each other? Or is there *an imbalance in power* that leaves one team more dependent on the other? This information is helpful to us later on in the intervention itself.

If we decide to go ahead, we notify both groups and fix the time for the intervention to take place. If possible, the meeting place should be a "neutral" one, not on the grounds of either group.

2. *Introducing the experience.* The introduction has three purposes:

a. It should create an atmosphere of goodwill and a problem-solving attitude toward the tensions. To create a "Win-Win" attitude and to decrease the "Win-Lose" attitude of participants. A "Win-Win" attitude means that both can gain from the situation, that neither of the groups need suffer, or lose, or be hurt in any way. A "Win-Lose" attitude conveys the belief that the situation between the groups can be settled only if one of them comes out on top and the other on the bottom; one needs to "win" (be right) and the other to "lose" (suffer, be hurt, or be wrong).

b. It should prepare the people to cooperate with us in performing a number of activities they are unaccustomed to. They should grant us *legitimacy* to do things in a different way.

c. It should enrich the experience and widen its implications for the participants by placing it within a *broader framework.* It is important that those who take part in this experience understand that it has broader applications. They may later generalize from it and draw practical conclusions on how to behave in other conflicting situations in which they may find themselves. The broader framework helps to create less personalized "I'll show him" attitudes and a more objective, balanced frame of reference to the situation.

We begin by giving legitimacy to misunderstandings between groups: "It is natural for two people or two groups that interact with one another to have points of difference." Most problems arise at the point of interaction between two groups. We draw on the newsprint two interlocking circles and mark the area of interface (refer back to Fig. 11.1).

One person interacts with others; one group interacts with other groups; one organization deals with other organizations—this is illustrated in the drawing. At the points of interaction (the interfaces), problems are bound to arise.

The question is not whether there will be any problems—they generally do exist—but how to deal with them? Will it be with a "Win-Lose" attitude or a "Win-Win" attitude? Has one of us got to be right and the other wrong—or may it be that we are both right? Has one of us to be the "winner" and the other the "loser"—or can we both win? The basic question is: How do we treat the problems between us? Do we try to win? Do we escape and run away from them? Do we try to "smear them over"? Do we compromise on them? Or do we try to solve them? To illustrate these questions we either draw on a newsprint or put up a placard: "Ways of Dealing with Problems (Fig. 11.2).

We explain that: The vertical axis depicts our willingness to confront a problem. The lowest point is one of complete unwillingness to confront the problem. The highest point is one of active confrontation. The middle point may be seen as some measure of willingness to confront.

The horizontal axis depicts our readiness to see both sides of the problem. On the left side a person is utterly unwilling and unable to see, understand, and accept the other person's viewpoints. At the point on the right a person can see, understand, and accept both sides of the problem. The middle point may be seen as some measure of willingness to understand and

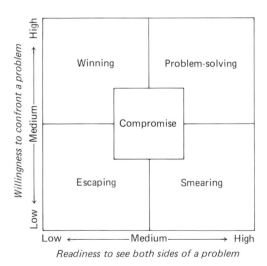

Fig. 11.2 Ways of dealing with problems

accept the other's viewpoint. When the two dimensions are joined together we get five typical ways of dealing with conflict:

a. *Escaping:* low willingness to confront and little understanding of the other side. You try to ignore the problem, not to acknowledge its existence; or you try to eliminate contact with the other person and escape the situation.

b. *Winning:* high willingness to confront and little understanding of the other person; you try to come out the winner, and have no feeling or sensitivity about what this will do to the other. This is a "Win-Lose" way of dealing with a conflict.

c. *Placating:* low willingness to confront and high understanding of the other side. This is "placating" the problem. You understand the other but don't want to rock the boat. You may be sweet and understanding, but meanwhile the problem is not confronted and solved.

d. *Compromising:* medium willingness to confront and some understanding of the other. The basic problem is not attacked but some way of living with it is found. Each person concedes something and a workable formula for getting by is developed.

e. *Problem-solving:* high willingness to confront and high willingness and ability to understand the other. The problem itself is openly confronted in a positive, constructive, problem-solving attitude; each party sees both sides of the problem and they work together to find a way of dealing with it. This is "Win-Win" way of dealing with a conflict.

Escaping, winning and placating do not solve problems. The causes and tensions remain and find an outlet. Sometimes compromise is helpful for a period and may be used. In the long run the only healthy solution to tensions between people is basically for them to confront those tensions and problem-solve together.

We sometimes develop this into a meaningful experience for the participants. Mixed subgroups are formed, in which each person, in turn, states which of the Ways of Dealing With Problems (Fig. 11.2) describes how he or she is behaving in the conflict we are dealing with. The person's name is marked in the appropriate place, on a newsprint illustrating Fig. 11.2. Other people in the subgroup then give the person feedback on how they see his or her behavior in terms of "Escaping," "Smearing," "Winning," etc.

We now explain that we will try to help the groups face the issues that exist in a problem-solving way. To do this we need people's cooperation and willingness to follow our instructions and do things in a way they are not accustomed to.

3. *The groups prepare their lists.* Each group now goes to a different room with one of the facilitators. (*Note:* In this intervention it is definitely preferable that two facilitators, or at least a facilitator with an assistant, work together.) When the two groups prepare their lists, one facilitator should be

with each group. Later, when the groups convene and when they break up into subgroups, two sensitive facilitators can lead the experience better than one. They support and complement each other; one rests while the other is active, and if the need arises they can help each other and consult together.

Before the groups break up into teams a time is fixed for them to finish their assignment. The teams are given 30 to 40 minutes for this. Throughout the meetings the facilitators are in touch with each other, and if need arises, they coordinate and lengthen this period.

In each separate group meeting the same procedure is followed. Each group prepares three lists on newsprint in the same order:

a. *First list:* The facilitator asks: "What are the things you like about the other group? What do they do well? What pleases you in their behavior?" Each person has to write his or her answers on a sheet of paper. After a few minutes, all the answers are read out and the facilitator puts them on newsprint. A heading such as "Things we like" is put on the top of the newsprint.

b. *Second list:* The facilitator asks: "Try to put yourselves in the shoes of the other group. Try to feel what they are feeling. What are the things people in your group do that hurt, interfere with, or displease the other group? What do you do that causes them difficulty and that they would prefer you not do, or do less? What don't you do that could have helped them? What do you think they want you to do?" People write their answers and the facilitator copies them on newsprint. The facilitator must be careful not to include disguised criticisms in this list. For example, a person may include in his or her list a statement such as, "I like things to be done well and effectively and this interferes with them." This is a veiled criticism and should not be included in this list. The person is told to keep it in mind and will be able to include it later in the last list.

Another way of dealing with a statement of this kind is to word it differently with the help of the person who proposed it. The different wording should place the burden of responsibility on the proposer. For example, "We make too many demands from them and pressure them." A suitable heading is put on the list, such as "Things we do that hurt them."

c. *Third list:* The facilitator says: "Write down the two or three most important things that you would like the other group *not* to do, or to do differently. Write down the things that really hurt you. Be concrete; be specific; don't give wide generalizations. Write only about behavior that you think they can change and do something about, and not with the intention of hurting them." In this list, which differs from the other lists, the facilitator tries to reach agreement among team members. Items that are not supported by the majority of the group are preferably not included. The final list should represent the essential things that are really hurting most of the people in the group. A suitable heading is put on the list.

4. *Lists compared; some problems settled; others defined.* At the appointed time the two groups meet as one. The lists of both groups will now be compared and commented on in this order:

1. Team A: First list
2. Team B: First list
3. Team A: Second list
4. Team B: Third list
5. Team B: Second list
6. Team A: Third list

In the interviews prior to the meeting, or during the meeting itself, we may have received impressions that one of the teams has more power over the other, and that the second team was the more dependent one. In such a case, the team with more power will be Team A in the order of reading the lists. The logic of this can easily be understood. The "stronger" of the two teams will thus be the first to state all the positive things it sees in the second team. It will also be the first to try to express its feeling on what is hurting the other team, and the first to hear what this really is.

The procedure is as follows:

a. Team A puts up its first list, and someone from that team reads it aloud.

b. Team B puts up its first list, and someone from that team reads it aloud.

c. Time is allowed for this to "sink in," and comments are encouraged. We will give all participants time to write down their thoughts for private use.

d. Team A puts up its second list, and someone from that team reads it out aloud and explains, if necessary.

e. Team B puts up its third list, and someone from that team begins reading it. After each item is read, the facilitator who is standing by Team A's list marks on it an item with the same or similar intent. In other words, the teams examine whether Team A could really feel which things it was doing hurt Team B. Similar items on both newsprints are marked. Items on Team B's list that Team A did not mention are circled. Team B members explain these items to Team A. Members of Team A may not argue back; they are requested to repeat what they have heard until Team B says this is exactly what it meant. Such an exercise demonstrates active listening on the part of both groups.

The facilitator may have to intervene a number of times during this step to ensure that people really do understand each other, *to clarify issues,* and to prevent people who want to keep it all "sweet and happy" from *evading the necessary confrontation.*

The facilitator may have to make explicit what a person is doing in attributing something to others. He or she may say: "You can in fact only say what *you* feel and how *you* are affected. You cannot say what the other person's intentions are. Only he or she can be witness to that." The facilitator may have to prevent participants from speaking in the first person plural ("we") and remind them that each is to *speak only for himself (or herself).* He or she may need to request people to speak *directly* to each other, looking at each other and not appealing to the facilitator. He or she may also have to remind people to speak in the second person ("you") and not the third person plural ("they"). Every now and then the facilitator intervenes *to sum up a point of agreement.* Another form of intervention is a summing up of this kind: "We may sum up this point by saying that Team A members realize that when they demand that Team B do it this way, the people in Team B feel that they are being pressured and feel nervous and irritated. Team B members realize that Team A did this not to hurt or belittle Team B but because the problems Team A faced necessitated their wanting it to be done in that way." This type of summing up clarifies to each group that the other group has understood what is troubling it and will take it into account in the future. A necessary contribution of the facilitator is *"meaning clarification."*

One person may make a remark or a statement. The facilitator should be sensitive to the hidden feeling or message underlying the spoken words, and tries to express this message to the listener. Then the facilitator asks the speaker if that was what he or she meant. If the speaker assents, the facilitator asks the people to whom the message was sent to repeat in their own words what the speaker was really trying to convey to them, and to continue this until the speaker agrees that they truly understood him or her.

When all items on Team A's second list have been dealt with, the same procedure is followed with the second list of Team B together with the third list of Team A.

When the lists have been dealt with, the time has arrived to focus on issues that still need attention. The facilitator should be active in this and try, with the participant's help, to draw up, on newsprint, a list of issues to be problem-solved.

These are issues that were not settled during the discussions on the lists. Probably they will include issues that may need further clarification and issues that need some form of agreement on how to deal with them in the future.

Sometimes in work teams the facilitator may suggest postponing dealing with an issue until people have received the opinion of an expert on it or collected information on how other teams have dealt with a similar problem. The remaining issues are divided between subgroups to be problem-solved.

5. *Mixed subgroups problem-solve the remaining issues.* Subgroups are now organized. Each should consist of about four people—two from each group. If one of the groups is smaller than the other, dividing into subgroups with an equal number from both groups is impossible. In such case we should at best make certain that the smaller group is represented in each of the subgroups.

Before people form into subgroups we explain to them what to do:

a. Each subgroup is given one or two issues to deal with.

b. The subgroup is to attempt to give recommendations to the total group on how to deal with the issue in the future.

c. The way to do this is to try together to suggest ways of dealing with the problem by brainstorming and similar open-minded techniques.

The subgroups now meet in different corners of the room or in adjoining rooms. The facilitators move among the subgroups, assisting, advising, and helping.

After a time period decided on beforehand by the facilitators, the groups convene and hear the recommendations. The time given to the subgroups for their meeting depends on various factors and cannot be arbitrarily stated here. It depends on the total amount of time available to the groups for this intervention, the number of issues available to the groups for this intervention, the number of issues left for them to deal with, the complexity and difficulty of these issues, etc. In any case, a time limit should be decided on so that the subgroup meetings will not struggle on indefinitely. Even if some issues have not been settled, much has generally been achieved. It is better to leave some matters for a later occasion than to stretch this session for too long.

6. *Summing up.* The groups reconvene. Each subgroup in turn presents its recommendation. Participants comment on them if they wish, and the facilitator tries to achieve a consensual decision and agreement of both groups on each issue in turn. All agreements and decisions are noted on newsprint, and matters not yet settled are written separately (for treatment at a later date).

When all subgroups have finished, the facilitator sums up points of agreement and understanding from the joint session of reading the lists (described in Step 4). The second facilitator can put these points on newsprint together with the agreements and decisions that came from the work of the subgroups.

A date is fixed for dealing with issues yet unsettled and people are invited to give their reaction to the experience they have been through.

This final "open expression" often has value of its own in bridging differences between the groups.

After the meeting, each member of both groups receives a typewritten copy of all the decisions and agreements that have been reached and a separate list of issues still to be dealt with. It is also worthwhile to attach a handout of Fig. 11.2—Ways of dealing with problems.

Variation 1

Sometimes almost all the issues can be settled in the joint session of both groups described in Step 4. In such a case the subgroup meetings can be skipped.

Variation 2

If there is time and the facilitator feels that people will be willing to cooperate, he or she can add a personal fantasy between steps 3 and 4. After explaining the different ways of dealing with tension, he or she suggests that people examine how they personally react to a conflict situation. The facilitator asks the participants to close their eyes and relax. "Now imagine you are walking along a long narrow corridor and you are deep in thought. Suddenly you lift your eyes and see at a distance, coming in your direction, a person you are in very intense conflict with. He is coming closer; now he reaches you. What do you do? What did you think of doing and what did you do? Open your eyes and think a few moments over what happened. Check to see if it suits any of the ways we mentioned before of dealing with a conflict situation. Think out how you generally behave in conflict situations. Anybody who wants to tell us about what happened to him or her is welcome to do so." This little experience sometimes helps people relate with more understanding to the conceptual scheme given beforehand.

Notes:

1. While in some of the other interventions described in this book the facilitator might drop the introductory lecturette, in this intervention we think it is a must. In our opinion it creates an "accepting" climate and a broader framework that readies people for the subsequent steps.

2. We wish again to stress that when we are dealing with an intense conflict, we will not settle for a single intervention, such as the one just described. We would probably use a combination of the different interventions described in this chapter—and, in addition, other interventions from Basic Steps in Team Development (see Chapter 6) and exercises such as Listening (see Appendix II) and Introductions and Expectations (see Appendix II).

Feedback on interventions

12

CHAPTER OBJECTIVE

To assist managers and consultants in using feedback for themselves as facilitators and as applied to the interventions used within the organization.

GUIDE TO APPLYING METHODS

What is feedback?

- It is a method of learning how to become more effective by polling participants.
- It is a method for gaining guidance on how to continue work with a group.
- It is a way for a facilitator to determine whether or not he or she must modify his or her ways.
- It is a method of channeling constructive criticism.
- It is a method of getting help when you are ready for it.
- It is a method of determining whether you have achieved a particular set of objectives.
- It is a method of determining the impact of your work.

Different purposes of feedback

The word feedback has such wide use in training, consultation, and interventions that it is often used indiscriminately to cover a wide field of activities serving different purposes.

Because of the wide connotation of this concept and because of the value attached to feedback, facilitators often—almost automatically—plan some form of feedback into their programs. But what is not done so often is to inquire what kind of feedback is needed. What should the feedback be about? What purposes will it serve? To whom is it given?

1. Is the purpose of the feedback to give the participants information about their own behavior, interpersonal processes, group processes?
2. Is the content of the feedback to be personal reactions to an experience, evaluation of a group's progress, evaluation of a facilitator's help, etc.?
3. Is the feedback given by people to others, to the team, to the facilitator?
4. Is the feedback to serve as an evaluation of the effectiveness of particular processes, or is it to help the facilitator decide how to continue the workshop or intervention?

Furthermore, if the facilitator has given thought to these matters, there are other questions that arise:

1. When should the feedback be asked for: at the end of a process, at the end of a day, at the end of a workshop?
2. What form would most suit a particular kind of feedback: an open discussion, a structured "round the room" survey of opinion, a questionnaire, an illustration, etc.?

In this chapter we will try to give some answers to the preceding questions and to differentiate between the different kinds of feedback.

We will try to estimate the advantages and disadvantages of the different kinds of feedback for different purposes.

We will present some examples of feedback instruments used for various purposes.

Different kinds of feedback

It is possible to differentiate between three broad classes of feedback:

1. As a learning experience for participants.
2. As a guiding experience for the facilitator.
3. As an assessment of the practical effects of the intervention.

Each of these three classes may be further subdivided in the following way:

1. Feedback as *a learning experience for participants:*
   a. A learning experience about oneself, behavior, feelings, motives, etc.

b. A learning experience about interpersonal, group, and organizational processes.

2. Feedback as *a guiding experience for the facilitators:*

   a. On the effects of the intervention on the participants.

   b. On the effectiveness of an intervention technique.

   c. On one's own style as facilitator.

   d. On how to continue.

3. Feedback as *an assessment of the practical effects of interventions:*

   a. Changes in the functioning of the group worked with.

   b. Changes that a group was attempting to instigate in the organization.

This chapter will include detailed descriptions of the second and third kinds of feedback. We will refer to the first kind just briefly, since it is beyond the scope of this book.

1. *Feedback as a learning experience for participants.* Feedback as a learning experience for participants about themselves, and about interpersonal, group, and organizational process is an essential method in human relations training.

Most forms of working with groups in these fields build heavily on some form of feedback. T groups use person-to-person spoken feedback as their major tool. Most structured experiences are based on some form of feedback. Feedback in this class of experiences may be given in various ways:

   a. Directly spoken feedback by one participant to another.

   b. Written feedback of some kind from a group to an individual (which that person compares with his or her own estimate).

   c. Feedback by an observer watching the team or individuals.

   d. Feedback by the facilitator.

   e. Feedback of a team to itself, evaluating its own performance on some scale.

   f. Filling in a questionnaire and receiving the interpreted results as feedback.

   g. Feedback through nonverbal methods.

   h. Feedback through illustrations, drawings, collages, etc.

To detail all of these forms of feedback and their uses is beyond the scope of this book. As already stated, most structured experiences and training methods depend heavily on feedback. The interested reader is referred to any of the handbooks of structured experiences in human relations training. We will concentrate on the two other kinds of feedback in the following two sections in this chapter.

2. *The section on "Feedback to facilitator"* deals with feedback as a guiding experience for the facilitator. We will examine the ways in which feedback can assist and guide the facilitator in his or her work. We will examine the different kinds of feedback which the facilitator may be in need of. We will try to evaluate when to try to get the different kinds of feedback. A number of tested methods of feedback will be illustrated in detail.

3. *The section on "Assessing the practical effects of interventions"* considers the methods of measuring change which might be related to the interventions. Change is considered in terms of the direct impact on members of the organization.

Recommended reading

1. Swartz, Donald H., and Lippitt G., *Evaluating the Consulting Process*, Journal of European Training **4, 5,** Fall 1975.

FEEDBACK TO THE FACILITATOR

Analyzing, describing, and illustrating various forms of feedback to the facilitator.

What purposes does feedback serve?

Feedback is the major method facilitators have for determining what participants are feeling about the things they are experiencing and what those things are doing to them. Feedback allows facilitators to gauge the relative effectiveness of their tools in order to decide what to use again, what to change, and what to discard. Feedback is a radar which signals to facilitators when they are on course and when they are not. The signals may guide them in changing direction.

Feedback lets facilitators know how they are functioning; it tells what is going well and what needs improving. In short, feedback is a *must* to any facilitator.

When feedback is to serve as a guiding experience to the facilitator it may be subdivided in terms of the different purposes it may serve: (1) To receive information on the effects of the intervention on the participants; (2) To serve as a guide on how to continue working with a group; (3) To estimate the relative effectiveness of, and make the necessary changes in, the techniques that were used; and (4) to learn what the facilitator needs to change in his or her way of functioning.

1. *To receive information on the effects of the intervention on the participants.* The purpose of this type of feedback is to tell the facilitator what is happening to the participants and *how they are being affected* by what they are experiencing.

Generally, and simultaneously, this type of feedback serves another essential function—to *make the participants themselves aware of what they are experiencing.* In other words, the participants are trying to put into words and define for themselves what has happened to them in order to report it to the group (and to the facilitator). Doing this helps them to clarify for themselves what they have experienced, what conclusions they have drawn, and what they have learned. The act of expressing this in public before the group serves a function of reinforcing what has been learned.

Feedback of this kind gives the facilitator information about what an experience has done to a person, and how that person feels about it. People may tell what happened to them during the experience. They may remark about the feelings they had, about the conclusions they have drawn, and so on. This material enables the facilitator to draw tentative conclusions on the following:

a. How did the intervention *affect the participants?* Did it affect them? Was the effect strong or weak? Did they learn from it? What did they learn from it? Did they enjoy it?

b. Were the effects on the participants *consistent with their expectations?* Was the experience what they expected? Did they think they were going to do something else and were they disappointed in what happened? Did they expect a different atmosphere in the group than the one that developed? Were they expecting to be personally more in the center of action? Were they expecting practical outcomes and instead got a human relations experience, or vice versa?

c. Were the effects on the participants *consistent with the facilitator's expectations?* Did he or she expect the intervention to develop in a certain direction only to have it take a completely different direction? Did the intervention achieve the purposes the facilitator had anticipated or expected it to fill? Did people learn, or do, or become aware of whatever the facilitator had expected them to learn, or do, or become aware of?

2. *To serve as a guide on how to continue working with a group.* The purpose of this kind of feedback is to receive from the participants attitudes, opinions, feelings, and preferences regarding *how to continue* working with them. The facilitator may have worked with the group for some time—a few days or months—and now wishes to know how to continue.

a. Do people want to continue with no change?

b. Do people want a complete change of direction and activities?

c. Do people want more of one kind of activity and less of another?

d. Do people want more individual development activities and less group-process oriented activities?

e. Do people want to deal more directly with their team's agenda items and less with learning experience?

f. Do people want to meet more often or less often?

g. Are the meeting hours what they would wish?

h. Do they wish to do more individual work and have less group activities?

This kind of feedback is given after people have experienced interventions, learning, and training together and the facilitator wishes to have information which will help him or her to decide how to proceed in future.

3. *To estimate the relative effectiveness of, and make the necessary changes in, the techniques that were used.* The same process, intervention, simulation, structured experience (techniques) may be used many times by the facilitator with different groups. Every group is different and conditions and timing for introducing a technique are rarely the same. Nevertheless, experience teaches a facilitator that whatever the variance in conditions, some techniques are almost always more effective than others. Also, there are certain approaches that fit the nature and style of the facilitator. Some techniques vary in effectiveness under different conditions. In one group or workshop they can have an unusual impact; in another group or workshop they are a failure.

The purpose of this kind of feedback is to give the facilitator information on the *relative effectiveness of interventions in different groups under varying conditions*—and over varying periods of time.

a. A facilitator may also wish to draw conclusions about the changes he or she should make in the process of an intervention. In one team the facilitator performs it one way, in another he or she does things differently. The question is: Are the results the same?

b. Two facilitators perform the same intervention in different ways. Which is the more effective: What changes should be made to get better results and greater impact?

c. There are variations in performing an intervention. Under which set of conditions is one variation more effective and under which conditions is the other variation better?

d. With the same kind of group, one type of intervention or process always seems to be more effective, and another type less effective. Is the facilitator sure about this? Do committees always prefer more problem-solving training and less team development? The facilitator needs feedback on this.

4. *To learn what the facilitator needs to change in his or her way of functioning.* Two facilitators may lead the same process in different teams and get different results. The difference in results may not stem from the team itself, the conditions, or the timing. Obviously, it does not arise from

using different processes, as the two facilitators are using the same process. The cause may be in the style, manner, behavior, attitude, and motivation of the facilitators.

Some facilitators seem to get results with all kinds of groups and all types of techniques. Some facilitators are effective in using one way of functioning and ineffective when they have to do something else. Some facilitators get good results whatever they do.

But all facilitators can learn. All facilitators can receive feedback about their style, their interventions, their mistakes, and their strengths. All facilitators can use feedback to improve their functioning. All facilitators need feedback to learn what they have to change when they work with groups.

When can feedback be given?

Some kinds of feedback are more meaningful at different times. People are more able and willing to give a certain kind of feedback after, say, a few days of training than after one day of training.

We would not expect to receive all the different kinds of feedback just because we feel we need them. We must suit the timing to the particular kind of feedback we wish to receive.

The following is a tentative rough estimate of the times which are most opportune to receive different kinds of feedback:

1. *In the middle of an intervention or process* (of a few hours). We sometimes receive unasked-for feedback of Type 1 (effects on participants), when participants express feelings about the process without the facilitator requesting it.

2. *At the end of an intervention or a process* (of a few hours). This is the most opportune time to get feedback of Type 1 (effects on participants). In fact, many processes are planned this way so that the last step in the process is some form of discussion or individual reaction to the process.

3. *At the end of a day.* If we are going to continue meeting the group on subsequent days or periodically in the future, this is the opportunity to get feedback of both Type 1 (effects on participants) and Type 2 (guide on how to continue). However, sometimes this may be too early for Type 2.

4. *After some days, mid-course, or after a number of periodic meetings.* We will have been working for some time and wish to know how to continue and what to change. This is the time for Type 2 (guide on how to continue). If the workshop is to last for more than a week, it may be difficult for people to remember the relative impact of each process. Sometimes, in such cases, we should try to get Type 3 feedback (estimating the value of the techniques relative to each other).

5. *At the end of a course or workshop.* This is the time when the facilitator may receive all types of feedback. In a short course of some days this

is the best time to receive Type 3 feedback (estimating the value of the techniques). If work is to continue with the participants, then Type 2 feedback (guide on how to continue) will be necessary. Type 1 feedback (effects on participants) about the entire experience is necessary. And finally, Type 4 feedback (for the facilitator himself) may be elicited.

How can feedback be given and by whom?

There are a variety of ways in which feedback can be given. Feedback can be spoken, or written, or acted. Each way has its advantages and disadvantages. Each way serves one purpose better than another.

Here is a tentative list of some of the ways commonly used:—

1. *Methods*

   a. *Open discussion.* The group is requested to react to the experience without any further stipulations. People speak whatever they wish, describing their own reactions, their feelings, what happened in the group, etc. People debate with one another. One point may be thrashed out thoroughly; another aspect may remain untouched. Some people may speak most of the time; others may remain silent. People may have spoken freely about whatever was important to them, but the facilitator may still remain in the dark regarding questions important to him or her.

   b. *A guided discussion.* This is the same as the former, with two differences: (1) at opportune lulls in the discussion the facilitator may ask a question regarding an aspect that was not touched on; (2) toward the end, the facilitator asks people who have not spoken how they feel about the matters discussed.

   c. *Round the room—open.* The facilitator requests participants to give their reactions individually in their seating order. Each person speaks on whatever he or she wishes. There is no give-and-take interaction among participants. Issues are not discussed or clarified. Each person gives his or her own reaction.

   d. *Round the room—closed.* The facilitator poses and writes down on newsprint a number of subjects or questions, and each person in turn is asked to react to these. For instance, the facilitator may request personal reactions, estimate of value to team, estimate of what can be applied, etc.

   e. *Written answers to a questionnaire.* The participants are given a questionnaire containing a number of feedback questions. Each person writes his or her replies and returns the questionnaire to the facilitator. There is no interaction among team members. The area of reaction is delineated by the questions themselves. This method may be made more open by a final question asking for any remarks or suggestions which participants may wish to make.

f. *Nonverbal techniques and collages.* Different forms of nonverbal techniques and collages have been developed to give feedback. The advantage, as in most projective forms, is freer expression of deeper feelings. The disadvantages are the same: difficulty in interpretation unless explained later verbally by the participants.

g. *Process observation.* A person or persons designated for this purpose gives the group feedback. This is more of a learning experience for the participants, and less a method of feedback for the facilitator.

h. *Interviewing.* Participants or other persons can be personally interviewed. The time needed for this form limits its use to very special circumstances.

2. *By whom.* Feedback to the facilitator can be received from a number of sources:

- The participants themselves.
- An observer of the group process.
- A co-facilitator.
- People who do not belong to the group.

Matching the form and purposes of feedback

We will attempt to summarize the different forms suitable for each type of feedback to the consultant. Some forms will be detailed and illustrated for guidance.

1. *Feedback to receive information on effects of intervention on participants.*

   a. *After a single intervention.*

      1) If the purpose is to receive the reactions of the participants to a particular intervention, the common way to do this is to ask for reactions at the end of the intervention.

      2) From the facilitator's point of view, *a guided discussion* is the simplest and most effective way of getting reactions. In short, people are asked for reactions and they speak about whatever they wish, when they wish. At opportune times the facilitator asks questions to which he or she wants answers, and, toward the end, brings in people who have not spoken.

      3) *Round the room "open" and "closed"* may be used if time is short.

   b. *At the end of a day.* At the end of the day, after participants have given their reactions throughout the day to all or some of the processes, the facilitator may wish to receive a *total reaction to the whole day's*

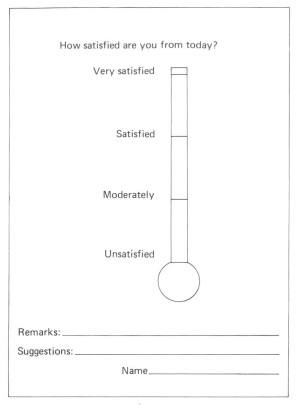

How satisfied are you from today?

Very satisfied

Satisfied

Moderately

Unsatisfied

Remarks: _____

Suggestions: _____

Name _____

Fig. 12.1 The barometer

activities. An excellent way of doing this is by means of The Barometer (Fig. 12.1). Each participant is handed a copy of "The Barometer" and requested to mark and answer it.

The mark on the barometer itself gives the participants "total reaction to the day's activities."

The lines at the bottom for remarks and suggestions allow the participant to express any strong feeling, reaction, or suggestion that he or she wishes to bring to the attention of the facilitator.

c. *At the end of a course or workshop.* The facilitator will want feedback on feelings of participants at the end of a course or workshop, and *the open or guided discussion* seems to be the best way of achieving this.

It is well worthwhile to tape, record, and take notes of what each person says. Often these notes are typed, duplicated, and sent to each participant.

In the summing-up discussion we do not generally find people who do not speak of their own accord. Should this happen, however, these people may be encouraged to speak.

In the summing up of a workshop, the facilitator will also wish to receive other types of feedback. These will be detailed later.

2. *Feedback as a guide to how to continue working with a group.* This feedback is generally requested after working some days with a group or in a mid-course of a workshop. It will also be needed after working with a team over a period of time.

The simplest way to obtain this feedback is through a guided discussion on "What do we feel about what we have done until now, and what do we want to do in our coming activities?" During this discussion the facilitator may introduce various topics on which he or she wants to hear the group's opinion; e.g., "Does the group want more (or less) skills training? Is there sufficient time for individual work? What kind of activities do people want more of? What kind of activities do they prefer less of? Are the times of meeting convenient?"

3. *Feedback to estimate the relative effectiveness of—and necessary changes in—techniques that were used.* There is a way to keep a constant check on the relative effectiveness of techniques, to see which techniques always have higher (or lower) impact; to see which are reacted to more favorably by a particular group, or kind of group.

The method we use is a simple questionnaire that participants fill in after a series of activities. (See Fig. 12.2.)

Each activity's importance / Activity	To me				For the group			
	No imp.	Some imp.	Imp.	Very imp.	No imp.	Some imp.	Imp.	Very imp.

Name _____   Group _____

Fig. 12.2 Questionnaire to evaluate activities

The questionnaire is given to participants at the end of a series of activities; if the group met only for a day—then at the end of the day. If the group is participating in a workshop, the questionnaire should be filled in every three days. People have difficulty in evaluating an activity that took place more than three days previously.

The questionnaire is handed to the participants and they are requested to list the activities in the order in which the facilitator calls them out. The facilitator has prepared a list of the activities which the group experienced, and reads them aloud slowly, at writing pace. After reading the name of each activity, the facilitator reminds the participants what the activity was. He or she should be sure that everyone understands what is being referred to.

People list the activities, one underneath the other, in the column headed "Activity." When all the activities have been listed, the participants are requested to answer by marking an × in the appropriate columns. After they have done this, and written their names and their group, they return the questionnaires to the facilitator.

The facilitator can summarize the group's responses when convenient. Generally, even a quick glance through the questionnaires can give the facilitator a broad impression of the reactions of participants. A facilitator who has done this a number of times can immediately evaluate the impact of the activities on the group as compared to other groups with whom he or she has worked. Individual reactions can also be noted. At the earliest opportunity the facilitator can summarize the group's total feedback on an unused questionnaire. The summary is done by listing the activities under Activity column and writing in the remaining columns how many people marked each activity. A picture of the total group reaction can be had by summing up each column.

A facilitator, or a group of facilitators working together, may use the questionnaire summaries to get an estimate of a number of things:

1. The relative impact of each technique, intervention, or process on *all* the groups that have experienced it so far.
2. The relative impact on *different kinds of groups.*
3. A comparison between the reactions he or she received to specific techniques and the reactions which *other facilitators* received.

The way to do this is to give mathematical weight to each category of importance and to sum up the summarized total which a group gave to each activity.

Every time a questionnaire is marked by a group, the sum total of the group's replies are entered on a *master list.*

Let us illustrate this. First we decide on a numerical value to give to each category of "importance." These values must be maintained throughout with all groups. Here is an example:

No importance = 0
Some importance = 3
Important = 7
Very important = 10

To the question "Importance to me," regarding a certain activity, the following replies were received in a group:

1 person marked "no importance"	1×0	$= \quad 0$
2 people marked "some importance"	2×3	$= \quad 6$
5 people marked "important"	5×7	$= \ 35$
2 people marked "very important"	2×10	$= \underline{\ 20}$
	Total	61

Dividing this total by the number of participants who filled in the questionnaire thus: $\frac{61}{10} = 6.1$ gives us the score of the group.

The same method of calculation is used for "Importance to the group" and the scores of each activity thus calculated. The group's score for each activity is added to the list which is kept together with the scores of other groups who have done the same activity.

The average score of each activity gives us an evaluation of how this activity is reacted to *in relation to the other activities.*

If we have sufficient data from different kinds of groups (work teams, managerial groups, etc.) we can compare the reactions to a specific activity in these *different groups.*

If we are careful to maintain a list showing which facilitator led such activity, we can *compare facilitators in different activities.* Also, a facilitator can see in which kind of activity he or she has high impact, and in which activity his or her impact is low.

There is much to be learned by maintaining a summary of group scores on activities. Checking these periodically may lead to dropping a technique or substituting another. Some activities may be found to have impact only in certain kinds of groups, and as a result will not be used with other kinds of groups. A facilitator may decide that it's necessary to change his or her method of leading a certain process or to learn how others do it.

4. *Feedback to learn what changes the facilitator must make in his or her functioning.* As indicated earlier, the most useful and valid feedback about the facilitator comes with increased trust. Thus, we do not request such feedback until the group has worked together for some period of time—at least until the second day of a workshop or after a series of sessions with a group.

Although we may not ask for specific feedback for awhile, we can get some important indications from general comments—and from what is *not* said. We also may talk privately with some of the more open members of a group and ask for personal feedback about our facilitating efforts.

The following factors are important to consider in evaluating the performance of the facilitator:

a. *Clarity of instructions.* Often a group does not benefit from a procedure because the members do not understand what they are being asked to do. Listen for feedback that comes through such comments as: "One thing at a time, please." "Now, what did you want us to do?" "Speak louder, please."

b. *Awareness of readiness of participants.* The facilitator may have been prepared for the group by one or two members of the team. He or she may have formulated a view of the entire team through their comments and his or her assessment of those two members. In a sense, the facilitator may have measured the readiness of the team to handle certain experiences during the workshop.

During the actual workshop, the facilitator will receive clear signs whether what he or she is doing is at the appropriate level for the group. Such feedback will help the facilitator modify the process to fit the readiness level of the group. For example, the facilitator might suggest to the group that each participant choose another person with whom to discuss a certain issue. The facilitator may sense the reluctance of the group to get that personally involved. They may only *be ready* to have more general discussions in total group or in groups of four.

c. *Keeping participants interested.* Boredom shows itself through the stares of participants, restlessness, yawning, side discussions, etc. This feedback is useful in correcting any tendency the facilitator may have to talk at the wrong level, talk too long, stay in one place too long, etc. In a sense, the facilitator can benefit from some experience as an actor. Some facilitators can use humor to break the boredom; however, such a "trick' provides only temporary relief. The deeper group message may be: "The facilitator is not reaching us." At appropriate times, such as during breaks or when trust level is higher, the facilitator should check on how he or she is coming across: "Have I any behaviors that may be bothersome to the group?" "How should I modify my approach?" For example, one facilitator was not informed that the team with which he was working had completed a series of listening exercises on a previous occasion. As part of the workshop, the facilitator had planned some work on listening. After a good start on perception, he could not understand why there was decreasing interest when he started some basics on listening. No one in the group felt comfortable enough to tell him of their previous experience. In the middle of the exercise, the facilitator commented on the lowered interest and finally got someone to explain.

d. *Degree of structuring.* Some groups need more leader direction and a series of fixed steps, and other groups need less of this type of *structuring.* As the facilitator observes each group, he or she can feel whether they are with him (or her) or are lost. If the workshop is a full day or more, the degree of structuring for the group should be assessed during the first break, so that the necessary modifications can be made. If the process is just a few hours, it is particularly important to get some data about the nature of the group before you begin.

e. *Degree of task vs. person orientation.* This factor is somewhat related to structuring. Some facilitators are more task oriented and others are more person oriented. It is important that the facilitator be aware of his or her nature. If one tends to be task oriented then his or her interventions are likely to be tilted that way, and vice versa. As the facilitator is working with a group, it is important to sense whether they need more task-oriented work; that is, more getting the job done, completing the agenda, finishing on time.

At times, the facilitator will get feedback that he or she and the group are not matching. Such feedback can come in comments such as: "That's too much." "Why did you cut me off?" At such times it is important to revise the schedule and allow more sharing of thoughts or feelings. At other times the feedback will say "We want to move along faster," or "This session does not seem organized enough." The revision requires more tightening of the agenda, being sure that tasks are completed, etc.

f. *Degree of openness about personal matters.* Facilitators vary on how much they talk about themselves and their own feelings about any given subject. It is useful to get feedback about whether one is taking too much or too little time in presenting his or her thoughts. On one occasion, the group felt that it could not open up with "an outsider." The facilitator had been introduced as an "outside consultant." When this feedback was received, the facilitator discussed with the group his long-term connection with their organization and also his interest in their work. After some questions and further discussion, there was much more of a feeling of working together.

ASSESSING THE PRACTICAL EFFECTS OF INTERVENTIONS

Methods for determining the kind of change (if any) that has resulted from the use of one or more interventions.

Our view of management or organizational development starts and ends with *Does it work?* We frequently review the interventions and other processes we use to determine how well they are working or if they are useful in a given situation. These views are detailed in the previous section of this chapter.

To highlight the practical aspect, we often use the following sequence: Development or training—Application—Evaluation of results—Back again to development. This sequence emphasizes that when we apply anything to an individual or group, that process or intervention must be evaluated for impact or we will rarely know the effects of our work.

Although evaluation or assessment can have its negative or painful moments, the primary outcome is a sense of being stronger. It is almost needless to say that we emphatically support assessment or evaluation.

Reviewing the purposes of the intervention to establish objectives

Under each intervention in this handbook, we have listed a series of purposes. It is important to review these purposes, for, as *written*, they are representative of what we feel can be accomplished by the intervention.

However, we recognize that each facilitator and each person or group is different. The purposes will often require some revision to fit the situation in which the intervention is being applied. Thus, we recommend reviewing the purposes so that they will reflect your objectives as the intervention is applied.

There are some useful steps to take in determining your objectives. As an example, we will use parts of the following checklist* to help us recognize and accept differences among team members."

1. *Being specific.* Look over the purposes as written and try to revise each one so that it is specifically related to you and your organization. If the general purpose is "to recognize and accept differences" you might want to specify *which* differences among team members you and your team want to work on.

2. *Relate to performance.* Include in your objective the kinds of behavior that show that the objective has been achieved. Thus, your criteria might include observing team members problem-solve with other employees who approach the problem from different points of view. You are considering their actual performance in handling the differences.

3. *Being realistic.* Consider the current situation in the team or organization. What can you really expect to have happen after the intervention? For example, you may wish all of the team members to accept differences; however, maybe only half of the team members can achieve much change in the first attempt at using this intervention. Reality would suggest that the objective should not reflect that all members will change.

---

*   From Pfeiffer, J. W., and J. E. Jones, *The 1975 Annual Handbook for Group Facilitators* (La Jolla, Calif.: University Associates, 1975), Ch. 6.

4. *Observable results.* Useful assessment requires that the results can be seen and agreed upon by other observers. Thus, your objectives should include the condition that "recognizing and accepting differences" not be just in the minds of the team members but be clearly visible to themselves and others.

If you apply this checklist to the purpose, it is more likely that later you will have a tangible way of knowing whether the interventions have had any practical effects on yourself, the team, or organization.

Establishing criteria for measuring results

Establishing criteria involves adding quantities and sometimes dates to the objectives. It usually requires fixing criteria that indicate the impact (results) of the intervention and the level of satisfaction with the impact. We find it useful to consider both kinds of criteria as we work on the outcome of the interventions.

We have discovered that setting the criteria for measuring impact is a task best handled by all or a representative group of people who will be potentially affected by the intervention.

If you are applying the intervention to yourself as a manager, you should think about the criteria that will satisfy you. If you are establishing criteria in a group, it is useful to display the detailed objectives on newsprint. If the objectives are written in the kind of detail suggested in the previous section, the criteria will be relatively easy to reach.

For example, if your objective specifies "accepting the differences that are causing trouble among team members," then the criteria-measuring impact could be:

> Team members can accept without long discussions the fact that people start problem-solving in different ways; some approach it by collecting information from many people; others will start problem-solving by collecting information from different books; still others will just sit back and think by themselves.

Such criteria may be difficult to establish prior to the initiating of the intervention. However, it is important to at least begin the criteria-setting process before the first steps of the intervention. That is, as you are setting the objective, you are getting at some of the factors that later will become criteria.

Keeping a record of such factors will give you a good start when you later sit down with others—or by yourself, if this is a personal intervention —to determine the criteria.

If the intervention covers the entire workshop, then we suggest waiting until the end of the workshop—usually before the step of evaluation and feedback to the facilitator.

If the intervention is part of a longer process within the organization, a subgroup of people who will be affected by the intervention might be convened to consider the criteria. Again, the specific objective should be openly displayed, and the group is asked to offer suggestions about the criteria.

After the meeting, these suggestions are organized into a series of criteria statements and circulated among the group for their comment and ultimate agreement. The final statement of criteria is circulated for their information.

In thinking through the criteria, one should raise the question of *how much* change is sufficient? This question relates to the levels of expectation. We have found that some people may see an intervention as impactful and others may not only because they had different levels of expectation about its results.

Thus, we strongly suggest (using the same example as we did earlier on team development) that you be very clear about the degree and kind of change you expect in each of the team members. For example, if you do achieve a certain change in say, four of nine team members—and that was all the change you expected—your level of satisfaction would be high. However, if you expected all nine team members to change, the feeling of satisfaction would be low. If you find that one team member takes more initiatives, and you had not expected any change of this kind, again your level of satisfaction would be high. So be sure to raise the issue of *how much* change is expected, as well as what kind.

Methods of determining the effect of the intervention

In this case, we want to determine whether the objectives have been attained according to the criteria we have decided on. Three methods are commonly used: (1) written reactions from organizational members; (2) interviews with organizational members; and (3) participants reviewing impact.

1. *Written reactions from organizational members*

   a. A week or so after the completion of the intervention, a letter explaining the intervention, including the objectives, is sent to all reactors (actual participants in the workshop or a representative group of people in the organization who may experience the impact of the intervention on workshop participants. In selecting the representative group, it is useful to think about the intervention and who is likely to have contact with the participants; which departments interface with the participants, etc.). The letter should also inform them that you will be contacting them again to receive their observations.

   b. About one month after the intervention, and then again from two to five months later, a questionnaire is sent out to each of the reactors with questions to be answered about each criterion statement. For example, if a criterion for change was related to accepting differences in handling problem-solving, you might ask the following kinds of questions:

1) Have you seen any members of the sanitation department in any group problem-solving situations in the last month? If you have, give their names.

2) What was the problem? Please state.

3) Briefly describe the manner in which the sanitation department member(s) approached the problem situation, including how they related to other people.

c. The answers to the questions are reviewed to determine whether the behavior of the intervention participants has been in the desired direction or not in the desired direction, as indicated in the objective. Figure 12.3 shows a method of tabulating results. One sheet should be made out for each criterion.

2. *Interviews with organizational members.* The interview approach is an alternative to the "written reactions," described in the former section. In this method, the reactors are identified and informed by memo. An interview schedule is set up about one month after the intervention and then again from two to five months later. Questions are developed around each criterion and the reactors are asked to respond. The results are tabulated on the same kind of form as shown in Fig. 12.3.

Criterion statement (state completely) _____

_____

Participants (full name)	In desired direction	Not in desired direction	Comments
1.			
2.			
3.			
4.			
5.			
6.			
7.			
8.			
9.			
10.			

Fig. 12.3 Responses to Intervention: summary sheet

The interview approach requires more time on the part of the interviewer. However, we do find that the results are richer. Often the interviewer can joggle the memory of the reactor. Also, it is sometimes difficult to get reactors to return the questionnaires; the interview eliminates that problem.

3. *Participants review impact.*

a. A team meeting is arranged about one month after intervention.

b. All the objectives are displayed on newsprint, one objective per sheet.

c. The team members are asked to first select the objective they feel has generated the greatest impact.

d. Each person is asked to record any of their experiences during the last month that were related to that objective. They should include in the recording what happened to them personally and what they have observed happening to others.

e. All participants who have selected the same objective are grouped in a fishbowl, and they discuss their observations in front of the rest of the team. The observing members are asked to record any experiences they have had in connection with this objective. The process is repeated with each objective.

f. The recorded observations are collected at the end of the meeting. The responses are organized on sheets similar to the one recommended in Fig. 12.3.

The effect of interventions can be realized in different ways. At times, the immediate effect of an intervention can be strong. Participants feel that they have benefited considerably. They return to the organization and after a week or so the glow is gone. In contrast, we have observed that an intervention that seemed to have moved slowly or did not appear to have much of an immediate impact may later be reported to have deep effects. Also, there is the person who made no comment during an entire day and seemed to be bored. Two weeks or a month later, he or she sends a letter stating how much practical benefit he or she derived from the intervention. Because learning takes different periods of time to be realized and is revealed in many different ways, we are cautious about making quick judgments of "change" or "no change." While it is important to be aware of the immediate signs of the intervention's impact, it is also essential to give it time before trying to measure the effects.

Further, we recognize that the impact of a given intervention will often lead to a revision of the plan or objective, and may be followed by the suggestion of another intervention or series of them. Thus, we highly recommend that the facilitator also remain aware of the passing comments that are volunteered during assessment. These remarks may be very helpful in evaluating the effectiveness of the intervention and suggesting how to carry on.

For example, a number of months after a workshop, one person remarked that he was laughingly reporting to his son about his workshop experience on learning how to listen. He was describing some of the other people who could not repeat the words of some other participant. His son was giving him some funny looks. He stopped talking for a second and said to his son, "Why are you looking at me that way?" Reluctantly, his son said, "Dad, are you sure they weren't looking at you the same way?"

Formats in using the interventions

13

CHAPTER OBJECTIVE
CHAPTER OBJECTIVE

To clarify the problems connected with choosing interventions, determining the proportion of each, deciding on the order and format or combination of interventions that naturally fall together.

INTRODUCTION

The interventions and processes described in this handbook are not single incidents that are gone through and finished with. Generally, we will use a number of these in a workshop. When training or helping a work team or a management team we will choose, change, or omit interventions according to the specific needs and conditions of the team.

Generally there will also be a logic behind the order in which we *sequence* interventions. It is understandable that we will not do "problem-sensing" after "dealing with basic problems."

A number of interventions tie up together in natural sequences that can be used in many different types of teams. It is worthwhile to be aware of the natural clustering of interventions that can often be used as one training or intervention unit.

In this chapter's next (second) section, *"What factors are given?"* we shall try to identify the "givens" of our work; i.e., what things we must take for granted, and yet be thoroughly aware of and clear about, when we begin our work in a particular situation. We will examine in detail who the *participants* are, what the *goals* and purposes are, and what the *resources* and *conditions* of the venture are. These will play a basic part in deciding what interventions we will use and in what sequence.

In the third section, *"To what should we give attention?"* we will deal with a number of prime factors that might sway our decisions in planning interventions. We will try to identify which objectives should sway our decision in deciding to use one kind of intervention in preference to another; we will examine considerations which may lead us to introduce a certain type of intervention possibly not in the expected natural sequence.

With these considerations before us we may wish to drop a certain process or add another. We will deal with the factors that could sway our considerations in *planning, choosing, mixing,* and *sequencing* interventions. We will consider the factors of visible results, impact on participants, applicability, learning and growth of participants, satisfaction from each meeting, and the facilitator's homework.

In the fourth section, *"What dilemmas must we balance?"* we will examine a number of dilemmas that we face in programming our interventions. Having a limited period of time means that we have to do one thing and not the other. Our decision will probably be swayed by the way we face these dilemmas. Whether we are conscious of it or not, it is probable that each of us has a preference of some kind that influences our choice in each of the dilemmas. It is better to be aware than unaware, and to make our choice consciously. The dilemmas we will deal with will be: *Task vs learning; task vs maintenance; group vs individual; group vs interfaces; cognitive learning vs experiential learning; planning vs flexibility;* and *participant responsibility vs facilitator responsibility.*

In the fifth section, *"Examples of some formats,"* we will give some practical examples of combining various interventions and sequencing them to serve as the broad outline for working with teams for specific purposes.

This section will contain five formats of groups of interventions that combine naturally to serve a specific purpose.

These formats may be used as guidelines in work with a team, adapting them to the needs of the team, deleting an intervention, adding another, etc.

WHAT FACTORS ARE GIVEN? (Identifying the given factors to be taken into account when planning interventions)

When beginning a series of interventions or a training project there are a number of factors that may be seen as "given." In other words, we see these factors as facts that to a certain extent we can accept as relatively unchangeable. We shall have to suit our actions and plan our work within the boundaries they set for us.

The three major sets of given factors are:

1. The participants.
2. Goals and purposes.
3. Resources and conditions.

Any experienced consultant knows that these too can be changeable. Management approaches us to begin working with Department A and we end up working with Department B. An organization comes to consult us on how to do long-term manpower planning and ends up with our working on job enrichment. Financial resources which seem at the beginning to be unavailable may begin to flow generously if tangible results are visible. In short even the "givens" seem to be flexible.

We will, therefore, begin with the assumption that we have passed the first stage of flexibility; we have now reached the point where we know with whom we will be working, what the goals or purposes to be attained are, within what broad boundaries are resources at our disposal, and under what conditions we will be working.

We would be well advised to examine these factors in more detail, because to a certain extent they determine what we do; what interventions we use; the sequencing of the processes; what we do more of and what less.

1. *The participants.* Who will we be working with; what are the characteristics of the participants; what kind of group will we deal with? These are questions worth answering and examining:

a. *What type of group?* Will we be working with a team or a group of people who are not a team?

b. *What kind of team?* Is it a management team, a committee, a work team—and if a work team, what kind? Production or service? Working in what field? Doing what?

c. *What size is the group?* Is it large, small, a team, a department? Can it be managed by one facilitator, or will we need more facilitators?

d. *What is the composition of the group?* Is it all men, all women, half and half? Some full time active members, and the rest not? Some old-timers and some newcomers? One the boss and the rest regular members?

e. *What are the characteristics of the group members?* What age are they? What education do they have? What other characteristics have they in common?

f. *How open do they appear to be?* How open are they to new experiences? Will they be ready to experiment with new ways of functioning; of doing things; of behaving? Will they be ready to undergo the kind of experiences we have planned for them?

Other important characteristics of the participants—such as interpersonal relations, team effectiveness, managerial style, cohesiveness, etc—will only be clarified after interviewing the team members or after a period of working with them. It is possible that these very factors may be the ones we will be working on with the team. Therefore, we do not include these among the factors that are "given."

2. *Goals and purposes.* What is to be attained? Why are we working with the team? What is to be achieved by the training? What goals are to be attained by the interventions? Let us detail these:

   a. *As seen by the group.* What are the purposes and goals as seen by the group we are working with? What do they hope to achieve by it?

   b. *As seen by the group's boss.* What does he or she want? Are his or her goals the same as those of the members of the group?

   c. *As seen by the initiator.* Management, or whoever approached us to do this work, may have different ideas about what they want us to do than the people with whom we will be working.

   d. *As seen by us.* We may see other goals, such as: This team may be the first one of the organization we are working with. As such, we may see it as a starting point from which to extend and widen our activities to other groups and other areas in the organization.

It is advisable to devote time to clarify these different views of goals and purposes before beginning to work with a group. Other purposes, expectations, and goals of other individuals, subgroups, adjoining groups, etc., will only become clear after some lapse of time.

3. *Resources and conditions.* What resources is the group/organization able to allocate to the project and what working conditions can we expect? What resources can we allocate? Let us detail these:

   a. *Time.* How much time can the organization allocate to this project? For how long can the team be relieved of its responsibilities in order to attend a workshop or course? Considering its other commitments, how often and for how long a period can we expect this team to continue meeting with us, etc.

   b. *Financial resources.* How much can the organization afford to spend on this project? How much is it willing to allocate? And so on.

   c. *Physical conditions.* What physical facilities will be at our disposal? Where will we meet? Will we be able to have an off-site workshop?

   d. *Our resources.* How much of our time can we afford to expend on this project—and for how long? How many of our facilitators (or consultants) will be involved, and for how long?

TO WHAT SHOULD WE GIVE ATTENTION? (Identifying considerations to be made when planning interventions)

In planning our work we will need to pay particular attention to a number of factors. In mixing and sequencing interventions, experiences, and processes, we will have to see that we are meeting the demands of numerous objectives. If we do not pay careful attention to this, we may be unpleasantly surprised to find our project tapering away and our contract with the client group terminated before planned.

In the list below we do not enumerate the conditions for succeeding in efforts of planned change in organization. There is sufficient material and literature on that subject. The more complex strategy of planned change in an organization differs in its demands from the shorter term strategy (and from conditions of attaining results) with one or two groups in a particular area of organizational life. In this handbook, we are not dealing with Organizational Development, in terms of the strategy of changing a whole organization.

We will try to focus on factors which we must give thought to when planning a series of interventions or a workshop for a group or a number of groups (in this case "group" may mean department). Specifically:

1. Visible results
2. Impact on participants
3. Applicability
4. Learning and growth of participants
5. Satisfaction from each meeting
6. The facilitator's homework

1. *Visible results.* When working with groups and organizations, there is no factor of greater importance than showing *tangible, visible* results and showing them *fast.* Everything may be fine, all going according to plan, the participants happy, and ourselves self-satisfied. But if there are no results to be seen, if nothing has changed for the better within a reasonable time, we are going to have a failure. There is a certain amount of credit given to our work, that is true. And we may gain from the credit. But there are limits, so results *must* be seen—and the sooner the better.

Attaining results also *motivates* the participants to make greater efforts in the future. Nothing succeeds like success. And success has to be seen and felt before it is acknowledged. The facilitator must take this into account when planning and sequencing his or her interventions. He or she cannot plan a series of interventions that take months to show any signs of a payoff. Participants (and sometimes their organization) must see tangible results on the way. They need to feel that they have attained something already. Motivation and commitment lag when progress is not achieved most of the time. This means that serious thought must be given right from the earliest stage to the introduction of processes that *show results.* A plan that does not do so may run into trouble.

Showing results means that we must finish things; we must ensure their implementation, ensure that there is someone responsible for implementation; fix dates of implementation and check the implementation.

Showing results means finding the correct balance between the "learning" and the "task" functions of our work. It means finding the correct balance between the "maintenance" and the "task" aspects of working with groups (both of these will be detailed later).

Showing results means finding ways to make results *visible*. There may be some results that people are not sufficiently aware of and which, therefore, they should be made aware of. This may entail sending typed copies of all decisions and changes decided on to participants after a meeting. It may mean sending copies of material that may be disclosed to other people in the organization. Visibility includes making the connection between the intervention and its results.

2. *Impact on participants.* Success in our work requires an impact on the people we work with. If working with us leaves people with a feeling that it is the same as everyday routine, we are not having the necessary impact. People should feel that they have had an experience. They must come out of interventions and workshops feeling or saying: "That was something valuable; that was worthwhile," or make such a connection at some subsequent time.

We have always found that if too many of the interventions and processes are not personally meaningful for those taking part, they "cool off." This poses a difficult problem of sequencing and mixing interventions and processes. Some interventions have to be made even though they leave less personal impact on people. There is some work that just has to be accomplished before going ahead, and not all of it is personally meaningful to all the participants. Therefore, in sequencing and mixing processes, we must give serious thought to a balance between "individual" and "group focus"; between "task" and "maintenance"; and between "cognition" and "experiencing." About this we will give more details later.

3. *Applicability.* People must recognize the realistic applicability of what they have learned. In fact, not only must they feel that it can be applied; they must also apply it. Who has not heard it said: "Well that is all very fine in a course and a workshop, but it won't work out back home." *Methods that are not applicable should not be learned.* Ways of functioning that will not meet the test of everyday applicability are not worth spending time on. If people come out of interventions and courses with the conclusion that what they acquired cannot be implemented, we have wasted our time. The major purpose of our work together is to implement practical, visible changes in everyday life. Not only must people feel that they have had an experience and that training has had an impact, they must feel that their everyday life is also affected.

This means thought and attention in planning interventions and in finishing them with their *practical implementation in everyday life*. This orientation requires decisions during the training period about what we are going to implement, by what date, who will be responsible, and when the implementation results will be reviewed.

It means *not overburdening* a workshop with more items than the participants can hope to implement.

It means finding the balance between time devoted to new learning and new experiences, and time devoted to *consolidating* what has been acquired and ensuring its implementation.

4. *Learning and growth of participants.* People we work with need to feel that they have learned something different. They should have the feeling that they have *"grown" as human beings* and have widened their horizons.

We should strive to attain the "aha" experience—the experience of suddenly understanding something which was not previously understood, the flash of enlightenment when things suddenly fit into place.

People need to make some sense out of the world in which they live. They strive to understand what makes things tick. They feel good when they "grow." When people have experiences that enrich them, they are gratified and wish for more. We hope to achieve some of this sense of growth through the interventions.

Our work attempts to help people learn and develop. One of our keenest tools is the ability to help people enrich their life experience and deepen their understanding of themselves and the realities of their everyday experiences.

If we disregard the use of this valuable aspect of our work we are not exploiting one of our major resources.

Thus, in planning, mixing, and sequencing our processes and interventions, we must constantly give thought to how we are going to attain a growthful learning experience. It means finding the right balance between the "cognitive" and "experiential" ways of learning (more about this later); it means finding the correct balance between the "task-oriented" interventions and the "learning-oriented" interventions (more on this later).

Thought and work must be devoted to creating and illustrating *"cognitive maps"*—such as the Johari Window and other devices that have opened many eyes.

The facilitator must first clearly understand what he or she is trying to impart to others. We must find the right balance between the personal growth processes and the task and group processes. We must give sufficient thought and attention to ensuring that the experiences which the group undergoes have personal learning and personal growth aspects.

5. *Satisfaction from each meeting.* We might call this "unit satisfaction." Each day and each meeting with a group over a period of time must be seen as a unit on its own, and not just a part of the whole process. *Each*

such unit must bear its own fruits in the sense that it provides people with satisfaction, growth, learning, and results. When we plan a series of meetings with a group, we may follow a line of work that sees everything in the "final payoff." We may set our sights on achieving something with a group, and in doing so may lose sight of what is happening on the way.

The concept of "satisfaction from each meeting" is used by us to stress the point that each meeting between facilitator and group must be a source of satisfaction and growth to the latter. The source of satisfaction or growth may differ in each meeting. Once it may be from seeing tangible results, another time from an "aha" experience; it may be from feeling that the team is dealing effectively with problems long disregarded; it may be an experience of personal growth, etc. Whatever it is, the aim should be to see that each "unit" of meeting with a team be a self-contained unit, and thus pay its own separate dividends.

When we plan a workshop or a series of meetings we have to give serious thought and attention to *each and every meeting* or part of the workshop as an entity. We stop thinking in terms of end results only and devote serious thought to each step on the way.

Thus, when we have planned something and find that it is missing the intended mark, we have to be sufficiently *flexible* to find the right process or action for that moment. We strive to maintain a constantly accelerating pace of interest and enthusiasm. We avoid having two meetings that are unsuccessful. If it happens, we are likely to lose in attendance and commitment in the future.

All this means that the facilitator has to do his or her homework well.

6. *The facilitator's homework.* It is said that the greatest conductors and musicians prepare themselves painstakingly and practice ceaselessly. However, in the training sphere it has somehow become accepted that the more experienced you are, the less you have to prepare yourself; the more you can rely on your intuition and experience.

Our experience has taught us differently. The more experienced you are the more you prepare for possible eventualities. The less experienced you are, the smaller your stock of tools, responses, conceptual maps, interventions, and reactions. The more experienced you are, the better able you are to estimate possible developments in meetings and prepare for them.

Possibly the worst facilitator is the one who has just passed his or her first stage of facilitating. Like a driver who is careful when he first gets his license, he may become more reckless as he gains assurance.

Every single meeting has to be carefully prepared for, taking into account as many possibilities and eventualities as can be conceived, developed, thought out beforehand, and prepared for. The enriching of people's experience, helping them grow, illuminating their confusion by conceptual maps, applying the intervention needed for the right situation—all these do not come mainly from "on the spot" intuition. They require careful thought and planning. The consultant and facilitator needs always to prepare him- or herself thoroughly before each meeting, planning what to do if such and such an eventuality occurs.

We have learned that hard work, detailed and thorough thinking, and careful preparation of everything that may possibly be needed, is the basis on which to build. Of equal importance is changing and suiting the intervention to the specific needs of the team with whom we are working.

If these are done there is a very good chance that the facilitator will have visible results and that the experiences will have an impact on participants. Most important, the participants will gain practical and useful skills from the experience.

WHAT DILEMMAS MUST WE BALANCE? (Identifying some dilemmas to be faced when planning interventions)

In planning the sequencing and mixing of processes and interventions we are faced with a number of dilemmas. The following are the ones we wish to mention here.

1. Task vs learning
2. Task vs maintenance
3. Group vs individual
4. Group vs interfaces
5. Cognitive learning vs experiential learning
6. Planning vs flexibility
7. Responsibility of participants vs responsibility of facilitator
8. One facilitator vs two or more facilitators

Finding the correct balance in each is not easy, but this list has already enabled us to take the necessary first step—to at least become aware of them. Now we will discuss each of these dilemmas in the following pages.

1. *Task vs learning.* We have already mentioned this dilemma. We are faced with the problem of how much emphasis to put on *achieving the purposes* of an intervention and how much on using the intervention *as a learning experience* for the participants.

Are we helping a management team to solve its problems, or are we training them how to problem-solve in similar situations in the future? Are we leading a team through a process to help them confront the role conflicts that are making their life difficult, or are we making available an experience which they can use in the future on their own?

Of course, the basis of learning is experiencing. But if the intention is to use the experience for other occasions, the process of presenting that experience must be handled differently.

We usually wish to attain *both* objectives. Nevertheless, we will be faced with practical concrete decisions if we wish to stress either. Generally, if it is wished that the learning be for future use, we will need more *time, practice,* and *theory.* We shall have to weigh the *cost* of using this approach against other possible training or development which the team may be in great need of. The decision is generally not easy.

2. *Task vs. maintenance.* How much of our meeting time are we going to devote to dealing with training programs, interventions, discussion of vital organizational problems, etc., and how much will we devote to *team building?*

We know that both are needed. Without *task achievements* and tangible visible results the effects of the interventions will not be considered of value. We also know that without dealing with the "maintenance" of the team there are going to be difficulties in getting results. Unless we deal with interpersonal tensions, hidden agendas, and all the usual interpersonal problems found in a team, we are going to have difficulty helping the team confront its task functions and *effectively apply what has been learned.* Choosing in this dilemma is no easy affair, especially if the team has a strong task orientation and emphasizes the importance of dealing with task activities.

The practitioner will have to weigh very carefully how much time he or she will devote to each of these two kinds of activity. There may also be problems in sequencing. The practitioner knows that task activities will be performed more effectively if maintenance has first been dealt with. But he or she also knows that dealing too long with maintenance will delay achieving what is termed "results" by people who have task orientation. Finding the ideal proportion and right sequence in this situation needs good planning and sensitivity to team reactions.

3. *Group vs individual.* How much of the team's activities will be devoted to *group*-oriented processes and how much to *individual*-oriented processes? Both are necessary; neither can attain its objectives without the other. But how to maintain a healthy balance?

Generally, the individual-oriented activities are such that people feel they have had an "experience" which leaves a strong impression on them. These are often experiences which affect a person's feelings and self image. Often when we go through these processes the atmosphere is charged with emotion.

But on the other hand, if we are to spend too much time on these personal needs, what will become of the group processes we also wish to deal with. In practice will we go through the process of "Are we doing what we should be doing?" (in Chapter 9), or will we choose one of the team building processes or simulations (Chapter 6)?

We need to find a balance between the two. The management team needs both effectiveness training and individual-oriented processes.

4. *Group vs interfaces.* When should we begin working on the problematic *interfaces* of the team? When should we begin dealing with problems

of tension and linkages between the team we are working with and other teams and individuals in the organization with whom the team is interdependent?

It is accepted by many consultants that first one works on the team itself, and later on its interfaces. But is this indeed so simple? When we are working with teams that serve, or work with, other people, is it possible for us to first "finish off" all processes dealing with the team as such—and only then move on to deal with its relations with others?

If we are working with a team of school teachers, do we deal only with the relations between the teachers themselves or do we need to work also on the relationship between them and their pupils? If we work with a nursing staff will it be any different? Can we so easily differentiate between the internal team problems and problems that stem from a different style of dealing with people outside the team (patients, for example)—treating them as a "task" or as "people"?

We have found the practice of dealing first with the team and later with interfaces as difficult to abide by. It creates a sequencing problem for which there is no simple solution. In certain teams and under certain conditions, we have to deal with problems of interfaces along with the team's problems. How one reaches the best mix depends on the experience, discretion, and sensitivity of the facilitator. Whatever the case, it is necessary to be aware of the danger in sequencing according to formulae, and attention and thought must be given to know the right moment to begin dealing with interface problems.

5. *Cognitive learning vs experiential learning.* In reaction against the classical learning methods, and taken with the effectiveness of experiential learning methods, some facilitators completely forgo classical methods such as reading, lectures, theory, and sometimes even modeling behavior (teaching by doing).

Experiential learning is the basis of most human-relations structured processes and simulations. The idea being that people learn best by experiencing for themselves that which has to be learned. People who draw their own conclusions from situations in which they find themselves, have learned a lesson. It is far better for people to discover the answers by themselves than to have their answers "fed" to them.

The question is not whether experiential learning is the major way of working with groups, but to find the right proportion of other methods that also enhance learning. *Reading* is often neglected, although reading can be a major tool to strengthen, deepen, and widen the effect of that which has been learned in an experiential way. Though long lectures may not suit many people, there are few who do not gain insight from a short *lecturette* that ties together loose ends into some understandable concepts. We believe that people will learn best from answers which they have found through their own search. However, many people must be guided into such a process. The facilitator may help in this process by modeling it before them or suggesting new possibilities which they had not thought of.

The problem facing the facilitator is not to choose either experiential learning or other ways. The problem is to find the right proportion in which to use the different methods.

Another problem is to find the suitable *time, conditions,* and *ways* to enhance the experiential method with other learning methods.

6. *Planning vs flexibility.* We find that if we do not *plan* our meetings thoroughly, methodically, and in much detail, we will not succeed in attaining our objectives. But we also find that if we are not *flexible* enough to change our plans in the course of the meeting, when the need arises, we may miss golden opportunities.

We may have exerted much thought, time, and resources in preparing a training session in problem-solving methods, but in the meeting itself we may run up against a hidden agenda of interpersonal tension that definitely interferes with establishing a problem-solving atmosphere. What should we do? Should we set aside our plans and deal with the interpersonal issue, or should we continue with the meeting as planned and make a note to deal with the problem on another occasion?

There is no simple answer. Sometimes we will continue as planned, and sometimes we will deal with the issue that has arisen. When we do continue as planned, we progress toward the team's learning objectives and the team feels it is moving ahead and seeing results. When we take a side step and deal with the interpersonal issue we help create conditions for more effective learning, and at the same time give the participants another essential learning experience.

Perhaps the best strategy is to plan *before* the meeting for all foreseeable eventualities, and thus be prepared if something like this does arise. Then we can deal with it effectively in a way that can be the best outcome for the team. In the meeting itself we will try as much as possible to attain the meeting's objectives. Yet, if the need arises, we will be sufficiently flexible to lay aside those plans, and meet the needs of the occasion.

Preparing for a meeting in this manner will not be easy for the facilitator. It requires much experience and pre-thought to be able to foresee possible developments, and to prepare oneself thoroughly to meet them. However, a facilitator who does this will soon see the fruits of his or her efforts in the satisfaction and growth of participants in a team which is making good progress toward its goals.

7. *Responsibility of participants vs responsibility of facilitator.* Who has the responsibility for the team attaining its objectives and getting results? The team, of course! The facilitator, of course! Sometimes we have heard others and ourselves say: "When things go right, the facilitator; when failures crop up, the participants."

As we seriously consider the burden of responsibility, it rests with both—*the facilitator and the participants*. Without the desire of the participants to change their present way of functioning, and without their willingness to invest themselves in learning new ways, all the facilitator's efforts will be wasted. On the other hand, if the team is willing, ready, and eager, but the facilitator does not function as he or she should, few positive results will be accomplished.

In the long run, it is the facilitator's responsibility to see first if the team is ready for learning and change. If not, then he or she should not begin working with it. Should conditions be ripe for work, and then, after some work with the team, the interest and commitment lags, the facilitator should not lay the blame on the participants. Either the first diagnosis of the team's readiness was erroneous or the diagnosis was correct and the facilitator has not been functioning effectively.

Thus, although the responsibility for success or failure lies with both the participants and the facilitators, it lies *more on the latter*. It is the facilitator's job, before undertaking a project, to decide whether the team can carry its part of the burden, and it is his or her responsibility to find the most effective procedures if he or she has decided that the team is indeed ready and able.

Some facilitators, under the guise of giving the client company the right to make its own decisions, avoid assuming sufficient responsibility. They will emphasize the importance of strengthening the client, and that the client's needs must go before the facilitator's needs. While we accept the basic idea, we know that the client has asked for help and in so doing is depending on our skills—our structuring. We know the team must become increasingly independent and assume primary responsibility for achieving its objectives. However, the facilitator usually will be in a better position to see beyond some confusing and distorting circumstances that may surround the team. He or she has the obligation to help the team see beyond the present and into some future ways of resolving the problem. That aspect of responsibility weighs heavily on the facilitator.

Everyone will agree that there is a joint responsibility for achieving the goal of the more effective team. Sometimes the onus of responsibility will be more with the team, and other times more with the facilitator.

8. *Single facilitator vs two or more facilitators.* Clients in need of help are usually looking for some direction. Frequently, direction is felt more clearly and confidently from *one* leader. However, we have found that with the complexity of many organizational situations, more than one facilitator is very useful. The dilemma is compounded by the increased fee that must be charged when outside consultants are required.

We analyze the situation to determine the number of facilitators required: What will be the effect of more than one facilitator? What loss will be felt by the facilitator if he or she operates alone? The answers to such questions help us to determine the optimum arrangements. Sometimes we will just have a lead facilitator who will carry out all direct contacts with the client. If circumstances suggest, the lead facilitator will use other colleagues to assist him or her, but not "in front" of the client. If, at some future time, additional help is required, the client must be prepared for the additional personnel. Usually, the concern over more than one facilitator is considerably reduced after some initial interventions have been introduced.

EXAMPLES OF SOME FORMATS (examples of ways of using different interventions together to achieve specific purposes)

When to use

The formats described here can be used in a number of ways:

1. As the framework of a workshop lasting a week or more.
2. As the framework of a two- or three-day workshop *followed by regular periodic meetings.*
3. As the framework of regular periodic meetings.

Purposes: Format 1: Helping a management team increase its effectiveness

Format 2: Helping a top management team deal with its organization's problems

Format 3: Helping a team define its goals and projects, then dividing the responsibility among members

Format 4: Helping a group with team building

Format 5: Training a team to improve its problem-solving ability

Note: The formats described here have been used by us on numerous occasions as frameworks for working with teams. However, in practice they have not always been carried out exactly as described here. The reasons are twofold: First, every team differs from other teams in its character, needs, and problems. Thus, we use the formats as rough outlines or guidelines to be suited in each case to the particular team, and deviated from according to developments taking place during work with the team.

Secondly, we generally intersperse team-building interventions (Chapter 6) and basic and standard methods (Appendix II) with the task-oriented interventions. Most teams require, to varying degrees, some form of team building. Team-building interventions and simulations may be regarded as the foundation of all our work.

We have not placed the team-building interventions in the formats presented herein (except Format 4), since team building depends so much on the character and the needs of the team.

We will try and intersperse the team-building interventions and simulations among the task-oriented interventions, taking into account the previously discussed considerations and dilemmas. Thus, we emphasize that, when reviewing the formats, it will still be necessary to add at appropriate intervals the team-building interventions and simulations described in Chapters 6, 7, 8, and 9, as well as Appendix II.

Format 1: Helping a management team increase its effectiveness.

Chapter Section

    2 Individual interviews and group feedback
    7 Resolving role conflicts
    9 What is hindering effectiveness?
   10 Defining and improving managers' jobs
    9 "Are we doing what we should be doing?"

According to need we will add to these five interventions, other interventions from: Chapter 5, Creative problem-solving; Chapter 9, Team effectiveness; and Chapter 4, Increasing your effectiveness as a manager. Of course, interspersed among all these would be appropriate team-building interventions and simulations from Chapters 6 and 8.

Format 2: Helping a top management team deal with its organization's problems.

Chapter Section

    2 Questionnaires and feedback (the intervention described therein), or
    2 Problem-sensing with groups
    5 How to begin dealing with a problem
    5 (Use the techniques of Chapter 5, Creative Problem-Solving, to work with the team on the problems)
   10 Establishing objectives
    6 Planning how to attain an objective

       Probably also:

    9 What is hindering effectiveness?
    9 "Are we doing what we should be doing?"

As usual: Team-building interventions and simulations dispersed at appropriate points.

Format 3: Helping a team define its goals and projects, then dividing responsibility for the work among members.

Chapter Section

10 Determining the team's responsibilities
10 Dividing the team's responsibilities or
10 Clarifying responsibility and authority in a team
10 Planning how to attain an objective
 9 Improving practical aspects of team functioning

   Probably also:

 9 What is hindering effectiveness?

Again: Team-building interventions and simulations should be interspersed among the interventions.

Format 4: Helping a group with team building. After completion of "Basic steps in team development" (in Chapter 6), the following additional interventions may be considered:

Chapter Section

2 Individual interviews and group feedback
7 (if needed) Resolving one-to-one conflicts
7 Resolving role conflicts
9 What is hindering effectiveness?
8 Developing an interprofessional team

Format 5: Training a team to improve its problem-solving ability.

Chapter Section

9 What is hindering effectiveness?
5 Stages of dealing with a problem
5 Defining a problem
5 Creative solutions to problems
5 Weighing proposals
5 Deciding between alternative solutions
5 Overcoming resistance to implementation
4 With whom should you make decisions?

As usual, teambuilding interventions and simulations should be interspersed among the interventions.

A final word

We have some final thoughts on the completion of this handbook. These ideas fall into three areas: (1) A summary of our frame of reference: A strategy for initiating and continuing constructive change; (2) Resistance to change; and (3) Change and development as a way of life.

A SUMMARY OF OUR FRAME OF REFERENCE: A strategy for initiating and continuing constructive change.

- Our values and those which we hopefully project when working with organizations are expressed in Humanistic Psychology.

- We recognize the everchanging, sometimes turbulent environment of present day organizations.

- We find that the needs of individuals and the needs of their organizations are often in discord and conflict. We seek ways to integrate these often-times conflicting needs.

- We believe that the level of interdependence between people in existing organizations has reached a stage that demands a significant change in the quality of human relations in the workplace.

- We find Open Systems Theory—that is, looking at an organization as a series of interrelating subgroups which must have a give and take with their external environment—as the most useful guide to analyzing and understanding the way an organization actually behaves.

- We support the view that change in organizations is more effective when it is synergistic. That is, we feel that unexpected and additional outcomes are gained through the combined action of a number of people, as contrasted with more individual and independent functioning of the people in the organization.

- Ideally, we aim our efforts to change individual behavior, group and organizational norms and culture, organizational structure, management style and practice, communication networks, and the technology and the ecology of the organization.

- We believe that changes in individual behavior require work on the behavioral, cognitive, and emotional aspects of the person. There is a greater chance of having a more permanent effect by working on all three aspects.

- We believe that bringing about change in organizations requires working at *all levels*—individual, group, intergroup, and total organization. Working at one level tends to reinforce the changes achieved at other levels.

- We recognize that a constant effort of organizational renewal is vital.

- We seek to build on constructive change mechanisms in the organization, such as individuals with ideas and the willingness to test those ideas, or departments that have demonstrated their creativity and interest in change.

- Our approach is *Client-Centered:*
  —We believe that client-initiated change is stronger and longer lasting.
  —We accept our client's needs as the major consideration in planning our work.
  —We try to help the client define his or her needs in the form of a set of problems to work on.
  —We honor the requests of clients to work within certain parts of the organization, even though we recognize the importance of change on many levels.

- Our approach is *Results-Oriented:*
  —Our interventions are aimed at helping individuals and groups change their own behavior. Our hope is that our client will also influence others in the organization to change their behavior in the desired way and possibly bring about more extensive organizational change.
  —We choose interventions that have practical and visible effects which are immediately recognized and, hopefully, will last over a significant period of time.

A summary of our frame of reference **389**

- Our *Method* includes:

  —Developing specific interventions for each particular aspect of the organization.

  —Establishing a balance between "task" problems and "maintenance" problems.

  —Developing change programs that have clearly defined goals and objectives and are planned and structured accordingly.

  —Establishing interventions that are structured and detailed enough to be used by others in the organization, while being open and flexible enough to suit different systems.

  —Involving the client and gaining his or her attention by using experiential learning methods, different grouping during training sessions, by reaching him or her through his or her different senses, and appropriately including lecturettes, readings, etc.

- We see our function as that of a change agent filling many roles, including: diagnostician, process helper, educator, trainer, facilitator, innovator, linkage creator organizational structure specialist, etc.

RESISTANCE TO CHANGE

We are aware of the forces within an organization that resist change. We are aware of society's needs to preserve institutions and cultures. In fact, the basic training we received as children and which has been reinforced in our adult lives emphasizes the importance of keeping our good way of life—or, negatively put, not rocking the boat. We have been taught to adjust to the norms; to parrot the "right" answers; to speak only when spoken to; to behave according to the rules of "good social behavior" to guess what the parent, teacher, or boss are looking for; to play the game. It is no wonder that change and creativity will be resisted.

Goodwin Watson, in his frequently referred to article, "Resistance to Change"* cautions us to be aware of the many factors that cause resistance in individuals, groups, and organizations. In organizations, he speaks of:

- The need to conform to norms.

- The need to keep a unit whole and totally connected to its culture—not allowing any part to change.

- The need of vested interests to maintain their own approaches.

---

* Watson, Goodwin (ed.), *Concepts for Social Change,* Cooperative Project of Educational Development Series, Vol. I (Washington, D.C.: National Training Laboratories, 1966).

- The need to hold on to things that are sacred; rituals, traditions.
- The need to reject outsiders and be suspicious of them.

As we work in organizations, these resistances must be kept in mind. Interventions can have an impact on a particular team. The members can leave the workshop with a "strong glow," a well thought through series of action steps, and the conviction that finally there will be some meaningful change. However, at almost every turn within the organization, they will meet the need to keep things as they are.

We raise these thoughts as *notes* of *reality*. As we have reckoned with these potential resistances and anticipated them, we have become more successful. The awareness of the resistance increases our use of careful and detailed planning, preparation for an intervention, thoughtful and flexible handling of the intervention, and often most important—*follow-up efforts*.

As a friend and colleague, Shel Davis, once remarked, "You have to keep the process open so you won't get killed as you gain success." By "open" he meant being aware of the resistances and being flexible enough to deal with them *before* and *as* they arise.

CHANGE AND DEVELOPMENT AS A WAY OF LIFE

We hope the message that change and development is *our* way of life has been expressed in a hundred ways throughout this handbook. At times it feels very strange to write a *handbook* about interventions when we stand for constructive and planned *change*.

We have thought about this observation which some colleagues have couched in the question: "Aren't you just giving recipes?" Obviously, we do not consider this handbook or our approach as characterized by—following a recipe. However, we do know that development and change are hard to come by and particularly difficult to keep going. Thus, we felt that offering a series of tested ways to achieve change is a useful step in building change and development as a way of life.

Each of us needs some degree of structure, help, or direction to get a process of change going. Each of us needs more help or less help in ensuring that such development will continue. We have found that:

- The more we can accept *change* as the norm instead of *fixedness* or adjustment, the greater the chance for creative solutions.
- The better we are in continuing our development, the more effective we are in helping others develop (through modeling).
- The more we are willing to take risks and experiment, the more rewarding are the outcomes (even though there are always some rough spots and tension).

- The more open we are with our thoughts and feelings (under appropriate circumstances), the more we can help promote responding and growing organizations around us.

- The more we build in evaluation of what we have tried, the more effective we will be during the next attempt of a similar action.

We sincerely hope that this handbook can be used as a take-off point for introducing constructive change in the lives of managers and organizations.

Glossary

Change Team: A group of people interested in, and empowered to bring about, planned change in a unit or an organization.

Consensus: A form of decision-making that involves the group discussion of thoughts about an issue until the participants reach an optimal and agreed-upon decision (as contrasted with decision by ballot).

Content: The subject matter of a discussion, problem, or area of work (as contrasted with process).

Evaluation research: An organized, step-by-step review of the impact resulting from an intervention with a group or organization using appropriate reporting of results on a periodic basis.

External consultant: A person usually trained in special area (organizational development, management development, management control systems, etc.) who can assist a person or team to work on problems and/or bring about planned, constructive change.

Facilitator: A person who helps another individual, small group, or large group review what is happening either within a person or among all participants; e.g., helping a group reach a shared decision.

Fishbowl: A method of group process in which two or more group members work together while being observed and listened to by the rest of the group who sit around them in a circle of chairs, so that there is an inner and an outer circle. The procedure aids in focusing on an issue of a subgroup that is of interest to the total group.

Humanistic psychology: A theory and practice of psychology which focuses on respect for the individual and a recognition of the strength and potential of each person to grow and continue to grow.

Interdependence: A relationship between two or more people in which there is a willingness to give and ask for help; a recognition of the skills and power of each person; a trust and respect that permits a high level of openness and honesty.

Interface: An area of connection or overlap between two teams or departments, (e.g., Accounting and Operations) which has the potential for unclarity and thus problems.

Internal consultant: A person within the organization who has the planning and implementing of constructive change as an identified formal or informal function. Usually there is a working relationship between an internal and external consultant.

Learning contract: An agreement, usually between two people, which has as its objective the learning of some skill and/or body of information; the steps to be taken; a time plan; and a method of evaluating the results.

Learning experience: Any event which has as its main purpose the learning or developing of a skill, the gaining of information, etc.

Linking pin: A person in an organization who spontaneously or by plan makes connections between departments or between levels of employees in the hierarchy of the organization. Usually such a person has another formal role or departmental base.

Lose-lose: A solution to a problem situation in which all parties lose; e.g., after a long discussion, no decision is reached even though all parties wanted some decisive action.

Management by objective: Or MBO; a procedure used to plan and execute action steps through setting clearly stated objectives with the necessary action steps, responsible parties, and time frame.

Newsprint: Large sheets of blank paper (about 2' x 3', available in pads) used to record information, ideas, etc. during a meeting so that all the data can be seen by all the participants.

Nonstructured intervention: A series of steps toward changing a team or organization that are determined by a group of people and grow out of the thinking and actions of the participants rather than being preplanned. The group may or may not have a formal leader (as contrasted with a structured intervention).

Nonverbal expression: Ways of communicating without talking or writing; e.g., gestures, ways people sit or stand, facial expressions, etc.

Open-systems theory: An approach to understanding organizations through looking at all the interfacing systems (i.e., departments, outside environment, political groups, etc.) and recognizing that all such systems influence each other and thus must be taken into account when planning change.

PERT: (Program evaluation and review technique) An established approach to planning that has resulted from computer technology and been applied to general planning within an organization.

Process: The manner in which a procedure or interaction between two or more people is played out; e.g., *how* a problem is solved as contrasted with the content of the problem.

Simulation: An exercise, like role-playing, in which a real situation is defined (including the roles of each person or group involved) and acted out. All necessary information is brought to the attention of the group and the results often allow for better preparation for a similar situation in the future.

Structured intervention: A series of steps which are planned and executed by a leader or facilitator with little opportunity for the participants to change the plan (as contrasted with nonstructured intervention).

Synergism: The creativity resulting from different people working together; more (and different types of) creative results than just the accomplishments of each individual in the group; e.g., the results of a "group think."

Variable: A behavior that is identified or measured during assessment or change procedure; e.g., "level of productivity," number of clear messages to employees.

Win-lose: A solution to a problem situation in which one party gains and benefits and the other party does not benefit, or loses. (At times the first party gains at the expense of the other party.)

Win-win: A solution to a problem situation in which all parties concerned *gain* from the resolution of the problem (as contrasted with win-lose).

Some basic and standard methods

Appendix II

INTRODUCTIONS AND EXPECTATIONS

Objectives

1. To "break the ice" with a group that is just beginning a workshop (either established teams or "strangers")
2. To become clearer about what participants are expecting from the anticipated experience.

Participants: From 8 to 20 people

Materials: Newsprint, felt pens, tape

Time: Not less than 45 minutes; depends on number of people

Detailed process

1. The facilitator states that he or she would like to have the group get to know or become better acquainted with each other. At the same time, he or she would like to know what the participants expected to get out of the session. Toward both of these ends, the facilitator suggests some steps.

2. The facilitator then suggests that the participants stand up and look around the room at the different people. They are asked to pick out someone who is not familiar and also looks like an interesting person. (*Note:* There is often reluctance or embarrassment. The facilitator should encourage the participants to walk around the room and not just pick the person sitting in the neighboring chair. When there is an odd number, it is suggested that a trio be formed.)

3. After the subgroups are formed, the participants are told the following:

a. The purpose of the pairing is to get to know another person, learn his or her expectations about the workshop or meeting, begin the process of active listening, and through introducing partners practice speaking in front of the group.

b. Ask your partner his or her name and "nickname"—the name that friends or family members have used that has special meaning. Also, find out how your partner got that name.

c. Collect other interesting information about your partner.

d. Ask your partner to explain why he or she came to the workshop and what he or she expected to get from it.

Remind the group that each person will have to introduce her or his partner after the interviews. Explain that talking is all right.

4. The interviews can last for about 20 minutes. At the end of 10 minutes the facilitator should remind the pairs that they have another 10 minutes and should begin the second interview.

5. At the end of the interviews, the group should reconvene and begin the introduction process. The facilitators should begin the introductions by modeling a short interesting statement of two minutes. (Note: A facilitator working alone should simply introduce himself or herself.) The person being introduced should be given a chance to make additions to the introduction. If time permits, other group members can ask some additional questions.

6. While the introductions are being done, the facilitator should have one newsprint for the nicknames and personal information and a second to list expectations.

7. After the introductions, the group can discuss the expectations and whether or not they can and will be achieved during the workshop.

8. The participants are then given a chance to reflect on what they have learned about the group and this process of discussing expectations before a workshop begins. The facilitator should ask them to record these thoughts in their notebooks.

ONE-WAY/TWO-WAY COMMUNICATION

Objectives

1. To help people recognize the benefit of two-way communication over just being "talked to."
2. To assist a group or team in having more of an exchange of ideas in their work.

Participants: From 10 to 20 people

Materials:
  1. Newsprint, felt pens, tape, pencils
  2. Notebooks
  3. Two charts with diagrams (Fig. II.1)

Time: About 1 hour

Detailed process

1. The facilitator begins with a very brief introduction to the exercise, mainly indicating that the objective is to help with communication within the team. If more warm-up is necessary, there may be a brief discussion of some problems that the team has had in communicating.

2. The facilitator asks for a volunteer to come to the front of the group.

3. The group is asked to turn to a clean page in their notebooks and get in a position so that each person can hear the volunteer.

4. The volunteer is instructed, in front of the group, that he or she will be giving directions to the group in drawing a series of squares. The participants are to draw the squares exactly as they are told.

5. The facilitator gives Part (a) of Fig. II.1 to the volunteer to study for about two minutes, and indicates to the participants that they *cannot* ask any questions during this part of the exercise. They must just listen.

6. The volunteer is asked to face away from the group and describe the diagram as clearly and precisely as possible while the participants attempt to draw it.

7. At the completion of the first phase, and without any discussion, the volunteer is given Part B. While he or she is studying this part of the figure, the facilitator tells the group that now they should turn to another clean sheet of paper to draw a second diagram of squares. This time they are permitted to ask questions of the volunteer, who is facing the group while describing the squares.

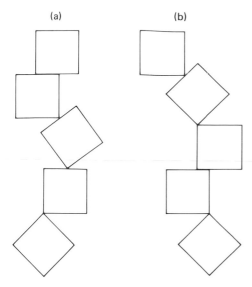

(a)   (b)

Fig. II.1 (a) one-way communication and (b) two-way communication

8. At the completion of the second diagram, the facilitator takes the diagrams from the volunteer and holds them up for the participants to compare with their drawings. If the diagrams cannot be seen easily, then the facilitator should draw copies of them on newsprint. Observations are elicited.

9. The group members are asked how they felt during the first phase as compared with the second phase, when they could ask questions. They are asked how often they had to guess how to make a square during the first drawing and then during the second drawing.

10. After a discussion of the exercise, the facilitator helps the group consider the application of this exercise to the work situation.

LISTENING

Objective

To gain an understanding of active listening and comprehending the message—as contrasted with repeating the words or just not hearing.

Participants: Groups of three in a workshop of about 15

Materials: Newsprint, felt pens, tape

Time: About 45 minutes

Detailed process

1. The facilitator asks the group to form into subgroups of three, just by choosing any other two people in the group.

2. The trio identifies its members as A, B, C.

3. In each group there will be an observer, a speaker, and a listener. The speaker can choose any subject he or she wishes so long as it is somewhat controversial; such as politics, some current event, a social problem, some controversial issue in the organization, etc.

4. The facilitator gives the following instructions:

a. The speaker begins with his or her comments about the subject.

b. The listener cannot start to speak until he or she has summarized what the speaker has said to the satisfaction of both the speaker and the observer. If the summary is not correct, the difference must be clarified first before the listener can make a comment.

c. For the first round participant A starts as speaker, B is observer, and C is listener.

d. After about ten minutes, B becomes speaker, C takes over as observer, and A is listener. Finally, after another ten minutes C is speaker, A is observer, and B is listener.

e. The trios may remain with the subject A raised, or each new speaker can select a different subject if he or she wishes.

5. After a total of 30 minutes the trios are invited back to the total group for discussion.

6. The facilitator suggests the following discussion questions:

a. What made it difficult for you to listen?

b. What helped you to keep your attention on the speaker?

c. What kinds of things kept entering your mind that made it hard to listen?

d. Were there any nonverbal things that distracted you while you were trying to listen?

e. What did you learn about yourself as a listener? As a speaker?

7. As the discussion continues, the facilitator tries to list on newsprint the blocks and aids to listening.

8. The participants are asked to think about their listening behavior at work and write down ways they might change such behavior for the better.

PROCESS OBSERVATION

Objectives

1. To give feedback to a team or group during regular meetings.
2. To learn the method and skills of process observation.

Participants: Up to 15 (total team)

Materials: Process reporting sheet

Time: The length of the meeting

Detailed process

1. This skill can be practiced at a meeting after there is some experience in small group training so that the process observer has experienced feedback and has seen process observation.

2. A decision must be made about the kind of behavior that will be observed during the meeting of the team.

3. Everyone on the team knows about the presence of the process observer and what is being looked for.

4. The report form is organized before the meeting. It includes the name of the group that is meeting and content examples that might be observed, such as the following:

    a. Pattern of *communication:* Is it one-to-one? Is it one-to-group? Is it all through the leader?

    b. *Leadership pattern:* Is it encouraging participants? Is it blocking creativity? Is it mainly evaluative? Is it building on suggestions? Is it just task oriented? Is it oriented to problem-solving?

    c. *Effect of leadership:* Does it stimulate people? Does it result in arguments? Does it help reach decisions? Does it encourage participation and commitment?

    d. *Growth of group:* Do you get a feeling that the group has developed during the meeting? Is there time to reflect on the process? Is there a sense of cohesiveness in the group?

    e. *Goals of group:* Do the goals come through? Did you notice steps towards the goals?

5. The sheet for the report form should have the areas being observed and sufficient space to record what is observed.

6. Before the conclusion of the meeting, there should be sufficient time for the report of the observer. After the feedback, the team members should have a chance to discuss the observations.

7. Finally, the team members should think through how they can change their method of operating to achieve more productive meetings.

ROLE-PLAYING

Objectives

1. To practice an exchange of ideas or feelings in a situation that is more controlled than real life.
2. To demonstrate a method or technique that might be used in the work situation.
3. To clarify to participants the feelings evoked by different kinds of behavior.

Participants: From 8 to 12 people

Materials: 1. Newsprint, felt pens, tape
2. Notebook

Time: From 1 to 2 hours

Detailed process

1. The facilitator wants to demonstrate some particular method of interviewing or evaluation technique.

2. Two participants are requested to volunteer and come to the center (or front) of the group.

3. The facilitator:

a. Defines the situation; for example it is an interview between a manager and an employee.

b. Explains the purpose of the interview.

c. Asks the participants whether they have preference for one role or the other.

d. Helps each person clarify what the role is. (Note: The role clarification can be done orally or it can be previously prepared and written out. When the role-play is previously planned, it is often useful to have the role and situation written out and the instructions given to the volunteers.)

4. The facilitator then explains to the participants that the objective is for them to learn the techniques through observing the interview, critiquing it and identifying the feelings that they have as they think of themselves in the same situation.

5. The facilitator starts the interview by suggesting a question, or just allows the volunteers to start on their own. In office interviews, we find it useful to have the interviewee pretend to knock on the door, and go through the usual exchanges before going right into the interview.

6. As the role-play proceeds, the facilitator might have to inject a question or suggestion to help the process move in the desired direction.

7. At an appropriate time, the role-play is concluded.

8. The volunteers are asked about how they felt playing the role and what they learned about the technique being considered.

9. Each participant is asked what feelings were evoked by specific behaviors of his or her partner.

10. The facilitator turns to the other participants for their comments. We find it useful to ask all participants to write down what they have learned and how the learnings can be applied in the work situation.

11. The facilitator might ask for another pair of volunteers to go through the same process. If so, the same procedure is followed. The same situation may be chosen but with different reactions from one of the participants.

12. At the conclusion of the role-playing, the facilitator makes some observations, usually noting the main points on newsprint.

BIDDING FOR NICKELS

Objectives

1. To demonstrate how competition among team members results in decreasing effectiveness in reaching a goal.
2. To demonstrate how collaboration can increase effectiveness in reaching a goal.

Participants: From 10 to 20 people

Materials: Newsprint, felt pens, tape

Time: About ½ hour

Detailed process

1. The facilitator says to the group, "I have a stack of nickels piled up in front of me, and I'm going to auction them off, one at a time."
2. The rules of this auction are as follows:
   a. The group counts off by fives: 1, 2, 3, 4, 5.

b. Number 1 has the first bid and must start with one cent. Number 2 can either bid two cents or pass—and so on until number 5. Then we start all over again with the second five people, with number 1 bidding one cent, number 2 bidding two cents or pass, etc.

c. The facilitator sets up on newsprint the form in Fig. II.2.

Round	Amount of highest bid
1.	
2.	
3.	
4.	

Fig. II.2 Results of bidding

d. As the round is completed, the facilitator records the amount of the highest bid in the right-hand column.

3. The facilitator takes the group through ten or more rounds or until the group begins to catch on, that is, they can get a nickel for one cent if a group of five collaborate.

4. The facilitator leads the discussion of how competition influenced the decision to increase the bid. Then, the discussion moves to the learning of how collaboration can result to "beat" the facilitator.

5. The facilitator tries to elicit thoughts about what kept members in the competitive mode and what moved them to the more collaborative orientation. The facilitator tries to identify work-related examples of how some competition has been counterproductive, as well as how certain kinds of competition and collaboration have been helpful.

BROKEN SQUARES

Objectives

1. To examine the interaction in group problem-solving.
2. To increase sensitivity to certain behaviors that may help or interfere with problem-solving.
3. In a team, to bring hidden agendas out into the open.

Participants: Any number of groups of six, consisting of five participants and an observer

Materials: 1. Newsprint, felt pens, tape
2. Instructions for participants and observers
3. One set of broken squares for each group of five people

Time: About 1 hour

Detailed process

1. There is a brief discussion of problem-solving, including: the importance of listening to one another; the fact that everyone can help in working on a problem; the importance of recognizing problems others have in solving problems.

2. The facilitator has the group divide into groups of six, or at least groups of five. If there are groups of six, one person is assigned as observer and is given a set of instructions.* A packet of the broken puzzles is also distributed to each group.

3. The facilitator reads the following instructions to all the groups:

In the packet there are five envelopes, and each envelope has pieces of cardboard that can be used to form squares. When you get the signal, you must form five squares of equal size. The task is not over until each participant has a completed square in front of him or her. During the square building you:

a. Cannot speak at all.

b. Cannot take a card from another person or signal that you want a card.

c. Can only get a card when another person gives it to you.

4. It is usually necessary for the facilitator to walk around to the various groups to enforce the rules of the exercise and observe what is happening between people.

5. When the exercise is completed, the facilitator engages the groups in a discussion of what has been learned. What were the feelings as the participants worked without talking? What did people notice about leadership? About effectiveness in doing the task? The observers' comments should be elicited. Finally, how can the learnings be applied in the work situation?

6. The facilitator may make comments on things he or she noticed and thus encourage people to speak about how what happened reflects a person's behavior, feelings, and position in real-life group situations.

Instructions to observer

1. Be sure there is no talking among group members.

---

* Instructions to the observers and directions for making the squares are given at the end of this exercise.

2. Be sure that participants just accept pieces and do not give them.

3. Pieces must be *passed* to another participant.

4. Look at the participants to determine the following:

    a. Who seems to be in a leading position?

    b. Did any participants just finish their own jobs and then sit looking bored or guard their own squares when others had not finished?

    c. Were there any moments of excitement or relief?

    d. When did the group suddenly realize how to solve the problem?

Directions for making a set of squares

1. Get some pliable pieces of cardboard at least six inches square.

2. Mark the lines on the five squares as indicated in Fig. II.3. Then lightly pencil in the letters.

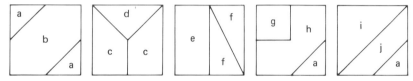

Fig. II.3 The squares

3. Be sure that when you draw the lines, all pieces marked by the same letter are of the same size. For example, all a's should be the same size.

4. Cut the pieces to their proper shape.

5. Place the pieces in five envelopes—which have been marked 1, 2, 3, 4, 5—in the following way:

    Envelope 1 has pieces i, h, e
    Envelope 2 has pieces a, a, a, c
    Envelope 3 has pieces a, j
    Envelope 4 has pieces d, f
    Envelope 5 has pieces g, b, f, c

6. Erase the letters from each piece before you place it in the envelope.

TOWER BUILDING

Objectives

1. To help develop a better working relationship within a team.

2. To experience different styles of leadership.

3. To experience the importance of planning in problem-solving.

Participants: Up to 15 people in subgroups of 5 or 6

Materials: 1. Table for each subgroup
2. Set of identical building materials for each subgroup, including such items as: colored construction paper, poster board, paper bag, paper cups, paper plates, yarn, string, paper clips, tape, scissors, felt pens or crayons, etc.
3. Newsprint, felt pens, tape

Time: About 2 hours

Detailed process

1. The total group is divided into subgroups of five people who can sit or stand around a table.

2. The following instructions are given:
   a. This is a silent exercise; there is no talking.
   b. Using *all* the materials each subgroup must construct a tower.
   c. When the towers are completed, they will be judged on the basis of:
      1) Height
      2) Strength
      3) Beauty
   d. You have 30 minutes to build the towers

3. The signal to begin is given and the time is noted. During the exercise the leader should see that there is no talking.

4. After 15, 20, and 25 minutes, the groups are reminded of the amount of time they have left.

5. The leaders should look for any significant incidents that help or hinder and actions that suggest competition, challenge, the ignoring of suggestions, boredom, leadership, planning, etc. Such information can be used for group discussion at a later time in the exercise.

6. At the completion of the towers, the facilitator gives the following instructions:
   a. The towers will now be judged
   b. To do this, each group should select one judge. The judges will select the winner on the basis of height, strength, and beauty.

7. The subgroups may be surprised that the facilitator is *not* judging and may need some help in seriously picking a judge.

8. The judges are brought to the middle of the group (in a fishbowl). While the other participants watch (without talking), the judges decide on

their method of evaluating each criterion. They have 15 minutes to make their decision on *one* winner.

9. The facilitator notes the indications of leadership, problem-solving, and the planning methods that may or may not be employed by the judges.

10. The judges make their decision and explain how they reached it.

11. The facilitator leads a discussion on what has been gained from the exercise, asking:

    a. What did all participants feel during the tower building?

    b. How did the judges feel in their role?

12. Highlights should be recorded on the newsprint, emphasizing the learnings about leadership, team-building, planning and problem-solving.

THE JOHARI WINDOW

Objectives

1. To increase the level of self-disclosure with a team.
2. To assist a team in discussing problems or issues that have not been generally discussed with all team members.

Participants: Six to twelve people. Can be used with a number of groups at one time

Materials: 1. Newsprint paper, felt pens, tape, pencils
2. Notebook

Time: About 2 hours

Detailed process

1. Present a lecturette on the Johari Window, including the fact that the Window is named after the originators, namely Joe Luft and Harry Ingham. The Window is displayed on a piece of newsprint as shown in Fig. II.4.

	Known to self	Not known to self
Known to others	Open area	Blind area
Not known to others	Hidden area	Unknown area

Fig. II.4 The Johari Window

The Open area includes things about you that are known to you and others. These are readily shared with others.

The *Unknown area* includes things that neither you nor others know about yourself.

The *Blind area* includes things that you do not know about yourself but that others know about you. For example, if you are overworking yourself, you may not realize it but it may be obvious to others.

The *Hidden area* includes things that are private or hidden from others. You know them, but others do not.

2. The Window can be used to help a group share information about a problem situation in which information has not been shared equally among team members. It can also be used as a way of sharing information about people on the team.

Using the Johari Window as a way of sharing information about people on the team. In carrying out the second suggestion (sharing information about team members), the following steps are taken:

a. Everyone in the group is asked to make a list of his or her own strengths and liabilities.

b. Then, on a separate piece of paper, the participant lists all the team members down the left side of the sheet, and on the top has one column for strengths and another column for liabilities. Each participant records the information on strengths and liabilities about each team member. The papers are then turned in to the leader.

c. Each participant makes out a Johari Window for him- or herself.

d. The leader reads the strengths and liabilities for each person as recorded on all the sheets that have been turned in. The participant copies the information in the appropriate area of his or her window. That is, if the information was known to the participant as well as to others, he or she records it in the Open area; if it was not known by the participant but only to others, he or she places it in the Blind area. The participant then completes the Window by recording items that are known only to himself or herself.

e. The group then discusses what they have gained from the shared information and from the use of the Johari Window.

Using the Johari Window to help a group share information about a problem situation.

a. When there is a problem to be reviewed by a team, all members are asked to write down everything they know about the problem. Then they record in a Window that they have drawn, what they think is known to themselves and others (Open), and what they think they know that is not known to others (Hidden).

b. The leader asks the group to read first from the Open area, and the information is listed on one piece of newsprint. After all the information is recorded, the leader then asks for all information listed in the Hidden area and lists that data on another newsprint. No time is taken to discuss the information until it is all on both sheets.

c. After all the information is on both sheets, the group is helped to discuss what has been disclosed through this process. Further, problem-solving steps are considered, on the basis of increased sharing of information.

THE LEMONS

Objectives

1. To increase the awareness of how people perceive similar objects in very different ways.
2. To help people to accept differences in others.

Participants: Eight to 10 people

Materials: 1. Newsprint, felt pens, tape
2. One lemon for each member of the group (similar fruits or vegetables can be used)

Time: About 1 to 1½ hours

Detailed process

1. The lemons are placed on a table that is in the middle of the group.
2. The facilitator has each person go to the table and select one lemon.
3. The following instructions are given:

a. Get to know your lemon in any way you choose except for marking or cutting into it.

b. Spend about the next five minutes on doing this. After you have completed "getting acquainted" you will be asked to introduce your lemon to the group.

4. After the facilitator is sure that each person has had enough time, the participants are asked to replace the lemons on the table.

5. The facilitator asks everyone to close eyes and then mixes up the lemons. He or she tells everyone to reclaim their lemons. (Participants may have some doubts about finding the right lemons, but they all will.)

6. Each person is given the opportunity to introduce his or her lemon.

7. The facilitator notes down in newsprint some of the distinguishing characteristics about the lemons for later discussion.

8. The ensuing discussion often includes the following:

a. Surprise that the lemons are really so different even though "I never think about it when I see them piled up in the store."

b. Awareness of the uniqueness of people, which is often referred to in the form of "All whites or blacks are *not* the same."

c. Surprise at how many different ways people followed the instructions of getting to know your lemon.

d. Thoughts about not wanting to let go of the lemon—becoming attached to the "darn thing." Sometimes, there are very personal thoughts that the lemon exercise helped bring to mind.

9. The facilitator uses the notes on newsprints to enrich the discussion and also helps the group relate the experience to their work relationships.

THE HELPING RELATIONSHIPS

Objectives

1. To increase skills in helping another person think through a problem.

2. To learn the difference between *helping* a person to work on his or her problems and *giving advice* to a person with a problem.

   Participants: Up to 15 people divided into groups of three

   Materials: Newsprint, felt pens, tape

   Time: About 1½ hours

Detailed process

1. The facilitator has the group divide into subgroups of three with A as a person with a problem, B as a helper, and C as an observer.

2. The facilitator asks one trio to volunteer to demonstrate the helping process in front of the group.

3. The person with the problem is asked to talk about any problem. The helper is asked to be helpful in any way that he or she can. The observer records the process steps taken by the helper.

4. The facilitator indicates that he or she will stop the process to point out the behavior of the helper that seems useful to the person with the problem and the behavior that seems interfering.

5. The facilitator records on two separate sheets of newsprint the helpful and the not-helpful actions; that is, one sheet headed by "Helpful" and another sheet headed by "Not helpful."

6. Some examples of helpful behavior are: Allows person to talk without interruption; shows interest in what person is saying; asks clarifying questions; keeps eye contact but does not stare the person down.

7. Some examples of not-helpful behavior are: interrupting the person; giving advice; making long-winded statements; looking bored.

8. After the demonstration has been completed, the trios form in different parts of the room.

9. The trios rotate through each member, so that each participant is helper, person with problem, and observer. The trio goes through three rounds.

10. The observer keeps notes on the helpful and not-helpful actions of the helper. The helping portion lasts for about ten minutes and the feedback to the helper takes about five minutes.

11. At the completion of the third round, the total group reassembles to discuss what has been learned. Applications to the work situation are identified.

CONDUCTING A PARTICIPATIVE MEETING*

Objective

To increase skills in organizing and implementing a meeting which will allow the maximum participation of all team members

    Participants: All members of the team or attendees at a meeting

    Materials: Newsprint, felt pens, tape (additional materials depend on nature of meeting)

    Time: Depends on meeting

Detailed process

Note: The agenda illustrated on the next page is an example of a full day management meeting.

---

*   Developed by John Shoup and Rick Mott in collaboration with Melvin E. Allerhand.

9:00–9:15	Opening
9:15–9:30	Warm up
9:30–10:30	Leadership Skills Technique
	Listening
	Perception
10:30–10:45	Break
10:45–12:00	Identification of major problem areas
12:00–1:00	Lunch
1:00–2:30	Work on solutions to major problem areas
2:30–3:00	Open discussion
3:00–3:15	Plan next steps
3:15–4:00	Evaluate

Opening (9:00–9:15). This part of the process is used for tone setting. It may include introductory remarks concerning special instructions, the goal of the meeting, an identification of the roles of team members and the role of the leader. It is also used to present a preview of the meeting.

Warm-Up (9:15–9:30). This step can be used in a number of different ways, depending on the kind of team you're leading. For a team that has worked together before, ask them to privately write down their thoughts on what they expect to see accomplished during the meeting. Then ask them to share their thoughts with the group. You should write down their expectations on a flip chart and display them in the room during the rest of the meeting.

For a team that is meeting together for the first time, you may want to take as long as an hour for the warm-up. A possible format for the warm-up could be the following:

- Ask each member to pair up with and interview one other, asking the following questions:

  What is your nickname?
  What is your background and experience?
  What do you expect to happen in today's meeting?

- Allow 10 to 15 minutes each for interviews.

- Reconvene the team and ask each member to introduce his or her partner.

- Record their expectations on a flip chart ard display it around the room.

People often come to meetings with the agenda items on their minds that never get expressed or dealt with during the course of a meeting. The warm-up can get these hidden agenda items expressed and oftentimes they can be dealt with during the meeting. If there are particular topics that do not fit into the planned agenda, allow time for open discussion, as shown in the illustrated agenda on the first page of this exercise.

Agenda Items (9:30–3:00).

9:30–10:30	Leadership Skills Techniques
	Listening
	Perception
10:30–10:45	Break
10:45–12:00	Identification of major problem areas
12:00–1:00	Lunch
1:00–2:30	Work on solutions to major problem areas
2:30–3:00	Open discussion

The agenda items represent the actual content of the meeting. It is important to keep the meeting moving according to your planned times for each topic. This is difficult to do and can be accomplished through proper preplanning (see the next section, on Preplanning) and practice.

Next Steps (3:00–3:15). This step of the process is one of the most important. It involves listing action steps that will be taken on the basis of what was covered during the meeting. Action steps should include the following factors:

Assigned responsibility
A timetable
Plan for follow-through

If you're dealing with a complicated problem, it may be wise to start a separate list for action steps that can be added throughout the course of the meeting.

Evaluation (3:15–4:00). During this part of the process, ask each team member to take some private time and write down his or her thoughts about what went on during the meeting. Go around the room and ask the participants individually to share their thoughts verbally with the team. Finally, ask them to pass in their written evaluations. These evaluations are helpful in planning for future meetings.

Preplanning

Preplanning this type of meeting is essential for it to be successful. The steps you should consider in preplanning your meeting are the following:

1. Brainstorm all the ideas you would like to get across in your meeting.
2. Write out the specific goals you would like to see accomplished in your meeting.
3. Use your list of ideas and goals to plan out your agenda.
4. Screen each of the five steps in the meeting process to determine their applicability for your particular type of meeting.

Possible uses

The five-step meeting process may not be applicable to all types of meetings. The following is a list of meetings for which the process has been applicable:

Staff meetings
Problem-solving meetings
Task force meetings
Planning meetings
Training sessions
Team-building meetings

Operating tips

You, or someone trained in conducting meetings, should be a *facilitator* of the meetings.

A facilitator is responsible for the meeting and is the one who preplans it. It is the facilitator's responsibility to pay attention to both the *process* and the *content* (agenda items) of the meeting. In other words, you have to pay attention to how you are conducting the meeting as well as the reason for conducting it. Either the facilitator or someone from another department (e.g., Personnel or Training) can be the formal leader.

Use flip charts in the meeting:

- They cause people to feel ownership of their ideas.
- They can display the progress of the meeting.
- You should write out your agenda in advance on a flip chart.
- Everything significant that occurs during the meetings should be recorded and displayed around the room.
- The sheets are useful for follow-up and should be typed up and distributed after the meeting.
- Use different colored marking pens (water color base) and have lots of masking tape so you can tape up sheets on the walls. (Don't worry, it doesn't mess up the paint!)

If you have trouble staying on the time alotted for each agenda item, check out with the team how they want to proceed. The result may be that you: (1) Revise the agenda and make the meeting longer. (2) Delete a topic in favor of covering it at another meeting.

Plan your meeting to meet multiple needs. For example, in addition to regular work topics, make training a part of your meeting.

Index

Index